OXFORD WORLD'S CLASSICS

THE COMPLETE INDIAN HOUSEKEEPER AND COOK

FLORA ANNIE STEEL and GRACE GARDINER were both married to members of the Indian Civil Service and lived for many years in India under the British Raj. Flora Annie Steel, the senior writing partner, was born in Harrow in 1847 to Scottish parents. She travelled to India with her husband, Henry William Steel, in 1868, where she quickly immersed herself in the local culture. She learnt to speak, read, and write Punjabi and various local dialects, and committed herself to improving the lives of local women. She helped to establish schools for girls and was appointed Inspectress of Schools for the Punjab in 1884. During a writing career which spanned five decades Steel published thirty books, including novels, short stories, and miscellaneous non-fiction. She is best-remembered as the author of *On the Face of the Waters*, her novel on the Indian Mutiny that was published to great acclaim in 1896. She died at the age of 82 in Talgarth, Wales on 12 April 1929; her autobiography, *The Garden of Fidelity*, which she had left unfinished at her death, was published later that year.

Grace Anne Marie Louise Gardiner, the daughter of the Rt Hon. Sir Joseph Napier, a lawyer and Member of Parliament for Trinity College Dublin, married John William Gardiner of the Bengal Civil Service in 1868. Her experiences of bringing up a large family in India are the perfect foil to Steel's experience of her only child growing up 'at home' in Britain. Gardiner died in England on 3 August 1919 at the age of 74. Together, the two women's experiences of twenty-two years in India lend *The Complete Indian Housekeeper and Cook* an authority and charm that reflect the full spectrum of the memsahib's life in British India.

RALPH CRANE is Professor of English at the University of Tasmania. He has published widely on colonial and postcolonial fictions, including editions of four Anglo-Indian novels.

ANNA JOHNSTON is Queen Elizabeth II Fellow in English at the University of Tasmania and is the author of books and articles on missionary writing and empire, and colonial and postcolonial travel writing.

T0054975

OXFORD WORLD'S CLASSICS

*For over 100 years Oxford World's Classics have brought
readers closer to the world's great literature. Now with over 700
titles—from the 4,000-year-old myths of Mesopotamia to the
twentieth century's greatest novels—the series makes available
lesser-known as well as celebrated writing.*

*The pocket-sized hardbacks of the early years contained
introductions by Virginia Woolf, T. S. Eliot, Graham Greene,
and other literary figures which enriched the experience of reading.
Today the series is recognized for its fine scholarship and
reliability in texts that span world literature, drama and poetry,
religion, philosophy and politics. Each edition includes perceptive
commentary and essential background information to meet the
changing needs of readers.*

OXFORD WORLD'S CLASSICS

FLORA ANNIE STEEL &
GRACE GARDINER

The Complete Indian Housekeeper and Cook

Edited with an Introduction and Notes by
RALPH CRANE and ANNA JOHNSTON

OXFORD
UNIVERSITY PRESS

OXFORD

UNIVERSITY PRESS

Great Clarendon Street, Oxford ox2 6DP

Oxford University Press is a department of the University of Oxford.
It furthers the University's objective of excellence in research, scholarship,
and education by publishing worldwide in

Oxford New York

Auckland Cape Town Dar es Salaam Hong Kong Karachi
Kuala Lumpur Madrid Melbourne Mexico City Nairobi
New Delhi Shanghai Taipei Toronto

With offices in

Argentina Austria Brazil Chile Czech Republic France Greece
Guatemala Hungary Italy Japan Poland Portugal Singapore
South Korea Switzerland Thailand Turkey Ukraine Vietnam

Oxford is a registered trade mark of Oxford University Press
in the UK and in certain other countries

Published in the United States
by Oxford University Press Inc., New York

British Library Cataloguing in Publication Data

Data available

Library of Congress Cataloging in Publication Data

Data available

Typeset by Glyph International, Bangalore, India

Printed and bound in Great Britain by Clays Ltd, Elcograf S.p.A.

ISBN 978-0-19-955014-2 (Hbk.)
978-0-19-960576-7 (Pbk.)

ACKNOWLEDGEMENTS

WE are indebted to the following for their assistance in the preparation of this edition of Flora Annie Steel and Grace Gardiner's *The Complete Indian Housekeeper and Cook*: Devleena Ghosh (University of Technology, Sydney), who checked and, where necessary, corrected the Glossary; Judith Luna (OUP), whose concise advice on an earlier draft enabled us to find a better voice for our Introduction; Rebecca Dorgelo, who provided timely and highly efficient research assistance. We would also like to thank our respective families for living with Flora Annie Steel and India through this and other joint projects. This edition is dedicated to Joy, Callum, and Rhiannon, and to Ron and Ruby.

Ralph Crane would like to thank the University of Tasmania for granting him Study Leave in 2008 and for the award of an Institutional Research Grant in 2009; Anna Johnston would like to thank the Australian Research Council (ARC) for the award of a Queen Elizabeth II Fellowship (2007–2011).

CONTENTS

INTRODUCTION

How could 'the English girls to whom fate may assign the task of being house-mothers in our eastern empire' survive but with a copy of Flora Annie Steel and Grace Gardiner's *The Complete Indian Housekeeper and Cook* packed carefully in their steamer trunks? From the moment they arrived in India—often newly married, inexperienced in both travel and housewifery, and suffering the culture shock that still confronts first-time visitors to India—these young women were on display as flag-bearers of imperial British standards. Imagine their horror when, on entering their new home, they found 'The kitchen is a black hole, the pantry a sink. The only servant who will condescend to tidy up is a skulking savage with a reed broom' (p. 6). What was an English girl to do?

Fortunately, Steel and Gardiner had plenty of specific, practical, and highly opinionated advice to give the girl who suddenly found herself a memsahib. They could explain how to 'make a hold' over her servants, how to establish and stock a storeroom, how to plan a menu, manage young children, treat bites from 'mad, or even doubtful dogs', and teach an Indian cook how to make fish quenelles. *The Complete Indian Housekeeper and Cook* promised its reader a comprehensive guide to domesticity in India, even if she found herself living in camps or in the jungle, on the hills or in the plains, whether she was the wife of an influential Indian Civil Service officer or a missionary.

The authors wrote from their extensive residences in India, in a variety of regions and domestic circumstances. Steel was by far the senior partner in terms of the actual writing of the book: it formed an early part of her professional writing career, and it is her biography that dominates our subsequent discussion. But Gardiner brought her own experiences to the book, and so the reader gets a rounded, binocular view of British India. Gardiner had come to India in the 1860s in her early twenties with her husband John William Gardiner, who had joined the Indian Civil Service in 1864, and brought up a large family in India. Sections of the book clearly draw on Gardiner's expertise rather than Steel's two years with her only child before Mabel was left with relatives to be brought up 'at home'. Indeed, across

the editions of *The Complete Indian Housekeeper and Cook*, we see
Gardiner's children growing up: by 1904, they include a 'fully quali-
fied M.D., and another an Associate of the Sanitary Institute, and a
ci-devant health visitor' who are rather dismissive of their mother's
dated views on parenting.[1] The commentary continually draws on the
two women's lived experience in various parts of India. So we learn,
between the lines, about a six-week-old baby being vaccinated by the
Civil Surgeon on the Mall in Simla, about being caught without provisions on an upcountry train trip to Karachi 'where on one occasion
the writer was twenty-four hours without the possibility of procuring
anything but whisky and soda and a biscuit' (pp. 218–19), and about
repeated failures in cooking potted sheep's head, a result indignantly
found to be caused by the head being skinned by the cook before
cooking. These compelling glimpses of a woman's life under the Raj
provide much of the charm and interest of *The Complete Indian Housekeeper and Cook* for the contemporary reader, and must have ensured
its popularity in the late nineteenth and early twentieth centuries,
creating a demand which warranted its many editions and reprints.

Flora Annie Steel

Flora Annie Webster (1847–1929) was born at Sudbury Priory,
Harrow, on 2 April 1847, the sixth child and second daughter (of
eleven children) of George Webster, the Scottish Parliamentary
Agent, and Isabella (née MacCallum), heiress to a Jamaican plantation.[2] When Flora was three years old the failure of the Australasian
Bank and her father's subsequent bankruptcy, which included the
loss of his wife's substantial fortune, forced the family to move to a
small villa overlooking the Harrow School cricket pitch. In 1856 her
father, whose reputation appears to have survived his bankruptcy, was
appointed sheriff-clerk of Forfarshire in Scotland and the family
moved to Burnside, a large old country house near Forfar, where
Flora would live until she married.[3] Apart from six months at a school
in Brussels when she was 13, Steel was educated at home,[4] where her

---

[1] *The Complete Indian Housekeeper and Cook* (London: Heinemann, 1904), 163.
[2] Violet Powell, *Flora Annie Steel: Novelist of India* (London: Heinemann, 1981), 1.
[3] Flora Annie Steel, *The Garden of Fidelity* (1929; Gurgaon: Vintage Books, 1993), 16.
[4] Ibid. 23.

mother encouraged her interests in amateur theatricals, reading, painting, singing, music, sewing, and other handicrafts.

On 31 December 1867 Flora married Henry William Steel, who was home on leave from the Indian Civil Service, and whom she had previously met as a three-year-old at a children's party and again while he was an undergraduate at Cambridge. Twenty-four hours later, on New Year's Day 1868, Flora and her new husband set sail for India, where she would spend the next twenty-two years of her life, chiefly in the Punjab, including lengthy periods of residence in Ludhiana, Dalhousie, and Kasur, near Lahore.

Henry was one of the new generation Indian Civil Service (ICS) officers, 'competition wallahs' who had come through a revised recruitment system that favoured intellectual over practical achievement.[5] Appointed at the lowest position in the executive branch of the Indian Government—Assistant Commissioner (3rd grade)—Henry reported to the Deputy Commissioner (known as the District Officer or Collector in other provinces). He would have assisted his superior in a wide range of tasks, for the Deputy Commissioner held executive power and was the key administrative figure in his district, acting as chief magistrate, principal revenue officer, and responsible for the police, the jail, the law courts, forests, roads, schools, hospitals, fences, canals, and agriculture.[6] Until he had passed his departmental exams—which focused on language acquisition, judicial process, revenue and treasury—Henry could only try small cases, imposing limited fines and prison sentences. The Punjab was seen as a plum posting (along with the North-Western Provinces), and among the provinces it had a reputation for paternalist if benevolent dictatorship, as a frontier state which had developed a characteristically mobile and locally engaged ICS culture. Crucially, the Punjab had 'held' during the 1857 Indian Mutiny and its Sikh troops had assisted in the recapture of Delhi, thus the region was to some degree sheltered from the aftermath of the Uprising. Henry had first joined the ICS in 1862, so all his service was under the post-Mutiny structure of government, which saw the Governor-General, now usually known as the Viceroy, maintaining governance but with oversight from both the

---

[5] For a fascinating study of ICS culture see David Gilmour, *The Ruling Caste: Imperial Lives in the Victorian Raj* (London: John Murray, 2005).

[6] Ibid. 90–1.

Secretary of State in Whitehall and the Council of India, a group of mostly retired officials who advised the Secretary at the India Office. Thus Henry joined a chain of command, through the Lieutenant-Governor of the Punjab, that was headed now by the British Government, rather than the East India Company. He represented the new ICS man: more accountable and less dependent on patronage for advancement.

The Steels' first posting was to Ludhiana, but the following April it was decided that, in view of her experiences of fever during the last hot weather, the now pregnant Flora should take a house in Kasauli, in the hills 90 miles away, where her husband would visit her each weekend. In July 1868 Henry suffered a particularly debilitating dose of fever and, through the good offices of Colonel Reynell Taylor, the Commissioner of the Punjab, the couple were posted to the hill station of Dalhousie where Flora gave birth to a stillborn daughter.[7] She gave birth to a second daughter, Mabel, on 10 December 1870, by which time she was actively involved in station life.

From this point on Flora convincingly played the role of *burra memsahib* to her rapidly promoted husband, and whenever they were posted to larger stations where there was a lively Anglo-Indian community she occupied herself with the organization of various community activities including theatricals and musical events. When the Steels were posted to remote stations where there were few or no other Europeans, Flora refused to succumb to the boredom experienced by many colonial wives who, like Olivia Rivers in Ruth Prawer Jhabvala's *Heat and Dust* (1975), found themselves faced with endless hours of idle domesticity. Instead she immersed herself in the local culture, learning to speak, read, and write Punjabi and the local language of whatever area her husband was posted to, and committed herself to improving the lives of the local native women. Flora regularly accompanied her husband on his tours of the districts that came under his charge; acted as a (self-taught) doctor to the local women and children, which gained her entry to a world hidden to most Europeans; instituted her own reading classes at the local boys' school in Kasur, where she was later invited by the Indians to help establish a school for girls, the first of many schools she started; worked on various health and education committees; designed the town hall

[7] Powell, *Flora Annie Steel*, 17.

in Kasur; assisted in the revival of traditional handicrafts (which even then were being threatened by Western commercialism), producing an illustrated monograph on *phulkari* embroidery which was published by the India Office;[8] and for a time was vice-president of the 'Victoria Female Orphan Asylum' in the Punjab.

In 1884 Flora was appointed Inspectress of Schools, with responsibility for girls' schools in an area of over 140,000 square miles that stretched from Peshawar to Delhi, and between 1885 and 1888 she served on the Provincial Education Board. As an active member of the Board, Flora introduced reforms and rewrote school primers, which were illustrated by another Board member, John Lockwood Kipling, the father of Rudyard Kipling. She shocked the Anglo-Indian community by living apart from her husband for a year in order to complete the term of her own public appointment as Inspectress of Schools. Henry was deliberately transferred to the other end of the Punjab in response to his wife pressing for an inquiry into rumours of corruption at the new Punjab University in Lahore, a pet project of the then Governor, after she learnt that a junior official in the Forest Department who could barely read or write had been awarded a diploma.

It is tempting to privilege Flora's portrayal of India and Indians, to be seduced by what Jonah Raskin, writing about Kipling's *Kim*, calls 'the illusion of intimacy'.[9] Certainly in theory, the nature of her life in India gave Flora an unusual insight into the lives of Indian women in particular and into native life in general. But as Jenny Sharpe reminds us, 'Flora Annie Steel, perhaps more than anyone else, embodies the memsahib in all of her contradictions.'[10] While she made a genuine attempt, in all her Indian writing, to interpret the country and its culture through Indocentric rather than Eurocentric eyes, she remained an ardent supporter of Empire and her knowledge of India was ultimately used to support Britain's imperial hold on the country.

Much of the knowledge that Steel gathered during her twenty-two years in India would find its way into the only two books she published before leaving the country in 1889: *Wide Awake Stories* (1884),

[8] Steel, *The Garden of Fidelity*, 115–16.
[9] Jonah Raskin, *The Mythology of Imperialism* (New York: Random House, 1971), 103.
[10] Jenny Sharpe, *Allegories of Empire: The Figure of Woman in the Colonial Text* (Minneapolis and London: University of Minnesota Press, 1993), 93.

a volume of folk tales written for children with notes by Captain R. C. Temple (published in England in 1894 as *Tales of the Punjab*, with expanded notes by Temple and illustrations by J. Lockwood Kipling), and a domestic manual she wrote with her friend Grace Gardiner. *The Complete Indian Housekeeper and Cook*, first published in 1888—which she began compiling while living in Kasur, a remote subdivision where the Steels were posted a year or so after Flora's arrival in India[11]—was produced as a guide for the many young women who, like the young Steel and Gardiner, found themselves thrust into a position of responsibility for the Anglo-Indian home.

The Anglo-Indian Memsahib

At the time Steel and Gardiner wrote *The Complete Indian House-keeper and Cook* in the third quarter of the nineteenth century the British Raj in India was at its height. The Victorian British, whether they served in the Civil or the Military, believed they were in India as rulers, and to do their duty. Their wives were expected to share in the civilizing mission of Empire. But for many women, India was a frightening place, which they ignored as far as was possible, retreating into their own closed, Anglo-Indian community where, as Margaret MacMillan puts it, 'they attempted to keep Britain alive in the midst of India'.[12] To do this they devised a complicated set of social customs—wonderfully caricatured in George Atkinson's *Curry and Rice: The Ingredients of Social Life at 'Our Station' in India*,[13] a series of satirical sketches of small-station life in the mid-nineteenth century—that both distanced them from the culture shock of India and provided a level of comfort through the dull routines they offered.

The primary role of the memsahib was to keep house: to supervise the housekeeping while doing few domestic tasks herself. The morning, the coolest part of the day, was usually the time reserved for this task. Otherwise a typical day for a memsahib—whose husband would have risen early and would be at work for most of the day—might

[11] Pat Barr, *The Memsahibs: The Women of Victorian India* (London: Secker and Warburg, 1976), 152.

[12] Margaret MacMillan, *Women of the Raj* (London: Thames and Hudson, 1988), 13.

[13] George Francklin Atkinson, *Curry and Rice: The Ingredients of Social Life at 'Our Station' in India* (1859; Chennai: Rupa and Co, 2001).

begin with a ride before breakfast, which would be followed by a cold bath before dressing to receive visitors to exchange gossip and drink lime sodas for up to four hours. A late lunch, or tiffin, which would usually run into several courses, would, contrary to the advice given in *The Complete Indian Housekeeper and Cook*, often be followed by a siesta (which might simply be lying on her bed with a book, trying to keep cool), before a late afternoon ride, another bath, dressing again, and another round of visiting. In the evening she would dress for dinner (even when in camp), which again consisted of several courses (typically soups, fish, joints, puddings, and savouries), and perhaps conclude the day with songs around the pianoforte. Many became bored with this routine, and took up sketching, collecting dried flowers, or similar activities, to fill in their endless hours of leisure time.

The Complete Indian Housekeeper and Cook sought to provide practical guidance to young memsahibs in India, 'giving the duties of mistress and servants, the general management of the house and practical recipes for cooking in all its branches' (title page). The first nineteen chapters on 'household management' cover everything from the duties of the mistress and the duties of the various servants, details about keeping livestock and maintaining a garden, to the specific challenges faced by Europeans residing on the hills, in the plains, living in camps and jungles, and working as missionaries. The second half of the book provides advice on cooking and recipes for a range of European cuisine, from soups to ices, and one short chapter on 'native dishes'. Together, these two parts of the book provide, in Steel and Gardiner's own words, 'the knowledge really required by a mistress [which] is of that half-practical, half-theoretical and wholly didactic description, which will enable her to find reasonable fault with her servant' (p. 220). *The Complete Indian Housekeeper and Cook* gave knowledge to the new memsahib by demystifying the Anglo-Indian household, which in turn gave her power over her servants.

The voice that emerges from the pages commands the reader's attention. Brisk, capable, humorous, strong-minded, and frequently ironic, it brings the English girl into a companionable association with other memsahibs, even if she is isolated on an out-station. It is unmistakably Steel's voice, familiar from her short stories, novels, and autobiographical writing, leavened with Gardiner's experience. *The Complete Indian Housekeeper and Cook* shows Steel's modern thinking on women's capacities. She 'strenuously denies' that, '*per se*, an Englishwoman cannot stand the hot weather as well, and perhaps better than a man' (p. 196). She believes that women are 'far more capable of undertaking the somewhat irritating drudgery of detailed accounts' and that 'middle-class households will run most economically, and what is more, most smoothly, where the man has the courage and trust to bring all his earnings to the woman' (p. 30). Managing a house is seen as a crucial test of a woman's character and intelligence: 'It is the fashion nowadays to undervalue the art of making a home; to deem it simplicity and easiness itself. But this is a mistake, for the proper administration of even a small household needs both brain and heart. A really clever woman always sees this, and, like George Eliot, the greatest of modern women, prides herself on being an excellent housekeeper' (p. 16). Steel is also funny: her account of the aggression saved by employing a thermantidote (an early air cooling machine) rather than a punkah wallah is now somewhat politically incorrect, but still amusing (p. 197), and the humour is often directed against Europeans as well as Indians. Smart little aphorisms pepper the practical advice: 'As to clothing, a woman who wishes to live up to the climate must dress down to it,' she states, advising against frills, furbelows, ribbons, and laces (p. 201). Steel's appealing voice and her sophisticated writing skills distinguish *The Complete Indian Housekeeper and Cook* from its competitors.

Throughout, *The Complete Indian Housekeeper and Cook* is determined to enable the memsahib to replicate, as much as possible, British domestic practices in a foreign climate. It is English seeds that are planted in the gardens (p. 143), English dishes that are served at breakfast, lunch, and dinner, and English standards that measure the duty of a mistress to her servants (p. 16). 'In regard to actual housekeeping, the authors emphatically deny the common assertion that it must necessarily run on different lines to what it does in England. Economy, prudence, efficiency are the same all over the world . . . Some modification, of course, there must be, *but as little as possible*' (p. 14). In this way British domestic practices were to be made universal, another component of the broader practices of 'raising up' other cultures to the high standards imperial proponents believed to be inherent in late Victorian British culture. The most demanding challenge for the memsahib was to insist on British ways of doing things against the experience and cultural assumptions of her Indian servants, and it was a battle royal that was played out daily in

Anglo-Indian households, if Steel and Gardiner provide a representative guide. But upholding standards was critical. Housekeeping in India had 'a political and social as well as a domestic side' (p. 5) and it was conceived of as a long-term project where 'a few generations of training shall have started the Indian servant on a new inheritance of habit' (p. 12). In this we see the '[a]utocratic high-handedness' (p. 79) that feeds popular images of the culturally narrow-minded memsahib who refused to engage with the extraordinarily rich and diverse cultures that surrounded her home.

Yet at the same time there is evidence of a real delight in India and the opportunities it provided for British women. Explaining the benefits of spending the hot season up in the hill stations, Steel writes:

Going to the hills is not quite as simple a matter as going to the seaside in England, but then there are the delightfully hairbreadth risks and miraculous escapes as a pleasant excitement, and there is always something new and wonderful. . . . We feel our hearts bound at the sight of the distant snows, and the sweet smell of the pines and wild flowers; and they re-echo a glad alleluia: 'I will lift up mine eyes unto the hills, from whence cometh my help'—and health! (p. 195)

Here is the other side of the Anglo-Indian memsahib, delighting in the adventures of travel in India, enjoying the risks and the novelties she encounters, and clearly engaged with the landscape that surrounds her. Similarly, in the chapters on camp life and jungle life, housekeeping challenges in these locations are seen to be thrilling rather than tiresome: indeed, the authors rather lament that the 'days of real camp life are, it is to be feared, numbered' (p. 148). Across these sometimes contradictory assessments of India and her people, *The Complete Indian Housekeeper and Cook* reveals the complex and fascinating world of the memsahib.

The Complete Indian Housekeeper and Cook

Many nineteenth-century household manuals addressed the construction of the ideal middle-class home, and *The Complete Indian Housekeeper and Cook* followed this trend. *Mrs Beeton's Book of Household Management*, first published in 1861, addressed the middle-class domestic British woman and, in doing so, brought her into being as an idealized type. Then, as now, cookbooks constructed a utopian domestic space—one which few achieved in precisely the prescriptive terms the books set out. But the idea of the bourgeois home presided over by the Victorian 'angel in the house' was crucial to imagining the British people and, by extension, the British nation. Isabella Beeton, like other authors, called on middle-class women to manage others—servants, other members of the household, and children—and developed a science of domestic management that could be taught and replicated, through both formal and informal systems of education.[14] Although the Victorian domestic sphere was placed in ideological opposition to the public world of men, commerce, and growing industrialization, in practice the home was where women managed consumption and it was therefore a crucial unit of the economy. Managing the labour of working-class servants, balancing domestic accounts, and ensuring that middle-class families lived well, but within their means, the middle-class housewife acquitted her duties to the family, her husband, and the nation as part of the linked Victorian values of domesticity and imperialism.[15]

The Complete Indian Housekeeper and Cook transplanted those British values to colonial climes. Here, the housewife had to manage servants marked by both racial and class difference; here, the accounts were carried on in a foreign currency and supplies were procured through bazaars and importers; here, her responsibility to uphold standards was overlaid with imperial assumptions about racial and cultural superiority (and, by corollary, vulnerability to the strangeness of India). At home, Mrs Beeton had assured her that 'Creatures of the inferior races eat and drink; man only dines . . . Dining is the privilege of civilisation.'[16] Steel and Gardiner's guide sought to provide the Anglo-Indian housewife living among those 'inferior races' with the means to sustain civilization in the face of colonial disorder: how to dine, rather than simply eat, in India.

Mostly Anglo-Indians of this era dined in remarkably similar ways to British families back home (interestingly, as Humble notes, Beeton

[14] Margaret Beetham, 'Of Recipe Books and Reading in the Nineteenth Century: Mrs. Beeton and her Cultural Consequences', in Janet Floyd and Laurel Foster (eds.), *The Recipe Reader: Narratives—Contexts—Traditions* (Aldershot: Ashgate, 2003), 22.

[15] Susan Zlotnick, 'Domesticating Imperialism: Curry and Cookbooks in Victorian England', ibid. 74.

[16] *Mrs Beeton's Book of Household Management*, ed. Nicola Humble (Oxford: Oxford University Press, 2000), 363.

included as many recipes from India as from Wales, Scotland, and Ireland combined[17]). The recipes in *The Complete Indian Housekeeper and Cook* show little evidence of the exotic landscape of their readers; instead, good, plain British cooking dominates. Earlier cookery during the East India Company era had engaged enthusiastically with Indian cuisine. 'Wyvern', for example, described the 'molten curries and florid oriental compositions of the olden time' in his *Culinary Jottings for Madras* (1878).[18] After the Mutiny—which augured in an inexorable shift from a predominantly male Anglo-Indian culture to a more diverse group of memsahibs, missionaries, and other advocates for British cultural values—the favourite meal of Company and military men, curry and rice, gave way to a European-based cuisine mimicking the table of Victorian Britain, even down to the French influences of the day.[19]

One searches with little success for Indian ingredients and influences in *The Complete Indian Housekeeper and Cook*. A chapter on 'Native Dishes' was added to the 1898 edition, and, even then, only a meagre eight recipes were provided 'by request'. The authors' disregard for Indian cuisine is self-evident: 'most native recipes are inordinately greasy and sweet, and . . . your native cooks invariably know how to make them fairly well' (p. 305). Occasionally Steel and Gardiner substitute a local ingredient for a standard European equivalent: using green mangos for Greengage and Cherry Rings (p. 293) is a rare example. Generally, though, Anglo-Indians are directed to consume British cuisine and, even in India, to guard against Continental influences. *The Complete Indian Housekeeper and Cook* sternly notes that, in the houses of adventurous gourmets in India, 'one is often treated to a badly-cooked dinner in the style of a third-class French restaurant, even to the *hors d'œuvres*' (p. 61). The concluding comment on the fashion of hybridizing English and French modes of breakfasting—'when, as is often the case, the breakfast hour is English, there is no real reason why English fashions should not be adhered to in every way' (p. 55)—can be taken as Steel and Gardiner's maxim for Anglo-Indian cuisine in general. Menus and the style of

---

[17] Ibid. p. xxix.

[18] Wyvern [Colonel A. R. Kenney-Herbert], *Culinary Jottings for Madras* (1878; London: Prospect Books, 2008), 1.

[19] Lizzie Collingham, *Curry: A Tale of Cooks and Conquerors* (New York: Oxford University Press, 2006), 115, 159.

eating should be carefully assessed against British standards: women
are warned against '[h]eavy luncheons or tiffins', consumed simply
because hot weather seems to preclude any other activity (p. 57). And the
pragmatic household economics of *The Complete Indian Housekeeper
and Cook* insists that families should live—and dine—within their
means, just as they would in Britain: 'a family with £1200 a year at
home would not dream of giving champagne and *pâte de foie gras*, or
spending thirty shillings in preserved fruit, bonbons, &c., for a very
récherché pudding. Why should it be done out here?' (pp. 60–1).

Steel and Gardiner's guide, like other similar household guides,
provides the memsahib with detailed advice on the management of
her Indian servants. The number and extent of her dependants was
one of the features that most clearly distinguished Anglo-Indian
and British households: David Gilmour estimates that the wife of an
Assistant Under-Secretary in Whitehall would have employed three
or four servants; in India, she would have been responsible for about
forty people.[20] Indeed the authors devote a forty-six-page chapter
(by far the longest in the book) to 'The Duties of the Servants', out-
lining in precise detail the roles of various servants, suggesting that
the management of Indian servants was the key to being a successful
memsahib, and that successful management was dependent on maintaining a position of imperial power and authority over her servants.
They also advise their reader at the outset that 'The Indian servant is
a child in everything save age and should be treated as a child; that is
to say, kindly, but with the greatest firmness' (p. 12).

The Complete Indian Housekeeper and Cook repeatedly positions
Indian servants as children, as other, and as representatives of a
degenerate culture which urgently requires British uplift. Not only
are Indians childlike, but they demonstrate 'a case of sheer ignorance
of facts well known to an *English* child; and it must never be forgotten that this is not the exception, but the rule' (emphasis added,
p. 80). Individual servants stand in for problems of Indian civilization, or its absence, so we are told that 'It would take page on page,
chapter on chapter, to tell the many evil habits in which Indian cooks
have been grounded and taught' (p. 79). These habits are darkly put
down to *dustoor*, or custom: 'pervading all things broods the stifling,
enervating atmosphere of custom, against which energy beats itself

unavailingly, as against a feather bed' (p. 6). In this way, Indian culinary and domestic practices are utterly elided: they are unmentionable because to detail them would attest to the richness and complexity of the traditional practices of everyday life, and would allow the possibility of cross-cultural adaptation and change. Anglocentric virtues must be made universal, through the manual's didactic regimes, in order to raise up the peoples of the Empire through domestic reform. The memsahib's duty, then, is not only to her particular household but to the other Anglo-Indian households present and future, who will employ properly trained servants, and beyond that to the Empire as a whole, which will benefit from a disciplined—in the Foucauldian sense—Indian underclass.

Dirt, disorder, and different cultural practices reverberate through *The Complete Indian Housekeeper and Cook* as threats to the universalized British domesticity that the handbook prescribes. These are the 'politics of contamination' that threaten the European colonial home as well as the bodies and minds of Anglo-Indians, and especially of Anglo-Indian children.[21] These contaminations are both literal and metaphoric. The manual is much concerned about the cook stirring eggs into a rice pudding with his finger, and the *khitmutgar* saving on washing up by hastily wiping cutlery rather than using the full Victorian armoury at each meal, and the storage of milk in dirty sculleries 'where the floor reeks like a sink, or side by side with raw meat in a safe' (p. 113–14).

But these literal contaminations have disturbing moral connotations, and they trouble the high-handed and brisk tone of the manual. When Steel and Gardiner declare that 'Dirt, illimitable, inconceivable dirt must be expected, until a generation of mistresses has rooted out the habits of immemorial years' (p. 86), it is clear that it is not only physical dirt that is of concern. In every chapter, the memsahib is warned to guard against 'the native's capacity for uncleanliness' (p. 114) and advised to discipline both herself and her servants in an obsessive regime of decontamination. In Victorian Britain, concerns about dirt led to increasing surveillance policing the borders between normal and dirty categories: categories of health, sexuality, and

---

[21] Ann Laura Stoler, *Race and the Education of Desire: Foucault's History of Sexuality and the Colonial Order of Things* (Durham, NC, and London: Duke University Press, 1995), 149.

money, for example.[22] In India, race complicated such ideas: Victorian concerns with gender and class differences were amplified through categories of racial difference, so that '[d]irt, illimitable, inconceivable dirt' attested to the popular imperial notion that other races were further behind the Europeans in terms of development and progress in 'civilisation'.

Yet it is not only Indian custom against which the mistress must be vigilant. The whole first chapter of *The Complete Indian Housekeeper and Cook* is devoted to 'The Duties of the Mistress' and here, as throughout the manual, the Anglo-Indian housewife is admonished by the authors. Against the tide of India, Steel and Gardiner chide, many women have failed to provide a bulwark of European standards. Throughout, lazy memsahibs and their domestic practices are roundly condemned, and particularly the 'absolute indifference displayed by many Indian mistresses, who put up with a degree of slovenliness and dirt which would disgrace a den in St. Giles, on the principle that it is no use attempting to teach the natives' (p. 11). Women who fail to learn Indian languages, by which to better instruct their servants, are castigated: 'No sane Englishwoman would dream of living, say, for twenty years, in Germany, Italy, or France, without making the *attempt*, at any rate, to learn the language' (p. 12). The authors tartly suggest European women in India need 'to ask themselves if a difference in longitude increases the latitude allowed in judging of a woman's intellect' (p. 12). Poor servants reflect directly on their mistress's intellect, character, and sympathy. Such judgements would have been common across metropole and colony but failing to maintain standards in Anglo-Indian homes has particular and pernicious consequences.

The future of British children was in the hands of the Anglo-Indian house-mother and, by extension, so too was the future of British civilization. The expansion of the Empire in the nineteenth century meant that measuring the birth rate, and the health, of the British at home and in the new colonies became crucial to measuring the success and status of the nation and its imperial vigour.[23] *The Complete Indian*

---

[22] Anne McClintock, *Imperial Leather: Race, Gender, and Sexuality in the Colonial Contest* (New York: Routledge, 1995), 154.

[23] Gillian Whitlock, 'The Silent Scribe: Susanna and "Black Mary"', *International Journal of Canadian Studies*, 11 (1995), 249–60.

Housekeeper and Cook urged its readers to take their responsibilities for maintaining the health and well-being of their household seriously, for the home is 'that unit of civilisation where father and children, master and servant, employer and employed, can learn their several duties' (p. 16). But it also urges that 'Life holds higher duties' (p. 11), which should not be compromised by wasting excessive effort on supervising domestic labour. In India, as evidenced by Steel's extraordinarily varied experience, those higher duties could include involvement in all manner of administrative, social, and philanthropic programmes associated with the British Raj. Yet *The Complete Indian Housekeeper and Cook* is explicit in seeing home management as part of a continuum with those imperial duties outside the home.

Steel and Gardiner consider the effective administration of the private sphere as central to the effective administration of the public sphere, and they confidently assign the memsahib a central role in the colonial enterprise. Towards the close of 'The Duties of the Mistress', the mistress-to-be is reminded that 'an Indian household can no more be governed peacefully, without dignity and prestige, than an Indian Empire' (p. 18). And this, according to the authors, requires that the boundaries between ruler and ruled be clearly maintained, regardless of the intimacy of their daily contact.

Nowhere is this intimacy—and the ambivalence of relationships between Anglo-Indians and the Indians they ruled—more evident than in the rearing of children, the future leaders of the Raj. *The Complete Indian Housekeeper and Cook* is as opinionated on this topic as one might expect:

Indian children are proverbially captious, disobedient, and easily thrown out of gear. . . . [W]e can only assure every young mother that there is no climatic reason whatever why discipline should be set aside in an Indian nursery, and that it is as possible to insist on cleanliness, decency, and order there as in an Indian pantry or cook-room. The whole secret lies in refusing to listen to the word *dustoor*, or custom. (pp. 94–5)

The chapter 'Hints on Management of Young Children' reveals significant revision and response to readers across the manual's many editions. Nursing, that is, breastfeeding, is very much the preference of the authors, even as the twentieth century dawns and new 'scientific' modes of formula feeding gain precedence. But whilst Steel and

xxiv   *Introduction*

Gardiner advocate mothers feeding their own children, the manual
explains the mechanics of employing a wet-nurse, when necessary.
Cashmiri women from Amritsar are the ideal, but those from Agra
'have got a great name' (p. 162). *Ayahs* or *dhaees* are servants with
special needs, and hence enhanced status and, it becomes clear in
the manual, considerable bargaining power. Steel and Gardiner are
scrupulous in detailing the precise clothing one must provide for
such women, as well as the cooking and eating utensils to which they
are entitled (pp. 162–3). While the language in which they describe
such women reveals an uncomfortably explicit commodification of
ethnic types and racialized bodies—Cashmiris are to be preferred
because they are 'very amiable, get very fond of their charges, are
simple in their ideas and unsophisticated, and not so grasping in
their expectations' (p. 162)—in other ways Steel and Gardiner are
clearly more liberal than their compatriots. They insist that a wet-
nurse must be allowed to see her friends, and warn that on no account
must she 'be treated as if she were merely an animated bottle' (p. 162).
That other Anglo-Indians might hold such attitudes becomes clear
in later editions. Steel and Gardiner express serious disquiet about
the correspondence they receive: '[t]he horror of native wet-nurses
universally expressed, even by missionary ladies', shocks them
sufficiently to make a point of addressing their 1908 readers explicitly
on the matter. They chide those 'who profess to love the souls of men
and women' but who 'find the bodies in which those souls are housed
more repulsive than those of a cow or donkey or a goat'. It is purely
'race prejudice' to fear that 'the milk of a native woman should con-
taminate an English child's character'.[24] Their readers' bigotry does,
however, reveal the unsettling nature of bodily intimacy across racial
boundaries as well as heightened sensitivities around the imperial
child. Sir Bampfylde Fuller voiced the concerns of many when he
warned: 'India enfeebles white races that cling to her breasts', using
the metaphor of the wet-nurse to explain the dangers of the Indian
climate for European constitutions.[25] One historian of the colonial
frontier in the Australian colonies has pointed out that the space
shared (and contested) by colonizer and colonized might be 'as close

---

[24] *The Complete Indian Housekeeper and Cook* (1904), 176.
[25] Bampfylde Fuller, *The Empire of India* (London: Pitman, 1913), 196.

as the bed shared with an Aboriginal woman'.[26] Steel and Gardiner's chapter on children reminds us that the domestic sphere provided many opportunities for informal and potentially destabilizing contact between Indians and their imperial rulers, and that the balance of power inside the home was not always as predictable as *The Complete Indian Housekeeper and Cook* mandated.

Steel after India

Henry Steel retired from the Indian Civil Service on 1 May 1889, and only two hours after his pension became due the Steels set sail for home. Encouraged by a friend, Richard Gilles Hardy, who would later become Commissioner of Lucknow, to turn her Indian experiences into fiction,[27] the following year Steel published her first story, 'Lâl', in *Macmillan's Magazine*; in all she wrote over thirty books and, of the many novels and short stories she wrote, over half were concerned with Indian or Anglo-Indian life. Steel returned to India twice more before her death in 1929, and her novel on the Mutiny, *On the Face of the Waters*, was published in 1896 to great acclaim.

Steel and Gardiner first published *The Complete Indian Housekeeper and Cook* in India in 1888–9, and probably little anticipated its eager reception. Demand for copies, and letters from readers, ensured a constant stream of revisions and new editions published back home in Edinburgh and London (see the Note on the Text in this edition for details). The authors continually updated and upgraded their manual, incorporating innovations such as reproducing chapters on the duties of servants as cheap pamphlets in Urdu and Hindi that servants in training could read or have read to them.[28] New fashions in cooking are incorporated, for example the addition of a chapter on vegetarian cooking in 1904 (here, as always, Steel's astringent humour is revealed: 'The writer, though practically a vegetarian, fails to see any difference between killing a cabbage and killing a chicken'[29]). Keeping details such as prices relevant was a constant problem, and Steel and Gardiner struggled, after they returned to England, to

---

[26] Jan Critchett, *A 'Distant Field of Murder': Western Districts Frontiers, 1834–1848* (Melbourne: Melbourne University Press, 1990), 23.

[27] Powell, *Flora Annie Steel*, 67.

[28] *The Complete Indian Housekeeper and Cook* (1902), x.

[29] *The Complete Indian Housekeeper and Cook* (1904), 370.

make sense of letters from memsahibs that reported widely varying costs in the different provinces. Still, they remained committed to their vision of the ideal housewife, and were quick to condemn any who slipped from their high standards, reiterating in the 1909 edition that 'this book premises a "woman's desire to look well to the ways of her household". It is not written for those who, in the words of a correspondent, "leave everything to my *khitmutghar*, and he manages everything".'[30] The manual's longevity and continued appeal was due to these careful efforts to remain up to date, and reading across the editions—which run for thirty-three years, from 1888 to 1921—it is possible to see the changes in India across this period. Issues such as health reveal this most dramatically, as the resourceful memsahib's pharmacopeia is expanded with the increasing number of effective drugs available and then, as professional medical services were more widely established in India, those skills are diminished as emergency treatments of last resort. It is a process of modernization that is seen ambivalently and often regretfully through Western eyes. In 1909 *The Complete Indian Housekeeper and Cook* recalls with some nostalgia the early years of the British in India:

India is fast being westernised . . . Motors are more amusing than bullock carts. Telephones are a convenience; electric fans a joy.

But all these things cost money, and cost more relatively in India than they do in England. So, undoubtedly, the cost of living has gone up. But then the standard of personal comfort has also gone up; so we must not complain.

Is it not the gospel of civilisation?[31]

Steel and Gardiner, both representatives of and keen advocates for the modernizing, civilizing mission of late Victorian Britain, reveal here the complex set of emotions that India stirred in her colonial officials.

In all her books dealing with colonial life in India during the Raj, Steel displayed her knowledge of the country and its customs. But with hindsight, later assessments prove that the 'so-called "knowledge" of India' displayed in Steel's fiction 'does not so much involve an open-minded responsiveness towards the country as the seeking of a *practical* kind of knowledge, a way of dealing with Indian life and

---

[30] *The Complete Indian Housekeeper and Cook* (1909), viii.
[31] Ibid.

people, and, by extension, of facilitating British rule'.[32] The publication of *The Complete Indian Housekeeper and Cook* certainly attests to the gathering of practical ways of dealing with the country, while also implicating household duties in the government of Empire.[33]

Such criticisms remind us that Steel was a woman of her time, whose thinking was inevitably influenced by Victorian certainties about the superiority of the British race, and an absolute belief in the British Empire in general and the British Raj in India in particular. But it is also evident that she was not averse to questioning the *way* Britain ruled in India, or accepting that in time India would govern herself,[34] which set her apart from the majority of memsahibs in the late nineteenth century. Steel did not shut herself off from India like so many of her countrywomen, and she tried to meet Indians in an emancipated way, even if her relationship always remained a paternalistic one. It is also evident that she sometimes nettled the British authorities in India with her criticisms, and that she was greatly admired by Indian women and girls in the areas where she worked. In her autobiography Steel describes a brooch given to her by the women of Kasur: 'the round, gem-set brooch they gave me was given with the simple explanation that it was indeed a token, since every jewel in it had been taken from those worn by their womenkind',[35] and recalls 'a crowd of some three hundred veiled women on the platform of the railway station' who had gathered to honour her as she departed for home.[36]

[32] Anne Fernihough, 'Steel, Flora Annie', in Janet Todd (ed.), *Dictionary of British Women Writers* (London: Routledge, 1999), 643.

[33] Sharpe, *Allegories of Empire*, 93.

[34] Steel, *The Garden of Fidelity*, 253.

[35] Ibid. 111.

[36] Ibid. 181.

NOTE ON THE TEXT

THE present text is that of the fourth edition, published by William Heinemann in 1898. The recipe chapters have been abridged, retaining over a third of the recipes in order to provide a representative selection which also keeps recipes of particular cultural and historical interest.

There were at least ten editions of Steel and Gardiner's domestic manual between 1888 and 1921. We have reproduced the 1898 edition because it represents the first full, revised version of the text that then served as the basis of later editions. Steel and Gardiner's prefatory comments about the editions are often misleading, perhaps because, prior to 1898, *The Complete Indian Housekeeper and Cook* was effectively self-published: first in India, in 1888–9; then in Scotland in 1890. The first edition is not held by any major library in India or the United Kingdom, so the book printed by Frank Murray in Edinburgh in 1890 is effectively the first extant edition, produced, according to its authors, 'within a few months of the first'. A seemingly constant stream of correspondence from readers motivated ongoing revisions: the addition of an index and several new chapters, as well as the revision of earlier material. *The Complete Indian Housekeeper and Cook* was one of only two works published by Steel—the most experienced and accomplished writer—during her residence in India, although she would reflect on her Indian experiences throughout the rest of her life and her subsequent publications.

By 1898 the text included forty-three chapters, including important chapters on account-keeping, comparative costs at different stations, and the varieties of Anglo-Indian life led on the hills and in the plains. In 1898 the book was taken up by the publisher William Heinemann, who kept it in print (and continued to encourage revisions and new editions) for the next twenty-three years. The twentieth-century editions show rapid developments in domestic, medical, and agricultural technologies, as well as the changing experience of Britons posted to India. The 1898 edition represents the culmination of Steel and Gardiner's high imperial experience of the nineteenth-century British Empire, and as such provides a fascinating snapshot of the daily lives of Anglo-Indians under the Raj at its height.

The authors' occasional inconsistent spellings of Hindustani, Urdu, or other Indian language words have been retained; variant spellings are noted in the Glossary, which has been prepared with the aid of Henry Yule and A. C. Burnell's *Hobson-Jobson: An Anglo-Indian Dictionary* (1886; London: Routledge, 1986) and Ivor Lewis's *Sahibs, Nabobs and Boxwallahs* (1991; Delhi: Oxford University Press, 1999). (Inconsistencies in the spelling or accenting of French and other European language words have also been retained.) In the course of the text the authors provide lists of common foods, essential kitchen utensils, common garden seeds, medicines, ingredients for various remedies, a table of measures, and the names of common Indian dishes and spices, together with their Hindustani or Urdu names. Various other words are clearly glossed as they appear in the text. These have not been repeated in the Glossary except where they appear elsewhere without a translation. The editors' comprehensive Explanatory Notes, which provide information that ranges across areas of cultural, historical, geographical, medical, and culinary interest, aim to provide sufficient background information to satisfy the reader's curiosity without overburdening him or her with detail. These notes are signalled with an asterisk in the text; all footnotes are by the authors.

SELECT BIBLIOGRAPHY

Biography

Violet Powell, *Flora Annie Steel: Novelist of India* (London: Heinemann, 1981).

Primary Texts

An Anglo-Indian, *Indian Outfits & Establishments: a practical guide for persons about to reside in India; defining the articles which should be taken out, and the requirements of home life and management there* (London: Upcott Gill, 1882).

George Francklin Atkinson, *Curry and Rice: The Ingredients of Social Life at 'Our Station' in India* (1859; Chennai: Rupa and Co, 2001).

W. H. Dawe, *The Wife's Help to Indian Cookery* (London: Elliot Stock, 1888).

Maud Diver, *The Englishwoman in India* (London: Blackwood, 1909).

G. R. Elsmie, *Thirty-Five Years in the Punjab, 1858–1893* (Edinburgh: David Douglas, 1908).

Mrs Eliot James, *Guide to Indian Household Management* (London: Ward, Lock and Co., 1879).

A Lady Resident, *The Englishwoman in India: containing information for the use of ladies proceeding to, or residing in, the East Indies, on the subject of their Outfit, Furniture, Housekeeping and the rearing of children, duties and wages of servants, management of the stables and arrangements for travelling to which are added receipts for Indian Cookery* (London: Smith, Elder & Co., 1864).

Chota Mem [Mrs C. Lang], *The English Bride in India, Being Hints on Indian Housekeeping* (1904; London: Luzac and Co., 1909).

Fanny Parkes, *Begums, Thugs and Englishmen: The Journals of Fanny Parkes*, selected and introduced by William Dalrymple (New Delhi: Penguin, 2002).

A Thirty-Five Years' Resident, *The Indian Cookery Book: A Practical Handbook to the Kitchen in India, Adapted to the Three Presidencies; Containing Original and Approved Recipes in Every Department of Indian Cookery; Recipes for Summer Beverages and Home-Made Liqueurs; Medicinal and Other Recipes; Together with a Variety of things worth knowing* (Calcutta: Wyman & Co., 1869).

Flora Annie Steel, *The Garden of Fidelity* (1929; Gurgaon: Vintage Books, 1993).

Annie Campbell Wilson, *Hints for the First Years of Residence in India* (Oxford: Clarendon Press, 1904).

Wyvern [Colonel A. R. Kenney-Herbert], *Culinary Jottings for Madras* (1878; London: Prospect Books, 2008).

Secondary Texts

Charles Allen, *Plain Tales from the Raj* (London: André Deutsch, 1975).

Pat Barr, *The Memsahibs: The Women of Victorian India* (London: Secker and Warburg, 1976).

Elizabeth Buettner, *Empire Families: Britons and Late-Imperial India* (Oxford: Oxford University Press, 2004).

David Burton, *The Raj at Table: A Culinary History of the British in India* (London: Faber, 1993).

E. M. Collingham, *Imperial Bodies: The Physical Experience of the Raj, c.1800–1947* (Cambridge: Polity, 2001).

W. Crooke, *The North-Western Provinces of India: Their History, Ethnology, and Administration* (London: Methuen, 1897).

Janet Floyd and Laurel Foster (eds.), *The Recipe Reader: Narratives—Contexts—Traditions* (Aldershot: Ashgate, 2003).

David Gilmour, *The Ruling Caste: Imperial Lives in the Victorian Raj* (London: John Murray, 2005).

Lawrence James, *Raj: The Making and Unmaking of British India* (London: Little, Brown and Co., 1997).

Margaret MacMillan, *Women of the Raj* (London: Thames and Hudson, 1988).

Geoffrey Moorhouse, *India Britannica* (London: Collins, 1983).

Daya Parwardhan, *A Star of India: Flora Annie Steel, Her Works and Times* (Bombay: Daya Patwardhan, 1963).

Mary A. Procida, *Married to the Empire: Gender, Politics and Imperialism in India, 1883–1947* (Manchester: Manchester University Press, 2002).

Joanna Trollope, *Britannia's Daughters: Women of the British Empire* (1983; London: Pimlico, 2006).

Further Reading in Oxford World's Classics

Mrs. Beeton's Book of Household Management, ed. Nicola Humble.

Robert Baden-Powell, *Scouting for Boys*, ed. Elleke Boehmer.

Empire Writing, ed. Elleke Boehmer.

A CHRONOLOGY OF FLORA ANNIE STEEL

Life	*Historical and Cultural Background*
1847 2 April: Flora Annie Webster born at Sudbury Priory, Harrow, sixth of eleven children of George and Isabella Webster (née MacCallum).	Charlotte Brontë, *Jane Eyre* Emily Brontë, *Wuthering Heights*
1848	Second Anglo-Sikh War (1848–9). Marquis of Dalhousie appointed Governor-General of India; embarks on a series of annexations under the 'Doctrine of Lapse'. Satara annexed. William Makepeace Thackeray, *Vanity Fair* Karl Marx and Friedrich Engels, *The Communist Manifesto*
1849	Annexation of the Punjab. Jaitpur and Sambhalpur annexed.
1850 Family moves to small villa overlooking Harrow School cricket pitch.	
1851	Great Exhibition, a celebration of modern industrial technology and design, held in London.
1852	Second Anglo-Burmese War (1852–3) leads to the annexation of Lower Burma.
1853	William Arnold, *Oakfield*
1854	Crimean War (1854–6). Jhansi and Nagpur annexed.
1856 Flora's father appointed sheriff-clerk of Forfarshire; family moves to Scotland and takes up residence at Burnside near Forfar. Flora is educated informally at home except for six months at a school in Brussels.	Earl Canning appointed Governor-General of India. Annexation of Awdh (Oudh). Hindu Widow's Remarriage Act (India) allows widows to remarry and to enjoy all the rights of a married woman.

Life	*Historical and Cultural Background*
1857	10 May: Indian Mutiny (1857–8) breaks out in Meerut. Matrimonial Causes Act (UK) allows divorce through the law courts. Under the terms of the Act, the husband has only to prove his wife's adultery, while the wife additionally has to prove her husband has committed incest, bigamy, cruelty, or desertion. Universities of Calcutta, Bombay, and Madras founded.
	Thomas Hughes, *Tom Brown's Schooldays*
	R. M. Ballantyne, *The Coral Island*
1858 Flora's eldest brother sails for India to take up a civilian post in Madras; her youngest brother born.	Government of India Act transfers rule of India from Hon. East India Company to Crown. Earl Canning appointed Viceroy of India.
	Charles Ball, *History of the Indian Mutiny*
1859	Charles Darwin, *On the Origin of Species*
	J. S. Mill, *On Liberty*
	Charles Dickens, *A Tale of Two Cities*
	Mrs Beeton's Book of Household Management begins to appear in monthly parts.
1860	Macaulay's Indian Penal Code enacted. Introduction of Indian indentured labour to Natal (1860–1911).
	William Howard Russell's *My Diary in India in the Year 1858–1859*
1861	8th Earl of Elgin appointed Viceroy of India. Indian Councils Act transforms the Viceroy's Executive Council into a miniature cabinet run on a portfolio system.
	Mrs Beeton's Book of Household Management published in volume form.

Life	*Historical and Cultural Background*
1863	Simla declared summer capital. Sir John Lawrence appointed Viceroy of India.
1864	The first of three Contagious Diseases Acts in Britain (also 1866 and 1869); intended to contain venereal diseases in garrison towns and ports, the Acts targeted working-class women.
	G. A. Lawrence, *Maurice Dering; or, The Quadrilateral: A Novel*
	A Lady Resident, *The Englishwoman in India*
1865	Lewis Carroll, *Alice's Adventures in Wonderland*
1867 31 December: marries Henry William (Hal) Steel, a civil engineer on leave from the Indian Civil Service, in Scotland.	Second Reform Bill (UK) enfranchises all male householders and male lodgers paying £10 rent per year for unfurnished lodgings, doubling the electorate.
	Karl Marx, *Das Kapital* (vol. i)
1868 1 January: Flora takes ship for India with her husband. Henry Steel posted to Ludhiana where Flora experiences her first serious bout of fever. Transferred to the hill station of Dalhousie, where Flora gives birth to a stillborn daughter.	Wilkie Collins, *The Moonstone*
	James Grant, *First Love and Last Love: A Tale of the Indian Mutiny*
1869	Suez Canal opens. Birth of Mohandas Karamchand (Mahatma) Gandhi. Earl of Mayo appointed Viceroy of India.
1870 10 December: birth of daughter, Mabel.	
1871 Posted to the isolated station of Kasur in the Lahore district, where the Steels are the only Europeans. Flora develops a keen interest in languages and customs of the local villagers.	Lewis Carroll, *Through the Looking-Glass*

Life	*Historical and Cultural Background*
1872 April: Steels return home on leave; Mabel is left with relatives to be brought up 'at home'.	Earl of Northbrook appointed Viceroy of India. Philip Meadows Taylor, *Seeta*
1873 Back in Kasur Flora acts as doctor to the local women and children. She is invited to open the first girls' school in the district, cementing her role as an educationalist in India. In Kasur Flora also designed the Municipal Hall, and assisted in the revival of local handicrafts.	Famine in Bengal.
1875 Flora lends her piano to the Government for use in the camp set up to accommodate the Royal Visit to the district.	October: Prince of Wales (later Edward VII) begins four-month-long visit to India.
1876 Visits Kashmir with Henry and two male friends.	Earl of Lytton appointed Viceroy.
1877 Flora and Henry leave Kasur. Home leave spent in Scotland, Oxford—where Flora met many influential figures of the day including Benjamin Jowett, John Ruskin, Walter Pater, and Charles Dodgson (Lewis Carroll)—and Italy.	Queen Victoria proclaimed Empress of India.
1878	Second Afghan War (1878–80). Wyvern [Colonel Arthur Robert Kenney-Herbert], *Culinary Jottings for Madras*
1879	*Boys' Own Paper* first published. Alfred, Lord Tennyson, 'The Defence of Lucknow' Mrs A. G. F. Eliot James, *A Guide to Indian Household Management*
1880	Marquis of Ripon appointed Viceroy of India.
1881 Second visit to Kashmir with Henry.	

Life	Historical and Cultural Background
1883 Flora rushes home to Scotland but fails to see her mother before her death. Returns to India in autumn, bringing daughter, Mabel, and youngest sister, Daisy, with her.	Ilbert Bill allows Indian judges to try Europeans.
1884 Third visit to Kashmir. Mabel returns home with her aunt in the winter. Flora appointed first female Inspectress of Schools in India. *Wide-Awake Stories: A Collection of Tales Told by Little Children between Sunset and Sunrise in the Punjab and Kashmir* (with R. C. Temple) published.	Marquis of Dufferin and Ava appointed Viceroy of India.
1885 Returns home to settle Mabel in a school. Appointed to Provincial Education Board (1885–8). Appointed vice-president of the Victoria Female Orphan Asylum in the Punjab.	Indian National Congress founded. Third Anglo-Burmese War. H. Rider Haggard, *King Solomon's Mines*
1886	Annexation of Upper Burma. Indian and Colonial Exhibition held in South Kensington, London. Henry Yule and A. C. Burnell, *Hobson-Jobson: A Glossary of Colloquial Anglo-Indian Words and Phrases*
1887	Queen Victoria's Golden Jubilee. Arthur Conan Doyle introduces Sherlock Holmes in *A Study in Scarlet*. H. Rider Haggard, *She: A History of Adventure*
1888 *The Complete Indian Housekeeper and Cook* (non-fiction), with Grace Gardiner, published.	Marquis of Lansdowne appointed Viceroy of India. Sikkim War. Rudyard Kipling, *Plain Tales from the Hills*

Life	Historical and Cultural Background
1889 1 May: Henry retires from ICS. The Steels return to UK; settle in Scotland.	Rudyard Kipling returns to Britain from India.
1890 First short story, 'Lâl', published in *Macmillan's Magazine*; Flora contributes twenty stories to the magazine between 1890 and 1897.	Arthur Conan Doyle, *The Sign of Four*
1891	Age of Consent Act (India) raises the age of statutory rape for 'consenting' Indian brides from 10 years to 12.
1892 Steels lease Dunlugas in Aberdeenshire.	Indian Councils Act expands the additional membership of the Viceroy's Executive Council to sixteen, of whom ten could be non-official, and increases their powers.
1893 *From the Five Rivers* (stories) published; *Miss Stuart's Legacy* (novel) published.	G. A. Henty, *Rujub, the Juggler*
1894 Flora returns to India alone to gather information for her novel on the Mutiny, leaving her husband and daughter to follow later. Meets Laurence Hope in Bombay. In Delhi Flora granted permission to examine the sealed archives of confidential papers relating to the Mutiny.	9th Earl of Elgin appointed Viceroy of India.
The Flower of Forgiveness and Other Stories (stories) published; *The Potter's Thumb* (novel) published; *Wide-Awake Stories* republished as *Tales of the Punjab Told by the People*.	
1895 *Red Rowans* (novel) published.	
1896 *On the Face of the Waters* (novel) published. The novel was rejected by Macmillan before being published by Heinemann.	

Life	Historical and Cultural Background
1897 The Steels establish a temporary base in London, where Flora becomes a lioness of the literary world. Flora organizes a Diamond Jubilee Banquet at the Grafton Galleries for 120 distinguished women and an equal number of male guests.	Queen Victoria's Diamond Jubilee.
The Gift of the Gods (novel) published; *In the Permanent Way* (stories) published; *In the Tideway* (novel) published.	
1898 *The Modern Marriage Market* (non-fiction), with Marie Corelli, Lady June, and Susan, Countess of Malmsbury, published.	
With her husband and daughter Flora makes a final visit to India as the guest of an old friend, now the Commissioner of Lucknow; performs hostess duties for him and carries out research for her novel *Voices in the Night*.	
1899 Flora and her family move to Talgarth Hall, near Machynlleth, North Wales.	Marquess Curzon of Kedleston appointed Viceroy of India.
1900 Much against her parents' wishes, Mabel marries her cousin, John Edward (Jack) Webster, a member of the ICS, and goes out to India.	
Voices in the Night (novel) published; *The Hosts of the Lord* (novel) published.	
1901	North-Western Frontier Province created. Accession of Edward VII.
	Rudyard Kipling, *Kim*
1902	Joseph Conrad, *Heart of Darkness*
1903 Birth of Mabel's first child, Patrick Webster, at Talgarth.	
In the Guardianship of God (stories) published.	

Life	*Historical and Cultural Background*
1904	Co-operative Societies Act (India) enables formation of cooperatives for supplying Indian farmers with cheap credit.
1905 *A Book of Mortals: Being a Record of the Good Deeds and Good Qualities of What Humanity Is Pleased to Call the Lower Animals* (non-fiction) published; *India* (text by FAS; paintings by Mortimer Menpes) (non-fiction) published.	Earl of Minto appointed Viceroy of India. Partition of Bengal.
1906 *A Sovereign Remedy* (novel) published.	All-India Muslim League formed.
1907 Birth of Mabel's second son, Neil, at Talgarth. Both children stay with Flora and Henry during their parents' absences in India.	Rudyard Kipling awarded Nobel Prize for Literature. A. E. W. Mason, *The Broken Road* Maud Diver, *Captain Desmond, V. C.*
1908 *India Through the Ages: A Popular and Picturesque History of Hindustan* (non-fiction) published; *A Prince of Dreamers* (novel), about Akbar, the first of a quartet of romantic historical novels about the lives of the four great Mughal emperors, published.	Robert Baden-Powell, *Scouting for Boys*
1909	Government of India Act, commonly referred to as the Morley-Minto Reforms, allows the election of Indians to the various legislative councils in India for the first time. Maud Diver, *The Englishwoman in India* Chota Mem [Mrs C. Lang], *The English Bride in India, Being Hints on Indian Housekeeping*
1910	Accession of George V. Baron Hardinge of Penshurst appointed Viceroy of India.

	Life	*Historical and Cultural Background*
1911	*The Gift of the Gods* (novel) published.	Delhi Durbar attended by George V and Queen Mary. Capital of British India shifted from Calcutta to Delhi.
1912	*King-Errant* (novel), about Baber, published.	Partition of Bengal revoked.
1913	Flora active in the Votes for Women movement; President of the Women Writers Suffrage League. Flora and her husband move to Court o' Hill, a late seventeenth-century house in Shropshire. *The Adventures of Akbar*, illustrated by Byam Shaw (juvenile novel), published.	Rabindranath Tagore awarded Nobel Prize for Literature. Leonard Woolf, *The Village in the Jungle*
1914	Flora travels to Jamaica with her eldest nephew to put family affairs in order. *The Mercy of the Lord* (stories) published.	First World War (1914–18)
1915		Gandhi returns to India from South Africa.
1916	[?] Pamphlet, *The Fruit of the Tree*, on the causes of the subjection of women, printed and distributed at Flora's own expense.	Baron Chelmsford appointed Viceroy of India. Mrs Besant's Home Rule League founded. Lucknow Pact between Muslim League and Indian National Congress.
1917	*Dramatic History of India: Twenty Playlets* (drama) published; *Marmaduke* (novel) published; *Mistress of Men* (novel), about Jehangir, published.	Montagu Declaration, promises gradual and progressive self-government for India within the British Empire.
1918	*English Fairy Tales* (illustrated by Arthur Rackham) (stories) published.	Suffrage granted in UK to women 30 and over, and men 21 and over.

Life	*Historical and Cultural Background*
1919 Seventeen of Flora's books in print with Heinemann. 3 August: Grace Gardiner dies.	The Rowlatt Act (India) indefinitely extends emergency measures enacted during the First World War, effectively allowing the imperial authorities in India to imprison anti-Government demonstrators without trial. A protest against the Act held in the Jallianwallah Bagh led to the Amritsar massacre on 13 April. Third Afghan War (May to August). Ceylon National Congress established.
1920	Non-cooperation Movement, led by Gandhi, begins in India.
1921	Marquess of Reading appointed Viceroy of India.
1922 Flora and her husband move to 'Beaufort' in Cheltenham where her youngest grandson, Neil, had won a scholarship to Cheltenham College.	
1923 Death of Flora's husband, Henry Steel. *Tales of the Tides, and Other Stories* (stories) published; *A Tale of Indian Heroes: Being the Stories of the* Mahabhrata *and the* Ramayana (stories) published.	
1924 *The Law of the Threshold* (novel) published.	British Empire Exhibition held at Wembley, London (and in 1925). E. M. Forster, *A Passage to India*
1926 Mabel's husband retires from ICS; Flora, Mabel, and Jack take a house at Minchinhampton in the Cotswolds.	Lord Irwin appointed Viceroy of India.
1928 Flora travels to Jamaica with grandson Neil to visit the family property. *The Builder* (novel), about Shah Jehan, published.	Simon Commission arrives in India to look into the state of Indian constitutional affairs and advise on the future of India. Equal suffrage granted to men and women in UK.

Life	*Historical and Cultural Background*
1929 12 April: dies at the age of 82 in Talgarth, Wales.	
The Curse of Eve (novel) published; *The Garden of Fidelity: Being the Autobiography of Flora Annie Steel, 1847–1929* published.	
1933 *Indian Scene: Collected Short Stories of Flora Annie Steel, 1847–1929* (stories) published.	

THE COMPLETE INDIAN

HOUSEKEEPER & COOK

GIVING THE DUTIES OF MISTRESS AND SERVANTS
THE GENERAL MANAGEMENT OF THE HOUSE
AND PRACTICAL RECIPES FOR COOKING
IN ALL ITS BRANCHES

TO

THE ENGLISH GIRLS

TO WHOM

FATE MAY ASSIGN THE TASK OF BEING

HOUSE-MOTHERS

IN

OUR EASTERN EMPIRE

THIS LITTLE VOLUME IS

DEDICATED

BY

GRACE GARDINER AND FLORA ANNIE STEEL

PREFACE TO THE PRESENT EDITION

THE great, and to some extent unnecessary, rise in the price of living during the last few years in India calls for a revision of economics in this book. I have therefore substituted for my experience of ten years back that of the winter of '97–'98, during which I kept a large house in one of the most expensive stations of Upper India.* Housekeepers may therefore rely upon the data given being realities of to-day. At the same time, I feel it a duty to record my sincere regret that it is becoming nearly as difficult to determine the fair price of a thing in India as it is in London, where a similar and sometimes actually the same article is offered at half-a-dozen different shops at half-a-dozen different prices. The old system of regulating price by consent is dying out, with many another custom which protects the poor. It seems to me, therefore, that housekeeping in India to-day has a political and social as well as a domestic side, and that those who, to save themselves trouble, or to avoid the loss of a luxury, consent to give a price which has no real relation to the intrinsic value or cost of the article, are sinning against a society the great mass of which is poor beyond belief.

The theory that a thing is worth what you can get for it has ruined commercial morality in England, and is at the bottom of all the difficulties between labour and capital. It is fast ruining India, which ere long will need that sign of civilisation—a poor rate.*

Perhaps so benevolent a consummation is desirable. The writer, however, prefers charity at home; the charity which will not, from laziness or negligence, either make it harder for others to live, or allow those others to degrade themselves by taking an unfair advantage of their neighbours.

F. A. S.

December 1898.

PREFACE TO THE FIRST EDITION

THIS book, it is hoped, will meet the very generally felt want for a practical guide to young housekeepers in India. A large proportion of English ladies in this country come to it newly married, to begin a new life, and take up new responsibilities under absolutely new conditions.

Few, indeed, have had any practical experience of housekeeping of any sort or kind; whilst those who have find themselves almost as much at sea as their more ignorant sisters. How can it be otherwise, when the familiar landmarks are no longer visible, and, amid the crowd of idle, unintelligible servants, there seems not one to carry on the usual routine of household work, which in England follows as a matter of course?

The kitchen is a black hole, the pantry a sink. The only servant who will condescend to tidy up is a skulking savage with a reed broom; whilst pervading all things broods the stifling, enervating atmosphere of custom, against which energy beats itself unavailingly, as against a feather bed.

The authors themselves know what it is to look round on a large Indian household, seeing that all things are wrong, all things slovenly, yet feeling paralysed by sheer inexperience in the attempt to find a remedy.

It is in the hopes of supplying a little experience at second-hand that this book has been written. In it an attempt has been made to assimilate the duties of each servant to those of his or her English compeer, and thus to show the new-comer where the fault lies, if fault exists. Also, as briefly as possible, to point out bad habits which are sure to be met with, and suggest such remedies as the authors' experience has proved to be successful. And here it may be remarked, that the very possession of the book may be held to presuppose some desire on the part of the possessor to emulate the wife who does her husband good, and not evil, all the days of her life, by looking well to the ways of her household.

One can scarcely begin a book of this sort by an essay on ethics; therefore the authors premise a certain sense of duty, and the educated refinement which refuses to eat more than the necessary peck of dirt.

In the Cookery Book, which follows as a second part, the authors have again worked from practical experience, not only of the recipes themselves, but also of the exigencies of Indian life in the present day. The age of the Nabobs* is past, the Pagoda tree* extinct as the dodo; and, though butcher's meat remains cheap, and most of the necessaries of life are reasonable, the rupee at one and fourpence and a fraction makes economy a grave question for most Indian officials. With young mouths at home eating beefsteak at a rupee and a quarter per pound, the number of those sadly depreciated images of Her Gracious Majesty which remain for *pater* and *materfamilias* is often but small.

So in the recipes the authors have given as wide a berth as possible to 'Europe stores';* to everything, in short, which makes a perusal of the daily rate of exchange a terror and a despair.

In order to simplify the training of servants as far as possible the authors have arranged to issue the various chapters on the duties of servants in the form of pamphlets in Urdu and Hindi. The price of each pamphlet will be from one to two annas; and it is believed that they will be found of great use, as, even when the servants cannot read, they can get some one to read to them.

The Cookery Book will be simultaneously published in Urdu at the lowest possible price.

F. A. S.
G. G.

PREFACE TO THE THIRD EDITION

IN sending out the third edition—the second having followed too closely on the heels of the first to need any preface—the authors have only to say that the whole book has been carefully revised, corrected, and brought up to date. The cookery recipes have been largely increased and simplified, and the work adapted, as far as possible, to the requirements of all parts of India. An English experience of three years has taught the writers that dirt, slovenliness, and want of method are not confined to one hemisphere, while civilisation is apt to bring other trials to the house-mother. Their advice, therefore, to those beginning to housekeep in India is—make the most of the patience, good temper, and old-fashioned sense of servitude, which Board Schools* do not teach.

LONDON, *November* 1893.

CONTENTS

CHAPTER I

THE DUTIES OF THE MISTRESS

HOUSEKEEPING in India, when once the first strangeness has worn off, is a far easier task in many ways than it is in England, though it none the less requires time, and, in this present transitional period, an almost phenomenal patience; for, while one mistress enforces cleanliness according to European methods, the next may belong to the opposite faction, who, so long as the dinner is nicely served, thinks nothing of it being cooked in a kitchen which is also used as a latrine; the result being that the servants who serve one and then the other stamp of mistress, look on the desire for decency as a mere personal and distinctly disagreeable attribute of their employer, which, like a bad temper or stinginess, may be resented or evaded.

And, first, it must be distinctly understood that it is not necessary, or in the least degree desirable, that an educated woman should waste the best years of her life in scolding and petty supervision. Life holds higher duties, and it is indubitable that friction and overzeal is a sure sign of a bad housekeeper. But there is an appreciable difference between the careworn Martha* vexed with many things, and the absolute indifference displayed by many Indian mistresses, who put up with a degree of slovenliness and dirt which would disgrace a den in St. Giles,* on the principle that it is no use attempting to teach the natives.

They never go into their kitchens, for the simple reason that their appetite for breakfast might be marred by seeing the *khitmutgâr*[1] using his toes as an efficient toast-rack (*fact*); or their desire for dinner weakened by seeing the soup strained through a greasy *pugri*.

The ostrich, who, according to the showman, *''ides 'is head in the sand and thinks as 'e can't see no one, as nobody can't see 'e,'* has,

---

[1] The object of this book being to enable a person who is absolutely unacquainted with India, its language and people, to begin housekeeping at once, the authors have decided on adhering throughout to purely phonetic spelling. The only accent used will be the circumflex.

fortunately, an exceptional faculty of digestion. With this remark we will leave a very unpleasant subject.

Easy, however, as the actual housekeeping is in India, the personal attention of the mistress is quite as much needed here as at home. The Indian servant, it is true, learns more readily, and is guiltless of the sniffiness with which Mary Jane* receives suggestions, but a few days of absence or neglect on the part of the mistress, results in the servants falling into their old habits with the inherited conservatism of dirt. This is, of course, disheartening, but it has to be faced as a necessary condition of life, until a few generations of training shall have started the Indian servant on a new inheritance of habit. It must never be forgotten that at present those mistresses who aim at anything beyond keeping a good table are in the minority, and that pioneering is always arduous work.

The first duty of a mistress is, of course, to be able to give intelligible orders to her servants; therefore it is necessary she should learn to speak Hindustani.* No sane Englishwoman would dream of living, say, for twenty years, in Germany, Italy, or France, without making the *attempt*, at any rate, to learn the language. She would, in fact, feel that by neglecting to do so she would write herself down an ass. It would be well, therefore, if ladies in India were to ask themselves if a difference in longitude increases the latitude allowed in judging of a woman's intellect.

The next duty is obviously to insist on her orders being carried out. And here we come to the burning question, 'How is this to be done?' Certainly, there is at present very little to which we can appeal in the average Indian servant, but then, until it is implanted by training, there is very little sense of duty in a child; yet in some well-regulated nurseries obedience is a foregone conclusion. The secret lies in making rules, and *keeping to them*. The Indian servant is a child in everything save age, and should be treated as a child; that is to say, kindly, but with the greatest firmness. The laws of the household should be those of the Medes and Persians,* and first faults should never go unpunished. By overlooking a first offence, we lose the only opportunity we have of preventing it becoming a habit.

But it will be asked, How are we to punish our servants when we have no hold either on their minds or bodies?—when cutting their pay is illegal, and few, if any, have any real sense of shame.

The answer is obvious. Make a hold.

In their own experience the authors have found a system of rewards and punishments perfectly easy of attainment. One of them has for years adopted the plan of engaging her servants at so much a month—the lowest rate at which such servant is obtainable—and so much extra as *buksheesh*, conditional on good service. For instance, a *khitmutgâr* is engaged permanently on Rs. 9 a month, but the additional rupee which makes the wage up to that usually demanded by good servants is a fluctuating assessment! From it small fines are levied, beginning with one pice for forgetfulness, and running up, through degrees of culpability, to one rupee for lying. The money thus returned to imperial coffers may very well be spent on giving small rewards; so that each servant knows that by good service he can get back his own fines. That plan has never been objected to, and such a thing as a servant giving up his place has never been known in the author's experience. On the contrary, the household quite enters into the spirit of the idea, infinitely preferring it to volcanic eruptions of fault-finding.

To show what absolute children Indian servants are, the same author has for years adopted castor oil as an ultimatum in all obstinate cases, on the ground that there must be some physical cause for inability to learn or to remember. This is considered a great joke, and exposes the offender to much ridicule from his fellow-servants; so much so, that the words, '*Mem Sahib tum ko zuroor kâster ile pila dena hoga*' (*The Mem Sahib will have to give you castor oil*), is often heard in the mouths of the upper servants* when new-comers give trouble. In short, without kindly and reasonable devices of this kind, the usual complaint of a want of hold over servants *must* remain true until they are educated into some sense of duty. Of course, common-sense is required to adjust the balance of rewards and punishments, for here again Indian servants are like children, in that they have an acute sense of justice. A very good plan for securing a certain amount of truthfulness in a servant is to insist that any one who has been caught out in a distinct falsehood should invariably bring witnesses to prove the truth of the smallest detail. It is a great disgrace and worry, generally producing a request to be given another chance after a few days. These remarks, written ten years ago, are still applicable, though the Indian mistress has now to guard against the possibility of impertinence. It should never be overlooked for an instant.

To turn to the minor duties of a mistress, it may be remarked that she is primarily responsible for the decency and health of all persons living in her service or compound. With this object, she should insist upon her servants living in their quarters, and not in the bazaar;* but this, on the other hand, is no reason why they should turn your domain into a caravanserai* for their relations to the third and fourth generation. As a rule, it is well to draw a very sharp line in this respect, and if it be possible to draw it on the other side of the mothers-in-law, so much the better for peace and quietness.

Of course, if the rule that all servants shall live in quarters be enforced, it becomes the mistress's duty to see that they are decently housed, and have proper sanitary conveniences. The bearer should have strict orders to report any illness of any kind amongst the servants or their belongings; indeed, it is advisable for the mistress to inquire every day on this point, and as often as possible—once or twice a week at least—she should go a regular inspection round the compound, not forgetting the stables, fowl-houses, &c.

With regard to the kitchen, every mistress worthy the name will insist on having a building suitable for this use, and will not put up with a dog-kennel. On this point the authors cannot refrain from expressing their regret, that where the power exists of forcing land-lords into keeping their houses in repair, and supplying sanitary arrangements, as in cantonments,* this power has not been exercised in regard to the most important thing of all; that is, to the procur-ing of kitchens, where the refuse and offal of ages cannot percolate through the mud floors, and where the drain water does not most effectually apply sewage to a large surrounding area. With existing arrangements many and many an attack of typhoid might be traced to children playing near the kitchen and pantry drain, and as in large stations the compounds narrow from lessening room, the evil will become greater.

In regard to actual housekeeping, the authors emphatically deny the common assertion that it must necessarily run on different lines to what it does in England. Economy, prudence, efficiency are the same all over the world, and because butcher meat is cheap, that is no excuse for its being wasted. Some modification, of course, there must be, *but as little as possible*. It is, for instance, most desirable that the mistress should keep a regular storeroom, containing not merely an assortment of tinned foods, as is usually the case, but rice, sugar, flour, potatoes, &c.; everything, in short, which, under the common custom, comes into the *khânsâmâh*'s daily account, and helps more than larger items to swell the monthly bills. For it is *absolutely impossible* for him to give a true account of consumption of these things daily, and so the item must in every case be a nominal charge far above actual expenditure. With regard to the best plan for keeping this storeroom, the next chapter must be consulted.

A good mistress in India will try to set a good example to her servants in routine, method, and tidiness. Half-an-hour after breakfast should be sufficient for the whole arrangements for the day; but that half-hour should be given as punctually as possible. An untidy mistress invariably has *untidy*, a weak one, *idle* servants. It should never be forgotten that—though it is true in both hemispheres that if you want a thing done you should do it yourself—still, having to do it is a distinct confession of failure in your original intention. Anxious housewives are too apt to accept defeat in this way; the result being that the lives of educated women are wasted in doing the work of lazy servants.

The authors' advice is therefore—

'*Never do work which an ordinarily good servant ought to be able to do. If the one you have will not or cannot do it, get another who can.*'

In regard to engaging new servants, written certificates to character* are for the most part of no use whatever, except in respect to length of service, and its implied testimony to honesty. A man who has been six or seven years in one place is not likely to be a thief, though the authors regret to say the fact is no safeguard as far as qualifications go. The best plan is to catch your servants young, promoting them to more experienced wages on the *buksheesh* theory abovementioned. They generally learn fast enough if it is made worth their while in this way. On the other hand, it is, as a rule, a mistake to keep servants *too long* in India. Officials* should be especially careful on this point, as the Oriental mind connects a confidential servant with corruption.

To return to written certificates. Their total abolition is impossible in India where the society is so fluctuating, but it would certainly be advantageous if a stand against them was made, except in certain cases. There is no reason whatever why further personal reference should not be requested. In the majority of cases this request *could* be complied with, to the great benefit of distracted housekeepers who, having engaged a cook adorned apparently by the seven cardinal

virtues,* find that the only merit he possesses is being the son of a
father who, having died in the odour of sanctity, left his certificates
to be divided amongst his children! But in this, as in all the difficulties besetting Indian housekeeping, *combined* effort is wanting. For
instance, it may safely be said that if Indian servants found cleanliness
necessary in every service they took, the present abominations would
soon disappear, for they are naturally obedient.

It is always advisable to give neat, durable, livery coats* for
wearing when on actual duty in the house. Broadcloth* is a mistake,
being hard to keep clean, and apt to get fusty. Good washing serge,
such as that to be got at the Elgin Mills,* is best, made to fit well, but
loosely, with sleeves of proper length and width. These coats, in the
case of table servants, should hang on pegs in the pantry, and only
be put on for actual attendance. If carefully brushed and put away
as the warm season* comes on, they will last for two years. For camp
work, &c., a commoner washing suit may be given, and in the hot
weather, cotton liveries of dark blue, which can be washed regularly
every week. Any little extra expense is better than having a servant
behind your chair who reeks of dirt and smoke; or, what is worse, a
whited sepulchre,* whose outside snowiness conceals warm clothes
which have been slept in for months.

Finally, when all is said and done, the whole duty of an Indian
mistress towards her servants is neither more or less than it is in
England. Here, as there, a little reasonable human sympathy is the
best oil for the household machine. Here, as there, the end and object
is not merely personal comfort, but the formation of a home—that
unit of civilisation where father and children, master and servant,
employer and employed, can learn their several duties. When all is
said and done also, herein lies the natural outlet for most of the talent peculiar to women. It is the fashion nowadays to undervalue the
art of making a home; to deem it simplicity and easiness itself. But
this is a mistake, for the proper administration of even a small household needs both brain and heart. A really clever woman always sees
this, and, like George Eliot,* the greatest of modern women, prides
herself on being an excellent housekeeper. It was written of her that
'*nothing offends her more than the idea that her exceptional intellectual
powers should be held to absolve her from ordinary household duties.*'* In
regard to expenditure, the mistress of a house has it in her power to
make debts, as to prevent them, for she, and she only, has the power

of preventing that extravagance in small things, which is but the prelude to a like recklessness in greater matters.

It is astonishing how few women know how to keep accounts; yet this is the first step towards economy, and a little method and care in this point saves infinite friction. One special fault which the authors believe besets most women is the habit of not showing all transactions on paper. For instance, in paying a minor bill, some *annas* or *pice* are allowed to remain as an advance to be deducted from the next payment, which must then either be written down less than it is, or paid less than it is written down. This is absolutely a false system, and is the cause of more dispute and hopeless addings up of balances than a novice can well imagine. So if you have two or more funds you nominally wish to keep separate, do not borrow from one and pay back to the other without showing the transaction; above all, do not receive small items of money and keep them off the paper altogether by saying, 'Ah, I paid that to So-and-so, therefore it is all square.' Accounts, in fact, do not come under the head of *Cookery*.

But on this subject we refer the reader to the special chapter on Accounts; here we may only warn young housekeepers not to descend to wrangling over prices or items. Make up your mind as to the fair price. Do not take an article at an exorbitant one simply because you want it. Some housekeepers in India nowadays cheerfully give the equivalent of one and sixpence per pound for bad beef, and by so doing are ruining the poor. Accept past deceit or fraud as *past*; tell the offender quietly that you do not intend to pay such a price again, and in cases of extravagance, give the order that in future the ingredients are to be brought to you before being put into use. If meat is bad, or dear, resort for a week to doing your own marketing, but do not sit for half-an-hour and squabble over it with your *khânsâmâh*. Make it a rule that all food which is to be used that day shall be personally inspected by the mistress, otherwise you may pay good prices for bad things. It must be remembered that half the faults of native servants arise from want of thought and method, and that mere fault-finding will never mend matters. A mistress must know not only where the fault lies, but how to mend it. So, in keeping accounts, a mistress *must* take the lead, and, knowing the proper prices of the different articles, and the amount which ought to be consumed, set aside all objections with a high hand.

Having thus gone generally into the duties of the mistress, we may detail what in our opinion should be the daily routine.

The great object is to secure three things—smooth working, quick ordering, and subsequent peace and leisure to the mistress. It is as well, therefore, with a view to the preservation of temper, to eat your breakfast in peace before venturing into the pantry and cookroom; it is besides a mistake to be constantly on the worry.

Inspection parade should begin, then, immediately after breakfast, or as near ten o'clock as circumstances will allow. The cook should be waiting—in clean raiment—with a pile of plates, and his viands for the day spread out on a table. With everything *en evidence*, it will not take five minutes to decide on what is best, while a very constant occurrence at Indian tables—the serving up of stale, sour, and unwholesome food—will be avoided. It is perhaps *not* pleasant to go into such details, but a good mistress will remember the bread-winner who requires blood-forming nourishment, and the children whose constitutions are being built up day by day, sickly or healthy, according to the food given them; and bear in mind the fact that, in India especially, half the comfort of life depends on clean, wholesome, digestible food.

Luncheon and dinner ordered, the mistress should proceed to the storeroom, when both the bearer and the *khitmutgâr* should be in attendance. Another five minutes will suffice to give out everything required for the day's consumption, the accounts, writing of orders, &c., will follow, and then the mistress (with a sinking heart) may begin the daily inspection of pantry, scullery, and kitchen. But before she sets foot in the back purlieus,* let her remember that if a mistress will not give proper appliances, she cannot expect cleanliness. If, however, this excuse is not valid, the authors' advice is— *notice the least dirt quietly, with the order that before going for his mid-day recess the servant in fault shall come personally and report its removal.* Let the mistress then send another servant to see if this be true; but let her guard against giving herself the least trouble in the matter. For here, again, Indian servants are like children, gaining a certain satisfaction in the idea that at any rate they have been *troublesome*.

We do not wish to advocate an unholy haughtiness; but an Indian household can no more be governed peacefully, without dignity and prestige, than an Indian Empire. For instance, if the mistress wishes to teach the cook a new dish, let her give the order for everything, down to charcoal, to be ready at a given time, and the cook in attendance; and let her do nothing herself that the servants can do, if only for this reason, that the only way of teaching is to *see* things done, not to let others see *you* do them.

Another duty which must never be omitted, so long as copper vessels are used for cooking, is their weekly inspection to see that the tinning is entire. No more fruitful source of danger and disease can be imagined than a dirty copper saucepan; and unless proper supervision is given, we advise every mistress who has any desire to avoid serious risk, both to her own family and her *guest*, to use nothing but steel or enamelled utensils.[1] In many jails also, nowadays, glazed earthenware utensils may be had, which will stand a charcoal fire, and are invaluable for milk, fruit, and soups. In fact, a much larger variety of articles can now be had of native manufacture than was possible ten years ago. It need hardly be said that, wherever practicable, it is clearly the Indian housekeeper's duty to encourage native industry, and at the same time, by never offering an unfair price or submitting to one, striving to prevent the evils of our civilisation going hand in hand with the good.

In regard to other household questions. The bearer's account for odds and ends is apt to be a source of trouble; indeed, a well-known Indian story tells of a bachelor who with a smile paid 820 rupees at the end of a year for *soot-sooie-button* (needles and threads and buttons). This was a palpable extravagance; yet the usual price charged and acquiesced in for matches, even in the hot weather, when the mere thought of fires is offensive, is 8 annas a month; for which sum 4 dozen boxes can be bought. It is wise, therefore, to limit the number of odds and ends, for which this servant is responsible, to the lowest ebb. *Jhârans* (dusters) are another source of trouble. Some ladies give them out every day, others once a week. The latter is perhaps the best way, if it ends in inspection, as you can then see the dirt better, and impose a fine for the using of glass cloths as sink swabs, and so on;

---

[1] Since writing the above, complaints that after a time the steel saucepans require tinning have reached the authors. These arise from a mistaken notion. The pans do *not* require tinning. If properly scrubbed with sand or Brookes' soap,* they will wear away to nothing without the necessity for tinning. There is no *copper* to require it, and the last film of steel is as safe as the first.

while in the daily plan, the dignity which doth hedge about* a perfectly clean cloth, gives a fictitious virtue to the servant using it! As a rule, one and a half-dozen coarse kitchen cloths, half-a-dozen glass, and half-a-dozen tea-cloths per week should suffice to remove all possibility of excuse from the pantry.

CHAPTER II

THE STOREROOM

THIS should contain proper shelves and receptacles. A row of common earthen *ghurras*—or earthen pots with lids—will be found most useful for rice, coarse sugar, split peas, *soojee*, &c. Empty tins—especially kerosene tins—of all sorts can be utilised by having suitable covers made for them. Great care is necessary in seeing that everything is tightly closed, or black ants and other insects will be a constant trouble. A two or three tiered table with strong wooden legs which can be stood in earthen saucers kept full of water, will be found most useful in the storeroom. On it all open tins, sugar, &c., can be kept in perfect security *if the saucers are kept full of water.*

In some things it is, of course, desirable to leave a certain supply with the cook, as it is extremely inconvenient to have to go to the storeroom for more potatoes, &c., if unexpected guests appear. But it is very easy to arrive at a fair idea of the weekly consumption of some few articles, and these it is best to give out in a lump, on the principle of avoiding all unnecessary trouble. Once the average has been fixed, any departure from it can be checked by recalling immediate control; this generally reduces the offender to reason at once. If *ghee* is used in cooking, it is well to buy it in quantities of a *seer* or two, and give it out. Otherwise one is never certain what abomination the *khânsâmâh* may not purchase. Even at the *best* houses it is no uncommon thing to find good dishes entirely spoilt by bad butter or *ghee*.

In India it is always advisable to limit quantity in the storeroom, since one is liable to sudden changes of station. It used, however, to be infinitely cheaper to import European stores for oneself than to trust to the most moderate firms in India; but nowadays, owing to the daily strengthening struggle for existence which affects even India, it is possible to get most things quite as cheaply from the larger native shops in the central towns. A comparison, however, should always be made, not only with store prices, but with those of the large export merchants. One great advantage of dealing with the shops is that large quantities need not be laid in at one time, and the risk of having to carry heavy goods from one station to another minimised; the disadvantage is the possibility of the goods not being fresh. But this also is minimised by the infinitely larger business done nowadays by native shops, so that some have supplies from England every month. Then the less any one has to do with tinned soups, fish, and cooked meat, the better. They are at best the means of evading starvation.

With some diffidence, the authors append a list of those things which ought to be in an Indian *godown* or storeroom—

FARINACEOUS FOODS

Cornflour.	Barley.	Semolina.	Flour.
Arrowroot.	Oatmeal.	Macaroni.	Soojee.
Sago.	Hominy.	Vermicelli.	Tapioca.

Indian flour from many local mills, notably at Delhi and Bombay, will be found quite equal to Snowflake American,* and more than half as cheap again. Indian vermicelli or *semâi* is no bad substitute for Italian, and *soojee* will take the place in all recipes of semolina. It is, in fact, the 'florador' of English shops. Wheaten groats or *dulliya* make excellent porridge. Rice, of course, is to be had of various kinds and prices in the bazaar. That called *bârsi muttee* is the best for curry.

CONDIMENTS AND PRESERVES

Olives.	Vinegar.	Store sauces.	Preserves.
Pickles.	Salad oil.	Syrups.	Dried herbs.
Chutnies.	Mustard.	Jams.	Tarragon vinegar.

Pickles are preferable when home-made, and sauces for common kitchen use are also better made at home. Where economy is an object, nothing on this list save the olives, vinegar, mustard, and salad oil need be bought. We strongly recommend getting the salad oil in five-pound tins through the Italian wine merchants, Acerboni & Co., Calcutta.* When the tin is opened, the oil should be decanted into bottles and sealed up. For high-class cooking this oil is the best frying medium in the world.

RELISHES

Norwegian anchovies.	[1]*Caviare.*	*Oysters.*
Anchovies in salt.	*Sardines.*	*Cheese.*
[1]*Pâte de foie gras.*	[1]*Lax.**	[1]*Sausages.*

These are not necessary, but a very small supply goes a long way. Potted meats are far better made fresh, and a saving cook will always have plenty of fish, tongue, game, or ham trimmings to keep up the supply. Parmesan cheese is a mistake; it never keeps fresh. Cornish sardines are cheap, and do well for toast.

DRIED FRUITS

Raisins.	*Plums.*	*Sultanas.*
Currants.	*Figs.*	*Prunes.*
Apricots.	*Apple rings.*	*Almonds.*

Country raisins (*munukkhâ*) do admirably. Dried apricots (*koobânee*), plums (*âloo bokhâra*), figs (*unjeer*), sultanas (*kishmish*), and almonds (*buddâm*) may be had in every bazaar; prunes, currants, and apple rings from home. The Californian fruits in tins* are extremely useful, especially in the hot season.

VEGETABLES

French peas.	*Mushrooms.*	*Tomatoes.*
French beans.	*Asparagus.*	[1]*Truffles.*

The fewer of these the better; but these five kinds will be found the best, the tomatoes especially.

[1] If expense is no object.

Miscellaneous*

Tea.	Gelatine.	Knife-powder.
Sugar.	Candles.	Soap.
Coffee.	Spirits of wine.	Plate-powder.
Treacle.	Essences.	Blacking.
Yeast powder.	Brookes' soap.	Matches.
Cocoatina.	Browning.	Kitchen papers.
Rutz pommade.	Beeswax.	Brown polish.

Soap may be had of excellent quality from the North-west Company; sugar, treacle, vinegar, and spirits of wine from Shâh-jehânpore.

Drugs*

Castor oil.	Cream of tartar.	Saltpetre.
Carbonate of soda.	Alum.	Sal ammoniac.
Tartaric acid.	Sulphur.	Linseed meal.
Borax.	Turpentine.	Methylated spirit.
Phenacetin.	Boracic acid.	Vaseline.

The storeroom should either contain another table, or there should be one immediately outside, where a pair of scales and a few tin measures can be kept. Here also the *khitmutgâr* can place in readiness the sugar basins, sauce bottles, &c., which require refilling. The recapitulation of all these minor matters would be superfluous were we dealing with English household management, but the want of method and comfortable arrangement is acquiesced in so calmly in India, that it becomes necessary to point out how easily convenience may be secured in these small matters.

For the information of new comers, we append an alphabetical list of the more common articles of general consumption, with their Hindustani equivalents; as before, a purely phonetic spelling has been adopted, which will, it is hoped, obviate all mispronunciation.

A

Allspice	*Kebâb cheenee*
Almonds	*Buddâm*
Alum	*Phitkurri*
Apples	*Sa-oo*
Apricots	*Koomânee*

B

Barley for horses	*Jou*
„ ground	*Udâwâ*
Beans	*Same*
Beetroot	*Chukunda*
Bone	*Huddi*
Brains	*Bheyjâ*
Bran	*Chôkâr*
Bread	*Rôtee*
Broad beans	*Bârklâ*
Browning	*Rung grævi*
Butter	*Mukkun*
„ clarified	*Ghee*
Butter-milk	*Lussee*

C

Cabbage	*Gôbee*
Candles	*Buttee*
Carrot	*Gâjer*
Cauliflower	*Phoolgôbee*
Cayenne	*Lâl merch*
Charcoal	*Kô-elâ*
Cheese	*Pun-eer*
Cherries	*Geelâs*
Chicken	*Moorghee*
Cinnamon	*Dâl-cheenee*
Claret	*Lâl sherâb*
Cocoanut kernel	*Khôprâ*
Cocoanut	*Neriyâl*
Coffee	*Kâffey*
Cream	*Mulla-i*
Crust	*Krâs*

Cucumber	*Keera*
Curry	*Kâree*
Custard	*Kustel*

D

Dough	*Mâ-wâ*
Dripping	{ *Kubâb-ki-churbee*
Drops	*Boonda*
Duck	*Butuk*

E

Eggs	*Un-dâ*
Essence	*Khooshboo*

F

Fennel	*Sômph*
Figs	*Unjeer*
Fish	*Muchchlee*
Flour	*Myda*
„ brown	*Âtta*
Flower	*Phool*
Forcemeat	{ *E-stuffin (stuffing)*
Fruit	*Phul*

G

Game	*Shikâr*
Garnish	*Sujâwut*
Ginger	*Udruk*
„ dried	*Sônth*
Glaze	*Leyzum*
Goose	*Hâns*
Gram	*Chunnâ*
Grapes	*Ungoor*
Guava	*Umrood*
Guinea-fowl	*Belâtee teetur*

H

Hare	*Khâr-gôsh*
Head	*Kullâ*
Herbs	*Hurra musâlâ*
Honey	*Shâhud*
Horseradish (Indian)	*Sôhâgnâ*

I

Ice	*Burf*
Icing	*Sufade leyzum*
Indian corn	*Mukâi*

J

Jam	*Merubbâ*

K

Kidney	*Goordâ*

L

Lemon	*Nimboo*
Lettuce	*Sulâd*
Liver	*Kulay-ji*

M

Mace	*Jowtree*
Maize	*Boota*
Mango	*Âm*
Meat	*Gôsht*
Melon	*Kerbooza*
Milk	*Doodh*
Mint	*Budeena*
Mulberry	*Toot*
Mustard	*Râ-ee*

N

Nutmeg	*Jâeephul*

O

Oatmeal	*Belâtee duliya*
Oil	*Tale*
Oil cake*	*Kull*
Onions	*Peeâz*
Orange	*Nuringee*

P

Palate*	*Tâloo*
Parsley	*Petercelli*
Partridge	*Teetur*
Paste	*Krâs*
Pea	*Mutter*
Peach	*Âroo*
Pears	*Nâsh pâtee*
Pepper	*Mirch*
Pickle	*Uchchâr*
Pigeon	*Kubooter*
Pineapple	*Unnunâs*
Plum	*Âloo bokhârâ*
Potato	*Âloo*
Preserve	*Mo-rubbâ*
Pumpkin	*Kuddoo*

Q

Quail	*Buteer*
Quince	*Beehee*

R

Rabbit	*Khârgôsh*
Radish	*Moolee*
Raisins	*Munukhâ*
„ sultana	*Kishmish*
Rice	*Châwul*

Roast	*Kubâb*	Turkey	*Peroo*
		Turnip	*Sulgum*
S		Turpentine	*Târpin*
Salad	*Sulâd*		
Salt	*Nimuk*	**V**	
Saltpetre	*Shora*	Vegetables	*Turkâree*
Snipe*	*Chchâhâ*	Venison	*Hern-ke-*
Soap	*Sâbon*		*gôsht*
Soup	*Surwâ*		
Spices	*Mâsâlâ*	**W**	
Spinach	*Sâg*		
Spirits of wine	*Tez shurâb*	Walnut	*Ukrôt*
Suet	*Chârbee*	Water-melon	*Turbooza*
Sugar	*Misree*	Whites of eggs	*Sufadee*
Sulphur	*Gunduk*	Wild duck	*Moorghâbi*
		Wine	*Sherâb*
T		Wood	*Lukri*
Tea	*Châ*		
Tinning	*Kulâee*	**Y**	
Tomato	*Belâtee bangen*	Yeast	*Kumeer*
Tongue	*Jeeb*	Yolk	*Zurdee*
Treacle	*Râb*		

Weights and measures are always a trouble in India, for they vary much; but for the purpose of recipes it is as well to consider the imperial *seer of* sixteen *chittâcks* as equal to two pounds. Hence—

8 *chittâcks* = 1 lb.   1 *chittâck* = 2 ozs.

Where other weights are not available, it is convenient to remember that forty *sikka* rupees go as nearly as possible to one pound; hence for practical purposes two and a half rupees equal one ounce.

Liquid measure is based on the same *seer* of eighty rupees' weight, and for practical purposes also it may be considered that one *seer* is equal to a quart. As a matter of fact, there is *no* liquid measure in India, and as the density of every liquid varies, you may get a greater quantity of poor milk than you will of rich. Nevertheless, good cow's milk will run as near as possible one quart to a *seer*, while distilled water would run one *seer*, two *chittâcks*, to the quart. But in nearly every place in the north of India, milk is sold to *natives* by the Lahori *seer** of twenty *chittâcks*, though not one European in a thousand dreams that he is paying one-quarter more than the recognised price when the wily milkman supplies him with the ordinary *seer*. This is one of the many ways in which the *sahib lôg* are made to pay for their position.

The following are useful memoranda in weights and measures *for cookery*:—

Liquids

1 Teaspoon	1	drachm.
1 Dessertspoon	2	„
1 Tablespoon	½	oz.
1 Sherry glass	1½	„
1 Teacup	¼	pint.
1 Tumbler or breakfast cup	½	„
1 Peg tumbler	1	„

In giving recipes not in this book to a cook, simplify them as much as possible by substituting measures for weights.

Those given in this book being simply proportional, it follows that any unit of measurement may be taken. A recipe can be made of any size, the only condition being that the same measure, whether tea-spoon or tumbler, be used throughout.

For verification, however, and help in reducing other recipes to the same form, it may be said that one tablespoon full and pressed down by the hand, is held to equal one ounce of most things, save suet, which is only half an ounce. One English egg also equals two table-spoons; therefore the tablespoon will be found the best unit, and it is the one adopted in this book.

Many English recipes speak of a gill: it is a quarter of a pint.

Weight and measures for medicines must be accurate. The latter requires a properly graduated glass, but in emergency it may be remembered that a drop is nearly, but as a rule not quite, one minim; and that a new rupee weighs 180 grains or 3 drachms, an eight-anna bit 90 grains or 1½ drachms, and a four-anna bit 45 grains or ¾ of a drachm.

Hence the following:—

Since one drachm, apothecaries' weight, equals 65.82 measured minims, then an eight-anna bit, which weighs 1½ drachms, is equal to, as near as possible, 98 measured minims, and a four-anna bit to 49 measured minims. Sixty minims go to one liquid drachm. Practically, therefore, a four-anna bit will be five-sixths of a measured drachm. On emergencies also, smaller weights can be made by beating a four-anna bit into a strip, and dividing it into three equal bits,— weighing, of course, fifteen grains each,—and so on to other subdivisions. Any native jeweller will do this.

CHAPTER III

ACCOUNTS

IT is perhaps a not sufficiently considered fact that all public servants in India are bound to keep written accounts showing their total yearly receipts and expenditure. Apart, however, from the question of duty, there can be none as to the practical utility of being able at a glance to see how the money has gone, and how much you can spare for those things which raise life beyond the mere thought for what we are to eat and drink, and wherewithal we are to be clothed. Again, in justice to your own honesty, it is wiser to have a safeguard against the risk of slander, which of late years has greatly increased in India, and must continue to increase until the great mass of the people cease to look on bribery as a part of the routine of life. It becomes a wife's duty, therefore, to see that this precaution is not neglected; and as it is, undoubtedly, better in every way that the person who makes the payments should be responsible for the accounts and keep the purse, it appears very desirable that at the outset married people should settle between themselves who is to undertake the duty. For ourselves, we believe a woman to be far more capable of undertaking the somewhat irritating drudgery of detailed accounts. At the same time, there is no reason why the husband should escape all responsibility, but we believe that, as in a lower rank of life, middle-class households will run most economically, and what is more, most smoothly, where the man has the courage and trust to bring all his earnings to the woman.

Men are apt to say, however, that a young girl entering on life can have no experience in such matters. True; therefore the sooner she buckles to the task the better, and with a very little help at first, and the usual monthly audit and consultation, there is small chance of failure, especially in these days of High Schools and University Extensions.* At the same time, even men are often woefully at a loss how to set about making a detailed record of expenditure, and to help such as find this a difficulty, one of the authors[1] appends a series of forms, which she has used for years with perfect ease and success.

Form A should be ruled in a foolscap folio of not less than thirty-three lines to a page, so that the whole accounts of one month can be entered in one opening—that is to say, in the two pages opposite one another; the totals of each heading showing, of course, on the bottom line, and so giving the monthly expenditure on each item. For convenience' sake it is a good plan to have the inventories of all household property, such as glass, linen, &c., entered at the end of this book. The number of columns in Form A may seem alarming, but it has been designed with the view of rendering all other daily record unnecessary. As every household differs in some detail, and every mistress may have some special fact she may wish to record, we advise that beginners should only rule one or two openings after the pattern given, which can then be modified if necessary; the idea being to keep all cash payments close to the daily total.

The general account Form B is to be made up monthly, and every item of receipt and expenditure, either direct or through a bank, must show in it. In order to facilitate the final yearly account, which is to show for future guide and reference the total yearly expenditure in the different departments, it is necessary to group the receipts and expenditure under different headings. Five will be found sufficient for receipts, and each of these is distinguished in the entries by a letter, or letters, thus—

1. P. Pay, and fixed income of all kinds.
2. T. Travelling or other special allowance.
3. S. Stock sold (see also under Expenditure).
4. B. Borrowed (*i.e.* loans repaid or moneys advanced brought into account).
5. M. Miscellaneous.

In Expenditure sixteen heads seem necessary, but these again may vary according to the idea the account-keeper may entertain of the meaning of the word miscellaneous, or with any special reason

[1] G. G.

for keeping some particular class of expenditure apart. These heads are—

1. C. Charity.
2. G. Food.
3. L. Liquors (including soda-water and tobacco).
4. D. Dress.
5. P. Postage and stationery.
6. F. Fires and lights.
7. H. Live stock (horses, dogs, cows, &c.).
8. R. Rent, garden, taxes.
9. W. Wages.
10. S. Stock bought (anything which may be sold again).
11. T. Travelling.
12. A. Amusements.
13. Dr. Doctor, sick-nurse, medicine.
14. B. Money lent or advanced.
15. I. Invested.
16. M. Miscellaneous.

Form B may be ruled in a smaller account book, which can, if desired, hold Form C—the yearly account—at the other end.

Life in India always partakes of the nature of a campaign, where light marching order is a great desideratum, so the multiplication of account books is to be avoided. Under the system thus explained, only expenditure on food enters into the daily account book, and therefore payments under the other headings must either be entered direct into the monthly account, which makes it somewhat lengthy, or a separate memorandum book must be kept. One of the authors would prefer to see the liquor columns in Form A, *i.e.* those for beer and claret, relegated to a regular cellar book, which can be bound up with the folio, and the space thus gained utilised as a column at the end for cash payments other than food, to be entered simply under its letter.

In filling up Form C, or the yearly account, the sums had best be entered in whole rupees, subject to the usual plan of treating all broken sums over eight annas as one rupee, and omitting those under eight annas.

Before quitting the subject, one of the authors[1] wishes to put in a plea for the column 'Miscellaneous' by reminding the reader that the bigger the total under this head can be conscientiously made, the richer people will be. This seems paradoxical, but it is only another

[1] F. A. S.

way of saying that the fewer absolutely necessary payments a man has to make, the larger will that residue be on which he can exercise that free will of disposal which alone constitutes possession. Those who, when Black Monday* comes round, have to pay all their income to the butcher, the baker, and the candlestick maker, are themselves positive paupers. A man with ten thousand a year may thus be as poor as a church mouse. The secret of riches lies in the art of having a margin. To gain this, cut down Europe stores, extra servants, and swagger generally. They are not worth that fatal five minutes when, after a glance at the monthly totals, you realise that you have not even a four-anna bit to lavish. Philanthropists talk of the benefits of a high standard of personal comfort. Doubtless; but what is personal comfort? One thing is sure. In the multiplication of pots and pans, and the enlargement of the necessaries of life, lies anxiety and slavery.

FORM A

Date	Daily Memoranda, April 1893	Dusters — Sent to the wash	Dusters — Given out to: Khit	Bearer	Ayah	Saises	Occurrences among Live Stock	Grain used — Gram	Ardawa	Bajra	Dallia	Fowls' mixture	Linseed	Date	Eggs	Loaves	Milk	Beer	Claret	Soda-water	Lemonade	Soup	Cash Payments — Meat	Sundries	R.	A.	P.
4	Sunday	..	..	..	..	..	Killed 1 fowl	8	2	2	1	2	..	4	6	2	2	1	1	2	1	2	Beef 2/, fish 8 as.	Apples 2½ as., potatoes 8 as.	3	2	6
5	Dirzie absent	4 glass, 6 tea, 10 old, 10 new	15	8	5	4	Bought 4 ducks	7	2	2	1	2	1	5	5	3	3	1	..	2	..	..	Mutton ¼	Suji 2½ as., tomatoes 2 as.	1	8	6
6	Carpenter half-day	..	..	..	..	..	Killed 2 chickens	7	2	2	1	2	1	6	11	2	2	2	1	4	1	..	Fish 6 as.	Tinning ¼, peas 2 as.	1	12	..
7	Gave out tin of oil	..	..	..	..	..	Killed 2 ducks	7	2	2	1	2	1	7	4	2 & 12 rolls	2	1	..	1	1	4	Brains 2 as.	Maida 2 as., rice 3 as.	..	11	..
8	Engaged Kurbdin 10/	15	15	..	..	..	Bought 1 sheep	9	2	2	1	2	..	8	3	3	3	1	1	2	2	..	Beef ⅛, fish 8 as.	Oranges 12 as., Dall 1 a.	2	13	..
9	Gave out saddle soap	..	..	..	..	..	Bought 40 quail	9	2	3	1	2	..	9	3	3	2	1	1	3	1	..	....	Sago 4 as., spices 2½ as.	..	7	6
10	Horses shod	..	..	..	..	..	Killed 5 quail	9	2	3	1	2	..	10	2	2	2	1	..	1	3	..	Kidneys 4 as.	Lemons 5 as.	..	9	..

FORM B

RECEIPTS.

1893. July

		Rs.	a.	p.
Balance from June		323	10	0
Pay for June	P	600	0	0
Office allowance	T	50	0	0
Dog-cart sold	S	180	0	0
Sale of Mutton—Club share	M	35	0	6
Total		1188	10	6

	Rs.	a.	p.
Receipts	1188	10	6
Expenditure	820	11	9
Balance	367	14	9

	Rs.	a.	p.
In Bank	250	0	0
In Hand	117	14	9
Total	367	14	9

EXPENDITURE.

1893. July

		Rs.	a.	p.
Donation to new Church	C	50	0	0
Other Charities	C	10	0	0
Cook's Account	G	50	8	0
Baker	G	5	4	6
Groceries	G	20	0	0
Beer and Soda-water	L	20	8	0
Dress	D	40	0	0
Stationery	P	12	6	0
Oil, Matches, &c.	F	11	4	3
Horses' Food	H	12	6	6
Varnishing Dog-cart	H	12	0	0
Farrier	H	2	8	0
Rent	R	80	0	0
Wages	W	100	4	0
Livery	W	15	6	6
Furniture	S	50	0	0
Amusements	A	20	4	0
Advanced Account, M. M.	B	10	0	0
Invested	I	250	0	0
Subscription to *Delhi Gazette*	M	48	0	0
Total		820	11	9

FORM C

1893.

Month	RECEIPTS						EXPENDITURE																	
	P.	T.	S.	B.	M.	Tot.	C.	G.	L.	D.	P.	F.	H.	R.	W.	S.	T.	A.	Dr.	B.	L.	M.	Tot.	Bal.
January																								
February																								
March																								
April																								
May																								
June																								324
July	600	50	180		35	865	60	76	21	40	12	11	27	80	116	50		20		10	250	48	821	368
August																								
Sept.																								
October																								
Nov.																								
Dec.																								
Total																								

CHAPTER IV

ESTIMATES OF EXPENDITURE

In consequence of the large number of questions on this point received by the authors since the publication of their book, they have compiled the following chapter from information supplied to them at first hand by friends living in the various Presidencies.* It is, of course, impossible to do more than give a rough idea of the probable cost, but they may mention that the error in the estimate, if any, will lie on the side of liberality. In all cases, the estimate is based on the requirements of a newly-married couple who desire both to have their cake and *to pay for it.*

It may be mentioned that in almost every station an authorised price list (*nirick*) used to be had, weekly, by application to the proper quarter, generally the Kotwâli. This list generally erred a little on the side of expense, and most things by bargaining could be had cheaper. This still obtains, nominally, but in large Europeanised towns and cantonments too much reliance must not be placed on it nowadays.

They have also received numberless inquiries regarding furniture and the probable cost of setting up house. They have therefore added a rough estimate for this from *data* supplied in every case by three capable authorities. With the modifications for each Presidency suggested further on, the following hints will be found useful:—

Furniture should rarely be imported. Those who can afford expensive things will always have an opportunity of buying them from other people at a reduction! In fact, the permanently fluctuating character of Indian society (to use an Irishism which need not be attributed to the nationality of one of the authors) is the first thing to be taken into consideration in furnishing a house. People are here to-day, gone to-morrow, and so solidities and fragilities of all sorts are a sheer nuisance. Therefore all the heavy things should be of the sort which you can sell by auction without a pang; all the delicacies of the sort that will pack. One of the authors was burdened throughout her long career by two white elephants of wedding presents—a priceless Wedgwood vase and an arm-chair. Of course it was open to her to get rid of them at a reduction, but, after a time, they became to her what a sickly child often is to a mother, a source of pride in her own care. There was a fierce resolve in each move, a fierce joy in each unpacking; for they arrived at the end of the twenty-two years' exile uninjured. She does not, however, recommend it as an example, since the safe transplantation of the necessaries of life, such as husband, children, books, and a piano, is generally sufficient strain on the nerves.

So let the young housekeeper go out armed with energy, hammers, tacks, brass nails, a goodly supply of Bon-accord enamel* (made by an Aberdeen firm, which is the best the writer has ever used), Japanese black,* varnish, &c., and then buy the old sticks in the bazaar, provided they are strong or can be made so by a few screws. Then, as was said to a friend of the authors', she will have the prettiest house in the station, with nothing worth a button in it! Wall-papers are everywhere—even in England—a mistake. Distemper* properly applied with dados* and friezes* of well-chosen colours is prettier and cleaner. The friezes especially serve to lower the obtrusive height of most Indian rooms. A very good way of producing a pretty effect is to take out a paper frieze, mount it on coarsest muslin like a map, and tack it with brass nails to the wall. If the room is *very* high, a band of contrasting distemper *above* it will bring the frieze within proper vision. Otherwise it will be lost in the rafters.

English carpets are always a mistake. A good jail* one for the reception rooms and cotton *dhurries* for the bedrooms answer all requirements.

Pictures are a great help in decorating, and no present can be more charming than a set of framed pictures fitted into a neat partitioned box with lock and key. One of the authors had a set of photographs from originals which kept alive her memories of art for many and many a long year in India, and now perform the same kind office for her in the wilds of Scotland. China and glass should always be chosen *cheap*, and the numbers noted and the address left, where they are purchased, in view of future matching. Lamps are best *very* plain, and with metal stands. Wire mattresses should never be omitted where possible, but nothing over 3 feet 6 inches in width is satisfactory. Wider ones sag in the middle. One of the authors[1] strongly recommends plain white double-width Bolton sheeting at 8¾ d. a yard as the best curtain material in the world. They can be dyed and re-dyed in the bazaar to any tint, and if that is kept light, and a bordering of fringe or cretonne added, the effect is charming, the folds being so soft. They require no lining, and if you order them to be dyed *kutcha* (not fast), you can change your tint at each move by having them washed, bleached, and re-dyed. The author did hers with Maypole soap,* which is invaluable.

Brass rings, hooks, picture cord, upholstery tacks, gimps,* wire nails, screws, brass picture nails, a few sets of neat hinges for screens, &c., will cost little, and be of endless convenience, while a set of carpenter's tools and a little perseverance will save their cost ten times over in a year. There is so much leisure in India, especially when the nursery is not full, that young housekeepers will find decorating and upholstering a delightful occupation. In taking out house-linen omit dusters and all but face towels of fine linen. With these preliminaries we proceed to particulars of estimates, &c., for each Presidency. These have been revised for the North-West, and, except in the item of bazaar account, for other places. By adding ten per cent to the food account, a fairly accurate estimate may be reached. It is a mistake to imagine, however, that *living* in India has gone up so enormously; it is the style of living.

ESTIMATE FOR BOMBAY*

	Rs.
House rent in Bombay itself	80 to 100
„ in Mofussil	50 to 60
Servants—three indoor, one outdoor, and washing	80
Stable servant, one	12
Keep of horse	20
Average bazaar account (excluding wood and stones, also milk and bread)	50
Fuel	8
Furnishing six-roomed house, including china, glass, &c.	1200

---

[1] F. A. S.

The prices of bazaar furniture are the same as those given for Madras. Blackwood furniture is famed, and it may be good in the damp climate of Bombay, but in more dusty places is a weariness to the good housewife's soul, by reason of its many crannies, which nothing bigger than a toothbrush will clean.

House rent in Bombay itself varies from Rs. 80 to Rs. 100 for one suitable to newly married couple, but rooms can be had in the Fort* from Rs. 60 to Rs. 80. In the country Rs. 50 to Rs. 60 would be a fair rent.

It is necessary to have a butler or boy, at, say, Rs. 20; a cook at Rs. 15; a *hamal* at Rs. 10; washerman at Rs. 5 a head. In Bombay itself water is laid on, elsewhere a water-carrier must be kept at Rs. 6; and everywhere some sort of servant is necessary to do the rough sweeping and attend to conservancy arrangements.

A really economical bazaar account for two people would be from Rs. 2 to Rs. 2.8 a day. This apparently does not include milk or bread. Beef is 2 annas a pound, and mutton 3 annas. Sufficient fish should be got for 3 annas to serve for one day. Milk is about 7 *seers* the rupee. Eggs are 6 annas a dozen.

Punkahs in Bombay itself are little used, and when required from March till June at meal times are often pulled by the *hamal*.

It is never advisable to take out furniture. Indeed, in Bombay due attention must be paid to the fact that one is in direct communication with England; and that therefore everything can be bought in the shops more reasonably than in any other part of India.

The damp is another potent factor in Bombay life, and stores should all be kept in stoppered bottles.

ESTIMATE FOR MADRAS*

	Rs.	a.
House rent (town)	100	0
„ (up country)	50	0
Indoor servants, five; outdoor, two	56	0
Punkah coolies, necessary all the year round	8	0
Stable servants, per horse	10	8
Average cost of horse per month (including stable, oil, farrier, &c.)	18	0
Average bazaar account	60	0
Firewood	8	0
Furnishing six-roomed house, including china, glass, &c.	1000	0

The prices of furniture are roughly—

	Rs.	a.		Rs.	a.
Dining table,			Small tables	1 to 4	0
3 leaves	30	0	Beds complete with		
Dinner waggon	9	0	mattresses and nets	10 to 25	0
Dinner chairs	2 to 2	8	Wardrobe with shelves	15	0
Long arm–chair	7	0	Hanging „	30	0
Camp tables	4	0	Commodes for		
Sideboard	40	0	bath-rooms	6	0
Couch	25	0	Dressing-tables	5	0
Whatnot	6	0	Washstand	5	0
Arm-chair	10	0	Chest drawers	14 to 20	0
Cane chairs	3	0	Chairs	2	8

The Madras Presidency is distinctly a cheap place to live in. Houses in up-country stations may be had from Rs. 25 to Rs. 70. These are very generally double-storeyed, and contain in the centre a drawing-room, and dining-room separated by a big arch; on either side, bedrooms and dressing-rooms with bath-rooms (not *fitted* bath-rooms); upstairs, either one or two bedrooms for hotter weather, with bath-rooms. The fewest number of servants compatible with comfort are cook, Rs. 10; boy, Rs. 10; matey, Rs. 6; tunny ketch, or cook's help (a woman), Rs. 4; waterman, Rs. 5; sweeper, Rs. 5; washerman, Rs. 6 to Rs. 8; two punkah coolies, at Rs. 4 each. These are full wages. A number of the Madras servants are Christians.

The bazaar account should never be more in economical houses than Rs. 1 each per diem, but this can be reduced. The authors are decidedly of this opinion, as the prices given from reliable sources are, if anything, cheaper than the Punjab. Beef is 3 *seers* per rupee, or 6 annas a *seer*; mutton, slightly cheaper; milk, 10 quarts per rupee in the country, 8 quarts in Madras; eggs, 3 or 4 annas a dozen; chickens, 4 annas; wood or charcoal is used in the cookroom, and is contracted for at prices varying from Rs. 6 to Rs. 10 a month; butter, 10 annas a pound.

The keep of horses is distinctly cheap. They get a grain called *kooltrie*, and as a rule the *syce*'s wife acts as grasscutter, just as the cook's wife acts as *tunny ketch* or kitchen slave. Cooking in Madras is largely done in earthen pots or *chatties*, and the general life is more

Oriental in its ways than in the rest of India. Wages are low, and it is necessary to guard against the importation into the compound of assistant relatives at almost nominal wages.

Punkahs in most stations are required all the year round during the day, but from 1st November to 1st April may be dispensed with at night. Two pullers are generally required for night work. The commonest plan, however, is to arrange a contract with a family, say for Rs. 8 a month. Meat will not keep more than a day.

Madras furniture is famed, and it is a mistake to bring out anything except as a pattern. As elsewhere, sales constantly take place, and all common things can be had in the bazaar. Some enamel, Berlin black,* or varnish soon makes the shabbiest things smart. The floors are matted, and the matting costs about 2 annas a square yard. Carpenters' and smiths' wages are from 8 to 12 annas a day; tailors, from 6 annas to 8 annas. It is advisable to bring out linen, glass, crockery, lamps, cretonnes,* and ornaments. The native furniture makers are *very* clever, and can copy anything even from a drawing, and upholster well. Briefly, the chief points in which intending settlers in Madras may have to modify advice given in other parts of this book is in regard to *climate*. Prices and customs appear much the same as in the Punjab. If anything, the former are cheaper, the latter more Oriental. Those going to Madras itself should apply to the registry of servants kept at the club,* and beware of *vagrants*.*

ESTIMATE FOR CEYLON*

	Rs.
House rent	60
Servants—four indoor, one outdoor, and washing at Rs. 5 a head	77
Stable servant	12
Keep of one horse and carriage	32
Daily bazaar account	50
House account, firewood, &c.	14
Baker	10
Milk	20
Furnishing six-roomed house	1000

These are the nearest figures available, but the data from Ceylon varied so greatly that it appears likely that the cost is different in different places.

The prices of furniture, native made, are roughly—

	Rs.	a.		Rs.	a.
Sideboard	50	0	Little tables	3	0
Dining table	30	0	Dining chairs	5	0
Easy-chairs	8	0	Small chairs	2	50
Dressing-table	5	0	Bed complete, with		
Washstand	5	0	bedding and nets	40	0
Wardrobe	20	0	Towel-horse	1	50
Teapoys	1	50			

Coir matting, Rs. 15 per roll of 60 feet, 1 yard wide.
Rattan matting, 25 cents per square foot.

It appears quite possible to live comfortably in some parts of Ceylon for Rs. 300 a month. House rent varies. In Kandy, one should be got for Rs. 50. In Colombo it may be Rs. 80 or more. Four house servants are quite sufficient; some authorities say three, and one outdoor servant, a garden coolie, who apparently does waterman's and sweeper's work combined; but the whole arrangements of Ceylon life approximate much more closely to England than in any other part of India. Their wages should be about Rs. 67; to this must be added washing at Rs. 5 a head, bringing the total up to Rs. 77. The servants may be Cinghalese or Tamil.* The former are Buddhists, the latter Hindoo, Christian, or Pariah. The former are largely employed up country. In Kandy it is apparently the custom to give some of the servants their food, allowing for it in the wage. All over Ceylon European servants* are largely employed.

The keep of a horse is by several authorities estimated at Rs. 50 a month, including the horsekeeper's wages. In Ceylon the servants do not live in the compound except the house coolie, who lives in the kitchen.

The daily bazaar account should, it appears, not exceed Rs. 50 a month, but this does not include milk or the bread account. Several correspondents put Rs. 3 a day as ample for the total commissariat expenditure for two people per diem. This is exactly what is said in the Punjab. English cooking-stoves are largely used, and coke or coal burnt; otherwise wood. As the currency is different in Ceylon,* it will be well to mention here that the rupee is considered equivalent to two shillings, and is divided into 100 cents. The weights used are the English pound and its divisions. The cost of firing is variously estimated from Rs. 15 to Rs. 30 a month. Provisions are fairly cheap, but not good. Beef about 4d., or 25 cents a lb.; mutton, double the price; milk, about six beer bottles for the rupee, but cows are very generally kept. Those of island breed cost about Rs. 50, and do not give more than three bottles a day. Indian ones, costing Rs. 80, give five bottles. The authors fail to understand this last piece of information, as the commonest Indian cow in India gives at least eight bottles, and many fourteen. Perhaps a reference to the chapter on Cows may be useful. Butter is not made at home; it is generally Rs. 1.25 a lb. Chickens cost about 45 cents.

In regard to furnishing, it is wise to take out ornaments, house linen, crockery, and cretonnes. Furniture is good and cheap. Sales go on constantly, at which the whole fittings of a house may be bought at half the cost price of new things. Wire mattresses and a few light chairs and tables might be imported. In regard to carpenters' and masons' work, whitewashing, &c., it is far cheaper to get it done by contract.

The climate of Ceylon varies much, but is damp throughout. Fires are never required in Colombo, or anywhere but in the higher hills; but, on the other hand, punkahs are seldom used except at meal times. You require no special servant to pull them, as in India. In furnishing, the damp, heat, and the redundancy of insect life must be considered. Draperies should be dispensed with as much as possible. There are capital shops of all kinds, and the hotels are excellent. The rest-houses throughout the country provide everything, including bedding and sheets. Keep for yourself and horse about Rs. 7 a day. The estimated expenditure for furnishing a six-roomed house is by three authorities placed at between £80 and £100.

As stated before, life assimilates itself to the European fashion despite the heat, even in the matter of calling.* The hours are from two o'clock till five o'clock, and new-comers do *not* call first.*

Estimate for Rangoon* and Burmah*

	Rs.
House rent, Rangoon	100 to 150
„ up country	60
Servants as in Madras, double the wage, say	90
Stable servant, one for two ponies	12
Keep of pony	16
Economical bazaar account	80
Estimate for furnishing	1200

The prices of furniture in Rangoon Central Jail* are—

	Rs.		Rs.
Dining tables	40 to 120	Wardrobes	45
„ chairs	4 „ 7	Hanging wardrobes	40
Arm-chairs	4 „ 7	Chests of drawers	30
Easy-chairs	10 „ 16	Bedroom chairs	5
Whatnots	12 „ 25	Dressing-table	10
Couch	18 „ 40	Washstand	8
Sutherland tables*	8 „ 16	Beds	18
Camp tables, 4 × 3	10	Commodes	7
Cane chairs	1 „ 5	Canvas chairs	7

Bamboo matting, 1½ annas per square yard.
Cane   „   3½   „   „   foot.
Covi   „   1½   „   „   „
Covi mats, 4 annas each.

The life in Burmah is absolutely different in many ways. The houses are two-storeyed, of wood, and are largely built on piles, because of the insects and the damp. Under any circumstances the lower rooms are seldom used except as dining-rooms. The upper verandah, especially that over the portico, is generally fitted up as a sitting-room.

The servants are all imported from Madras or Bengal, and when asked to go up country insist on very high wages. The Madrassi is often what he is pleased to call 'Romukatlick' (Roman Catholic); he almost always speaks English. The Bengali is nearly always Mahomedan. It is advisable to keep the household of one nationality or the other.

Horses are seldom kept in Burmah, the native pony being an admirable animal. A fair price for one is Rs. 250. They are fed in Rangoon on 'crushed food,' which is sold in bags at Rs. 7 for about 168 lbs., or the equivalent of 12 *seers* per rupee. The keep of a pony can be calculated on this basis with reference to the estimates for the Punjab, remembering that 3 *seers* should be sufficient per diem.

All country produce is dear, and meat very bad. Mutton has to be imported from Madras; beef is tough, and people live largely on fowls. The *seer* is not used in Burmah; the *viss*, a weight of about 3½ lbs., taking its place. Milk is about six bottles the rupee, and is often adulterated. Butter unobtainable. Many people do not eat it, and when they do, have recourse to tinned butter from England. In Rangoon good reliable milk can be obtained for children from the Lunatic Asylum. Vegetables are also imported from Madras and Calcutta. So is fruit. In fact, at first sight Burmah appears to be the last place on which the eye of annexation would be cast!* Still, it is said to be very beautiful, and life there very pleasant, when once the initial strangeness has worn off. The following are current prices of supplies translated into pounds: Mutton, 8 annas; fish, 6 annas; beef, 6 annas; goat's flesh, 6 annas; fowls, 12 annas each; ducks, 1 rupee; potatoes, 1½ annas; vegetables, 4½ annas. With these prices the authors wonder how the usual boarding contract of 1 rupee 8 annas to 2 rupees which prevails all over India can extend to Burmah. But it does. Nothing shows the lack of care in housekeeping, which is so remarkable throughout the East, more than the fact that with ever varying prices the authors have always to go back to the one old formula, '*Oh! from three to four rupees a day for two people.*' Certainly, if it can be done for this in Rangoon, it ought to be as much less in other parts of India as it undoubtedly is in the Punjab.

Punkah coolies, being very dear, are seldom kept—the syce, or the gardener, when one is kept, pulling them for meals between the 15th March and the breaking of the south-west monsoon in June.

Furniture is dear, but good. The extreme damp makes it impossible to have much drapery. It is very desirable that frames, brackets, &c., should be screwed together, and not glued. The extent of saturation in the air can be estimated by this fact alone. The heat, however, is never very great. On the other hand, fireplaces are unknown. The rainy season begins in June, and there is a ceaseless pour for ten or twelve weeks. During this time, the weather-bound inmates of the house amuse themselves in trying to prevent their Lares and Penates* from being reduced to a pulp. Upper Burmah is drier, and Mandalay* is colder. Mosquitoes are numerous and obtrusive, and unless punkahs are kept going, must be endured till the veil of night (a mosquito net) falls between them and you.

During the rainy season the greatest care should be taken, not only of your photographs, but of yourself, as the damp heat is most depressing and relaxing. In Rangoon itself there is, however, plenty of gaiety and amusement.

ESTIMATE FOR MONTHLY HOUSEHOLD EXPENDITURE IN THE PUNJAB AND NORTH-WEST PROVINCES* FOR A NEWLY MARRIED COUPLE

	Rs.
House rent	60 to 80
House servants	58 „ 70
Stable servants, two	11
Keep of one horse, including farrier, oil, and litter, with grain at 20 *seers* per rupee, and a ration of 3 *seers*	9
Bazaar account for two people	60
Charcoal and wood	10
Bearers' account, oil, matches, odds and ends	14
Furnishing house completely	800

The prices of furniture are the same as Madras; if anything, cheaper.

In the Punjab and North-West a house containing dining-room, drawing-room, two bedrooms, dressing-rooms, bathrooms, and verandahs, with suitable servants' accommodation, may be had from Rs. 40 to 80 per mensem. In most cases the landlord keeps up the garden in a perfunctory way, but this is seldom satisfactory. By far the best plan is to arrange, at a slight reduction in rent, that the landlord shall only supply bullocks to work the well twice or three times a week, while you keep and pay for the gardener. The landlord is bound to keep his house in habitable and sanitary repair, to whitewash the outside once a year, the inside every two years. There are no taxes, except in some cantonments a very trifling fee for clearing away refuse.

The number of servants can scarcely be reduced below seven. Bearer and valet, Rs. 10. Cook, Rs. 14. (Though many people give cooks Rs. 30 and Rs. 40 because they can cook a few indigestible *entrées*, a perfectly good cook can still be had for Rs. 14.) Upper *Khitmutgâr*, Rs. 10. Under ditto or *Musolchi*, Rs. 6 to 8. Water-carrier, Rs. 6. Washerman, Rs. 10. Sweeper, Rs. 6.

Many ladies manage without an *ayah* or female servant; but if one is necessary, she is generally, in small establishments, the sweeper's wife, and a wage of Rs. 8 is given. Without the *ayah* this brings the total to about Rs. 65 a month. This represents the total cost of the house servants. They find their own food, and houses are provided for them by the landlord. If it is desired still further to reduce the servants, this can be done by combining the duties of upper *khit* and bearer by giving them to a Mahomedan who will do both works. But any arrangement involving the necessity for more underlings is to be deprecated, such as the employment of that unpresentable drudge a *chokra* (lad) or *matey* (assistant). The *musolchi*, or torch-man, so called in most Presidencies, is quite enough in the way of anomalous domestics, and even his duties vary so enormously, that it seems likely he is a vestige of prehistoric times who—when his real occupation dissolved into darkness with the invention of hur-ricane lanterns—remained on in the house as general servant and substitute. As a rule, the fewer domestics you have the better they will perform their duties. Nothing, in fact, upsets the smooth work-ing of a household like *too much leisure* or a too minute division of responsibility. Above all, nothing is more insensate than the multi-plication of *khitmutgârs*. If a man cannot wait on six people, he is not worth keeping as a table attendant. But, with the curious perversity which characterises so many Indian customs, one often sees three table servants waiting on two people, while the whole cleansing work of a large, dusty, dilapidated Indian bungalow is left to one man, who is also scavenger, dog man, poultry man, and general scapegoat. The authors' advice therefore is—*Cut down the table servants and increase the sweepers.*

The bazaar account varies enormously according to the housekeep-ing: this is even more true nowadays than it used to be. Briefly, the bazaar account may still, for two people, average from Rs. 40 to Rs. 60 a month; though with very little more to show for it, Rs. 100 will not cover the bill. Provisions are still cheap on the whole; indeed, when beginning to housekeep last winter the revising author was immensely struck by the fact that the rise in the cost of actual food bore *no relation whatever* to the increase in the general cost of living. As an instance, fuel had not advanced a *cowrie*, but cooks were asking double for the charcoal contract. The author did not give it. Nor would she take joints of meat for 5 and 6 rupees, when, by weighing them, it became evident that the price per lb. was half as much again as she gives for the best meat in London. She did without them. Roughly speaking, prices are now, in one of the dearest stations in the North-West, as follows: Meat, from 3 to 6 annas a *seer*; milk, from 8 to 12 quarts or *seers* per rupee; eggs vary very much, from 3 annas to 6 annas a dozen; butter, which is now mostly bought from central dairies, is R. 1 a lb., but from the bazaar it is cheaper; while vegetables, if they have to be bought, are most reasonable. Bread is absolutely unreasonable. Its cost, taking wheat at 12 *seers*, should be less than one anna a pound. It is nearly three, or, roughly speaking, tenpence halfpenny a quartern. The usual practice is to subscribe for a basket of vegetables every, or every other, day from the public gardens. There is a fixed price for this, varying from Rs. 2 to Rs. 4 per month. It is also usual to join a mutton club. This is a joint-stock feeding company of any number of members divisible by four, who agree to divide a sheep into four quarters and take their share, hind and fore, and the appurtenances thereof, in turn. One member is secretary, and is responsible for the management and quality of the meat sent out. This can be done by private feeding under private shepherds—the total cost per month being divided among the shareholders—or by contract, the object being to secure wholesome, well-fed meat. This is a plan adopted in many small stations, but not so necessary in big ones. It is very generally adopted in regard to beef, especially about Christmas time. Fowls are cheap, but not as a rule good, unless fattened at home. Small chickens cost about 4 annas, large roasting ones 12 annas. The fuel used is charcoal. This should be contracted for with the cook, and from Rs. 10 to Rs. 12 a month is *ample*, including hot water for baths. In like manner, what is called in London lodgings the 'cruet' should be contracted for, and Rs. 1 or Rs. 1.4 a month is ample for salt, pepper, spices, and onions; about 8 annas a month for oil; and 1 anna a piece for the tinning of cooking pots. It is a mistake to get this done cheaper, as the tinman in that case only uses pure *lead*. As it is, an inferior alloy has to be guarded against. A good test is the finger; a perfectly clean one, newly washed, and *not greasy*, should show no suspicion of black on it if rubbed sharply on the newly-tinned vessels. Some housekeepers buy their charcoal in bulk and give it out daily. This is only a good plan in out-stations, where it is possible to get the charcoal burned for you by contract. The custom of giving a daily fixed sum for soup is iniquitous and absurd. Occasionally for very strong, clear soup meat may be allowed, but for the good wholesome household purées and broths, &c., the bones and cold meat (which cannot be long kept in India) are ample. The cook will, of course, say it is impossible to make clear soup out of bones and cooked meat, even if he does not deny the possibility of its being made at all; but this is a mistake.

And in India, where eggs are so cheap, there are always shells and whites waiting to be used.

Another barbarous extortion is a fixed price for *ghee*, or frying butter. A fixed sum may be given per month for suet; a better plan is to buy a fixed quantity yourself weekly, and see it properly melted down.

It is well to bear in mind that *ghee* is a favourite article of your servants' diet, and that a pot of it in the cookroom is peculiarly handy for all sorts and conditions of men. In trying to legislate for Supply,* the following simple rules known to all experienced housekeepers may be useful.

Average consumption per person:—

Bread (per week), one and a half quartern loafs	6 lbs.
Sugar „	¾ lb.
Tea „ (*ample*)	¼ lb.
Butter (per week), exclusive of cooking, but inclusive of afternoon tea	½ lb.
Milk (per day), including *café au lait* for breakfast, and a milk pudding.—(N.B. *Never stint milk*)	1½ pints.
Meat (per day), for a party of two, including soup, per person	1 lb.
Meat (per person) for a party of four	¾ lb.

(In a large household the meat item can easily be kept down to ½ lb. per head *per diem*.)

In India bread is sold by the loaf. It is generally about 12 ounces in weight, and from 8 to 16 are given for the rupee.

Furniture in the bazaar is cheap; if anything, below the Madras prices—but ugly, of course, until the buyer puts his or her taste into it. As a room, however, is worth nothing unless it is, like the nautilus' shell, a true guide to the growth of its inhabitants, this is no drawback. Very often in taking a house one is asked to take over the reed screens (*chicks*) and matting (*chitai*) of the former occupant. In this case be sure both are in good repair, and remember that the former, when new, cost from 8 annas to Rs. 1.4 each, and the latter is to be had for Rs. 1 per hundred square feet. In bringing out cretonnes, or, indeed, any kind of ornament, the height and size of Indian rooms must be considered. They require boldness both in colour and design.

ESTIMATE FOR CALCUTTA AND BENGAL*

	Rs.
House rent up country	60 to 70
„ in Calcutta (a flat)	200
Servants—four indoor, two outdoor, and washerman	58 to 80
Punkah coolies	49
Stable servants	12
Keep of horse in Calcutta	20
„ „ up country	10
Bazaar account in Calcutta	100
„ „ up country	60
Fuel	10 to 12
Estimate for furnishing house in Calcutta	3000
Up country	1500

Calcutta-made furniture has an almost European finish, and is proportionately dear.

In regard to Bengal the authors have great difficulty in giving estimates, owing to the great difference in the information given by authorities. Calcutta is a very expensive place; apparently causelessly so, as the prices of country produce are quite reasonable. House rent is ruinous in the well-drained and watered parts. Consequently, most people with small means live in boarding-houses, where two or three rooms with board may be had for Rs. 300 a month for two persons, or they rent furnished or unfurnished flats. Up-country houses vary from Rs. 40 upwards, and living is practically the same as in the Punjab.

Servants' wages are a little, but not much, higher in Calcutta, and it is rare to keep either a sweeper or water-carrier for your own exclusive use. These servants are generally shared with your neighbours. Tailor's wages are very low, only Rs. 8 a month.

Horses up country cost practically the same as in the Punjab. In Calcutta hiring is much resorted to. The prices in Calcutta appear reasonable. Meat, 8 *seers* the rupee; eggs, 5 annas a dozen; milk, 6 *seers* the rupee; chickens, 4 annas; ducks, 5 annas; bread, 10 loaves the rupee, or about Rs. 6 a month for two people. Fuel may be contracted for from Rs. 10 to Rs. 12 a month; vegetables plentiful. Two annas' worth of potatoes and another anna's worth of vegetables should be sufficient daily. The tendency appears to make the bazaar accounts very long, and to allow half an anna or quarter of an anna daily for trivialities like herbs (!), salt, pepper, &c. Considering that salt is 10 *seers*, retail, the rupee, this means a daily consumption of six ounces of salt!!

Punkahs are used from 15th March to 1st November, and for day and night work three are required. This averages Rs. 9 for the year. The mosquitoes are large, venomous, and *untameable*. They bite with as much zeal at the end of the day as at the beginning, and have a discriminating eye to open-work stockings.

For the convenience of those proceeding to India for the first time, a few notes are appended on the principal Hill Stations:—

BOMBAY possesses two Hill Stations—Mahableshwar and Matheran,* both connected by railroad, and some add Bhandala* as another resort and change from Bombay. As the rains are exceptionally heavy in the two first stations, every one leaves them during the rains; which procedure is different from other hill stations. Matheran is a smaller and quieter place, and where expense is an object it has the advantage that it is accessible from Bombay. In both places there are hotels, places of public amusement, and houses are let by the season furnished; but, as in all hills, they require to be supplemented by comforts and elegancies of all kinds. There is a weekly market; mutton, potatoes, and strawberries are excellent. Bhandala can scarcely be called a hill station. Its elevation is about 2000 feet on the edge of the *Ghauts*. It is a very small place, and is a military sanatorium; no doubt the difficulty in obtaining houses would be great, but it might serve as a change during convalescence.

CEYLON.—Newera Elliya Hills*—Rail goes within a few miles' easy drive of the principal sanatorium, Newera Elliya, which is a plateau with an artificial lake. It is only ten hours' journey from Colombo, and in consequence travellers must be prepared for sudden and rapid changes from heat and cold; such as leaving a temperature of 94° to find themselves by evening in sharp frost. The manner of living is much the same as in any part of Ceylon, but fewer servants are required, and provisions are slightly more expensive owing to their having to be brought up by rail, &c. Dress: what would be required in April or September in England.

MADRAS.—Ootacamund and Coonor.*—Rail runs from Madras to Mesapolium,* where there is a small hotel. *Dhoolis*, ponies, or tongas can be hired there for Coonor and Ootacamund. Coonor can be reached by breakfast time, and Ootacamund a full 1½ hours farther. Rail is in process of construction all the way to Coonor. Coonor has the milder climate, and is suited to invalids who could not stand the climate of Ootacamund. Houses in both places are hired by the season, and are distinctly cheap for hill stations, being Rs. 50 to Rs. 80 per mensem. Food is good and cheap, excellent markets in both places, English churches, doctors, libraries, all kinds of amusements, most hospitable society. Kodai Kalnal,* in the Pulney Hills, is a resort which becomes more popular every year, especially to those who have children. Rail to Ammani Kamir, where there is a rest house, thence by transit vans drawn by bullocks at a charge of Rs. 10; each contains two passengers, with their baggage. House rents, Rs. 75 per mensem during season, less if taken by the year. Living rather more expensive than at Ootacamund. Perfect climate.

BENGAL, Darjeeling.*—Access very easy. Railway runs right into the station. This is the dampest of all hill stations, and care is needed for the preservation of clothes, &c., and a suit of good waterproof is almost a necessity. Most excellent hotels. Both living and house rent are dear, and the place is apt to be over-crowded. Society very gay. Leeches and ticks are a perfect pest. Scenery finest of all the hill stations.

UPPER INDIA.*—Naini Tal, Ranikhet, Landour, Mussoorie, Kasauli, Simla, Dhurmsala, Dalhousie, Murree. The resident in Upper India has all these hill sanitaria to choose from. The mode of living in all is nearly the same, and for this the chapter 'On the Hills' can be consulted. Choice will depend on requirements of the individual in regard to society, cheapness, accessibility. The most accessible of all these, now that the railway is opened, is Kasauli. To invalids who cannot stand a long fatiguing journey this is a great desideratum. It is not pretty, but is fairly healthy, though, owing to its being a sanatorium for British troops, outbreaks of cholera have taken place from time to time. Simla is nearly forty miles farther, and can be reached by tonga. It is a very large place, very expensive, very gay, very pretty. Educational advantages good. No one should go up that has not a bag of rupees and many pretty frocks. For the North-West Province Naini Tal is perhaps the most accessible; a charming place, but somewhat shut in. Mussoorie and Landour have practically the same route, the pony track diverging about 2½ miles

down the hillside. Landour lies on the right, Mussoorie on a somewhat lower hill on the left. The latter is a larger and gayer place;
the former the most healthy, and is the military sanatorium.
Mussoorie is the cheapest hill station; hotels very good, especially
'The Charleville.'* Society rather mixed. House rent fairly cheap,
and provisions also; but the distances from the bazaar are great,
and many people allow their cook a pony. The scenery is not very
pretty, with the exception of the Doon,* which is unique. A large
number of retired officers, resident in the Doon during the winter,
come up for the summer to Mussoorie. Educational advantages good.
Dhurmsala and Dalhousie are both difficult of access, being more
than fifty miles from the railway. This makes the carriage of goods
troublesome, though there is a good cart-road. Dalhousie is the prettiest and healthiest of all hill stations; water excellent; gravel and
granite soil, which dries quickly; good, but not very gay society;
style of living and prices in both places fairly cheap and good. The
houses in Dalhousie are the best, being built of good stone. Dhurmsala is nearer the perpetual snow-line than any other hill station. The
pleasantest way of reaching Dalhousie is by three daily marches, as
there are excellent rest-houses, scenery beautiful, climate fairly cool.
Murree is by far the most convenient hill station north of Lahore,*
and is, in addition, the usual starting-point for Kashmir.* Excellent
shops, where all things necessary for the trip can be hired or purchased.
With the exception of Ooty,* it is perhaps the most English place in
India. The only drawback to its healthiness is its water-supply, and
the large number of troops with their bazaar followers* camped out
on the surrounding hills. It is six hours by tonga from Rawulpindi,*
and it is necessary to make arrangements to be met at the thirty-eighth
milestone by dandies or ponies, as the tonga does not go beyond that
point. House rent and provisions much the same as at other hill
stations; good society; you can be as gay or as quiet as you like. There are
several small stations scattered beyond Murree, such as the Gullies
and Thandiani,* all of them very healthy and very quiet.

Since writing the above the water-supply has been altered, and is
now good.

CHAPTER V

HINTS ON BREAKFASTS, DINNERS, LUNCHEONS, ETC.

———◆◇◆———

BREAKFASTS in India are for the most part horrible meals, being hybrids between the English and the French fashions.* Then the ordinary Indian cook has not an idea for breakfast beyond chops, steaks, fried fish, and quail; a *menu* rendered still less inviting by the poor quality of both fish and meat. Tea made and poured out by a *khitmutgâr* at a side table, toast and butter coming in when the meal is half-finished, and the laying of the table for lunch while the breakfast-eaters are still seated, combine to make new-comers open their eyes at Indian barbarities. Of course, if breakfast be deferred till eleven or twelve o'clock, it is better to lean towards the French *dejeuner à la fourchette*,* since under these circumstances lunch would be a crime; but when, as is often the case, the breakfast hour is English, there is no real reason why English fashions should not be adhered to in every way.

A breakfast table should never be crowded by flowers or fruit, but should depend for its charm on the brightness of china and silver, and on the cleanliness of the cloth. A dumb waiter is a decided con-venience, if, as will be invariably the case where the mistress is wise, servants are not allowed to stay in the room at breakfast. It should never be a set meal; and even if the English plan of helping oneself cannot be fully carried out, it is at least not necessary to have a tribe of servants dancing round the table ready to snatch away your plate at the least pause. Breakfast is *par excellence* a family meal, a special opportunity to show forth mutual helpfulness, an occasion when the hostess can make her guests feel at home by admitting them to the familiar friendliness of the *vie intime*.* If the servants after handing round the first dish wait outside, a touch on the handbell will bring them back when they are wanted. Then, if the bread, butter, tea, sugar, milk, and jam are (as they should be) on the table, it is surely no great hardship so far to remember the wants of others as to pass an empty cup?

When there is a large party at breakfast, it greatly conduces to the familiar comfort of all to have small sugar basins and cream or milk jugs at intervals down the table, and there should be at least two plates of butter and toast. In regard to the former, the *khitmutgâr* should be generally discouraged from making it the medium for a display of his powers in plastic art;* it is doubtless gratifying to observe such yearning after beauty, even in butter, but it is suggestive of too much handling to be pleasant.

Most of the recipes given under fish and eggs are suitable for breakfast, while a variety of appetising little dishes can be made by using white China scallop shells, and filling them with various mixtures. An inch or two deep of nicely-minced chicken, covered with tomato or *brinjal* scallop, or with a nicely-seasoned batter—the whole to be crumbed over and baked—is always liked. Hunter's sandwiches,* kromeskys,* and croutons* of all descriptions are also suitable; but it should be remembered that any elaborate side-dish has too great an apparent connection with yesterday's dinner to be agreeable to the fastidious. Indeed, this lingering likeness to the immediately preceding meal is always to be striven against; and the mistress of the house where you have duck for dinner, and duck stew next morning at breakfast, may be set down as a bad manager.

In regard to tea and coffee, it may be possible to get these made satisfactorily by the servants in India; but, except in the largest establishments at home, the mistress usually does it herself.

Luncheons should invariably be laid on the table as lunch, and not as dinner; that is to say, most of the dishes should be on the table and not on the sideboard. Like breakfast, it is not a set meal, and the courses need not be observed strictly; unless indeed it is a formal entertainment. It is absurd to see people at lunch or breakfast sitting with empty plates before them, because some one else is eating an *entrée*. Apart from comfort, luncheon in a large family is far more economically served thus, as cold puddings, &c., of which there is not enough to hand round, can be neatly arranged in small dishes and placed on the table. Lunch in economical houses has to be more or less a made-up meal, or waste becomes a necessity. Where there are children, it will, of course, be the nursery dinner, and it will be found a good plan to begin with well-made soup or broth. Nothing is more nourishing than well-made mutton broth with plenty of rice or barley in it, and the meat stewed down into the soup. This, with an honest milky pudding eaten with stewed fruit, is as wholesome a dinner as it is possible to give. Of course, if Indian bairns are fed upon curry and caviare, their taste for simple dishes will become impaired, but there really is no reason *why* they should be so fed.

Servants in India are particularly careless in serving up cold viands;* having a contempt for them, and considering them as, in reality, the sweeper's perquisites. So it is no unusual thing to see puddings served up again as they left the table, and pies with dusty, half-dried smears of gravy clinging to the sides of the pie-dish. This should never be passed over; but both cook and *khitmutgâr* taught that everything, even down to the salt in the salt-cellars, must be neat, clean, and pleasant to look at, as well as to taste.

Heavy luncheons or tiffins* have much to answer for in India. It is a fact scarcely denied, that people at home invariably eat more on Sundays, because they have nothing else to do; so in the hot weather out here people seem to eat simply because it passes the time. It is no unusual thing to see a meal of four or five distinct courses placed on the table, when one light *entrée* and a dressed vegetable would be ample. Even when guests are invited to tiffin, there is no reason why they should be tempted to over-eat themselves, as they too often are, by the ludicrously heavy style of the ordinary luncheon party in India. If the object of such parties is, as it should be, to have a really pleasant time for sociable conversation between lunch and afternoon tea, stuffing the guests into a semi-torpid state certainly does not conduce to success. Yet if the *menu* be large and long, it is almost impossible for a luncheon guest to persist in refusal without making himself remarkable. He has no refuge, and, like the wedding guest, must accept his fate, although he knows the result to be that—

> 'A sadder and a wiser man
> He'll rise the morrow's morn.'*

Afternoon teas are, as it were, outclassed by tennis parties, and as these latter are a form of entertainment suitable to the limited purses of most people, a few hints may be given as to the refreshments required, &c. To begin with tea and coffee. It will be found best to have at least two teapots, and not to put more than three teaspoonfuls of tea in each. Anything more tasteless or injurious than tea which has been 'stood strong' and then watered down cannot be imagined. Cream should invariably be given, and for this purpose the milk must

not be boiled; even in hot weather milk will stand for twelve hours in
a wide-mouthed jar placed in an earthen vessel of water, especially if
a little carbonate of soda be dissolved in the milk, while boracic acid
will keep it sweet for days. Lump sugar costs very little more than
grain sugar, and looks infinitely nicer. Coffee is best made double or
treble strength in the morning, and diluted with boiling water when
wanted. If not sufficiently hot, the bottles containing it can be placed
in a saucepan of boiling water. This is the most economical plan,
as this strong coffee will keep several days; it is also the most satisfactory, as it enables the mistress to be sure of the quality of her coffee.
A recipe for this coffee will be found under the chapter on the '*Khitmutgâr.*' Hot milk and cold-whipped cream should be served with
coffee, and brown crystallised sugar, or what is still nicer, pounded
sugar-candy.

For other beverages, claret cup, hock cup, and cider cup may be
mentioned, and if a novelty is desired, it will be found that in the
hot weather *granitos* and *sorbets** will be much liked. They are simply
claret and hock, or sauterne cups made with water, and frozen to a
semi-liquid state. A good recipe will be found under the heading Ices
in the Cook's Guide. In the matter of cups, the common mistake is
to make them too complicated. Their chief object in India being to
quench the thirst, it is *unkind* to have them too strong. Indeed, if once
people begin it, they will find that a quarter of a tumbler of hard-iced
milk with a bottle of soda poured over it is about the best tennis drink
in the world. In cold weather ginger wine, cherry brandy, milk punch,
and other liqueurs may be given.

In regard to eatables, plain bread and butter should invariably
be a standing dish. Many people do not care for cakes, and yet find
a cup of tea or coffee better for something to eat with it. Brown
bread and Devonshire cream is a great favourite, and so are freshly
made and buttered scones enriched with an egg or a little cream.
Cakes and bonbons suitable for tennis parties are legion, and, as a
rule the one thing to be observed in selecting them is to avoid sticki-
ness or surprises. It is not pleasant to find the first bite of a firm
looking cake result in a dribble of liqueur or cream down your best
dress. In this connection, it may be mentioned that the ordinary
large teaspoon is a fearful weapon of destruction at garden parties,
especially when one's saucer is crowded up with cakes; and people
who go in for this form of entertainment should always use small

apostle spoons,* which are to be had very cheap. A supply of small plates is also a great boon.

The refreshment tables should be very neatly laid, and adorned with flowers. The trays give an opportunity for many little daintinesses in the shape of embroidered cloths, and there should always be a sprinkling of small tables covered with tea-cloths for the convenience of the guests. In ordinary tennis parties in small stations it is infinitely more convenient and pleasant to have two Sutherland tables with trays on them—one for coffee and the other for tea—whence the lady of the house, or, in her absence, the guests themselves, can supply a cup of tea or coffee without calling for the *khitmutgâr*. There should be room on the table for a plate of bread and butter, and one of cakes.

Ices are best served in India in regular ice-glasses, as they do not melt so fast, being less exposed to the air.

In England, the fashion of having various kinds of sandwiches at afternoon tea has of late gained ground but as it means a necessary disregard of dinner, it is not to be encouraged by any one who sets up for being a gourmet. A few recipes of the latest novelties have, however, been given in the proper place.

The art of dinner-giving is a difficult subject to approach. Many people openly assert that the native plan of sending dinner on a tray to the person you desire to entertain, would remove mountains of *ennui** and trouble for both host and guest. But there must be something wrong in a hospitality which demands self-devotion on both sides. As a matter of fact, the big dinner-party fails just in proportion to the effort made in giving it. A hostess who is dead tired with cooking and arranging flowers all day, must be exceptionally gifted if she can perform her duties to her guests as well as if she came to them fresh. It may be laid down as an axiom that, to be pleasant to all parties, a dinner must not rise too much beyond the daily level in cooking and serving. Hence follows the corollary, that if you wish to give neat, well-served dinners you must live neatly, and have even your water-gruel served tidily. Therefore, whatever your style of living may be, entertain your friends in that style, and there will be reasonable prospect of your succeeding. It must not be forgotten that the dinner is not the end in itself. It is the means of making your guests enter into that contented frame of mind which conduces to good fellowship; and, to an ordinarily sympathetic guest, the sight of an anxious host or hostess is fatal to personal placidity. '*If they serve you up a barbecued puppy dog, keep a cool countenance and help the company round*,' says the young husband in 'Heartsease' to his tearful wife.* Never was better advice given, if we supplement it with the words, '*and have it out with the cook afterwards.*'

Everyday dinners, then, are the test of capacity for entertaining; the effort at success should be made there, and not intermittently, when, with a sigh, you accept the inevitable necessity of asking the Browns, Joneses, and Robinsons to a fearful feast. With the number of servants in Indian houses, there is no reason why the table should not be laid, and the dinner routine gone through with the same details when you are alone, as when there are guests in the house. In addition, it is fatal to a cook to let him get slack under any circumstances, while there is really no more reason why your husband should be treated to an ill-considered meal than your guest; perhaps less, since the guest will not complain, and the husband most certainly will.

It is no use, however, giving imaginary *menus*. They are like a swimming belt—the learner finds himself quite as helpless once the support is removed as he was at the very beginning. The only royal road is thought and imagination. It requires little to convince any one that a dinner of beef olives, rolled shoulder of mutton, stuffed quails, and roly-poly would be nauseating in the extreme. A successful dinner-giver will train this innate sense of taste till it becomes equally certain that mock-turtle soup is not a fit prelude to a dinner, though it may make an admirable lunch.

In India, of late years, the style of dinner-giving has vastly improved, and it is rare now to come across the saddle of mutton, boiled fowl, and almond soup, which was considered *de rigueur a* few years ago. But it is a question if the present style is not a little pretentious for the salaries and position of many who adopt it. Rs. 1800 a month cannot be held equivalent for more than £1200 a year, or even less, if the enormous preliminary expenses of India are taken into account. Both servants and house rent out here average higher in proportion to income than they do at home, whilst, taking one thing with another, living is little, if at all, cheaper. Of course, where there is a family, the actual worth of an Indian income sinks to at most one-half, as far as its applicability to *personal* expenditure goes. Now, a family with £1200 a year at home would not dream of giving champagne and *pâte de foie gras*, or spending thirty shillings in preserved fruits, bonbons, &c., for a very *récherché* pudding.* Why should it be done out here? There are plenty of inexpensive dishes that are quite as nice to eat, and a housekeeper really does her work better if she manages, as can be done, to please her guests more simply.

As it is, one is often treated to a badly-cooked dinner in the style of a third-class French restaurant, even to the *hors d'œuvres*. In regard to the latter, it is doubtful if they should ever be considered a legitimate part of the *menu* at private houses, though exceptions may be made occasionally in favour of fresh oysters. The real *raison d'etre* of the *hors d'œuvre* is *not* to stimulate the appetite. To do this it must be taken ten minutes before dinner, like bitters.* It was at first nothing more or less than a restaurant dodge to while away the time (and increase the bill) whilst the dinner that had been ordered was being prepared. It therefore ceases to have any meaning in a private house, where, it is to be presumed, the guests will not have to wait for their dinners. On the other hand, it may be laid down as an axiom that no dinner, even a purely family one, is complete without a dressed vegetable of some sort or kind.

Without going into detail, it may be remarked that clear soups are far more wholesome than thick cloying ones, except in summer, when, the subsequent dishes being of a light character, the vegetable purées are in their proper place. The ordinary glutinous Indian soup is most unwholesome, and is admirably described in the *Cuisinier des Cuisiniers* in these words: '*Cette pâte epaisse et gluante, est une vraie colle sur l'estomac, qui, toujours indigeste, dérange ses fonctions.*'*

The present habit in India of serving the remove before the *entrées* is opposed to tradition, though that is no reason why it should be wrong. It has one advantage, in allowing the cook more time to dish the *entrées* neatly; but if the fashion is to continue, the *name* of the latter will surely need revision. An *entrée* is distinctly an *introduction* to the heavier meats. For ourselves, we believe this new idea has arisen from the fact that in most French cookery books and *menus* the *relevés* are printed first, and the *entrées* after. But this does not mean that they were served first, but simply that in those anti *à la Russe** days, the 'top and bottom' were shown before the four corners. Gastro-nomically, it is a mistake, for it crowds the made-dishes and sweets together, and forces those who are obliged to stick to plain diet to finish their dinner of soup, fish, and roast without a pause.

Cold sweets before the hot is a barbarism only to be equalled by serving a cheese *fondu* before jelly as a pudding.

Menu cards are a great convenience, and the ordering of a dinner is more likely to be consistent if the mistress makes it a rule to write out the *menu* on an ordinary china *menu* slate every day. It is also a means by which she can check the idle cook's constant excuse, '*Kuchch hukm nahin milla*' ('I had no order').

In regard to the decoration of the table, the tendency is to overdo it. Bright glass, clean linen, and brilliant silver are the first require- ments; after that, fancy may have play, so long as flowers are not strewn about the table to fade '*wisibly under the werry eyes*.' Such a sight is extremely depressing. One thing must be said in regard to the table-cloth. In India this is a limp rag, without a bit of gloss, or a suspicion of blue.* Insist on a rinsing in blued starch-water and iron- ing while wet. The napkins, too, without being stiff, should have some backbone; they should not, however, be twisted into fancy shapes, but one pattern should be adopted and adhered to throughout. Those who are particular about their table-linen will, of course, provide themselves with a cloth-press.* One great advantage in its use is that it necessitates the cloth being folded up and put away between each meal, and so checks a variety of evil Indian habits born of a table always ready spread. Wines and liquors of all sorts should be in the bearer's charge, and it is he who should put the decanters on the table at dessert.

The present fashion of making dessert into a *troisième service*,* with the servants perpetually handing round wines and sweets, is detestable. The dinner ends, as it began, with a bustle and a clatter of spoons and forks, instead of a calm. So soon, therefore, as the dessert has been once handed round, it should be placed on the table and the servants enjoined not to meddle with a spoon, a fork, or a plate, within hearing of the table. Then comes the time for conversation, and not, as now, for a hurried bolt of the ladies into the drawing-room before the *khitmutgârs* have done prancing round with distracting choco- lates, pralines, or pickled ginger. '*How can you taste your wine with half a pickled orange in your mouth?*' asked the uncle in *Punch** of the undergraduate nephew, who was winking wisely over a glass of port! How can you, in like manner, feel that you have had a good dinner if some one is perpetually pressing you to spoil it with a bonbon?

In serving coffee to the gentlemen, it should *never* be poured into cups. Some are sure to like *café noir*,* and it is horrible to have only half a cup; while if the cups are fairly filled to meet this want, they will still more horribly overflow if milk is poured into them. So let the coffee be served in the pot on a tray, with brown sugar, boiled cream or milk, and a liqueur bottle of best cognac for those who like it.

In India it is customary to speed the parting guests with cigars, &c. The best plan is to have a table in the verandah, and servant in attendance with soda-water, whisky, cigars, &c. More guests avail themselves of the privilege when served in this way.

CHAPTER VI

THE DUTIES OF THE SERVANTS

━━━◆◆◆━━━

IN the following chapter the authors have adopted the division of labour which obtains in Bengal and Northern India. In Bombay, Madras, Ceylon, and Burmah the manner of life is so different, that residents in these Presidencies will find it necessary to piece the duties of the various servants together into a new classification. Nevertheless, it is none the less certain that the work has to be performed, whether the worker be called by one name or another; also, that the majority of servants, from Himalaya to Cape Comorin, are absolutely ignorant of the first principles of their various duties. The *masaul* doing the lamps in Bombay is quite as likely to do them badly as his congener, the Bengali bearer, while the Madras butler's besetting sins are not far removed from those of the Oude *khitmutgâr*. The authors, therefore, believe that, given this slight difference in classification, the following brief outline of household duties will be found useful all over India. To facilitate this alteration, they give a comparative table showing the work assigned to each servant and the approximate wages demanded by good servants of each class at the present time in the various Presidencies.

BENGAL	BOMBAY	MADRAS	CEYLON	BURMAH
1. Bearer, 8 rs. to 10 rs. Head of house, valet, housemaid.	1. Butler, 15 rs. to 30 rs. Head of house, valet, wait; does marketing.	1. Butler, 15 rs. to 30 rs. Head of house. As Bombay.	1. *Appu*, 20 rs. to 25 rs. Head of house. As Bombay.	1. Boy, or butler. Same as Madras. Double wage.
2. Cook, 14 rs. to 40 rs. As a rule caters also.	2. Cook 15 rs. to 20 rs. Cooks.	2. Cook, 10 rs. to 25 rs. Cooks.	2. Cook, 20 rs. Cooks.	2. Cook. As Madras.
3. *Khitmutgâr*, 8 rs. to 10 rs. Waits at table.	3. *Masauls*, 10 rs. to 15 rs. Waits at table.	3. Mateys, 10 rs. to 15 rs. Waits at table.	3. Boys, 12 rs. to 15 rs. Waits at table.	3. Mateys, 20 rs. Waits at table.
4. *Khansamah*. 10 rs. to 20 rs. Housekeeper and head waiter. Head, as it were, of the commissariat department. A useless servant.	4. None.	4. None.	4. None.	4. None.

BENGAL	BOMBAY	MADRAS	CEYLON	BURMAH
5. *Musolchi*, 5 rs. to 8 rs. Scullery man.	5. Cook's Boy, 5 rs. Do.	5. *Tunny ketch*, 5 rs. Cook's help; a woman generally.	5. Kitchen coolie, 5 rs. to 10 rs. Scullery man.	5. Cook's coolie, 10 rs. Kitchen help.
6. *Mehtar*, 5 rs. to 7 rs. Sweeps, under-housemaid.	6. *Humal*, 10 rs. to 15 rs. Does bearer's and superior sweeper's work.	6. *Musolchi*, 8 rs. to 10 rs. As Bombay.	6. House coolie, 10 rs. to 12 rs. Superior sweeper and inferior bearer's work.	6. *Humal*, or house coolie. As Madras. Double wages.
7. *Bhisti*, 6 rs. Carries water.	7. Waterman, 6 rs. Carries water.	7. Waterman. 6 rs. Carries water.	7. None, except in country.	7. Waterman. Double Madras wage.
8. *Ayah*, 6 rs. to 10 rs. Lady's maid, nurse.	8. *Ayah*, 12 rs. to 20 rs. Do. do.	8. *Ayah*, 12 rs. to 18 rs. Do. do. Does needlework.	8. *Ayah*, 20 rs. Do. do. Does needlework.	8. *Ayah*. As Madras.
9. *Dirzi*, tailor, 10 rs.	9. *Dirzi*, 15 rs.	9. *Dirzi*, 10 rs.	9. *Dirzi*. Seldom kept.	9. *Dirzi*. Seldom kept.
10. *Dhobi*, washerman, 8 rs. for two persons, 12 rs. for a family.	10. *Dhobi*, 5 rs. each person.	10. *Dhobi*, 5 rs. each person.	10. *Dhobi*, 5 rs. each person.	10. *Dhobi*, 5 rs. each person.
11. *Syce*, or grooms, 6 rs. to 7 rs. Does groom's work.	11. *Ghora wallahs*, 10 rs. to 15 rs. Do.	11. Horsekeepers, 7 rs. to 10 rs. Do.	11. Horsekeepers, 12 rs. Do.	11. *Syce*, 12 rs. Do.
12. Grasscutters, 5 rs. to 6 rs.	12. Grasscutters, 6 rs.	12. Grasscutters, 6 rs.	12. None kept. Women bring grass.	12. Grass generally bought.
13. Gardener, *Mâlee*, 5 rs. to 30 rs.	13. *Mâlee*. As Bengal.	13. *Mâlee*. As Bengal.	13. Gardener, 10 rs. to 12 rs.	13. Seldom kept.
14. *Gow wallah*, cow man, 5 rs. to 6 rs.	14. Seldom kept.	14. Cow man. As Bengal.	14. Not kept.	14. Not kept.

It will be seen that the chief difference in the distribution of household work lies in the head man in Bengal being the bearer; and in Madras, Bombay, &c., the butler. The difference is greater than it seems on paper; for while the bearer is invariably a Hindu, the butlers are Christians or Mahomedans. In the former case the whole of the household goods, barring those connected with food, are placed in charge of one man; in the latter, everything, without any exception. In Bombay the various duties of the servants are not so marked as in Bengal; but most of the house-servants dust, sweep, wait at table, and cook, if required to do so. Roughly speaking, butler and *hamal* divide the bearer's duty in Bombay, while in Madras they are performed by the butler and *musolchi*. Both in Madras and Bombay an inferior sweeper, either male or female, is kept. Details regarding the duties of the Bengal servants will be found below, with a few recipes for things required in their work. Each of these can be had in tract form, translated into Hindoo, so that they can be given to the servants, but this is never so efficacious as verbal order, quiet, authoritative, unyielding, yet kindly.

DUTIES OF THE BEARER

The implements required by the bearer are—

6 Soft dusters.	1 Tin Putz pomade.
1 Feather broom.	2 Funnels.
1 Bottle home-made	1 Bottle brush.
furniture polish.	1 Ice breaker.
1 Clothes brush.	1 Salver for cards.
1 Corkscrew.	1 Bottle benzine.
1 Pair scissors.	Hammer, tacks, glue,
1 Chimney brush.	string, &c.

The bearer should be the head servant, and the greatest care should be exercised in engaging one who is honest and respectable. Being his master's valet, the other servants give weight to his opinions, and follow his lead, knowing that he has opportunities for private communication with the authorities. Ear-wigging,* it must be remembered, is supposed by the Oriental to be all-powerful. The discipline and respectability of the servants' quarters depend to a great extent on the character of the bearer, who should be held responsible.

The bearer must be an early riser. He has charge of every single thing in the house, save those in the dining-room and pantry, and any loss or breakage has to be accounted for by him; therefore it is to his own advantage that he should keep an eye on the under-servants. In addition, one of the greatest alleviations of Indian discomfort lies in his hands; that is, keeping the house free of mosquitoes. To do this he must in the hot weather shut every window before dawn. They may be opened afterwards; but if they are not shut between four o'clock and six o'clock mosquitoes will come in.

His next duty is to remove the lamps used the night before to the lamp-room, taking those used in the bedrooms from the *ayah* or *khitmutgâr*, as the case may be, whose duty it is to bring them out to the bearer. This should be done at the opportunity afforded by the taking in to the bedroom of the early cup of tea. He should also call upon the *khitmutgâr* to remove coffee cups, tumblers, &c., that may have escaped notice. He should not remove them himself.

When the sweeper has swept the outer verandahs, the upper and lower windows should be thrown open, but not till then, or the dust will come in.

One day a week the drawing-room should receive a thorough cleaning, summer and winter; and after a dust-storm a complete turning out is also necessary; but on other days the sweeper should, with a soft brush and dustpan, sweep over the whole room, shaking mats, &c., outside, as they are apt to harbour vermin. The bearer meanwhile should remove the flower-vases and place them on a table in the verandah, fold up newspapers and put them in a certain fixed receptacle, replace books in the bookshelf, restore chairs to their proper place, and sort everything up as far as possible. It is a good plan to have a separate basket for all papers, envelopes, &c., found on the floor anywhere about the house, as it is then a sure find for lost letters or memoranda. Punkahs and thermantidotes* often blow scraps of paper off tables.

When this is done the whole room should be carefully dusted.

The weekly turn-out should include a polish to all articles of furniture, a smart beating of the backs of the carpets, and a cleaning of windows. Dirty windows are the sign of a bad bearer. If the bearer is valet also, he should now attend to his master's room, brushing and folding the clothes used the day before, tidying the dressing-table, and not forgetting to dust the mirror.

As a rule, the gardener or the mistress arranges the flower vases, but it is the bearer's duty to take them back into the drawing-room when they are ready. He should remember that as he is responsible for all the ornaments and the many valuable things left lying about a drawing-room, it is to his interest *not* to let strangers in. On the weekly cleaning day the flower vases should be thoroughly washed out with soap and water, taking care to remove all sediment with a bottle brush. If soap and water fails to restore the polish of the glass, a few drops of sulphuric acid in the water is infallible.

After breakfast the bearer should be in attendance on his mistress at the godown,* and report *openly* to her anything which has occurred in the compound during the last twenty-four hours which she ought to know. He need fear no enmity from other servants if he does this fearlessly, openly, and honestly.

If he has charge of the wine, he should ask for what is needed, and keep his mistress informed as to the supplies in his charge. He should see the grain weighed out for the horses, cows, and poultry, and should never fail to report anything unsatisfactory in their management.

The bearer should be ready to receive callers from twelve o'clock till two. Unless his mistress has told him to say '*durwâza bund*' (the Indian equivalent for not at home), he should *at once* usher the visitors into the drawing-room and present their cards* to his mistress, wherever she may be. He must never do this with his fingers, and a small tray for receiving the cards should always lie on the verandah, or hall table.

One of the most important parts of a bearer's work is the charge of the lamps, and yet not one man in a thousand knows anything about it. Most lamps in India burn kerosene oil, and the great secret of making them give a good clear light is cleanliness. When a tin of kerosene has to be opened, it is only necessary to make a hole in two opposite corners of the top, about the size of a pea. This can be done with a round nail and hammer. As a full tin of oil generally runs twenty-five bottles, the bearer should have that number ready. He should then decant the whole tin into the bottles, and at once report any deficiency to his mistress. By this means fraud on the part of the supplier will be detected at once, and also the very common adulteration of the oil, as the bearer will be able to see if it runs clear and uniform in tint to the very bottom. To fill the lamps the reservoirs should be removed from their stands to a separate table and most carefully filled with a funnel by means of a proper can or an old teapot. If any kerosene is spilt on the reservoir, it should be thoroughly removed. If it is necessary to remove the burners, before replacing them the loose ends of wick should be squeezed dry by drawing them downwards through the fingers over a basin or empty tin kept for the purpose. The burner should then be held to the light, to see that all air-holes are free from dust or dirt. Any clogging is fatal. When the burner is replaced, the wick should be very slightly turned up and *cleaned*, not cut, by gentle rubbing with a duster and a final squeeze between finger and thumb. If any threads or unevenness appear, they may be carefully removed with the scissors, but as a rule scissors should never *touch* the wick. If due care in filling the reservoirs at a different table is observed, and the chimneys and globes are never touched with greasy fingers, it is hardly ever necessary to use water in cleaning them, a chimney brush and dry duster being quite sufficient. The overpowering smell of most Indian lamp-rooms is simply due to wasteful carelessness in filling.

The wick of a lamp should *never* coil round in the reservoir. Even the best oil has a sediment, and when the wick lies in it for weeks and weeks, the fibres get clogged, and so the oil is prevented from rising through them. Therefore, when a new wick is put in, it should only just reach to the bottom of the reservoir; if the lamp is kept well filled, as it should be, it is surprising how long even this little bit of wick will burn brilliantly; and though this plan involves more frequent change of wick, and a slight excess in the amount used, this is more than compensated for by the satisfaction of clear white light. Once a week every reservoir should be completely emptied and wiped out with a rag. The oil from them should be put with that squeezed from the wicks, and filtered before it is used again.

Candlesticks must be cleaned every day, and every trace of grease removed with hot water.

In the evening, when the bearer lights the lamps, he should also see that each bedroom has its candle and box of matches; at the same time, he should satisfy himself that the sweeper, *bheesti*, and other servants have done their work. On bringing the lamps into the drawing-room he should tidy it up, remove bits of thread, torn papers, &c., from the floor, draw the curtains, and if there is a fire, see that the wood-box is full. If the bearer is also *âbdâr*, i.e., serves the wine at table, it is his duty to inform the *khitmutgâr* what wine-glasses will be required, and satisfy himself that they are duly placed on the table. If the *âbdâr* has to serve a large number of people, especially in the hot weather, when guests are naturally in a hurry for something cool to drink, it requires method and preparation to be successful. The ice should be broken into pieces before dinner is announced, and wrapped in a napkin. The best way of breaking up ice is to use a short sharp steel skewer; a large darning-needle fixed in a handle answers well. No hammer is required, as the lightest pressure with the sharp point will split the ice. The soda-water should be ready to hand, champagne wire removed, claret uncorked, and the wines for dessert decanted in scrupulously clean decanters. The *âbdâr* should not dodge round the table in serving the guests, but go round methodically, beginning with the lady at the host's right hand.

The bearer should always be on guard against the ravages of white ants, fish insects, and other vermin; and in the rainy season he must not forget the periodical airing of all woollen clothes, blankets, rugs, &c.

Another important work of the bearer is making the beds, excepting, of course, those in the *ayah*'s charge. It may generally be asserted that no native servant has the faintest idea how to make a bed, and therefore those mistresses who desire to make their guests comfortable will do well to give at least one practical lesson on this subject, insisting on the mattress being turned, the sheets evenly spread and separately tucked in, and the pillows well shaken up. An Indian bed too often consists of a hard felted surface, with more than a suspicion of crumbs, and covered by frantically crooked sheets and blankets, which the slightest movement reduces to chaos, while a sudden turn lets them loose in disastrous avalanche on the floor.

Recipes for the Bearer

1. **Armenian Cement.**—Half oz. isinglass soaked in water till soft. Strain, add 2 oz. spirits of wine, and dissolve with gentle heat. Dissolve ¼ oz. selected mastic pearls in 2 oz. spirits of wine. Mix both solutions whilst warm. Powder 1 drachm gum-ammoniac, and mix on a slab with enough solution to damp it through. It will then incorporate with the rest of the solution if stirred over gentle heat. Strongest cement known. It will join polished steel.

2. **Ants, to keep from Tables, &c.**—Tie a rag dipped in castor oil round the legs of the table or cupboard.

3. **Ants, White, to keep away.**—Tar the floor with thin tar. Infallible, and cleanly. Indigo in the concrete is said to be efficacious.

4. **Brass Work, to clean.**—Cut a lime in half, rub over the brass, wash the article thoroughly in soap and water, dry and polish. One teaspoon of sulphuric acid mixed in quarter of a pint of water, and used instead of the lime, is still better. Sapolio* and Brookes' soap also do well, but Putz pomade is the best.

5. **Brass Work, Benares, to restore the Gold Colour.**—Coat the ornament with a paste of powdered sal-ammoniac and water. Heat over, or rather in, a slow charcoal ash fire, rub dry, and polish with bran.

6. **Brass Work, to preserve untarnished.**—Coat lightly with pale paper varnish.

7. **Bottle Wax.**—One lb. resin melted with ¼ lb. suet and ¼ lb. shellac.

8. **Bottle Paste or Dextrine.**—Wet 2 oz. arrowroot with 2 oz. cold water. Soak 80 grains gelatine in 14 oz. water for one hour. Bring to the boil. When the gelatine is quite dissolved, add the arrow-root, and boil for four minutes. Pour into a bowl to cool. When nearly cold, add 1 oz. spirits of wine, in which 6 drops of pure glacial carbolic acid have been mixed. Stir well, bottle, and cork. It will keep for months.

9. **Carpets, to remove Ink Stains.**—Wash, if possible, while still wet, with fresh, hot boiled milk. Sponge again and again with hot water. Time and patience must be plentifully used. A weak solution of oxalic acid may be tried if the stain is very dark, but the risk of injuring the colour is very great. It is, however, possible to re-dye the injured portion, with a result certainly preferable to a black spot.

10. **Chairs, to prevent the Leather from Cracking.**—Rub with white of egg beaten thin with water.

11. **Chimneys, to prevent Cracking.**—Set in a pan of cold water, and gradually heat to boiling point. Let the chimneys remain in the water till cold.

12. **Cloth or Velvet Embroidery, to clean.**—Bake a very thick *chapâtti* (unleavened cake) of coarse *atta* and water. When barely cooked through, take the inside doughy part, form into a roller, and with the palm of the hand roll in over the embroidery. The fluffs and hairs stick to and come away on the dough, which also acts, like bread, as a cleanser. Excellent for velvet.

13. **Dubbin for Boots.**—Melt 2 oz. mutton suet, 4 oz. black resin, and 1 pint fish oil. One of the best dressings for boots is plain castor oil. Vaseline is also good.

14. **Glue, Strong.**—Digest by gentle heat in a corked bottle 3 oz. rectified spirits of wine with 4 oz. of fine pale shellac. The Chinese use nothing else for all their wood-work. Excellent for pianos.

15. **Furniture Polish.**—Mix in a bottle equal parts of linseed oil, turpentine, vinegar, and spirits of wine; or half a teacup shredded beeswax dissolved in 1 teacup turpentine.

16. **French Polish.**—Put into a bottle enough pale shellac slightly broken to fill it one-third, fill up with spirits of wine. Digest in the sun.

17. **Grease Spots, to remove.**—Rub with oil of turpentine and air in the sun; or place a double fold of blotting-paper* over the spot, and rub with a moderately hot poker.

18. **Patent Leather, to preserve.**—Use plain boiled linseed oil. The easiest plan to make a good drying oil is to powder 2 oz. of litharge and 1 oz. oxide or sulphate of lead. Put into a pint bottle of linseed oil, agitate occasionally for ten days. Set in the hot sun for two more, then decant the clear portion.

19. **Scouring Drops.**—Mix 2 oz. rectified spirits of turpentine with 2 drachms essential oil of lemon or cloves. Rub on with a clean rag till the stain disappears.

DUTIES OF THE SWEEPER

The implements required by the sweeper are—

1 Native broom for verandahs.	1 Scrubbing brush.
1 Dust-pan and brush.	Soap.
1 Carpet-switch.	6 Dusters of all sorts.
1 Hearth brush.	Set boot brushes.
1 Ash-pan.	1 Turk's head for cleaning walls.
1 Dust cloth.	1 Carbolic or Phenyle bottle.
1 Slop pail.	1 Wooden spud.*
1 Bath-room basket.	1 Tin whitewash and brush.
1 House flannel.	1 Comb and brush for dog.

In most houses the sweeper is engaged simply because he is the husband of the *ayah*. This is an immense mistake, as the whole cleanliness of the house depends upon him. Again, his duties give him the *entrée** to every room, therefore the trust reposed in him must necessarily be great. He is, in fact, the under-housemaid, and should never be allowed to degenerate into the dirty, unkempt drudge, whose sole notion of work is to raise a dust-storm with a broom, and try experiments on the relative fragility of your pet ornaments by flicking them with a greasy duster. Housekeepers will find a rupee or two more well expended in securing the services of a man who is presentable, and who is both fit to, and capable of, receiving orders direct.

Care should also be taken that the sweeper is not imposed upon by every other servant; as a rule, he is simply hunted from pillar to post, and made to do odd jobs for everybody; the *khitmutgârs* being special offenders in this way, calling on the sweeper at all hours to clear up their messes, and generally to be the scapegoat for their dirty habits.

When a large number of servants are kept, making a full compound, and there are also dogs and poultry to be looked after, we *strongly* recommend the employment of an under or mate sweeper, who should do the outdoor work. So much of the cleanliness and consequent healthiness of a house and compound depends upon the sweeper, that it is *worth while* to make sure the work is not scamped; and the plan here advocated, of having two sweepers, will be found to be far more satisfactory in large establishments than the employment of an upper and under bearer, neither of whom will do any real cleaning. The under-sweeper (who will seldom require more than five rupees a month) should have the charge of the servants' houses, compound, and stableyard, look after the dogs and poultry, sweep the verandahs, remove the refuse from the cook-house, and be generally responsible for outside cleanliness. The upper sweeper should be virtually the under-bearer, leaving the head man available as butler and valet.

The sweeper's first duty in the morning is to see to the bath-rooms and empty the slops, taking care to observe all regulations as to the disposal of refuse, and to keep everything sweet and clean. His next is to sweep the verandahs, then the dining-room and hall, and lastly, the drawing-room. If there has been a fire, he should, after placing the dust-cloth over the rug, proceed to remove the ashes, and thoroughly clean the hearth. It will be found a good plan to make the sweeper keep a pot full of colour-wash to take the place of hearthstone. With this he should wash over the inside of the arched recess which in most Indian houses does duty as a fireplace; by thus removing the smoke and dust marks, the hearth has a much tidier appearance. Once a week, every room in the house should have a complete cleaning out, beginning with the upper windows and walls, and finishing with a rub down to all the doors and frames. Such of the boots and shoes as have not been cleaned over-night should now be attended to: in some houses the bearer cleans the boots, and he always remains responsible for their being ready when wanted, and should always keep clean the patent leather, and the finer kinds of shoes; but in many respects it is better to make the sweeper do the dirty work.

After each meal it is the sweeper's duty to go into the scullery, and, under the *khitmutgâr*'s orders, remove all refuse to *its proper place*. In large stations there is generally a recognised place for the refuse heap, which is periodically cleared away by conservancy carts;* but in other cases the best plan is to dig a long trench, three feet deep by two broad, in some convenient corner of the garden, piling up the earth on one side only. As the sweeper throws in the refuse he should cover it with dry earth from above, taking care not to use the trench in various parts, but work steadily from one end, and to fill it up only to about two feet, and after that to make it level with pure earth. When one trench is filled, another may be dug alongside. In this way all refuse becomes valuable manure for the garden.

The sweeper's last duty at night is to see that everything in his charge is clean, and to give both scullery and kitchen a final sweep-out. On this depends much of the health of the household. The sweeper should always have on hand a supply of carbolic or phenyle, and should be instructed how to use it, or whitewash if that is preferred. His duties in regard to dogs and fowls will be found under those headings. The following recipes will be found useful for the sweeper:—

1. **Boots, to black**.—Remove every atom of dust or mud with the brush, or, if necessary, a damp cloth. Put on the smallest possible amount of blacking, and leave it to dry thoroughly, then polish as hard as you can. Do not forget to take the laces out before blacking laced boots or shoes. If the leather feels sticky, too much blacking has been used. For brown shoes, use one tea-cup shredded beeswax dissolved in one tea-cup turpentine, or the usual brown boot polish. Polish with a silk cloth.

2. **Chitai Matting, to clean**.—Wash with strong salt and water. Dry at once with a soft cloth.

3. **Grey Wash for Fireplace**.—Make a *gharra* full of rather thick whitewash, colour with powdered charcoal, and add a little rice-water or glue.

4. **Iron, to clean**.—Use powdered bathbrick* and oil, with plenty of elbow-grease.

5. **Red Wash for Fireplace**.—Mix one pice worth of *hirmchi* with one pice worth of *géru* in sufficient rice-water to make the whole to the consistency of whitewash.

6. **Rust, to remove.**—Take powdered polisher's putty (or crude peroxide of tin) mixed with a little oxalic acid and water. Apply on the rust spot as a paste for a few minutes. Wash off carefully, dry and polish. Both Brooke's soap and Putz pomade are excellent for metal work.

7. **Whitewash Marks on Wood, to remove.**—Mix 1 oz. salt with 1 oz. linseed oil and 4 oz. of water. Rub on with a damp duster till the spot disappears.

8. **Windows, to clean.**—Remove varnish or putty marks with spirits of wine. Wash with soap and clean water on both sides of the pane. Polish with a dry rag. If the polish has gone, it may be restored by dry, powdered tripoli,* and a very fine polish may be given by dusting powdered chalk, tied up in a piece of muslin, on to the glass, and then rubbing it off with a dry, clean rag. Greasy cloths will never clean glass.

9. **Windows, to preserve Glass from Paint.**—Make the painter or varnisher use a thin slip of glass as a guard. Put this close to the woodwork, when all surplus stuff will be smeared on it, not on the real window glass below.

DUTIES OF THE COOK

The implements required are mentioned hereafter.

The first duty of the cook is to have a tidy cook-room, and for this his mistress is mainly responsible in the first place. We cannot insist too often on the folly of expecting cleanliness when there are no appliances rendering it possible to be clean.

The cook-house, then, must be airy and wholesome. The floor should be of broad, flat bricks, such as are used for mosques and public buildings, set close in really good mortar. There will then be no difficulty in getting it swept and *washed* out every day.

No better mode of cooking exists than the *chûla* arrangement for charcoal, at present in use in most parts of India, and which closely resembles that seen on the Continent. It is convenient, economical, safe, and suitable in every way to the requirements of the climate. But it is *not* necessary that the whole erection should be made of mud and loose bricks, as is very generally the case. Good bricks, well set and surmounted by a strong sheet of iron clamped to the bricks, with holes cut to correspond to the round brick *chûlas* below, will make as good and as cleanly a kitchen range as any cook need desire. A hot case with an oven beneath it can be built on one side, and leave the cook no excuse for bad cooking. Such an oven is very simply made; it is merely a framework of sheet iron with a door in front, let into the bricks with a place for charcoal below and above, and a space of about one inch left between the iron and bricks at the back to act as a flue.

The expense of such simple arrangements is trifling in the extreme, and no practical cook who has ever personally superintended the working of that diabolical invention, a native *tizâl* or oven, will ever allow one in her kitchen. The mischief it can do to the best made cakes is simply incredible; and it is impossible to say which is more difficult, to get the lid *on*, or, having succeeded in that, to get it *off* again. The mere sight of a *tizâl* with two crooked legs, the missing third supplied by a tottering pile of bricks, and three inches of dust and ashes inside to prevent the utter cremation of the wretched cake, is enough to dishearten any one. No one need be astonished if, in the frantic effort to get the lid full of burning coals off or on, the whole frail structure collapses, and *khitmutgâr*, charcoal, ashes, cake, and tins are mingled in hopeless confusion. If the initial expense is not a bar, we strongly recommend every housekeeper to have a kerosene oil stove with an oven* on a table in a verandah, where she can use it for dainty cooking.

A point which must be insisted on in a cook-room is the raising of the washing-up place or sink so far from the ground that the refuse water will fall into a proper and movable receptacle outside, and *not* filter into the ground. It cannot be right that food should be cooked in a house whose very foundations are saturated with sewage. The sink, then, should be at least two feet from the ground, with a high ledge round, and a stand for water vessels on one side. These are best made of old kerosene tins with iron handles, and in each should be a tin-dipper—any empty tin will serve the purpose. Every kitchen should contain two tables—a dishing-up table, which is best close beside the range, if not part of it, and a working table. Besides the latter there should be another stand for two water vessels, as it is by no means advisable that water which has been standing, so to speak, in the *sink* should be used for cooking.

The cook should be provided with a cupboard which locks for his stores, and an open bunker for his charcoal. Shelves for saucepans, and a row of hooks for different utensils, are of course necessary.

With regard to the utensils themselves, the best and safest are the steel saucepans now so much used at home, though nothing *cooks* better than copper.[1] It is, however, a constant source of anxiety, any slight fit of indigestion rousing suspicions of the *dêgchies*; so that, if possible, it is best to use nothing but enamel and steel, especially when cooking for children. The number of utensils must, of course, vary with the style of establishment, but a small household, no less than a large one, requires the little conveniences and refinements which are so often conspicuous by their absence in Indian cook-rooms. The following list only gives absolute necessaries, if clean and wholesome cooking is expected. The Urdu name is given against each.

6	Stewpans or saucepans, of sizes, with covers	*Dêgchi*
2	Frying-pans	*Fry-pân*
1	Omelet-pan, enamelled	*Momlet-pân*
1	Large kettle with cock	*Kittli*
1	Colander	*Turkâri ke chulni*
1	Wire frying basket	*Tôkri*
1	Egg poacher	*Unda poach-dân*
1	Large boiler	*Dêgchâ*
2	Small tin saucepan	*Sârse-pân*
1	Mortar and pestle	*Imâmdusta*
1	Curry stone*	*Sil*
1	Gridiron	*Gridârni*
2	Iron charcoal stoves	*Ungêthi*
1	Roaster	*Kubâb-dân*
1	Chopper	*Châppa*
1	Saw	*Âri*
6	Kitchen knives	*Chûri*
6	Forks	*Kârnta*
6	Metal spoons	*Chumchâ*
1	Gravy strainer	*Grævy ke chulni*
1	Potato muller	*Âlu mulne ke lukri*
2	Graters	*Grâte-dân*
3	Dredgers	*Mirich, âtta,* and *nimuk dâns*
2	Ladles	*Chumchâs*
1	Whisk	*Kûchi*
12	Bowls, of sizes	*Piyâle*
1	Coffee mill	*Câffé ke chukki*

[1] See remarks, page 19.

1	Coffee roaster	*Câffĕ senk-dân*
1	Set scales and weights	*Turâzu*
1	Meat safe	*Dûli*
1	Hair sieve	*Chulni*
2	Wire sieves	*Chulna*
1	Jelly-bag	*Jeli ki thaili*
1	Mincing board	*Mêz*
1	Paste board	*Crâs ke mêz*
1	Rolling-pin	*Bêlun*
24	Dusters and cloths	*Jâhrun*
	Moulds *à discrétion*	*Sâncha*
	Pie dishes	*Pi-deesh*

If high-class cooking is attempted, a *bain marie* becomes absolutely necessary for the sauces; but this can easily be made in any bazaar out of an old kerosene tin cut down to six inches, the edge turned over an iron wire, and handles put at each side. This, half filled with water, in which four small bazaar-made tin saucepans can be plunged, is all that is necessary, and the whole arrangement need not cost more than two rupees. In fact, a very little supervision and ingenuity suffices to fit up a cook-room properly at a small cost. Small enamel pans are now to be bought in most shops, and there are an infinity of labour-saving trifles which repay their cost in kitchen work; such as egg-beaters, bread crumb mills, vegetable slicers, &c., which it is well worth while to add to the above list.

Having thus placed the cook in a decent kitchen, with decent appliances, the harder task remains of getting him to keep it in a decent state. This will never be accomplished unless the mistress takes the trouble of seeing that her orders are obeyed. The sweeper should go into the cook-room twice a day—once before breakfast, and once after dinner—at both of which times every particle of refuse should be removed, and the sink swept and washed clean. The ashes must also be removed, and the whole place put into thorough order, saucepans hung up, waterpots re-filled, tables washed down. A little method is all that is required, for once the sweeper and the *bheesti* are on the spot, it is no trouble to the cook to insist on their doing their duty thoroughly.

Even supposing the kitchen is kept in a cleanly state, it by no means follows that the food will be cooked cleanly, and the mistress must always be on her guard against the dirty habits which are ingrained in the native cook. The strictest morning parade will not prevent him stirring the eggs into a rice pudding with his finger, but a practical illustration that the method is both troublesome and ineffectual may do some good. In the same way, once the saving of time resulting from proper appliances is brought home to the cook, you may trust him to use them; but not till then.

It would take page on page, chapter on chapter, to tell the many evil habits in which Indian cooks have been grounded and taught; but in the Cookery Book published as a companion to this volume, most of them are mentioned in the various recipes as things not to be done. There is therefore no need to detail them here.

In regard to catering, the authors much prefer the less common system of allowing the cook to do the marketings, without the intervention of the *khansâmâh*. If one man is responsible for the quality of the provisions, and another for the preparation of them, it is impossible to get a firm grip of blame on either, in the event of unpalatable food. One throws the fault on the other, and even if the *khansâmâh* is held responsible, it must always be with a mental reservation, if the mistress be herself a practical cook; for the best food will not stand bad cooking, any more than good cooking will take the place of good food. It is certainly a great satisfaction to be able to award praise or blame with a free hand, and for this reason alone divided responsibility is objectionable. Again, the man who is to do the cooking alone knows *what* he intends to make, and what sort, size, and quality of ingredients he requires. The bazaar is seldom so far away but that the cook can get to it before breakfast if he arranges his work methodically, while the commission he of course makes on every article is so much inducement for him to work well. As half the comfort of life depends on the actual cooker of food, it is as well to keep him pleased with himself and with his service. Yet for one mistress who makes a point of commending a well-cooked dish, how many are there who never dream of praise, and whose only criticism is unmeasured and often unreasonable blame?

There are certain delusions current in cook-houses in India, such as the belief that it is the *yolk* of the egg which clears soup, against which it is useless to argue. Autocratic high-handedness is the only weapon of any avail. As an instance in point, one of the authors ordered potted sheep's head several times, and in spite of minute instructions the result was failure. At last the head was ordered for inspection, and it was *skinned*. The reply to an indignant query as to why strict orders had been disobeyed, was that sheep's heads were always skinned—it was *dustoor, i.e.* custom; together with the remark that skinning or not skinning had nothing to do with the non-setting of the jelly, which every one knew came from *bones* and not skin. The offender was told to boil an unskinned head for twelve hours. He came next day with a new light on his face. '*Mem Sahib*,' he said, '*do they by any chance make gelatine of skins, for, as the Lord sees me, I can hardly cut that jelly with a knife!*' Here was a case of sheer ignorance of facts well known to an English child; and it must never be forgotten that this is not the exception, but the rule. An Indian cook does not understand why eggs will not rise if whipped slowly, or why syrup will never crystallise unless stirred. He often stands confounded before his own failures, unable to tell *where* he has gone wrong, or how; and if his mistress is a practical cook, he will give a smile of wonder and relief when she points out what he must have done to have caused that specific result. The consequent testimony, '*Béshukk—âp such furmâta hai—aisa hua*' ('Without doubt, your honour speaks truth—it was so'), will go further to raise a mistress in his estimation than any amount of theoretical knowledge she may display. It must not be forgotten either that the best cooks are liable to failures. The fire may be too slack, and yet the delay of increasing it may be *worse* than making the best of what you have. Attention may be distracted for half a second, and lo! the custard curdles, the caramel burns. In cooking, as in other things, the charity born of sympathy covers a multitude of sins.

In regard to the actual duties of a cook in India, they are confined entirely to cooking. He has nothing whatever to do with the morning tea, boiling the kettle, making the toast, &c. That is the *khitmutgâr's* work, and even when poached eggs are taken it is best not to make the cook responsible, for the early morning is his marketing time. In the same way he is in no way responsible for the proper serving of breakfast, only with the dressing and dishing up of the hot dishes, whatever they may be. Tea, coffee, eggs, milk, toast, butter, &c., are in charge of the *khitmutgâr*; and so is the afternoon tea. Beyond this, everything which comes to table is in the cook's care, and he must arrange with the table servants how the various dishes and sauces are to be served.

A considerate mistress will always look a day or two ahead in her orderings, but the cook should be encouraged to act on his own responsibility in minor details, and be praised when he has contrived some fresh pudding or side-dish. This is an immense relief, especially in the hot weather, when one racks one's brains in vain to think of something new, and everything that comes to mind seems a Dead Sea apple of dust and ashes.*

Never let a cook *run down* in his cooking, even when he is in camp; for it is a dead certainty that once the niceties of dishing up and dressing are disregarded, a general slackness will set in. '*I can't cook well'm,*' said an English servant to one of the authors; '*there ain't really enough cookin' to do; my 'and gets h'out.*' This is still more true with an Indian servant. So insist on everything being done every day in the same style. Then, if a friend comes into dinner unexpectedly, you need have no anxieties. The dinner may be plain, even frugal, but it will be correct, even to the most minute details.

Between the Scylla of sheer pitchforking of viands on to the dish, and the Charybdis of what cooks call '*sujāwut,*' or decoration, *simply as decoration*, the mistress will find it a little hard to steer a middle course; but the one fault is as bad as the other, and cutlets coloured pink with cochineal, and green with spinach, may be to some minds as unappetising to the look as a heterogeneous mass of chops and garnishing swimming in a loose gravy, which shows by a high-water mark on the dish that it underwent a tide on its way from the cook-room. A good cook is not made, he is born; so if you are lucky enough to find one, do anything to keep him—short of letting him know that you are anxious to do so.

Finally, if in the hot weather the results of his hands are poorer than usual, and he shows a captious dislike to criticism, give him a blue pill,* or present him with a bottle of Eno's Fruit Salt.* It is very bilious work stooping over a hot fire with the thermometer above 100°.

DUTIES OF THE KHITMUTGÂR

The implements required by the *khitmutgâr* are numerous—

1 Set of plate brushes.	1 Knife board.
2 Chamois leathers.	1 Tin for washing knives.
1 Box plate powder.	1 Jug mop.
1 Box polishing paste.	1 Wooden butler's-tray.
1 Brazier or *angithi.*	1 Toasting fork.

1 Earthen butter cooler.
2 Galvanised iron pails.
1 Decanter drainer.
3 Wooden or tin tubs.
1 Plate rack.
1 Scrubbing brush.
1 Hot case.

Kitchen paper for wrapping
   spare plate.
1 Bread pan.
Wire covers for jam, &c.
1 Silver basket.
Endless dusters and tea cloths.
1 Pair butter spats.*

This servant is a curious mixture of virtues and vices. As a rule, he is a quick, quiet waiter, and well up in all dining-room duties; but in the pantry and scullery his dirt and slovenliness are simply inconceivable to the new-comer in India.

The best of them will, if put to it, give a final polish to your teacup with some portion of his own clothing; or place fresh-made mustard on the top of the old to save the trouble of cleaning out the pot. Much of this is, of course, due to heredity, all Mahomedans of the lower classes being apparently blind to dirt; but more is the result of almost every table-servant beginning work as what is called a *musolchi*—a nameless, abject, adjunct of the scullery, who washes up by the light of Nature. Dirty habits thus grow unchecked by the mistress's eye, and cling to the learner long after he has risen to higher things; whereas, if the sensible plan, advocated elsewhere, is adopted, of having no *musolchi*, the *khitmutgâr* would have to learn his work thoroughly from the beginning. But whatever may have been his training in the past, the mistress should insist on her *khitmutgâr* washing up, in the present, with his own hands. Plate, glass, teacups and breakfast cups, &c., should be washed in the pantry. Dinner plates and dishes should be washed either in another scullery, if available, or in the verandah; for if the pantry and scullery work are done together, there is no possibility of keeping the pantry as it should be—sweet, clean, and free from flies. In addition, there is a certainty that the same greasy water will be used for plates and cups alike.

The pantry should be provided with a washing-up table, and at least three wooden or tin tubs. A supply of cold water can easily be secured by placing a cask against one of the outside walls with a few inches of leaden pipe, and a tap inside, while a sink below the tap is also easily made to connect with a removable zinc tub outside. This will be found a great convenience, and, as such, an immense help towards cleanly habits. The cask should be filled by the *bheesti* every day, and the tub emptied morning and evening by the sweeper. The scullery or verandah should also have a washing-up table, a plate rack, and at least two wooden tubs, and a pail for scraps.

In regard to dusters, tea-cloths, &c., the supply must be much larger than is necessary for an English household. The best plan is to give out the week's supply to the bearer, and make him responsible for issuing the fixed daily number of clean cloths, and taking back the same number of soiled ones. Otherwise your fine glass cloths will be used for scrubbing the kettle, and being black with grease and dirt, will fall to pieces in a few washings from the manipulation necessary to remove the filth.

One thing must be fought against root and branch, and that is the extraordinary want of forethought, and desire to save themselves much washing-up, which leads every *khitmutgâr* to vary his waiting at table by constant dives into the pantry, whence he returns breathless with a hastily-wiped spoon or a forgotten butter-knife. Everything required for each meal should be in the dining-room before that meal is announced, and a running accompaniment of washing should be ruthlessly repressed. If milder measures fail, lock the pantry door before sitting down to meals for a few days, and fine one *pice* for every missing article. Good habits are quickly learned when there is no possibility of continuing bad ones. In regard to details of the *khitmutgâr*'s duties, it will, perhaps, be as well to begin with the things he is to leave undone, since his offences are by no means of the negative order.

Therefore he should not lay the table for any meal more than one hour before that meal is to be served. He should not devise ingenious patterns with the spare silver. He should not attempt to fold up the cloth unaided, and so reduce it to creases. He should not make a separate journey to the pantry for each separate article, but use a tray, like a reasonable human being. He should not wash up glass, china, plates, and silver in one small *dêgchi* with a rag tied to a stick. He should not clear away the table and lay it for the next meal whilst the family are still at table. He should not use the table napkins as kitchen cloths. He should not conceal, or attempt to conceal, a dirty duster about his person when waiting at table. He should not leave things to be washed up till they are wanted. Finally, he should not say the kettle is boiling when it is not. This is an inexcusable offence, but universal.

The *khitmutgâr*'s first duty is to send in the *chôta hâzri* to the bedrooms at the appointed hour. The tray should be covered with a tray cloth, and a cosy be invariably provided for the teapot. This done, the sweeper should be called to sweep the dining-room, and the *under-khit* should then throw open the windows, shake out the curtains, dust and polish chairs and tables, whilst the head *khit* turns his attention to the sideboards, burnishing up the set silver, if any, and putting everything in order. He should also remove the flower vases, see that they are clean, and place them ready for re-filling on the gardener's table on the verandah.

Before laying the table for breakfast or any meal, the *khit* must first inquire of the cook what dishes are to be served, otherwise he cannot know what articles will be required. This is rarely done, and is at the bottom of half the frantic dives into the pantry of which we have complained above.

The *khit* should then lay the table carefully, placing on the sideboard every extra which may be wanted, and he should satisfy himself that the *under-khit* has put a sufficiency of plates and dishes into the hot case. This can easily be made in the bazaar out of an old tin-lined packing-case. A few wire shelves and a pan of charcoal will turn it into a very efficient plate-warmer. These rules are to be observed at every meal. In regard to breakfast, specially, it may be noticed that every dish should be brought in at once on the butler's-tray and placed either on the sideboard or table, according to the custom of the house. If a person refuses one dish, another should be handed at once, as there are no set courses at breakfast. Nothing save meat dishes and plates should be removed from the table until the guests have risen, and butter, &c., taken from their places to be handed round, should be returned to the same spot. Washing up must never be commenced till the family have left the dining-room, as the pantry is generally close by, and the clatter is annoying. Everything should be cleared away at once; the cups put ready to wash in the pantry, the greasy plates outside; the jam, sugar, butter, bread, cruets, &c., returned to their places; the cloth brushed, folded, and placed in the press.

When all this is done comes the time for washing up.

Then the knives should be put to stand in an upright tin made for the purpose, and sufficient hot water poured in to cover the blades only. The silver should next be placed in one of the tubs in very hot water. The *under-khit* should meanwhile be scraping off the remains from the plates outside, and placing everything to be washed in a large tub of hot water. Cups, plates, dishes—every bit of china—should first be washed in clean hot water and then rinsed and well rubbed with *the hands* in clean cold water, and set to drain on the table. When all are washed the tubs should be emptied and put aside, and then, and not till then, should drying be commenced. In this way one tea-cloth will do the work of six, which are used a little, then thrown on the floor, then taken to soak up greasy water, then perhaps used to rub down the table. Everything, as it is dried, should be put in its proper place.

The *under-khit* should follow the same rules with the meat plates, &c., except that they should be set to drain in the rack, and not wiped at all. He should then take the knives in hand and clean them, not forgetting to wipe the handles with a damp cloth. The *khit* meanwhile should be busy on the silver, putting each article as he washes it into a pan of clear, cold water, whence it should be taken piece by piece, wiped dry with a soft cloth, polished with another, finally rubbed with a chamois leather, and put, as it is done, into the plate basket. These rules for washing up apply to every meal. After breakfast the *khit* should attend his mistress to the storeroom and ask for everything he may want for the table.

Lunch should not be laid till half-an-hour before the time for serving it. If due method is observed in washing up, a good two hours' recess will have elapsed between the end of breakfast work and the laying of lunch. This is quite sufficient leisure for any but the idle. As at breakfast, the *khit* should inquire what dishes are to be served, and make arrangements accordingly. Washing up follows the same lines, the upper *khit* taking glass and silver. Between lunch and afternoon tea-time (which is often irregular in time) the *khit* should not leave the house, but should occupy himself with the spare silver, which cannot have too much elbow-grease. The *khit* will thus be at hand to bring tea at any time, should the advent of visitors require it to be brought, either earlier or later than usual; if the kettle is boiling, which it should be, on a charcoal brazier in the verandah, a sharp servant will appear with the tray, toast, cakes, &c., less than five minutes after it has been ordered. Yet how often has not every Indian visitor been kept wearisomely waiting for the tea, the offer of which he was unwise enough to accept.

When his mistress goes out, the *khit* is once more at leisure, if he has been wise enough to see to his preparations for dinner between lunch and tea-time. Dessert should then be arranged, and creased tablecloths or napkins taken to the *dhôbi* (washerwoman) for an iron. A *khit* should always be reminded that an untidy table, dull glass, and tarnished silver tell his character far more truthfully than his *chits* (certificates) tell it; and that even should he lose the latter, as *chits* through some fatality are always being lost, he need fear no difficulty in finding, and keeping, a good place if his glass, china, and silver attest his industry.

The procedure at dinner is much the same as at lunch; but special care should be taken to avoid delay between the courses. Vegetables, especially potatoes, should be handed with the joint, and not ten minutes after, when people have finished their meat. To facilitate carving at the side-table, the cook should never put sauce or gravy in the dish, but in a separate bowl. A servant should never put anything down, even for an instant, on the dinner-table, and he should never dodge round the table, but serve steadily from right to left.

Silver should receive a special cleaning twice a week, and once a week the pantry should be cleared out, and everything in it receive an extra wash. Water carafes must be emptied every night and set to drain in the decanter drainer. Silver should be counted over every night, and glass and china once a week. If a breakage is not reported, and the mistress discovers it, cut the *buksheesh* money remorselessly; not so if it is reported, since accidents will occur.

Dirt, illimitable, inconceivable dirt must be expected, until a generation of mistresses has rooted out the habits of immemorial years. Till then look at both sides of your plates, and turn up the spare cups ranged so neatly in order in the pantry. Probably one-half of them are dirty.

The following recipes will be found useful by the *khitmutgâr*:—

1. **Brass, to clean.**—Use Putz pomade, or rub with finely pounded bath brick mixed to a paste with sweet oil, or powdered sal-ammoniac mixed in the same way with water. Polish with equal parts of bran and whiting.

2. **Bread, to freshen.**—Soak the loaf for one minute in boiling water, then bake till dry in a hot oven.

3. **Butter, to keep sweet.**—Press the butter into the bottom of an empty jam jar, then invert the latter in a soup plate of water. This keeps out the air effectually. If the butter is kept actually in the water, the latter should always have salt or boracic acid in it, and be changed every day.

4. **Coffee, to make Essence of.**—For every two tablespoons of ground coffee take one breakfast cup of cold water. Place in a wide-mouthed jar and stand all night. Place the jar in a *dêgchi* of water, and let the whole come to boiling point. Strain and bottle. It will keep for a week, the addition of an equal quantity of *boiling* water making it hot enough to use. Similar essence may be made in any machine by adhering to the same proportions of coffee and water.

5. **Glass, to clean.**—Wash in warm water with *bâsun* (parched gram flour) mixed to a paste with water, and use like soap. Rinse well, and polish. The stains or rims in neglected water carafes, decanters, &c., are best removed by a few drops of strong hydrochloric, or, at a pinch, sulphuric acid in a tumbler of water. This should be poured into the carafe and well shaken. Rinse thoroughly in clean water, as the acid bites into the glass.

6. **Plate, to clean.**—Powder, mix, and bottle four ounces each of common salt, alum, and cream of tartar. Add a teaspoon of this mixture to every quart of water. Boil the plate in the water for five minutes. Remove and plunge in cold water. Dry and polish, using a little powdered chalk tied in a muslin bag, and dusted over the silver during the final polish. Elbow-grease is the only secret of bright plate. Every now and again wash with Sapolio.

7. **Table Linen, to remove Wine Stains from.**—Put a soup plate under the stain while wet and squeeze a lemon or pour boiled milk over it. After five minutes wash out with water. A careful servant will remove all small grease stains from table linen as they appear by rubbing bread on them, and see all creases ironed out.

8. **Tea, to make.**—Use boiling water, and warm both tea and teapot before the fire. Fill the pot at once with the amount of water required. Infuse for five minutes, and decant into another well-warmed teapot.

9. **Toast, to make.**—Cut *stale* bread into thin even slices. Hold at some distance from the fire at first in order to dry it, or if there is an oven, place in that; then closer to give it a golden brown tinge. Toast should be crisp and yellow brown, not tough and dirty white, streaked with burnt black. Place the toast when made in the toast-rack at once. The Christy bread-knife* enables any one to cut even, thin toast out of new bread.

The Duties of the Musolchi or Scullion

The implements required by the scullion are, as a rule, confined to a pail of greasy water and a rag swab. The wisdom of having such a servant at all is doubtful; but if the most prominent duty of a table attendant—cleanliness—is delegated to a nameless drudge on six rupees a month, a very great deal of supervision must be exercised by the mistress to ensure obedience to orders. In most houses the scullion is an unknown quantity, a gruesome ghoul of spurious cleanliness, bearing, as his badge of office, a greasy swab of rag tied to a bit of bamboo.

It is said that good *khits* will not work unless a *musolchi* is kept; but this is not the authors' experience, and one of them has never allowed such a servant in the house; though in the cook-room she acknowledges a drudge may be necessary in a large family. Indeed, it seems absurd that *khitmutgârs* should be above the washing of valuable glass and china; for it must be remembered that if *once* a *musolchi* is admitted to the pantry, he will be used for everything and anything. There is no objection whatever to his doing the preliminary clearing of the dinner-plates in the verandah, as elsewhere advised. Indeed, this *is* the scullery-maid's duty, and the *musolchi* should be a scullion, and nothing else; the pantry is a step above him, and on no pretence should he be allowed to flourish his swab there. Under the system, or no system, which obtains in most houses, the *musolchi* and the sweeper are the only two servants who ever condescend to clean anything. Curiously enough, in these cases they acquire a strange similarity in dress and demeanour; possibly because, being everybody's slave, they lose all spirit and self-respect. Both slink from sight, and become furtive even in *their* methods of work, and both contrive to assimilate an incredible amount of pure griminess around their own persons.

In many so-called good houses the *musolchi* is the motive-power underlying the simulated activity of the Mahomedan servants. He lights the early fire, makes the tea and toast, and prepares everything for the *khitmutgâr*, who is generally a lordly relative. It is he who washes up the early breakfast cups and saucers, and makes it possible for his real master, the *khitmutgâr*, to lay the table leisurely.

Breakfast over, the lordly one retires for recess, while the *musolchi*, left in sole possession of the pantry, proceeds to wash up everything in one poor pennyworth of water, with an intolerable amount of greasy cloth. *Jharans* (cloths) here, there, everywhere; all more or less filthy, all more or less capable of leaving a fine bold smear on your plates and dishes. The process, as patented by the unchangeable law of *musolchi*-dom, is simple:—

1. Plates are plates, and include cups and saucers, teapots, side-dishes, and milk-jugs.
2. Spoons are spoons, and include knives, forks, toast-racks, &c.
3. Water is water, so long as it is fluid.
4. Cloths are cloths, so long as they hold together. After that they are used as swabs.
5. The floor is a floor, and nature made it as a table.
6. Variety is pleasing; therefore always intersperse your stone-ware plates with china teacups.
7. At the same time, union is strength; so pile everything together, use one water and one cloth, and do not move from your station till everything is dried and spread carefully in the dust.
8. Only one side of a plate is used by the *sahib logue*; it is therefore purely unreasonable for them to cavil at the other side being dirty.

The cleaning of knives follows, and *musolchi*-dom has long ago reduced this to a science in the way of destruction. Given a little of his own productions in the way of broken china, and a slanting wooden board destitute of leather, and the *musolchi* will produce an Indian knife, *i.e.* a two-edged pliable spatula, out of the best shear steel, in an incredibly short space of time. In extreme cases he has been known to clean your silver with bathbrick; and being invariably a slave to his work, he may be seen all day wiping and smearing, smearing and wiping, whilst the *khitmutgârs* lounge on their beds or smoke pipes in the kitchen. Such a state of affairs will, however, never be allowed by a good mistress. Even if a *musolchi* be kept, which is by no means advisable, he should be a responsible servant on good wages; indeed, it is an admirable plan, if *khitmutgârs* object to washing up, to keep one *khit* and put on a *musolchi* on higher wages; it generally settles the matter.

Where a *musolchi* is really needed is in the cook-room. There, just when clean hands are necessary, the scouring of a saucepan may become imperative; and some one to stand between the cook busy at his pastry board and the fire which requires fresh fuel, is a vast aid in preventing the thousand and one trivial accidents and dangers that beset the culinary art. Only those who have actually cooked a whole dinner know the immense relief it is to have some one at hand to prevent those sudden interruptions, which seem invariably to come at the most critical moment.

The *musolchi*, then, finds his proper place amongst the pots and pans, and the utmost he should have to do with plates and dishes should be the clearing away of bones and fragments from the dinner-plates, and, perhaps, a preliminary washing of the same,—the *khit-mutgâr*, however, being held entirely responsible for the cleanliness of every dish, plate, cup, saucer, or article of any kind or sort which he puts on his master's table. By keeping the *musolchi* in the kitchen, and at the same time recognising him as your servant and *not* a general drudge, another advantage is secured. He can be trained as a regular cook, and should be taught to look forward to promotion during the time his superior may be on leave, or sick. It is an immense comfort to know that a sudden attack of ague in the kitchen need not result in starvation to the dining-room.

THE DUTIES OF THE BHEESTI

With the implements required by the *bheesti* the mistress has little to do beyond providing him with a few clean dusters and seeing that he has a sufficiency of hot and cold water cans, and at least one filter.

Bheesties are, as a rule, the cleanest servants in an Indian household, and are, as a class, more ready to turn their hands to an odd job than any of the others. The duties, however, in which he comes absolutely under the mistress's eye are few.

The first is to bring daily a supply of drinking water from some approved source, see it boiled in the vessel set apart for the purpose, and put it to cool in earthen pots beside the filter. These earthen pots should be emptied out every day, as also the filter and every receptacle of filtered water. As often as not, if this rule be not strictly enforced, filtered water is quite, if not more unsafe, than that drawn fresh from the well.

The *bheesti*'s next duty is to keep a supply of fresh water in the bathrooms, and to heat the water required for the morning baths. It will be found a good plan to give out, or allow, the wood or charcoal for this purpose quite separately from the kitchen fuel; for complaints of stinting on the one side, or extravagance on the other, are sure to arise as an excuse for tepid baths, or large consumption. The water-jugs, carafe, sponge, and soap dishes are in the *bheesti*'s charge, and it is his duty to keep them clean and duly filled with fresh water. We strongly advise the placing of an ordinary three-*gurrah* filter close to the servants' houses, so that those who desire it can always have a supply of fresh water. Such little evidences of care for their health are duly appreciated by the servants; and, in addition, the removal of one of the chief causes of epidemic disease—impure drinking water—is a source of safety to the entire household.

In regard to the supply of water in bathrooms, the *bheesti* must be made to scrub out the earthen vessels at least once a week, and boiled water should be put in the carafes.

What is generally called a 'Punjâb tub' will be found a great convenience for heating bath-water. It consists of an ordinary wooden cask, with a small iron cylinder in the middle. The cylinder is open both top and bottom, and has a grating about a foot from the latter. The cask being filled with water, some live charcoal is put into the cylinder, and the water soon becomes hot, with a very small expenditure of fuel. If the Punjâb tub be placed in the verandah near the pantry, it will be found an exceedingly useful aid to the *khitmutgârs* in heating water for washing up, and thus taking the place of the English boiler.

Filters are often a source of great trouble, and the following, recommended publicly by an authority, will be found excellent:—

Cut the bottom neatly off a quart bottle. This may be done with an ordinary steel file well moistened by oil of turpentine, or by tying a hank of cotton thread dipped in turpentine round the bottle, setting light to it, and immediately dipping the bottle into cold water. Get a new cork, and through the centre put the glass tube of a Maw's feeding-bottle* (to be had in any bazaar), pushing it well through and letting the indiarubber tube remain as in the feeding bottle. Cork the bottle tight, place a bit of sponge in the neck to prevent the tube getting clogged, and fill the bottle with, if possible animal, charcoal finely pounded—but free from dust—and silver sand, in equal parts. Place another sponge at the open end of the bottle, and either close by tying a bit of muslin over, or get a tight fitting tin cover made in the bazaar; it must, of course, be perforated with small holes. If this filter be placed in an ordinary *gurrah* of water, and the indiarubber tube attached to the glass tube be allowed to hang over the side into a proper vessel, such as a *surâhi*, water will filter over rapidly when once it has started. This must be effected as with a baby's bottle, by squeezing the nipple, or by sucking it. In this case, the nipple should be removed afterwards. The advantage of this filter is the ease with which it can be cleaned and renewed.

But it has lately been discovered that the addition of even a few grains of alum to a gallon of water is the best filter there is. In fact, if the water is first boiled, then put to cool in a small-mouthed vessel in a clean place, with two grains of powdered alum to every gallon, it will, after an hour's settling, and careful decanting to another vessel, be practically as pure as it is possible to get water.

Permanganate of potash added till the water is faintly pink destroys most bacilli. It is also put into wells nowadays, about 2 oz. every week or so for a well in constant use.

The Duties of the Ayah

The implements of the *ayah* are few, and consist chiefly of dusters, brushes, &c.

The *ayah*'s duties naturally vary immensely with her situation. If there are no children, she is virtually a lady's maid, while if an English nurse is kept, her responsibilities are almost *nil*. On the other hand, when she is really head nurse, she is of all the servants the most important.

In the latter case, again, her duties would vary very much according to the part taken by her mistress; so that it is hardly worth while treating of the *ayah* simply as a nurse. We may only remark that with very few exceptions, the Indian *ayahs* are singularly kind, injudicious, patient, and thoughtless in their care of children; but to expect anything like *common sense* from them is to lay yourself open to certain disappointment.

Unless you can get a woman from a regular *ayah*'s family, the Mahomedan ones are apt to be a nuisance; and the reason which leads many ladies to employ them, viz., the dislike to a sweeper or low-caste woman,* is in itself foolish. For no one who has lived long in India can fail to see that the sweeper is very often cleaner in his ways, and certainly in his house, than the Mahomedans. Nor does it follow that because a woman belongs to the sweeper caste she should necessarily do all the dirty work of the establishment. But to whatever class she belongs, the *ayah*'s household duties are virtually the same, except that she will not condescend to the broom if she is a Mahomedan. In this connection it may be remarked that the degradation which attaches to the mere act of cleansing anything in India is mainly responsible for the inconceivably filthy ways of its inhabitants. Most of them cannot afford to pay for a cleanser, and so learn to live on contentedly in dirt.

We will begin with the duties of an *ayah* as housemaid and lady's maid. At the time specified by her mistress, she should knock at the door of the bedroom and bring in the early tea, placing the tray on the table, or wherever her mistress directs. She should never forget to *salaam* to her mistress, and ask if anything is wanted, and what time her mistress desires to rise. She should then draw back the curtains and leave the room, remembering to take away the lamp, dirty boots, &c. Having unbolted the bathroom door whilst inside, she should now go round to the outside, and put everything in order, taking special care that the water is fresh, and the jugs, basins, &c., scrupulously clean.

At the appointed time, she should bring in the hot water, carefully close the outer door, and after putting towels, soap, &c., in order, go into the bedroom and collect such clothes as her mistress may want. She should never place these in the bathroom till the water has been brought in by the *bheesti*, and the outer door closed. When all is ready, she should take her mistress's dressing-gown and slippers to her. During the bathing time the *ayah* should be arranging and dusting the dressing-table, and carefully putting away everything that is lying about. The bed should also be turned down, and the dress which her mistress is to wear carefully looked over, and hung ready on the back of a chair. Whether the *ayah* does her mistress's hair or not depends upon individual capacity and custom; but most *ayahs* have to do the brushing of the hair, and they generally do it very gently and well.

As soon as her mistress has left the room, the *ayah* should open the windows and put everything in thorough order, making the bed last of all. Not till everything save dusting is finished should the room be swept, especially if she has to call in another servant with a broom. Once a week a more elaborate cleaning should take place, boxes, &c., be moved, lest vermin of any sort should lurk behind them, and both windows and doors receive a polish. Her mistress's room done, the *ayah* will see that the bathroom is set in order, squeeze out the sponge, dry and fold the towels, &c.

If there are no children, she has little else to do during the day, except to lay out walking things, boots, parasols, &c., as may be required. To ensure these being ready, she should come with the other servants after breakfast to take her orders; and if she desires to please, will take her recess between breakfast and twelve o'clock, so as to be on the spot when her mistress is most likely to require her. When the order is given for luncheon, she will take hot water to her mistress's room, and at the same time ask what dress she proposes wearing in the afternoon and evening. At dusk she will go to the bearer for candle and lamp, draw the curtains, if necessary light the fire, and be ready on her mistress's return from her evening drive to take her wraps. While her mistress is dressing for dinner, the *ayah* should arrange everything for the night; turn down the bed, &c., see that fresh water is in the carafe, and lay dressing-gown and slippers ready for use. She must not forget to see that there are matches at hand, and that anything likely to be required is in its place. If a lady guest comes to the house without a servant, the *ayah* of the house should attend to her wants exactly as if she were a mistress, and any neglect in this point should be punished at once.

Where there are no children, an *ayah* should always have time to hem dusters, give out the *khitmutgâr*'s cloths, and do many little odd jobs about the house. Indeed, a really good woman will be an immense help, and put her hand to anything, from arranging flowers to sewing on buttons. Being the only woman-servant in the house, the *ayah* should be treated with consideration and respect. Whether she be a sweeper or not, it should be generally understood that you hold her to be the equal of any other servant in the house. If she has charge of children, this point must be still more insisted upon, and you should endeavour to instil into her a sense of her great responsibility, and the confidence you have in her. To treat, however, of the *ayah* as a nurse would involve a chapter on the management of children,* and lead us into controversial waters.

One thing is certain: Indian children are proverbially captious, disobedient, and easily thrown out of gear. Whether this be the fault of the mother, the *ayah*, or the climate is a moot point; perhaps the safest plan is to attribute it to all three. The more frequent employment of English nurses is no doubt improving the régime of Indian nurseries; but even now it is no unusual thing to see an English child eating his dinner off the floor, with his hands full of toys, while a posse of devoted attendants distract his attention, and the *ayah* feeds him with spoonfuls of *pish-pash*.* Appetite is no doubt variable in Anglo-Indian children, but it is possible that a little more pomp and circumstance, and a wholesome conviction that food is not forthcoming except *at* meal-times, would induce Sonny or Missy Baba to treat dinner with graver circumspection. Where, save in India, do we find sturdy little tots of four and five still taking their bottles and refusing to go to sleep without a lullaby? Without going further into the subject, we can only assure every young mother that there is no climatic reason whatever why discipline should be set aside in an Indian nursery, and that it is as possible to insist on cleanliness, decency, and order there as in an Indian pantry or cook-room. The whole secret lies in refusing to listen to the word *dustoor*, or custom.

Few mistresses have been long in India without having had the trouble of scandals between the *ayah* and other servants. In this connection, one word of warning. A steady, well-doing woman may lay herself open to deliberate slanders by her very virtues; and in sifting a story of this kind, it must not be forgotten that the Mahomedan men-servants as a rule have no shame, and will say anything.

The following recipes will be found useful to the *ayah*:—

1. **Brushes, to wash.**—Dissolve one teaspoonful of carbonate of soda or brush powder in a basin of hot water, and whisk the brush on it till clean, taking care not to wet the back lest the ivory or wood should split. Dry in the shade, with handles upwards.

2. **Dentifrice.**—One oz. betel-nuts roasted to charcoal and ground fine, 1 oz. lump sugar, cream of tartar and Peruvian bark, of each ½ oz., powdered cinnamon, 1 drachm. Pulverise. Or equal parts of betel-nut charcoal and common salt. Both these whiten the teeth.

3. **Grease Spots, to remove.**—Use a hot iron and blotting-paper. A piece of cardboard split to a rough edge, and rubbed gently on the spot, will often remove grease from silk. But no house should be without benzine.

4. **Hair, to wash.**—Bruise one dozen soap-nuts *(rēta)*, and steep for an hour in a pint of hot water. Pound one tablespoonful of poppy seeds *(kish-kâsh)* on a curry stone, and steep in half a pint of hot water. When wanted for use, strain the water from the soap-nuts into a basin, using pressure to extract all the juice. Into a separate basin strain the liquor from

the poppy seeds, which should look like milk. Wash the hair thoroughly
with the *rĕta* water, rinsing it well out before using the poppy-seed milk.
The latter should only be lightly rubbed on to the hair, and just rinsed out.
It gives the hair a beautiful softness and gloss, without being greasy. It is
also a specific against scurf.

5. **Hair Wash.**—Dissolve in two quarts of boiling water 1 oz. of borax
and 2 oz. of camphor; use to wash the hair, rinsing it well.

THE DUTIES OF THE 'SYCE' OR GROOM

The implements required by the *syce* are:—

2 Dusters.	1 Burnisher.
1 Chamois leather.	1 Body brush.
1 Sponge.	1 Mane comb.
1 Set blacking and harness brushes.	

The stable may seem outside the domain of the mistress, but as
a matter of fact, so many Englishmen in India are over-busy, that,
unless the mistress keeps an eye on the horses, the animals are apt
to be neglected. Now, if the good house-mother's proudest boast is
that not even 'the cattle within her gate'* fail to feel her kindly care,
she will often find it necessary to take an active part in teaching the
syce his duty, and seeing that the horses receive proper attention. It
will, in the authors' opinion, be invariably found a good plan to *limit*
the number of servants employed in the stable as much as possible.
The old plan of a *syce* and a grass-cutter to each horse is a thing of
the past, and the number of *syces* or grooms should have reference
merely to the amount of harnessing and out-work necessary during
the day.

If one grass-cutter be given to each horse, one *syce* to every three
horses will, as a rule, be found sufficient. The *syce* should be made
responsible for the horses under him, and any complaints he may
make about the grass-cutters should be attended to at once. He is thus
placed in a position of responsibility, and for the extra work involved
may be given a small increase of wage. His duties also become those
of an English groom. Every morning after breakfast he will come for
orders, and again after dinner at night; since, if a horse is to be taken
out early in the morning, a good *syce* will wish to know it, in order that
he may arrange that the animal gets its feed in good time.

The routine of an ordinary Indian stable should be as follows: At daybreak the horses should receive quarter of their daily allowance of corn, and in hot weather this may be preceded by a limited drink of water. In cold weather this is not necessary; a light grooming should then be given, night clothing removed, the bedding gathered to one corner, and the stall cleaned. After this the grass-cutters should go out for their daily bundle of grass, under orders to return by twelve. It is not by any means necessary for grass-cutters to go out every day for grass, as they can quite well cut a double quantity in the time allowed. In fact, in large stations they invariably do so, and sell one bundle before returning home. Supposing, then, six horses are kept, it will only be necessary for at most four grass-cutters to go out, so that two can remain to help the two *syces*.

The *syce* must be ready at the door to take over the horses which have been ridden, and he should invariably have a light saddle-cloth with him to throw over the horse before leading him away. It is not, of course, necessary, but it will be found a good plan, after district or cross-country work, to put on bandages for the first hour after the horse comes in. The *syce* should have orders first to loosen the girths, then to bandage the legs, then remove the saddle and set to work at once, first with a wisp, then with a pad or cloth, and finally with hand and arm-rubbing. Remarks have been made* on the omission of a curry-comb* in the list of implements for the *syce*. This is no oversight. A curry-comb is an abomination, and quite unnecessary. Except under unusual circumstances, there will always be two men at leisure to attend to one horse; and as freedom from chill and its many consequent evils depends in a great measure on quickness of grooming after work, it should be a recognised rule in the stable that the grass-cutters are not on *one* particular horse, but on all.

As soon as the horse is groomed, he should be watered and given a small supply of grass. Meanwhile the horses which have not been out will have been exercised, and when all have been looked after and watered, the whole stable should get the mid-day meal of corn. At three the horses may again be watered, at four they get the next feed of corn and should be thoroughly well groomed, so as to be ready for the evening exercise. On their return from this, they should get their last feed and be made up for the night. With regard to the *times* of feeding, people will, of course, consult their own convenience; but it should never be less than three times a day: the gram* should be given dry or merely sprinkled with water, and should be mixed with, at least, an equal quantity of chaff or chopped hay, to ensure thorough mastication and digestion. The horses should invariably be given water not less than half-an-hour before, and *never* immediately after, his gram. It is a mistake to feed horses out of their stalls.

In regard to the food, variety is a thing to be looked to, and horses kept from year's end to year's end on nothing but gram are seldom in such good health as those whose food is judiciously changed. Almost every grain may be given, mixed with either bruised barley, gram, or oats. A small corn-crusher will be found both economical and convenient where many horses are kept; you are then certain of getting the food unadulterated, and the horses prefer freshly-crushed grain. Each grass-cutter in turn grinds the corn for the day, and, roughly speaking, it takes five minutes to crush one horse's rations.

The quantity of food must vary immensely with the work given, but it may be remarked that, considering the small amount of work horses do in India, they generally get too much corn. The recognised scale of forage for the largest carriage horses in full work in England is per diem—

Hay	12 lbs.
Corn	12 lbs.
Chaff	2 gallon measures.
Bran	2 quart measures.

For ponies of 14 hands in full work the English allowance is—

Hay	10 lbs.
Oats	8 lbs.
Chaff	2 gallon measures.
Bran	2 quart measures.

In the country in England, a ten miles' drive to the county town and back is supposed to be nothing out of the way; but in India, if any distance over ten miles has to be *ridden*, an extra horse is laid out. Much, of course, depends on the grass, and for this reason it is always advisable to make the grass-cutters bring their bundles into the verandah for inspection at twelve o'clock. If the gram, oats, &c., be kept in lockers in the same verandah, the mistress can then see the grain taken out, and so, at very little trouble, avoid the *buniya's* bill. It is not necessary to weigh out the grain; and if a week's supply is put into the lockers every Monday morning, and the feeds measured with a wooden corn-measure, you will scarcely ever be out more than half a *seer*. Under the ordinary system of a *buniya*'s account, you are never certain what kind of stuff the horses are getting, while any change in quantity or kind in the food leads to troublesome complication, and gives cover to cheating. Once, if not twice a week, horses should have a bran mash, a recipe for making which will be found at the end. It also tends to keep horses in health to give them some green food—a *seer* or two of carrots, green wheat, lucerne, grass, or even sugarcane—and if the mistress takes a pride in her horses, which it is to be hoped she will always do, this little treat will be given during her daily visit to the stable. It will be a distinct pleasure to most women to hear the whinnyings and neighings which will then follow at the first glimpse of the *Mem Sahib*.

Always encourage your *syce* to speak to you at once if anything ails the horses, and never neglect such information. If a horse is reported lame, it does not take much trouble to put on your hat and go out to see. Even if you know little what to do, it impresses the *syces* with your anxiety, and they themselves will look on the matter more seriously.

In cold weather always give out blankets to all the stable-servants, to prevent them from stealing the coverings of their horses. These blankets should be of good quality, marked with your initials, and should be attached to the *service*, and not given to the individual. At the commencement of the hot weather they should be washed and put back into store. The same procedure should be adopted with regard to the horse-clothing, otherwise it will be used to wrap up bundles, &c. &c. Do not grudge warm clothing to your horse; if he is decently groomed, his skin will be very susceptible to the changes of temperature; and with good clothing, he will keep in condition on less food. It is false economy to deny him what is equivalent to an extra feed of corn.

It is not always possible to have *good* stables, but it is in every one's reach to have clean, wholesome ones, by knocking ventilators through the walls near the roof, and converting stalls into loose-boxes by movable bamboos. Heel-ropes should never be seen in a private stable, and the mere sight of them condemns the management. It is said that some Waler horses* require heel-ropes, owing to a bad habit of rubbing mane and tail, especially during hot weather; but there can be no doubt that such symptoms point to disease, and these cases may therefore be treated as abnormal. The floor of the stable is nearly always of mud, but it should be quite level; and once a week at least it should be *leped* or plastered with a thin paste of cowdung, sand, and water, as should be the walls to a height of four feet. Stables should always have a verandah in front, and it is wonderful how greatly a cheap bamboo or grass chick to the arches will reduce the temperature in the hot months. The *syces* should not be allowed to sleep *en masse* with wives and families in the spare stalls or verandahs, as they disturb the horses, but *one* man must always do so in case of sudden illness.

If horses are picketed out at night, as they often are during the summer, the safest and most comfortable plan is to have a wooden post about four feet high permanently let into the ground. The horse should have a light iron chain to his headstall, with a ring at the end large enough to slip over the post. If the bedding be arranged round the post in a circle, the horse can always shift his quarters without fear of entanglement or breaking loose. The best bedding in India is rice straw; but where grass is plentiful, many people use *drubh*[1] grass, which a horse will seldom eat.

The best manger for a horse is a square of hemp matting or *tât* on which the gram can be spread on the ground. This enables the horse to eat in a natural position, and prevents bolting; nose-bags are an abomination in a private stable. Watering buckets of galvanised iron are the best; and though it is more reasonable to allow a horse an unlimited supply of water all day long, by means of a suitable receptacle in his stall, yet without constant supervision it is hard, on this plan, to ensure the water being fresh. Therefore, unless unusual care can be given, it is best to keep to the bucket. Hay should never be in a rack. The seeds and spikes are apt to fall into the horse's eyes, and it also conduces to greediness.

In regard to grooming, body brushes, &c., the real secret of a good coat lies in sheer, honest, hard work. As the *khitmutgâr* when pulled up about the dulness of the plate cries loudly for *pureah* (plate powder), so the *syce* will clamour for brushes and curry-combs when brought up for neglect. Elbow-grease is more effectual on a horse's coat than anywhere else—which is saying a good deal—and,

[1] A kind of coarse rye grass.

while it is quite possible to get on without a brush, it is impossible to dispense with the hand and arm. In fact, a *syce* who does not take off his coat and turn up his sleeves before beginning to groom his horse, knows nothing of his work. There is a great art in making a horse look smart, which is seldom thought of in India; but if the *syce* sees that his employers expect it and notice it, he will soon learn, like an English groom, to take a pride in the appearance of his horse. The following rules should be impressed on all the stable helpers:—

1. Give water before and never after food.
2. Do not soak the corn. It may be damped for ten minutes.
3. Report the least injury or symptom of illness.
4. Beat the grass well, and let it dry a day before using it.
5. Always have two men to groom a horse.
6. Never wash a horse's legs except on rare occasions, and then dry carefully at once.
7. If you must steal, steal from men, and not from dumb animals.

The *syce*, however, has other duties besides keeping his horses. He must look after the saddlery and harness, also the dog-cart or carriage, unless a coachman is kept. For saddlery there is nothing like good English soft-soap. If washed with this once a week and carefully dried, scarcely anything else will be required. A recipe for dubbin is, however, given at the end; though we doubt if anything home-made can be cheaper or better than the soaps and *mom roghan* sold by the N. W. Soap Company at Cawnpore.*

Bits and stirrup-irons should be cleaned with dry sand or pounded brick and burnished with a regular steel burnisher. If washed in water, they must be dried at once. In hot weather constant care is necessary to prevent insects getting to the saddle stuffing and it is a good plan to have bags of camphor and *nim* leaves tacked along the top of the saddle-horse or stand. Girths, if white, should be sponged and pipe-clayed, then dusted out; *numdahs* or saddle-cloths dried in the sun and brushed, instead of being utterly neglected.

Carriages, when it is necessary to wash them, require plenty of water, and not half a bucketful, as the *syce* seems to think. But in India the roads are seldom so muddy as to make daily washing necessary. A dry duster is generally sufficient for the most part, and splashes can be removed from the wheels gently with a sponge. A spoke brush or carriage mop is rather a dangerous implement in a native's hands, and we prefer to give him nothing but soft dusters, a sponge, wash-leather, and carriage brush. It is always necessary to have a large dust cloth which will completely cover the carriage almost to the ground. Without this, the most careful *syce* will not be able to send his carriage out as neat as it should be. If the hood is movable, the best plan is to have a hook and pulley to the roof of the coach-house, and so keep the hood out of harm's way when it is not in use.

Harness requires care to keep it strong, and it is usual to put a little lamp-black in the composition used for it. A good recipe for harness paste is given at the end. The mountings should be kept bright with powdered whiting, and the patent leather portions carefully polished with drying oil. Whips should be hung up by the lash, otherwise they will warp.

The following recipes will be found useful to the *syce*:—

1. **Waterproof Harness Dressing.**—Melt 2 oz. mutton suet with 6 oz. beeswax (*kuchcha môm*). Add 6 oz. powdered sugar-candy, 2 oz. soft-soap, 2 oz. lampblack, 1 oz. powdered indigo, and 1 teacupful of turpentine. Use like boot blacking.

2. **Wheel Grease.**—Melt and strain into a tin 2 lbs. fat and 1 bottle common mustard oil.

3. **Waterproof Brown Harness Dressing.**—Melt 1 lb. mutton fat, 5 oz. beeswax; boil and skim. Then add 1 pint turpentine.

4. **Saddlery, to clean.**—Wash with soft-soap. Then apply with a sponge the following recipe: Warm 1 *seer* milk, add ½ *chittâck* dilute sulphuric acid, and when cold 2 *chittâcks* hydrochloric acid. Strain and bottle.

The Duties of the 'Dirzie' or Tailor

These are almost too well known to require description; indeed, they are only referred to here in deference to request. The tailor's duties, briefly, are to give his mistress eight hours *at least* of steady sewing work. If, as is usual, he gets a Sunday holiday, his hours should be longer, but in daily work the tailor should be in his place by eight o'clock A.M., and work till five o'clock, with a break of one hour for food in the middle of the day. In the hot weather it is better to make him work from seven o'clock till eleven, and again from three till seven P.M.

Few *dirzies* can be trusted to cut out without any supervision, and it is far better for the mistress either to do it herself, or to order the tailor to show her the patterns tacked on to the stuff before the fateful scissors are brought into use. In most large towns, however, *dirzies* are to be found who are to all intents and purposes dressmakers, and excellent ones into the bargain. They have not, of course, much taste, and their original draperies are almost always woodeny; but small dressmakers at home have the same faults. The price charged by such *dirzies* for making a dress varies from five to ten rupees, and as a rule they finish their dresses very neatly indeed. To ladies in out-stations, Butterick's, Schild's, or Weldon's paper patterns* will be found invaluable; and by giving the bust and waist measurement when ordering the pattern, there is seldom any radical alteration necessary. If, in addition, the lady is wise enough to have an accurately modelled dress form* on which to fit the bodice, the *dirzie* is quite as likely to produce a good fit as the most expensive dressmaker. The difficulty about dress forms is their unwieldiness. Several kinds, however, pack into a fairly small space, while the bazaar dress form, to be had from Butterick's for about fourteen shillings, folds up like an umbrella, and can be altered to any size. All that is necessary to make the bodice part of this form efficient is a wadded bodice made to button over the wire frame. It then answers quite as well as many more expensive kinds, whilst it is nearly as portable as an umbrella. It is an excellent plan to pay five shillings at Redmayne's,* or any other good dressmaker, for a scientifically-cut bodice pattern,* made to actual measurements.

The *dirzie* should always be supplied with a locking box for his work, a sheet for spreading on the ground, an iron and an ironing board. He is supposed to supply his own scissors and thimble. Where a permanent *dirzie* is not kept, it is an admirable plan to have a man in regularly once a week or fortnight to do general repairs. It must not be forgotten, however, that there is an appreciable chance of infection in giving work out to be done in the bazaars, as the natives are almost criminally lax in all kinds of infectious disease. A permanent tailor almost always saves his own wages, especially if in spare time he is set to do embroidery. Many of them are excellent hands at many kinds of silkwork. Indeed, one of the authors had a complete set of curtains embroidered by her tailor when regular work was slack.

THE DUTIES OF THE 'DHOBI' OR WASHERMAN

The *dhobi*'s duties do not bring him much under the eye of the mistress, but there are a few points about his work which require notice. To begin with, it is necessary to fix the place where he is to wash, and insist on his keeping to it. Those who have children, and indeed all who regard their own safety, will arrange for all the washing to be done at their own well. It is both disagreeable and dangerous to have one's wearing apparel steeped in water in which the clothes of smallpox and cholera patients have been cleansed. Yet, if the *dhobi* be allowed to wash at the *ghât*, there can be no certainty that such may not be the case. The *dhobi* should also be carefully watched to see that he does not wash other people's clothes at the same time as those of his ostensible master. It will be found almost impossible, especially in large stations, to prevent the *dhobi* from doing extra washing, but there is no reason why he should wash them in your compound. For this reason it is advisable, every now and again, to make a raid on your *dhobi*'s house, and ruthlessly confiscate any clothes in process of being washed or ironed, which do not belong to you. This generally leads to an *éclaircissement*,* in which you, being in possession, have a strong position. As a rule, where there are ladies and children, the *dhobi*'s wife comes to count over the dirty clothes, and in many houses this is done twice a week—the clothes given out on Monday coming back on Thursday, and those given on Thursday on Monday. As there is no difficulty—except during the rainy season—in drying the clothes, there is no hardship in giving out the dirty linen even three times a week; in fact, on an emergency, twenty-four hours is sufficient for a small wash.

In regard to the method of cleansing adopted in India, nothing can be more primitive or ineffectual. Cold water, bad soap, and much beating on stones remove the dirt with less certainty than the buttons, and in the effort to bring a presentable *jâogân* (wash) to his mistress, with the least possible labour to himself, the *dhobi* is apt to forget that lace and embroidery is an integral part of underclothing. There is, however, no reason whatever why the recent improvements in cleansing clothes which have revolutionised laundries at home should not be adopted in India. 'Sunlight,' 'Paraffin,' 'Scotsman,' and other soaps* make almost all handling needless, the only necessity being warm water and thorough soaping. These, however, owe almost all their efficacy to the paraffin they contain, and this may be used in its pure state with equal advantage. The procedure adopted in most home laundries in England is as follows: A boiler is filled with water, to which one tablespoon of paraffin or kerosene oil has been added to each gallon of water, with a sufficiency of soap to make it blend. The clothes are dipped in this, well rubbed with soap, rolled tight, and set to soak for three hours. The fire is then lit, and the whole boiled for one hour, after which the clothes are removed, well rinsed in two waters, and hung out to dry. No rubbing of any kind being required, the saving in wear and tear is enormous.

Flannels only require steeping for a quarter of an hour, and should *not be boiled*; or if they are simply well rinsed out in warm water in which soap and paraffin have been mixed, they will be found quite clean. They should be at once wrung out and set to dry in the shade. When half dry, pull out carefully and iron. This prevents shrinking.

Table linen should always be ironed whilst still wet, or it will not glaze. Borax should also be put with the blue.

Coloured clothes are the better of a little alum in the water, and coloured woollen stuffs and embroideries should be washed in water in which bran has been boiled.

It is a good plan to order all flannel things, socks, &c., to be returned the day after they are taken, as this ensures rapidity in washing and drying.

The *dhobi* requires a table, a box for the clothes, an ironing blanket, and a heavy sheet for carrying the dirty clothes.

He will also be the better for a polishing iron—that is to say, one with a convex copper surface. Without some such thing the shirts will never look glazy. It is made moderately hot and rubbed up and down till the polish appears.

It will be found useful to have a supply of 'Maypole Soap' of different tints for renovating blouses which fade. The directions are given on each packet.

CHAPTER VII

HORSES AND STABLE MANAGEMENT

So much has been said on this subject in the duties of the *syce*, that little more is required save to mention the diseases to which the horse is most liable, and give a few recipes for remedies. Of course in regard to the former, it is impossible here to do more than give an outline of a few emergent ones, and their treatment by remedies likely to be at hand. In India one is often beyond reach of all skilled aid, and it is a cruel thing to sit by and see a favourite dying without knowing how to help it in the struggle for life. Fortunately, danger shows itself in very nearly the same symptoms as it does in man, therefore it is not, as a rule, hard, even for the untrained, to diagnose the class of disease. The chief point to be borne in mind is the difference in the normal rates of pulse, breathing, &c., between the horse and its master. The horse in health and at rest breathes about ten times in the minute, and with great regularity in inspiration and expiration. The pulse, which is most conveniently felt a little before the angle of the lower jaw, and close to the edge, beats from thirty-five to forty-five beats a minute. In fever it may run as high as ninety beats. The normal temperature of the horse is 99.5°.

In health the membrane of eye and nostril is of a pale pink. Variations from the normal in these matters point to the same disturbances as similar variations would in the human being.

High fever, quick breathing, shivering, and expanded nostrils point to urgent mischief in the breathing apparatus. Loud, noisy cough and discharge from the nose and eyes generally point to bronchitis; while dulness, disinclination to cough or move, total loss of appetite, and heaving of the flanks, show the mischief has gone down to the lungs. Both these diseases may be treated as they would be in man. Heroic remedies in such cases are past for humanity, and are rapidly passing away for the horse also. Twenty years ago the least fever in a horse was treated by bleeding. The removal of sixteen pints of blood was considered a slight matter, and 'Bleed till the animal faints' was no unusual direction. We are wiser now, and disease of the respiratory organs must be treated by poultices, fomentations, expectorants, diaphoretics, and with stimulants* in the advanced stages.

When high fever is accompanied by great restlessness and obvious pain, shown by a constant looking round at the flanks, there is probably disease of the digestive organs. Care in observing the state of the dejections,* and inquiries as to the beginning of the symptoms, will generally enable an intelligent person to make a fairly accurate guess at the particular organ affected. Here, again, the horse should be treated with common sense; for diet, temperature, pure air, and nursing are to the full as potent remedies with animals as with man. It is not sufficient to give a ball as a drench,* and then leave the patient to all the draughts of heaven, and indigestible, unsuitable food.

In the following list, remedies suitable for the first symptoms of gradual, and for the immediate treatment of emergent, diseases will be found. Beyond this it is better to consult skilled aid if possible, or, at any rate, a better authority:—

1. **Cooling Lotion for Sprains.**—1 oz. sal-ammoniac (*nau-shâdur*), 1 oz. nitre (*shôra*), 1 pint water. Apply on a light bandage, and keep constantly moist.

2. **Condition Powder.**—4 oz. each of long pepper (*pïpul*), ginger (*sônth*), black pepper (*kâla mirch*), and a root called *kootki*. Grind and mix. Give 1 oz. in the evening corn. The addition of 4 oz. of black salt (*kâla nimuk*) to the recipe makes it more alterative.

3. **Colic Draught.**—Three drachms assafœtida (*hing*), 2 drachms black pepper, 1 drachm ginger, mixed with half a bottle hot spirits and water; or 1½ drachms camphor given in the same way; or linseed oil, warmed, half a bottle, turpentine 2 oz.; or 1 pint hot beer, mixed with 2 oz. pounded *ajwain* seeds. Some colic draught should be ready in every stable.

4. **Colic, Treatment of, in Emergencies.**—Give any of the remedies as above on first symptoms. Clothe warmly, exercise gently by walking up and down. An immediate clyster of warm water is incomparably the very best remedy. Therefore, no stable should be without a common tin clyster pipe,* which can be made in any bazaar for a few annas.

5. **Cough Balls.**—4 oz. assafœtida, 2 oz. nitre, 2 oz. raw sugar (*gûr*); make into sixteen balls. One three times a day when there is no fever.

6. **Cough and Fever Ball.**—One drachm aloes, 1 drachm tartar emetic, 2 drachms nitre, made into a ball with warm *gûr*. When the horse develops cough and fever suddenly, repeat, if necessary, every twelve hours.

7. **Cold, Treatment of.**—Mashes, warm clothing, ½ oz. nitre in gruel. Young bamboo leaves are good for a dry cough.

8. **Gruel, Linseed** (*ulsi*).—Boil 8 oz. bruised linseed in four quarts of water; add salt and enough cold water to make it drinkable. Some horses take it quite thick.

9. **Embrocation for Sprains.**—Half pint vinegar, 2 oz. turpentine, 2 whites of eggs. Mix thoroughly and bottle.

10. **Mash, Bran and Linseed.**—Boil 1 lb. whole linseed for two hours in enough water to keep it fluid. Add enough bran to make it of the consistency of an ordinary bran mash. Give slightly warm.

11. **Mash, Bran.**—Pour as much boiling water as the bran will take up on 2 lbs. of bran. Cover and stand for quarter of an hour. Give whilst warm.

12. **Sprains, Treatment of.**—If there is heat, foment constantly with very hot water, or place the foot in a stable-bucket of hot water for at least a quarter of an hour four or five times a day. When the heat is gone, use cooling lotion or embrocation. Every stable should use Elliman's embrocation;* it is invaluable. Obstinate sprains with heat may call for leeches.

13. **Sore Back.**—Wash with salt and water, dress with carbolic or boracic, or powdered indigo or Holloway's ointment,* and keep covered with a damp cloth.

14. **Shoeing.**—This is a fruitful source of lameness, as the smiths constantly cut the hoof too much, especially at the back. They thus alter the natural angle at which the foot should touch the ground, and cause unnatural strain on the sinews. Good shoes are thin, light, flat, and not too much curved in at the back. They should fit the hoof, and not require the hoof to be fitted to them. As a rule, a set of shoes will last two months if they are changed about after a few weeks' wear.

15. **Wounds, to treat.**—Wash thoroughly, pick out every bit of dirt or grit, if necessary stitch together with silk, and dress with carbolic or boracic dressings. It is well to have a bottle of some wound lotion ready in the stable.

CHAPTER VIII

COWS AND DAIRY

————◆————

REGIMENTAL and jail dairies* are in favour nowadays, but the revising editor says frankly that she distrusts both. She has seen the demand for butter, cream, and milk at some of these institutions treble in a week, and yet be satisfied by guaranteed supply. How was this done? In England such fluctuating demand can be met without much risk of impurity by tapping other sources. In India there is nothing to fall back on save the bazaar. And if this has to be done, the editor prefers to do it herself. Besides, this much is patent, that despite regulated dairies, typhoid increases in India by leaps and bounds. Therefore, when she paid her last short visit to India she bought a cow at once, and trusts that most housekeepers will follow her example. It is infinitely more trouble, but infinitely safer. It has another advantage. Even where there is no intention of stinting, bought milk is always scrimp milk, and half the most wholesome food of adults and all that of children requires a practically unlimited supply. With this warning, the experience of thirty years is reprinted without alteration.

No animal is more misunderstood in India than the cow. Left to the *gow-wâla*'s guidance, she becomes a wild, untrustworthy creature, given to alarming fluctuations in the quantity of milk, and absolutely refusing at times to produce any butter at all.

It is as difficult to choose a cow as to choose a horse. The size of the udder bears very little relation to her milking powers, the best test for which, after actual trial, is the width of the cow when looked at from behind. If she is wide, and the udder plainly visible, she will be a good milker. A cow gives most milk with her third, fourth, and fifth calves.

When a cow calves, do not listen to the cowman's protestations. Give a warm bran mash, or some linseed meal or oatmeal, or *dulyâ* gruel, and reduce the quantity of *bhoosa* or chopped straw. A cow before calving must have a reasonable amount of exercise; but if this is given, there will be no need for all the spices and *ghee*, the raw

sugar and oil, without which the *gow-wâla* predicts instant death.
The practice of leaving the calf with its mother is a detestable one,
and is at the bottom of half the difficulties attending cow-keeping in
India, as it tends to keep these animals in that semi-state of domesti-
cation in which, if they give milk one year, they are dry the next. But
unless you begin from the beginning, and educate a heifer with her
first calf, you must accept defeat on this point. One of the authors
once, by dint of great patience, trained two young heifers in the
English fashion. The calves, after being licked, were tied in a separate
house and never saw their mothers again, being fed in a pail with
skim milk, linseed tea, and fresh milk. Great was the dismay of the
compound, as two months passed by, and both calves and mothers
prospered. Fate, however, sent the author into camp for three weeks,
and on her return she found a grin on that *gow-wâla*'s face which
did not long remain there. Both calves were sucking the mothers, in
the absence of *huzoor-ki-ikbâl* (your honour's mightiness), by which
alone, the man said, they had been reconciled to the unnatural and
impious arrangement. On one point, however, firmness will produce
the best of results. If the calf dies, insist on the *gow-wâla* making some
arrangement to produce milk as before. It can be done by patience,
and in this, as in most matters in India, it is wisest to adopt the plan
followed by the House of Commons in regard to factories consuming
their own smoke*—that is, give the order, and leave the method to
personal ingenuity.

The milk of a cow is usually fit for use on the fourth day; if it stands
boiling without turning to curd, butter can be made from it. But from
the day the calf is born the cow should be milked regularly after the
calf has had a good suck—that is, about five times a day—and the
milk brought for inspection. *Gow-wâlas* invariably object to this plan,
as they do to everything which savours of novelty. They look on the
beestings, or first yellow milk, as their perquisite, and for this reason will tell the inexperienced mistress gravely that the milk cannot
possibly be used for ten days.

Although the calf, under the present detestable arrangement, has
to suck a little before the cow will give down her milk, it should never
be allowed to suck again, or, in fact, to do more than bring down
the milk. After the cow has been milked *quite dry*, it may be allowed
to finish up. The practice of leaving 'something,' equivalent in the
cowman's mind to '*ek thun*' (one teat), for the calf, invariably ends

in semi-starvation for the poor little beast. It is no uncommon sight to see a really fine cow followed by a wretched, starveling, stunted calf, covered from head to foot with the scab from *sheer weakness*. Such a sight is a disgrace to the mistress who allows such cruelty to be done in her name. The cowman covers the result of his own theft or neglect, viz., a diminution of milk, by encroaching on the already scanty allowance left for the calf, which is often thus reduced to a mere drop or two; nor does he attempt to stay its hunger by giving it linseed tea or gruel. The only certain plan, therefore, is to have your cow milked dry, and then give a regular allowance for the calf, which, after a day or two, will learn to drink from a tin kettle as if it had been born to it. Half or three-quarters skim-milk, provided it is sweet, may be given to the calf for the first six weeks, after which it will thrive capitally on skim alone, especially if a little linseed gruel is mixed with it. It is well worth the trouble to look after the calves; for, if well nourished, they will sell for from ten to twenty rupees as yearlings; whereas, in the ordinary disgraceful method, the calf fetches nothing in the market. The skim-milk must be slightly warmed, and the total allowance for the calf should never be less than three quarts a day for the first two months. This is less than half the English allowance. If you have not this amount of skim to spare, make up with linseed, hay tea or *suttoo* (parched and ground gram) gruel.

It is most important to secure a good milker as *gow-wâla*. The quicker a cow is milked, the more readily she gives down the supply. The habit of milking with the thumb bent in to use as extra pressure is bad. The best cowmen—Mahomedan *goojurs* from the lower hills—adopt the English plan of milking straight with closed fist. The pressure on the teat is thus even, and the risk of hurting the cow lessened immensely. In fact, a *goojur* seldom has to hobble his cow, because he milks as a calf sucks, but the Poorbeâh *gow-wâlas* drag and knuckle away till the cow, perforce, becomes restive.

The food of the cow is another matter which is thoroughly misunderstood. Grain in quantities is given, but no pains are taken to see that it is properly prepared. If you want a cow to give milk, you must make sure that it eats enough in *bulk*. Therefore the grain must be used to induce the cow to eat more *bhoosa* or grass than she would otherwise do. The daily allowance for a cow giving eight to ten *seers* of milk should not be less than 4 lbs. of sweet or *til* oil-cake;

2 lbs. of *binôla*, or cotton seed; 2 lbs. of *kurra*, or the husks and rough grindings of gram. It would be well to increase this allowance by 2 lbs. of ground barley or grain if the cow keeps thin. Everything should be soaked in water overnight, and next morning it should be added to the daily allowance of white *bhoosa* or straw, and the chopped-up grass, cabbage leaves, green wheat, green millet, &c., which should *always* form part of the cow's food. Dry *churrie*, or millet stalks, chopped fine, is excellent food. Where a *gow-wâla* has only one or two cows to look after, he can quite well bring in a small bundle of green grass, which he can cut whilst grazing the cows. This should be chopped and given with the other stuffs.

As a rule, if the food is properly prepared, a cow giving ten quarts of milk will eat 16 lbs. dry white *bhoosa*; 8 lbs. green food; 4 lbs. turnips; 4 lbs. chopped *churree*; 2 oz. salt.

These allowances, properly prepared, should be sufficient for the best cow, and should ensure wholesome rich milk, yielding about 1 lb. butter to ten quarts of milk.

The whole secret lies in having a good *gow-wâla*, who will look after his cow day and night, groom her well, and take a pride in her. *Bhoosa* should always be well washed before giving it, and if the food can be steamed so much the better. Green wheat increases the yield of milk, but thins the quality.

Grazing is so bad in Upper India, that it will be found advisable to send the cows out for three or four hours a day, not more, chiefly for the sake of the exercise. Variation in the quantity of milk is a sure sign of carelessness in feeding. Sometimes, at the beginning of the hot weather, the milk turns easily, and will not make firm butter. Change the diet for a few days, giving barley instead of gram, and reducing the quantity of oil-cake. Give saltpetre (½ oz.) instead of salt, and keep the cow in a cool, airy, shady place out of doors. A steady decrease in the supply of milk before the sixth month after calving means either disease or starvation, and requires prompt attention. If the *gow-wâla* is not in fault, give a drench as noted in the end. It can do no harm, and may avert serious illness.

Cows should be watered at least three times a day, and the bearer, or some head servant, should *see* that they are given water immediately before they are taken out to graze. This is the surest way of preventing them drinking from tanks and dirty puddles. The *gow-wâla* should, of course, have strict orders to prevent them from doing so, but the best preventative is to make sure that they are not thirsty when they leave your compound. Besides, if a cow is watered regularly, it will not drink except at those times.

Milking should also be as regular as possible, and the hours so fixed that the intervals may be nearly equal. There can be no doubt that it largely increases the supply of milk if the cow is milked three times in the twenty-four hours, say at 5 A.M., 1 P.M., and 8 P.M. Some cows always require to be hobbled, but if a generally quiet cow gives trouble in milking, look at her udder yourself at once, and if it seems hot and tender, rub in gently camphor and butter ointment, and cut down her grain.

Finally, remember that a cow, though hardy, will not stand neglect. On the other hand, she well repays care; and where, with her food merely flung to her, she will give one quart of milk, she will give two if she is properly fed. It will perhaps interest the reader to know that wheat straw and cotton-seed are only now coming into repute in England as the best dairy food. The authors are sure that sweet *til* cake would also make its mark as a butter producer. It is, however, only procurable in England at prohibitive prices.

Dairy Management.—The cow's udder should always be wiped with a damp cloth before milking is commenced, and the most scrupulous cleanliness is necessary, both in regard to the milker's hands and the pail.

As cream never rises so well after being once disturbed, and the rising commences *at once*, milk that is to be set for cream should always be put into the cooler whilst still warm. It must, of course, be strained through a hair sieve into the cooler. Opinion is divided as to whether cream rises best in shallow or deep vessels; but it certainly keeps sweeter in deep jars, where less surface is exposed to the air. In warm American climates milk is set in stone jars, immersed in cold water, and the cream is said to rise splendidly, even through eighteen inches of milk. But if the weather be cool, nothing can be better than shallow tin pans capable of containing about three inches deep of milk. These should be set on a scrupulously clean shelf, if possible in a room set apart as a dairy; at any rate, in some place where the milk shall be beyond the possibility of contamination. There is scarcely anything so easily tainted as milk, and nothing which, when so tainted, is more dangerous to health. Yet it is no uncommon thing in India to see it set in a dirty scullery where the floor reeks like a sink, or side by side with raw meat in a safe. In such a place, and left to the native's capacity for uncleanliness, milk will not keep sweet for three hours, unless it is boiled; whereas, in a proper dairy, and properly treated, it will keep good for thirty-six. As a rule, however, twenty-four hours will be found most convenient, as the skim milk will then be available for the calf. Of course, during the hot months milk *must* be scalded or treated with boracic acid; but in the cold weather the English routine can be carried out. The cream separator* is revolutionising dairy work at home, but as yet the machines are on too large a scale for private use in India. Next to it, the Devonshire plan of scalding the milk after twelve hours' setting seems most productive of cream butter.

The cream need not be churned every day, except in the hot months. A small-sized atmospheric churn* will be found the most useful, as butter comes in it very quickly; it can also be used for milk butter; but if this cannot be had, an ordinary plunge churn* made of tin will do as well; that is to say, a cylinder of tin, fifteen inches long by five in diameter, with a cover, through which passes a wooden or tin plunger, with flanges pierced with holes. This is, at any rate, a quicker and more cleanly plan than having the butter made by the *khitmutgâr* in a slop basin by means of a fork. A very good churn is made at the Roorkee workshops,* where prices, &c., may be had on application. Every third or fourth day is quite sufficient in the winter to churn butter, which is always sweetest when made from slightly sour cream; the reason being supposed to be that the membraneous envelope in which the fatty portions are enclosed breaks more readily when slightly weakened by fermentation, and thus the oily matter is completely set free from it. Butter that is absolutely pure, and that contains little or no caseine,* will keep sweet for weeks. This is the reason why clarified butter or *ghee* keeps so long. The curdy matter sinks to the bottom when the butter becomes liquefied by heat, and is strained away. Sometimes butter will not come. The cream thickens, and little grains of butter may be seen in it; still it will not separate. In cold weather this may arise from too low a temperature, in which case add a teacupful of hot water, or place the churn in hot water if the cream is thin. In warm weather, it generally comes from too high a temperature, when a lump of ice is the best remedy. Otherwise set the churn aside in an earthen vessel filled with cold water for an hour or more, and then begin churning again. Sometimes a teaspoon of vinegar will bring butter when all else fails; but with an atmospheric churn difficulty of any sort is rare. The best temperature for making good, firm butter is between 60° and 62°.

Opinion is divided as to whether butter should be washed in water or not. It is said to keep better if the buttermilk is simply well squeezed out of it; but in India, unless there is personal supervision, we advise plentiful washing in many waters, for this simple reason—a native can *see* if the water still runs milky, and has no excuse for leaving the butter until it runs clear; but he can always say he thought it was all right on the dry system. When washing in water is adopted, the best plan is to pour off the buttermilk carefully, and fill the churn up with water two or three times, working the plunge gently. The butter may then be removed to a basin, and washed carefully with wooden spats. Finally, it should be finished in strong salt and water in which a little boracic acid has been dissolved if the butter has to be kept, and then *beaten* on the spats till all the moisture is extracted. If it is desired to keep it fresh, the best plan is to make into ½ lb. pats, wrap them in coarse muslin, and place in strong salt, boracic, and water in a cool place. Butter so treated will keep good for a month or two. If the slight taste of salt on the outside is a fault it can be scraped off. Another good plan is to press it into the bottom of a jar or basin, and invert this in a saucer of water, the object being to exclude the air as much as possible. Butter for use at the table should be pressed into wooden moulds, or made into pats with proper fluted butter spats. The *khitmutgâr* should never be allowed to exercise his talent for plastic art upon it, as is often the case.

During the hot months cream butter is still possible, but the out-turn per quart or *seer* of milk will be very small. The milk must be scalded or treated with boracic, and in either case the cream must be skimmed after twelve hours, and the butter made at once. On the whole, the authors think it better to make milk butter in the hot weather. It is a plan which is largely pursued in Scotland, and if properly made, no fault can be found with the butter. The morning's milk, after being well scalded, should be set aside in a stoneware jar in a cool place, and the evening's milk added to it, either raw or scalded, according to the heat of the weather. Early next morning, the whole should be found *sweet* but coagulated, when it should be churned in the stone jar by means of a native or *mudhâni* churn, which is not unlike a chocolate miller.

If milk butter has a cheesy taste, you may be sure that *jâmun* or stale curd has been used to make it coagulate. This is not at all necessary, especially in hot weather, unless the milk is over-boiled; but *gow-wâlas* frequently do it to save themselves trouble. The remedy is simple. If the milk does not coagulate in twenty-four hours, unless stale curd is added, keep it for thirty-six, or until it *is* fit to churn. Milk butter seldom comes under two hours' churning, but the out-turn is larger than with cream.

The following dairy recipes will be found very useful:—

1. **Butter, to clarify.**—Put it in a basin and let it oil with as little heat as possible. The hot case is the best place for effecting this. Decant the clear portion into jars and give the residuum to the cook, who, by applying extra heat, will make *ghee* of it. This clarified butter will keep good a long time, and is only to be distinguished from butter by its grain.

2. **Butter, to pickle.**—Wash good fresh butter in strong brine, make into ½ lb. pats, and wrap each in a muslin cloth. Lay by in a jar and cover with strongest brine—that is, water saturated with salt. It will keep sweet and fresh for two months, and is very useful for camp. The addition of a teaspoonful of boracic acid to every quart of water makes it keep better.

3. **Butter, to salt.**—Allow ½ oz. salt and a teaspoon of pounded sugar to each pound of butter. Mix intimately and press into jars. Cover with a well-salted cloth. Before salting butter wash well with boracic.

4. **Cream Cheese.**—This may be made as milk cheese, using half cream and half milk. The latter alone should be heated so as to bring the whole to blood heat. This is generally preferred to the cheese made by simply tying thick cream in a coarse cloth and letting it drain.

5. **Cheese, Milk.**—To every quart of warm new milk add a tablespoon of essence of rennet. The curd should set in four hours. When firm, cut into dice and drain. Place a coarse muslin in the cheese mould, lay in the curd, salting it a little. Weight, and increase the pressure daily for three days. The cheese should then be fit to handle, and may be turned for more pressure if required to keep, or laid aside in vine leaves for a day, and then eaten fresh. If made with a quarter cream, these cheeses, properly kept, are equal to the best Stilton.* A cheese mould is easily made from a round wooden box or *dibya*, such as may be found in every bazaar. A few gimlet holes are all that is required to make an excellent mould.

6. **Cream, Devonshire.**—Set the milk in shallow tin pans for twelve hours. Remove carefully to a charcoal stove, and heat till the cream shrinks

to the middle and wrinkles. Stand for another twelve or twenty-four hours before skimming. It should be quite thick and leathery.

7. **Float Whey.**—This should be made when cheeses are being done. Take all the whey and heat just below boiling-point, when a little scum of curd should rise to the surface. Add new milk gently till the milk thickens to a sufficient quantity. Then add a little cold water to reduce the temperature. When nearly cool, remove the floating curd and drain on a sieve. Serve in a glass dish with cream and sugar.

8. **Ghee, to make.**—Heat the butter in a pan till the flaky sediment begins to brown or comes to the burn (*julna pur âgya*). Strain into jars. *Ghee* has a nutty taste, due to its having browned a little, but it will keep for years.

9. **Hatted Kit.**—Warm two quarts of new milk and pour it over four quarts of buttermilk. Let the whole stand till cold. The top should then be a firm curd. Remove, drain, and set for two hours in a china mould with holes in it. Turn out and serve with fruit syrup or cream.

10. **Junket.**—To one quart of warm new milk add one tablespoon brandy, two of sugar, and one of essence of rennet. Set in a warm place, and in two hours it should be fit for use. Grate a little nutmeg over the top, pile on Devonshire cream, and serve.

11. **Milk, to keep Sweet.**—Add some of the following boracic water to milk when you wish to keep it, and place the jug in an earthen jar full of water or on ice. Milk may be kept sweet during the hottest weather by this means for at least twenty-four hours, which enables the cream to rise. This is a great advantage for tea, for which scalded cream is oily. To every quart of water allow one dessertspoon boracic acid. Keep in a bottle corked. One or two tablespoons to a quart of milk.

12. **Rennet, to make.**—Take the maw of a young kid not more than one month old. Empty of curd, and fill with salt. Tie the bag round and hang up to dry. In a week empty out the salt, split the maw open, and dry in the sun. When wanted for use, steep a piece the size of a rupee in a wineglass of tepid water for four hours. Vell, or rennet skins, can sometimes be bought from the cheesemakers in the bazaars.

13. **Rennet Curd or pure Casein Rennet.**—Set three quarts of milk as for Devonshire cream, stand till every particle of cream has risen. Skim carefully. Add two tablespoons of vinegar to the milk, and heat till it curds thoroughly. Wash the curd in several waters, kneading it thoroughly. Dress, dry, and powder. This is nearly pure casein, but can be made purer still by

dissolving the powder for twelve hours in a weak solution of carbonate of soda, and then throwing it down again by adding sufficient vinegar.

14. **Rennet, Essence of.**—Is generally bought, but, as a rule, it is only a solution of pepsine, which can be made at home.

15. **Sourcog.**—Set a quart of milk in a glass dish till it coagulates. Sprinkle with sugar and nutmeg, and, if liked, pour over a little brandy. Serve with sweet cake or fruit. This is the Scotch form of junket.

In regard to the diseases of cows it may be remarked that they are somewhat delicate animals, especially when artificially fed, and that even slight ailments require to be promptly alleviated. Even imperfect digestion on the part of the cow cannot fail to render its milk less wholesome for consumption. The following facts will be useful in diagnosing any variation from the normal:—

In health the cow's temperature is from 100 to 102 degrees. The pulse, which is most conveniently felt (as in the horse) at the angle of the lower jaw, or just behind the fetlock in the metacarpal vein, beats about forty-six beats a minute in the adult animal. The respiration is fifteen per minute, and, as a rule, is very regular and deliberate. The cow goes 284 days in calf as a rule. In England it is considered bad management if she does not calve every eleven months. In India, to ensure anything approaching this, the very strictest orders are necessary.

The following is a brief list of the more ordinary ailments of both cows and calves, with appropriate remedies:—

1. **Calving.**—Give oil-cake or the chief grain food for a month before calving. It is laxative. As a rule, there is little trouble in the actual calving, and it is only necessary to give warm drinks for a day or two after calving, and keep the cow from chill. Sometimes, but not often, it is necessary to give an aperient, or an ergot of rye drench if the cleansing is not all right.

2. **Chill.**—Cows are very liable to chill and slight fever or shivering. Keep warmly clad, and give 1 *seer* hot linseed gruel, in which ½ a *chittâck* ginger and *ujwain*, and 1 *chittâck goor*, have been boiled. Add 1 teacup country spirit if necessary.

3. **Cud, Loss of.**—Generally a symptom of the approach of other disease. If no sequel comes on, treat by mild purgatives and the alterative powder.

4. **Diarrhœa.**—Change the food. Give a full dose of castor oil, and then the recipe for diarrhœa in calves, only four times the quantity.

5. **Diminution of Milk, sudden.**— Another constant forerunner of active disease. If when this occurs causelessly the cow appears sluggish, give 1 oz. nitre and 4 oz. powdered sulphur shaken up in a quart bottle of water.

6. **Hoven.**—This comes from indigestion, especially from a surfeit of green watery food like young wheat. The stomach swells from the gases evolved during fermentation, and in extreme cases rupture ensues. It is the bovine form of colic, and should be treated the same way. Give the carminative draught, or linseed oil warmed, half a bottle turpentine 2 oz., raw opium 20 grains. Where nothing else is at hand, lime water may be tried. If remedies fail to stop the swelling, and the animal is in absolute danger of bursting, open the paunch with a trochar. The puncture to be made exactly in the centre of the flank between the last rib, the lumber vertebræ, and the ileum; that is to say, in the centre, at equal distances from the back bone, the last rib, and the big projecting bone above the haunch bone. If you have no trochar, you may relieve a desperate case with a penknife and any kind of tube, the object being to allow the gas to escape. A hollow flexible probang may be passed into the stomach through the mouth for this purpose.

Hoven is often followed by a sort of inflammation of the various stomachs. Warm beer or porter and carminatives may be given, in conjunction with mild aperients and stimulants.

The following are useful remedies:—

7. **Aperient.**—Twelve oz. Epsom salts,* 2 drachms powdered ginger.

8. **Carminative for Cattle or Horses.**—In 1 quart country spirit digest for eight days 3 oz. each of ginger, *ujwain*, and cloves. *Dose.*—One tumblerful mixed with a very little hot water, in which ½ oz. nitre has been dissolved. Give in hot gruel.

9. **Cooling Draught at any time.**—One oz. nitre, 4 oz. powdered sulphur, 1 bottle of water. Half at a time.

10. **Alterative Powder for Indigestion.**—Sulphate of copper 1 oz., Glauber's salts* 1 lb., resin 2 oz., nitre 2 oz. Powder and divide into ten doses. One night and morning.

11. **Alterative and Carminative Powder.**—Equal quantities of black salt, black pepper, long pepper, and *kootki*. *Dose.*—One oz. in the grain.

12. **Cleansing Draught at Calving.**—Half pint warm beer boiled with ¼ oz. ergot of rye.

13. **Stimulant Draught for Chills or Colic**—Opium ½ drachm, ginger 2 drachms, allspice 3 drachms, *ujwain* 4 drachms. Give in gruel. Or hartshorn 1 oz., ginger 3 drachms, water 1 pint, or carbonate of ammonia 1 drachm, ginger 1 drachm, in hot beer. This is a good powder to have ready.

14. **Ointment for Sore Teats.**—One oz. wax, 3 oz. *ghee*, 1 drachm alum, ¼ oz. sugar of lead.

15. **Ointment for Hardness of the Udder.**—This generally comes from chill. Treat as for that, and rub in gently 1 oz. *ghee* rubbed up with ½ oz. camphor.

16. **Astringent Draught for Diarrhœa in Calves.**—Quarter oz. prepared chalk and 5 grains of opium in a pint of slightly sweetened rice water, or ½ pint of beer boiled with ¾ oz. black pepper. Give 3 oz. of castor oil as a preliminary.

17. **Ointment for Scaldhead in Calves.**—Plain sulphur ointment, made by mixing equal parts of *ghee* and powdered sulphur.

18. **Aperient for Calves.**—Two oz. Epsom salts, 2 drachms *ujwain*.

19. **Linseed Jelly for Calves.**—Half-pint measure of bruised linseed, 3 pints water. Boil for ten minutes. Mix with skim milk.

20. **Hay or Churri Tea for Calves.**—Infuse 2 lbs. chopped hay or *churri* in 2 gallons of boiling water for two hours. Strain, squeeze, and mix the liquid with the milk.

CHAPTER IX

HINTS ON POULTRY

ONE fowl costs as much as another to feed, while some are good layers and some are not. The first thing to do, then, is to choose your fowls, and not waste time in keeping birds that will not repay care. Of course, if you wish to go in for fancy breeding, a pure breed to start with is necessary, but for ordinary purposes Light Brahmas or Houdans* may be met with in most big stations. The latter are the better layers, but they are slightly more delicate, and though they feather earlier than any other breed, they are not quite so soon ready for table as the Brahmas. Silver Dorkings* are an excellent all-round breed for India.

The first thing after getting decent fowls is to find them a suitable house. Most people think that any hole or corner will do for a fowl-house; the idea of whitewashing never enters their head, yet they are surprised if the birds droop and sicken, and wonder why the animals are so infested with insects.

It may safely be said that the fowl-tick or blood-sucker is responsible for most of the failures in fowl-keeping in India; therefore no pains should be spared to prevent their gaining a foothold in the fowl-house. If it is too expensive to build a mud lean-to with a galvanised iron roof, and burnt brick doorways in which iron staples for the door-pins can be built, it is still possible to do much towards making the ordinary wooden roofs and lintels insect-proof; for it is in the crevices that these pests lurk by day, coming out at night to fasten on the birds. Common cloth stretched as a ceiling, and tarred, will mend matters to some extent, and a thorough *lepe* (plaster), with the usual mixture of cowdung and sand, to which some phenyle has been added, will keep the walls free. But in one station the writer was completely vanquished by the insects, till a large, mud-brick dome, like an oven, was built, with small lattice-work bricks here and there for ventilation, and an arched doorway just large enough for cleaning purposes. This was thoroughly mud-plastered inside, and a huge fire lit, which vitrified the whole of the dome. In fact, the great object of having an iron or domed roof is that you can purify the place by fire, which is the only effectual way of doing it.

The perches should be about one foot from the floor, which should invariably be two inches deep in sand. They are best made by permanently fixing two uprights in the ground. The uprights should have slots in them, in which a horizontal bar can be fixed, and whence it can be taken out to be cleaned. The bar should not be quite round, and the diameter should be large enough to prevent cramp in the feet. With regard to a run for your fowls, give them as much liberty as you can, and rather than confine them to close quarters, go to the expense of a few yards of wire-netting. It will well repay its cost. If possible, net in a shady bit for your fowls, for they get fever if much in the sun. If this is impossible, spend eight annas on a grass thatch, elevated about two feet from the ground, where they can take shelter. Put a pile of wood-ashes somewhere about, and a heap of lime. Then the fowl-yard will be ready.

The next point is food. As with all animals, *variety* is the great secret. If you only keep a limited number of fowls, the leavings from the table will secure this. And even when you have many, the fear of trespassing on time-honoured bad habits, and the sweeper's perquisites, should not prevent you from giving your fowls what is the *very best* thing for them, viz., the constant variety afforded by what is called in India the sweeper's tin, in other countries the pig's pail. It will be better to give the man an extra eight annas a month—though this is not necessary if his wages are, as they should be, sufficient for him to live upon—than to deprive the fowl-yard of *its* perquisites.

Taking all round, a fowl will thrive well on 2 oz. of mixed grain in the day, supplemented of course by green vegetables, onions, &c. For thirty-two fowls, then, four pounds of grain will be enough; and we should recommend 1 lb. barley, 1 lb. gram, ½ lb. boiled rice, ½ lb. bran, and 1 lb. of whole wheat.

The last thing at night, or after dinner, the cook should have orders to put on a big pan, containing the remains of the day's vegetables, cabbage leaves, cuttings of turnips, potato peelings, &c. These should remain on the embers all night, and be warmed up next morning on the fire where the kettle for early tea has been boiled. The mess should be given hot to the sweeper or fowl-man, who will strain away excess of water and mix in the ground barley, grain, and bran. The consistency should be such that it will just *crumble* in the hand. The fowls should then be let out, and the food given to them while still warm. It must never be thrown on the ground, but be spread in shallow earthen saucers. It is well to have plenty of these, to prevent crowding. After this the fowl-house should be cleaned out, the eggs collected and given in, the door closed again and kept locked. Water must be given in earthen saucers, and it will be found a great preventative of disease if a few drops of Douglas' mixture be mixed with it. A recipe for making this is given at the end. At twelve o'clock the fowls should be again fed with boiled rice, in which a few handfuls of soft food—which should have been saved for this purpose from the morning's meal—should be mixed. If the fowls have a run where grass is not to be had, a little should be gathered and thrown to them. The last thing before roosting-time the fowls should have their whole wheat mixed with a little of the gram. Twice a week at least they should get a little animal food; a liver boiled and minced is best, as it is cheap; but if the soup meat is given regularly, as it should be, this is not necessary.

The great mistake in India is not giving enough *variety* or enough *green food*.

Diarrhœa is almost always caused by too much whole grain, and when it appears the ration of boiled vegetables should be increased. Keeping the key of the fowl-house door has a very beneficial result in the number of eggs the birds lay. The sweeper will remark it is '*âp ki ikbâl se*' ('your honour's mightiness'), but he is a fulsome flatterer.

One warning may be given. If you have a clean, thriving set of fowls, don't make a lazaretto* of their run by turning the *khansâman*'s bazaar chickens into it. Put them in quarantine, and give them a kerosene bath first. The same remark applies to clucking hens, which are often fetched in from the bazaar in order to set eggs. The best laying boxes are earthen pans, half filled with clean dry sand. If you intend to raise chickens, get an incubator without delay. It is, to begin with, an amusement; secondly, an immense saving of bother and expense. Hearsom's Champion* is very successful; one to hatch twenty-five eggs costs £4, 7s. 6d., delivered on board ship in London. It is no trouble, and with a little supervision the bearer will look after it perfectly. But even if you do not have an incubator, by all means get a foster-mother. This is a contrivance also of Hearsom's, Regent Street, London, for rearing chickens without the aid of a hen. It consists of a chamber warmed by hot water kept at an even temperature by a small kerosene lamp, a glass-protected run for damp weather, and a wire run beyond. One for twenty-five chickens costs £4, 5s. packed free on docks. In India, where, owing to the climate, very little heat is required, this will be found large enough for fifty chicks if an extra wire run is added. A pamphlet detailing the method of using is sent with each machine; or, if further information is required, send to the same address for the 'Problem Solved,' a brochure costing 1s. Endless are the tragedies from which these two admirable inventions, incubator and foster-mother, will save you. The sweeper will never come to report, with a lurking delight, that the clucking hen which with '*infinite trouble he had produced at your honour*'s *command, having laid an egg, now manifests no desire to sit longer*'; nor will he appear with a dismal little tassel of fluffy dead chicklings in his hands to inform you, still with that fiendish undercurrent of joy, that the hen, '*having doubtless taken fright, became unaware of the chicks, and trampled on them, God knows why!*'

With a foster-mother you are gladdened every day with perceptible growth; and one of the authors can testify that out of about 700 chickens put into the foster-mother, not ten have *died* before they were eaten! They were all *killed*.

The food of young chickens is not such an elaborate affair as the orthodox fowl-man makes out. They require nothing for twenty-four hours; after that a crumbly omelette made from the white, yolk, and shell of an egg, all beaten up, and fried with a little dripping, then rubbed up with parched wheat and bread crumbs, is the best possible food. After forty-eight hours the little creatures may have free run of the foster-mother, and will eat anything and everything. The staple, however, should still be parched, or raw, wheat ground to groats, mixed with boiled rice, chopped onions, and curd made of the skim milk. The remains of the curry minced and mixed with the rice causes flutterings of eagerness; so will chopped cress. In fact, young chicks, being always hungry, should always be in process of being fed; and as they will eat anything and everything, the chicken fancier will find it a good plan to have all the table scraps set aside after every meal for the foster-mother. Do not, however, give them whole grain, or they will gorge themselves on it, and very probably die of indigestion. It is false economy to stint growing chickens, the great object being to get them ready for the table as soon as possible. This should be in ten weeks at most.

The best plan for fattening is the French country plan. Give the birds as much rice and milk, boiled to a stiff paste and mixed with a little Indian corn meal, as they can possibly eat. Do not coop them, but reduce their run. In ten days they should be quite fit for table. If necessary, fatten still more with Indian corn meal boiled to a paste with kitchen grease or sweet oil, and made into pellets, with which the birds must be fed. About six hens should be allowed to each cock if rearing is to be carried on; but if the production of eggs is the object, the fewer cocks the better.

Ducks.—The best breed for India is the Rouen, as the young birds are very hardy. Indian sweepers will insist on feeding ducklings with a feather, on a mess of ground *dâl* (lentils), garlic, and water. It is not in the least necessary. If you have a foster-mother, duck-lings, chickens, and young turkeys will all thrive together on the same food, so long as there be plenty of green stuff and plenty of variety. The writer has seen young Rouen ducklings, three weeks old, which already reminded her irresistibly of green peas. This was the result of a foster-mother, no water to splash in, and plenty of *dry* food. The old ducks, however, rejoice in a slightly different diet. The daily ration should be increased to three ounces by the addition of bran, and the whole should be made liquid by skim milk or water. Wheat need not be given, a feed of split gram soaked being substituted for it. Ducks in India are peculiarly liable to rheumatism, and, as they do not really require water, it is best only to allow them an occasional swim, and even then to limit the time.

Rouen, Pekin, and Aylesbury ducklings,* if kept dry and fed on barley meal mixed with Indian corn meal, will be quite fit to eat at six weeks old. They never require fattening, as a duck will eat till it cannot stand; so will young Houdan chickens. The writer has seen them huddled up almost unconscious, simply from having gorged themselves. Young ducklings often suffer from a mysterious inability to stand on their legs; they topple over backwards, and lie sprawl-ing on their backs. An incredible but nevertheless practically effective remedy is to cut their tail feathers to the quick with a pair of scissors. It sounds useless, but the writer's practical experience has proved that in most cases it is a cure.

Turkeys are very easy to rear in India, at any rate in Northern India, owing to the dryness of the climate. The chicks, which at home require the utmost care, thrive splendidly, and seem as hardy as ordinary fowls. One great advantage of the foster-mother is that the young turkeys can be brought up with chickens, who by their superior liveliness seem to brisk up their companions and incite them to eat. One great secret of success is the giving of fresh sweet milk curds, made by coagulating the milk with alum. With this and a plentiful supply of chopped green food, notably cress, there is no difficulty in rearing turkey chicks. They will shoot the red,* and pass through the fledging without any drooping, or necessity for peppercorns. Turkey chicks love warmth, and will stand being hatched out later on in the season than either fowls or ducks.

A full-grown turkey must be allowed at least four ounces of grain in the day, and as much green food as it can eat. It must not be forgotten that these birds are regular grazers, and if kept in any way in confinement, require chopped grass, lettuce, turnip tops, whatever is to be had, even lucerne grass. Turkeys may be fattened the same way as fowls, with rice and milk, but as they are poor feeders, they must be stuffed. As a rule, the dark turkeys are the biggest and hardiest.

Quails do best in the ordinary pit dug in the ground, but care must be taken to avoid flooding in the rainy season. Any suspicion of damp is fatal, though the mere sprinkling of the floor with water does no harm. Quails thrive best on *bâjra* or small millet, but a mixture of ground wheat may be given. Green food, notably cress, is greedily eaten. The best plan of feeding quails is to fill two or three large earthen vessels with grain, renewing them to full measure when getting low. In this way the quails always have enough to eat, and they need not be disturbed so often. They require plenty of fresh water. At first—that is to say, immediately after capture—a rather large percentage of quails die in the pit; but after a time they get accustomed to captivity, becoming almost too fat. The time for laying in quail is April and September. Partridges may be kept the same way, but a larger proportion die at first.

Guinea-fowls are noisy, troublesome birds to keep, and have a mania for laying in other people's premises. Another disadvantage is, that if intended for breeding, the birds must be in pairs, as they are monogamous. This does not matter if they are only kept for eggs or for eating. The chicks are tender, and require a good deal of insect food. On the whole, it is best to let other people rear and keep guinea-fowls; you can generally buy the eggs!

Geese.—There is not a good breed of geese in India, but some birds might be imported which would be free of the wild, rank taste of the ordinary Indian goose. If hatching the eggs is tried in the incubator, it must not be forgotten that the temperature must be kept high, as they are said to require great heat. The treatment is the same as for ducks, but the grain required will be at least four ounces.

The following recipes will be found useful in the fowl-yard:—

1. **Bumble-foot.**—This is common in Houdans and other heavy birds, and is often caused by too high perches. It is an abscess, and can only be treated by the knife, and afterwards by cauterisation or carbolic dressing.

2. **Diarrhœa.**—Give a piece of camphor the size of a pea three times a day, also plenty of green food.

3. **Douglas' Mixture.**—One teaspoon sulphate of iron (*kussees*), 6 drops strong sulphuric acid (*têz-âb*), 1 quart bottle water; dissolve. About 30 drops in a large pan of drinking water.

4. **Fever.**—Fowls constantly get simple fever in India, when they droop, look languid, and feel burning hot. Give ½ grain quinine and 3 grains camphor.

5. **Inflammation of the Air Passages.**—Give ½ grain ipecacuanha and 2 grains camphor thrice a day. Feed on boiled rice, and keep warm.

6. **Insects, to get rid of.**—Place live charcoal in an earthen dish on the floor of the house, when empty; sprinkle over it red pepper and sulphur. Close all doors and openings, leave for two hours. Or, take water ¼ pint, common salt 6 oz., strong sulphuric acid ¼ pint, black oxide of manganese 2 oz. Mix in an earthen pan, and leave as above. This evolves chlorine gas.

7. **Roup.**—Separate any bird showing signs of heavy cold in the head, as it may be roup, which is most contagious. Give half a grain of blue vitriol (*nila tootya*) in meal once a day. Sponge away all mucus, and anoint nostrils and mouth with carbolic oil, ten drops to the ounce. If very bad, blow the oil down the nostrils by means of a quill. Some of the volatile powders sold by poultry fanciers are very good for this disease.

8. **Ticks, to remove.**—Rub the bird well with kerosene oil, repeating the operation next day. These pests are generally found under the wings.

9. **General Hints.**—Camphor is a great stand-by with fowls, and a bit as big as a pea should be administered on the first symptom of dulness. The golden rule of fowl-yards, however, is this, '*Give the birds plenty of green food and they will doctor themselves.*'

CHAPTER X

DOGS

MOST people leave their dogs to the tender mercies of the sweeper, whose intentions may be good, but whose ideas are certainly limited.

A new-comer will always be astonished to see even rough-haired dogs given a wadded coat at night, and, stranger still, taken out to exercise with it on in the morning. Some people defend this practice, and the writer has heard those who ought to know say that the variations of the climate demand it. Yet the variation is nothing compared to that experienced by an English dog, who leaves a warm fireside to plunge into a snowdrift outside. The fact is, it is not the variation of the climate, but the draughty houses, that gives inflammation of the lungs to Indian dogs. A dog loathes a draught. You will often see a dog in an English room get up and deliberately move himself from the draught of door or window. In India he is often tied up in a whirl-wind, or worse still, is fastened up in the shade, as a sequence to a hot race in the sun after horse or dogcart. Give a dog freedom, and you will find he will invariably choose a snug corner, preferably under a table or bed; therefore, if you deny him freedom, give him comfort at least. The writers can only say that after having kept dogs of all sorts and conditions in India for twenty-one years, the wadded coat or *jhool* still appears to them not only useless, but hurtful. Certainly, a long-haired dog never has such a good natural coat when he is given an artificial one, as without it.

On the other hand, a certain amount of care is necessary not only to keep the dog from chill, but from the sun also. Therefore, during the heat of the day, even in the cold weather, it is kindest to keep your favourite tied up. Kindest in many ways; for during the busy hours a dog may roam away unobserved, to come back, with an equally unob-served bite, which may bring on hydrophobia.* Therefore, keep your dog as much in your sight as possible.

Another bad Indian habit is the washing of dogs. If carefully brushed, combed, and properly fed, even long-haired dogs seldom require washing more than once a month. Then choose the best time of day, about twelve o'clock in winter, or eight in summer, and let him be thoroughly and immediately dried. Soap spoils the gloss of a dog's coat, as it spoils human hair, and a beaten-up egg will do the cleansing work quite as well. If you suspect fleas or parasites, the addition of a teaspoonful of turpentine to each yolk will do wonders. Water in which a dog is washed should only just have the chill off. The sweeper should have orders never to wash the dog without asking permission; but every day after the morning run, brush and comb should be diligently employed, long hair being parted and cleansed by brushing different ways. If this is really well done, parasites will be unknown. It is a mistake in India only to feed a dog once a day; and though the morning meal be only a saucer of porridge, or bread and milk, it should invariably be given. The eagerness with which the dog will look for the mouthful or two shows that he needs it. If you value your dogs, never give the sweeper so much a month for dog's meat, but take the trouble to order so much *âtta* to be made into *chupâtties*, so much meat or milk.

It is the fashion nowadays to keep house dogs without meat, but their teeth proclaim the absurdity of feeding a carnivorous animal on slops alone. Variety is the great thing. Give a dog *chupâtties* and milk one day; liver, vegetable, and rice the next; porridge and milk the third; soup and *chupâtti* the next, and so on, arranging as a rule to have meat or soup three times a week. With regard to the kind of meat, the coarser bits are best, and in hot weather the head or the liver is most suitable. The proportion of meat to *chupâtti* or rice should be small, and the gravy and meat should not be put to the broken *chupâtti* till just before meal-time, as dogs loathe pappy and slithery food. Curry, spices, turmeric, &c., should be tabooed; but once or twice a week a pinch of powdered sulphur may be sprinkled on the food. Seeing how intensely a dog enjoys bones, it is cruel to deprive him of such a pleasure; so even when no meat is given, a bare bone or two may be conceded, if only to clean and sharpen the teeth; but chicken or game bones should be withheld, as they are liable to stick in the intestines. Water should be in a fixed place where the dog knows it is to be had. If a dog seems out of sorts and will not eat his food, do not worry him, or tempt him to eat. He has probably got a fit of indigestion, and means to cure it by that best of all remedies—starvation.

In regard to exercise; running after a cart is not good for little dogs, who find sufficient work in keeping up; though it does not hurt bigger ones who are fleet enough to make excursions, and linger behind, secure of being able to overtake their belongings. But no dog does without real, active exercise, for which a dreary constitutional with the sweeper—generally at the end of a chain—is but a poor substitute. Even long-haired dogs will thrive in the hot weather if their food is regulated, and they get real exercise morning and evening. The fatness of pet dogs is proverbial, but this comes far more from want of exercise than over-feeding. To see a dog really enjoy life, one should see him in camp, when he has a ten-mile run in the morning, which he increases to thirty by side-walkings! With what keenness will he not go at porridge and milk, then curl round in some snug corner with a sigh of satisfaction, and sleep steadily till the sound of master looking to his guns awakens him to fresh delights. How different is this life to that of the 'sweeper's dog,' who goes for a *raol* (constitutional), has his skin blistered with soap every morning, and is fed for 365 days of the year on meat in the last stage of jaundice with turmeric.

The following will be found useful in treating simple diseases as a preliminary; though all dog lovers should buy Hugh Dalziel's book on the 'Diseases of Dogs,'* price 1s. It may be said that a pulse of a dog taken inside the knee, or from the heart, is in health from 90 to 100, the temperature about 98°, the breathing about 20 per minute.

The doses for dogs must naturally vary with the size of the dog, also with old age. Briefly, a mature dog of the largest size stands the same dose as a man. Taking this as a basis, it is easy to apportion the dose for any drug. Dogs under a year should be given three-quarters of the dose for their size; under six months one-half; under two months one-eighth.

1. **Bad Breath.**—Black salt, 1 oz.; sulphur (*gunduk*), 1 oz.; sulphate of iron (*kussis*), 1 oz. As much as will lie on an eight-anna bit daily in food.

2. **Cold with Cough.**—Nitre, 30 grains; ipecacuanha, 5 grains; powdered opium, 1 grain. Divide into five doses.

3. **Diarrhœa.**—Catechu (*kuth*), 1 drachm; chalk, 2 drachms; mixed cinnamon and cloves, ½ drachm; opium, 6 grains. Twelve powders, one three times a day.

4. **Eczema Ointment.**—Boracic ¼ oz., bismuth ½ oz., oil 4 oz.

5. **Emetic.**—One teaspoon of dry salt on the tongue is a speedy and safe emetic if a dog has been eating garbage.

6. **Eye Lotion.**—½ oz. boracic, 1 pint water. Bathe night and morning.

7. **Indigestion and Want of Condition.**—Bicarbonate of soda, ½ oz.; carbonate of iron, ½ oz.; powdered chiretta, 1 oz. Make with treacle into sixteen or twenty-four balls, according to the size of the dog. Give one twice a day.

8. **Mange.**—Ethiops mineral,* ½ oz.; cream of tartar, 1 oz.; nitre, 2 drachms. Sixteen to twenty-four doses. Night and morning.

9. **Mange Ointment.**—Powdered aloes (*ilva*), 2 drachms; white hellebore, 4 drachms; sulphur, 4 oz.; cocoanut-palm oil, 6 oz. Add 1 oz. of mercurial ointment if the dog is suffering from red mange. Muzzle the dog, rub in well, leave for three hours, and wash out thoroughly.

10. **Tonic Alterative during the hot weather, or Distemper.**—Quinine and sulphate of iron, 20 grains to 1 drachm; powdered chiretta, 6 drachms. Make into twenty pills with treacle.

11. **Worms.**—Keep the dog without food for twelve hours. For each pound of the dog's weight give 1 grain of powdered betel or *areca* nut, followed in an hour by a full dose of castor oil.

12. **Rheumatism.**—Twelve grains bicarbonate of potash and 2 grains iodide of potassium twice a day for a big dog. A red herring well rubbed with nitre, given with potatoes or porridge six days running, is a favourite remedy.

13. **Sore Ears.**—Goulard lotion,* 1 oz. glycerine, and boracic ¼ oz., sweet oil 4 oz. If it seems necessary, add ¼ oz. carbolic. Bathe ears and apply.

CHAPTER XI

GARDENING

If the native of India is unsympathetic in his treatment of animals, who have at least the power of expressing pain, he is still more so in his treatment of plants, whose very claim to individual life he derides. It is best for those who desire to have a garden to watch their gardener carefully when he is watering that row of mangy pots with which even the most hardened criminal conceives it to be his duty to ornament his master's doorstep. It consists possibly of a parched mimulus, a few sodden-looking pansies, some seeds struggling to life, a pot of maidenhair fern, and a stolid cactus. To these various individualities *mâli* plays the part of indiscriminate Providence, and rains alike upon the just and the unjust, never observing the mimulus expectant for at least one drop more, the cactus bristling at the impertinent intrusion, or every yellow leaf of the pansies crying mutely for a pause. Now, unless you have sympathy with the flowers, unless you can see from the look of the plant what it needs, and feel intuitively *that wire-worm* at its roots, you may sow seeds and water them, but you will never gather the real fruits of gardening. There may, of course, be a few native gardeners in the real sense of the term, but the writer never came across one, and it is safest, therefore, to regard the *mâli* as a mere executive, and insist on his obeying orders and nothing more.

The expense consequent on the necessity for irrigation prevents many people from cultivating a garden; but where cows and horses are kept, and where the soil is fairly good, it need not be so expensive. As a rule, the well-bullocks are not made to work for, and produce, their own living; but this should be the first detail insisted upon. Summer and winter the bullocks should grow their own green fodder, and so help to lessen their own expense.

There are two things necessary for a supply of good vegetables, which is, perhaps, the primary object of the garden, viewed from the standpoint of domestic economy. The first is good and plentiful manure; the next is good seed. In regard to the first, there should never be any difficulty where cows, horses, and fowls are kept; though the *mâli* will invariably expect to be allowed an unlimited order for a supply from outside sources. By far the best and cleanliest plan is to have all the stable and cow house droppings put on to the land at once, and not piled in a heap. There is always some plot unused in a garden, and here the manure can be thrown and ploughed in *at once*. This effectually prevents the volatile parts of the manure from flying off into space, and as these are the most valuable portions, the plan is economical as well as efficient. Roughly speaking, it saves about one-quarter of the fertilising power to put the manure into the soil at once. Another advantage is, that it becomes thoroughly mixed with the soil, and the white ants—which invariably follow manure—have ravaged and gone before the seed is put into the ground; whereas, with ground fresh manured, they are certain to do mischief to the crop. Even if the home farm does not supply enough fertiliser for the garden, it is false economy not to purchase elsewhere. It costs just as much to water a bad crop as a good one. Do not trust the *mâli* to ask for manure when wanted. His belief in Providence is too strong for him to be a safe guide; and as he looks on the manure as his perquisite, he will keep the fact of there being none to put on, dark, if possible; though, when driven to a corner, he will be shameless in his demands. It may safely be asserted that garden ground cannot be too well manured; but as this may convey little impression to the mind of the mistress, it may be remarked that the best strawberries the writer ever saw in India were raised on ground manured fifty tons to the acre. Therefore, while it is evident that no fertiliser should be lost from the gardener's point of view, the mistress will find it a convenience in another way, since it is far more wholesome to have refuse thrown on the land at once and ploughed in, than to have it fermenting in heaps about the back premises. The next desideratum is good seed. As a rule, it is better to import from home; at least, such is the experience of the writer. And it is, perhaps, wiser to deal with regular exporters of seeds, such as Carter, Sutton, Cannell, &c.,* than with smaller firms, who have not the experience of sending seeds to India. Haage & Schmidt, however, at Erfurt, Germany,* have excellent and extremely cheap seeds for the main crop, and are accustomed to export. The best results in the writer's experience are obtained when the cold-weather seeds are ordered so as to arrive about the middle of July. Flower seeds should be ordered in a separate tin, as it is well not to open them till the middle of August. And here a strong protest must be entered against the indiscriminate handing over to the *mâli's* tender mercies of the seeds. Most people are aware of the curious Indian dispensation, by which it becomes possible to have a *dâli*, or basket of fresh vegetables, every morning, by simply keeping a gardener, and omitting the apparently more necessary condition of having a garden. In the same way it becomes possible to have a garden, and to have that garden stocked with fair English seeds at almost nominal prices. *Mâli* will produce the seeds from his *bhaibund* (brother craftsmen), who have invariably some mysterious reason for possessing them. Now those who have no desire to encourage social piracy, actively or passively, will do well to give out the seeds packet by packet, or, what is better still, to *see* them sown. If the order to have so many drills ready for such and such seeds is given in the morning, it is no trouble to go round for five minutes in the evening and see the *mâli* sow them. In this way it is possible to ensure a regular rotation of vegetables, and your evil passions will not be roused when, in the pleasant morning saunter round the garden, the *mâli* points with pride to half an acre of French breakfast radishes, saying delightedly that they have all come up, every one, and *Huzoor* had better perhaps get some more of that super-excellent seed! Half an acre of radishes! Equanimity is naturally gone for the day.

The climates of India are so variable, that it is impossible to lay down absolutely what seeds are and are not desirable; but, unless the garden is something more to you than a mere duty or provision, it is well to keep steadily to the more certain kinds of seeds. In choosing these from a seedsman's list, it is also well not to select new and expensive varieties, as the older and cheaper kinds will probably serve your purpose quite as well.

It is also impossible, owing to the variations in climate, to give decided rules as to when certain seeds should be sown; indeed, this varies with almost every station, and certainly with the facility for, and kind of, irrigation. Canal water and congenial soil mean a month's advance over well-water and an unkind soil. The calendar at the end of this chapter will, however, be found suitable for most fair garden soils in Northern India, and the following pages will, it is hoped, supply enough information to enable the mistress to prevent the *mâli* from spoiling good seed. General remarks on the soil, method of sowing, and watering will be given first, and afterwards the cultivation of the commoner vegetable will be treated more in detail.

Soils.—Almost every plant requires a different kind of soil, and it is positively waste of time trying to make a plant grow when its home does not suit it. Luckily the gardener can make the soil, to a large extent, to suit all requirements by adding manure, leaf mould, sand, or clay.

Manure, as has been said before, is best applied fresh to the land. What the native *mâli* calls black earth or *kâla mutti*—a substance like black snuff—is almost inert. What is required is good, half-rotted cow manure. Stable manure in India does very well to put on to the ground day by day when fresh, but is no good for the dung-heap.

The best plan to secure good mould for pots, or mixing, is to half fill a large trench with fallen leaves in January and February, add a few baskets of quicklime and bone dust, cover with fresh cow manure, and flood with water. Next autumn it will be ready for use. It can be sifted through a string bed set up on end. Soils are also to be doctored by adding to them what they want, as, for instance, the addition of sand to stiff clay when carrots are to be grown, or the addition of stiff tank clay or loam to sandy soils. Soil for seed-beds and seed-pans must also vary with the seed to be sown, but the foundation of all is well-rotted, enriched leaf mould, prepared as above. Without a plentiful supply of this it is *useless attempting to grow flowers.*

Another good manure, where a stimulant is wanted, is bone dust. Get the sweeper to collect old bones and have them pounded, buying them from him, if necessary, ready prepared. You will get them very cheap. Some of this may be mixed with soot or charcoal dust, and applied dry to the land; but the best way of using it is by treating it with half its weight in sulphuric acid mixed with its whole weight in water, that is, two *seers* each of bone dust and water to one of sulphuric. Put the dust in a big *hândi* (or earthen vessel), and pour the acid and water over. It will dissolve the bones and make them into a soft paste, which will dry into a powder. A half handful of this, mixed with a large watering-can of water, will be sufficient for about fifty pots, and increase their growth wonderfully. *Reh*, or salt soil, is very difficult to treat, but the best chance lies in washing out the salt, by flooding copiously with water. But, of course, where the *well* is salt, this only increases the evil. Where this is the case, it is best to content oneself with growing plants which stand the salt, a list of which will be given later on.

Sowing.—In all cases, in pots or beds, the soil should be watered first and allowed to dry until it is friable. Seeds should invariably be sown in the evening if out in the open; at any rate, until November shall have reduced the fierce heat of the sun. Every seed requires a different way of sowing, and a varying proportion to the amount of surface sown. This will be given under its own proper heading. Proper labels should not be neglected; and as the expense of ordinary wooden ones is almost nominal in India, there is no excuse for the too common cleft stick with a bit of paper, which the first inquisitive parrot or squirrel makes off with, to the confusion of the sower. If the written side of the label be put underneath, instead of up, the subsequent watering will not wash it out, even if it is written in pencil.

Watering.—Pot seeds are best watered (on a small scale) with a jug. By putting the lip against the edge of the pot, seeds and seedlings can be gently flooded without injury. *Mâli*, however, in his unregenerate state, loves a thunderstorm produced by an ill-conditioned rose. He will thereafter wonder placidly why the seedlings damp off, and, as usual, lay it down to some disastrous combination of the planetary bodies. If the ground has been moistened before sowing, seeds will not require to be watered again for two days, except in very dry weather. Growing vegetables require a great deal of water in India, especially root crops, and at the most vigorous stage of their growth they can scarcely receive too much.

In pot culture, watering is an art dependent entirely on sympathy. One thing should never be forgotten. Rain water, in fact dirty water, is infinitely more satisfactory to pot-plants than pure water. The water from the baths should never be wasted; while cold tea, mixed with water, has a marvellous effect in making geraniums bloom. Indeed, all pot-plants thrive with it, and it is this which makes the cottager's window plants in England so profuse and *brilliant* in bloom. Liquid manure of some kind is always a necessity for pot-plants. A little fresh cow manure and a handful of leaf mould stirred into the water and allowed to settle will materially enrich the water with food for the plant. As a rule, pot-plants in India are starved. Another great fault in India is a waste of ground. Where there is so much to spare, this may seem a trivial mistake, but it is not. It gives an unnecessarily large area to be watered, and this means sheer waste of the *mâli*'s time. He *loves* watering, finding it far easier to sit and drive the bullocks than to hoe and weed; but in the market gardens outside the large towns in India, you will not see one inch of ground vacant. It is far better to have a small garden well cultivated than a vast semi-desert. In India nearly everything is best grown on ridges, to keep the leaves of the plants from being flooded.

Hoeing and Dressing.—In pots the surface of the ground should never be allowed to cake. This is not only to let the air into the roots of the plants and admit the water, but also to let the gases *out* of the soil. It is now well known that plants assimilate almost as much through their leaves as through their roots; therefore, as well-manured soil is always giving out gases charged with volatile atoms, an open surface increases the food supply of the plant. The only exception to the rule is in the case of root crops, such as carrots and beetroots. Here the tendency of the open surface to increase the growth of root is favourable to forking, which is *most* undesirable; therefore, the disadvantages of hoeing may be held to outweigh the advantages.

Transplanting.—Here is the crucial test of a gardener. *Máli* believes his thumb to be all-sufficient for planting, whilst the addition of a forefinger provides him with the best of trowels. With his marvellous trust in Providence, he will sit down contentedly in the sun with a basket of young lettuce plants (plucked up by the roots decisively by the aforesaid finger and thumb), and proceed to slide along in a sitting posture, leaving a curious plantigrade trail behind him, bordered on either side by dejected little plants thrust into the ground by one swift action of his thumbs. That is *his* notion of transplanting; but it must be scouted, trampled on, absolutely exterminated if good vegetables are desired. '*Koi nahin mur ja-éga*' (not one will die), he will say proudly, and possibly none will actually perish. But the check means a month's delay, a month's extra watering, a month of absolutely unnecessary expense. An old teaspoon is a capital transplanter; but it is worth while to purchase for a trifle a French transplanter, as it will amply repay its cost. This instrument is not unlike a pair of sugar-tongs, with a cheese scoop instead of the bowl part. This scoop is sharp-edged, and enters the ground easily. Then by pressing the tongs the earth between the scoops is pressed together, and the plant comes out absolutely unharmed. But whatever means is taken to ensure the desired end—leaving the roots undisturbed—it must be ensured; for vegetables checked in their growth will never recover themselves.

Insects.—Care is the best preservative. Soot and lime does much, but kerosene oil* is incomparably the best for India. Two tablespoons-ful rubbed up with some *bâbool* gum-water, and mixed with two gallons of water, will, if sprinkled over a seed-bed, keep away most insects.

The following list gives brief details of the best way to raise most garden seeds:—

1. *Artichokes* (*Artichuk*).—Sow in seed-beds in August. Soil light-ened by leaf mould, sand, and enriched with manure. Transplant when six inches high into prepared places three feet apart. Manure again in January, and water copiously. It is not necessary to sow seed where plants of a good sort already exist. In such cases strong suckers about fifteen inches high should be cut out of the old roots, taking care to choose those which can be so cut with plenty of young roots. These should be treated as seedlings. Thrive in salt soils, and will stand any quantity of manure.

2. *Jerusalem Artichokes* (*Artipeach*) thrive in sandy light soils well enriched. Plant the tubers in May like potatoes; ridges two and a half feet apart, tubers three inches deep. Once in a garden it is difficult to eradicate them, but it is a mistake to let them grow again from the small tubers left behind in digging the crop. In England, big tubers are selected and planted in rows for next year's crop. This might be done with advantage in India.

3. *Asparagus* (*Pallâgâs*).—Sow in drills in August, each seed about two inches apart; soil highly manured. Transplant in Novem-ber to specially prepared beds. Dig a trench at least four feet deep, two feet wide, and fill up with alternate layers of six-inch well-rotted cow manure, and eight inches garden mould, until the bed is about six inches above the surrounding level; another trench may be dug alongside, just leaving a water channel between. The last two layers of earth and manure should be mixed, and the young plants (or divided old roots) put in about eighteen inches apart. In planting them a large shallow hole should be dug, and the roots spread out carefully in every direction, the object being to get the bed a network of shoot-bearing roots. The crown of the plant should be two inches below the surface. The beds must be kept free of weeds, open, and neatly dressed to two feet wide; and twice a year top-dressings should be given. As aspara-gus beds have to last for several years, it is well in making them to work in a good quantity of ground bones, as this is the most lasting of

all manures. The results will surprise those accustomed to the usual green tendrils called '*pallâgâs*' by the *mâli*.

4. *Broad Beans (Sêm).*—Sow in September in rows on ridges. One seed every four inches. Soil fairly rich, and very well worked. It is better in many ways to sow in a seed-bed, and transplant when two inches high, as in this way you are certain of germination. Earth up once or twice, and nip back the top shoot to make the flowers set. The first flowers seldom *do* set in India. The refuse chalk from soda-water machines is good for a bean manure.

5. *French Beans (Belâti Sêm)* give trouble, but are natives of India. As a rule, they are sown out of season. They will not stand any cold, therefore they must either be sown in July and sheltered from the frost, or be sown in a hot bed in February and transplanted. The dwarf kind is said to bear six weeks after sowing, but the writer has never been successful with them except in the hills.

6. *Beetroot (Chuckunda).*—One of the most easily grown vegetables. Thrives in a salt soil. Sow in drills where it is to remain, dropping one seed into holes four inches apart. A pinch of soot and dried fowl manure in each hole makes the seed germinate better. Each seed produces three plants, and must be thinned out to one. The others will transplant, but are not so good generally. The ground for beetroot should be deeply trenched, or the roots will branch. Birds eat the young plants, which are just the colour of the ground. The seed germinates in three days.

7. *Cabbages, Broccoli, Cauliflower, Kale (Gobi, Phool Gobi).*—All require about the same treatment. Sow, beginning in July, in seed-beds well manured; quarter ounce seed is sufficient for a bed 4 feet by 5 feet sown broadcast. When the plants show their fifth leaf, transplant to a seedling bed three inches apart. Again transplant five inches apart finally, when sticky and strong, to the ground. All the cabbage tribe are gross feeders, and it is therefore best to manure the hole for each plant separately, as it would take too much to manure the whole field. The cabbage tribe require constant earthing up, and each time manure should be added. The seed germinates in three days.

8. *Carrots (Gâjer)* are most uncertain germinators, and in market gardens at home the seed is always germinated before being put into the ground, by being put in a warm place in a box mixed with a very little wetted sand. In this country the seed will sometimes lie for six weeks in the ground, and as the insects are very fond of it, the English

plan might be tried with advantage. Trench the ground to three feet at least, and mix with sand and leaf mould, and sow in drills nine inches apart. Thin out twice; once when about six inches high, and again for immediate use. Carrots *do not like* a freshly-manured land. If the seed is germinated on wet sand, it should only be allowed to 'chip'; that is, to show a white streak, not to send out a germ. It should then be gently mixed with dry sand and sown; about half an ounce should be sufficient for four rows twenty feet long.

9. *Celery* (*Celari*).—Sow in July in boxes or pans, and prick out when about two inches high; four plants in a pot. Give incessant attention to ensure rapid growth, for on this depends the success of celery. When strong, vigorous, young plants, at least six inches high, they may be put in the open; but unless great care can be given, it is best to put the plants in single pots for a fortnight or three weeks more, especially for the first crop. The easiest way of planting celery out is to dig a row of circular holes about six inches apart. They should be nine inches across, and at least a foot deep. Fill to within three inches of the top with a mixture of two parts rotten manure to one of earth. Water the plants constantly with liquid manure, and when they have come to maturity, *not before*, earth up and blanch for a fortnight. The art of celery-growing consists in rapid, continuous growth, gained by well-rotted old manure and leaf mould. The best soil for growing celery is made by mixing old manure with water and a little mould to a thick paste, putting it first in the pan, and over that half an inch of finest leaf mould mixed with sand and a little charcoal dust. Celery plants should be pricked out in a similar composition. Fresh manure is *not* to be applied, save mixed with water as liquid manure. Celery may be sown in March, and the young plants kept through the summer will come on rapidly when the cold season begins. But they are apt to be stringy.

10. *Cucumbers* (*Keera*)—*Kukrees* and cucumbers grow lavishly, and give no trouble anywhere. But they may be had a month earlier by sowing in a hot bed in January. Require well-rotted manure. English seed grows well, but the flowers sometimes fail to set unless artificially hybridised. The native cucumbers are, however, excellent, and the *Kukree* or downy cucumber is an unjustly neglected vegetable, being far more wholesome than the cucumber.

11. *Egg Plant* (*Brinjâl, Baingun*).—Leave this to the *mâli*. He understands it; but insist on having a supply from April to November.

12. *Endive (Salâde).*—Treat as for lettuce; but before cutting for table, endive must be blanched. Gather the plant together with one hand, and tie round about three inches from the top. Earth over with *dry* earth, or put a pot over. In six days they will be ready, and in ten they will begin to spoil, so do not earth too many at a time. Stewed endive is as good as sea-kale, but few people know it.

13. *Lettuce (Salâde).*—Begin trial-sowings in August, and continue every fortnight till February. Sow in pans protected from ants, as they are very partial to lettuce seed. The soil should be a mixture of old manure, leaf mould, and sand. The seeds sometimes take a long time germinating. Prick out the young seedlings, when they have four leaves, into very rich shady beds, and transplant again into the open. The object in all salad-plants is to secure rapid growth, and yet check the tendency to run to seed. This can only be effected by *careful* transplanting and the *richest* of soils. Briefly, endive and lettuces cannot be too highly manured, or too often hoed and weeded. The *mâli*'s pet plan of pulling seedlings up by the roots cannot be allowed. Lettuces need a good deal of water. If the seed sown is good, there should be no need of tying up, as the plants should heart of themselves. In England, at the approach of winter, lettuce and endive crops are taken bodily up by the roots, and packed away with earth and sand in dark sheds, where they keep for months. It would be interesting to try this during the summer in India. Lettuces should be planted along the spaces between other vegetables and by water-courses. They do better singly, and it saves space.

14. *Melons (Kurbooza).*—English melons grow perfectly if sown in heat in January. The *mâli* understands melons very well as a rule.

15. *Onions (Peeâj).*—Leave to the *mâli*; if he can grow anything, it is an onion.

16. *Peas (Mutter).*—The rows should be single, at least twenty feet apart, leaving room for a strip of other vegetables between each, and the direction should be invariably from north to south. The row should be dug about eighteen inches deep and at least eighteen inches wide. Good leaf manure should be forked into it, and the whole watered. About two days after it will be fit for sowing. Good pea-growers plant each seed singly, like beans; but even if sown in drills, one pint of peas should sow a row thirty yards long. The *mâli* will use twice that quantity, and insist on a double row. Do not listen to him. For early peas it is best to sow in seed-beds, and transplant when four inches high. This is done in all the

nurseries at home, and it is said vastly to improve the yield of the pea. It is of great advantage in India to have all the first crops and seeds near the well, so that they may be carefully watched and tended together. The seed should be sown at least three inches deep for large peas. With decent management peas should be on the table from November till the first week in May, as sowings may be made every week, and some of the rows kept back from flowering by judicious stopping. Peas require earthing up, and a top dressing of fowl manure is of great benefit.

17. *Radishes* (*Moli*).—The *máli* loves those that run eight to the pound, and his soul delights in half an acre of them. Therefore, give him fifty seeds to plant every three days throughout the season, and in this way, and this way *alone*, you will checkmate him, and enjoy first-class radishes from September till May without a break. Never prepare a special bed for radishes, but put the seeds in between rows of carrots or lettuces, or anywhere there is room. This saves both space and watering. The best radishes are undoubtedly the common French breakfast radish.

18. *Spinach* (*Sâg*) requires to be sown in a light soil not too freshly manured. The seed is best steeped in water for twenty-four hours before being sown, and one ounce should sow one hundred and fifty feet of drill. The ground cannot be too highly manured, and a plentiful supply of liquid manure, made of soot and pigeon's dung, may be given with advantage. The white beet spinach is most useful in India, giving a continuous supply from November to May. It is best sown in seed-beds, and transplanted into drills eighteen inches apart. It cannot be too highly manured.

19. *Tomatoes* (*Belâtee Baingun*) thrive splendidly. Sow in June, July, and August in seed-beds, and transplant when two inches high into well-manured beds. Thence they may be removed when six inches high to the open; plant in rows about two feet apart, or what is better, make ridges two feet broad and plant on either edge. As the plants grow, bend branches or bamboos across the ridge like hoops, and train the tomatoes against them. Any attempt to stick tomatoes at a later period will result in snapping off the best shoots, while the fruit will never grow so well when the plant is prostrate. Get the *best* seed for tomatoes; they are worth it.

20. *Turnips* (*Sulgam*) require a light soil, and do well where other vegetables would starve. Sow in drills, and weed out to six inches apart; the weedings, if carefully planted, do very well in India.

21. *Parsley (Petercelli), &c.*—Parsley may be kept in pots all the year round, and the curled varieties are really pretty in the verandah. Always have parsley, thyme, and marjoram amongst the pot-plants, and, if possible, chervil. Omelets and salads will gain thereby.

The following is a brief calendar for the kitchen garden, beginning with July, when the first English seeds should be put down.

July.—Sow first sowings of the cabbage tribe, also celery and tomatoes. Continue sowings of hot-weather vegetables, and sow Cape gooseberry and roselle. Bud orange tribe, also roses, including peaches, plums, &c. Manure and earth up Jerusalem artichokes.

August.—Continue sowing cabbage tribe. Sow artichokes, asparagus, and tomato. Begin trial sowings of lettuce, spinach, and beetroot; also, if the season is favourable, a row or two of peas may be put in a sheltered spot.

September is a very busy month. Regular sowing of radishes should be commenced, also mustard and cress, &c. Towards the middle of the month the whole first crop of peas, turnips, carrots, beetroot, onions, spinach, &c., should be in the ground, and from this time fortnightly sowing should go on till the middle of December. Roses should be pruned in the last week of September, and strawberry plants put out.

October.—Every kind of English seed may now be sown, and the gardener needs to be at work all day to keep pace with the growth of his seedlings and get them into the ground. Irrigation must be constant, and plentiful food given to the young plants in the way of manure. It is also the season for making up the paths and trimming the garden generally. If help is wanted, October is the month for the extra coolie. Sow barley for cattle.

November.—Sowings as before, and careful thinning out of beetroots, carrots, and turnips. In the middle of the month cease watering fruit trees and lay open the roots. Put down rose cuttings and those of the orange tribe. Sow barley for cattle.

December.—Peas, turnips, and lettuce may still be sown till the middle of the month, but the germination will be slow. Figs, grapes, peaches, &c., should be pruned, and the open roots, exposed last month, covered in with manured soil. This should be done at the very end of the month.

January.—Sow cucumbers and squashes in hot-beds for early crop, and continue sowings of radishes, cress, and small turnips.

Water and manure well towards end of the month to stimulate spring growth.

February.—Sow squashes, cucumbers, and melons in the open ground, and sowings of native spinach and other vegetables for early crop, especially *brinjâls*. Make sowings of parsley in pots for the hot weather.

March.—Remove old soil from asparagus, cover with old manure, and water. Plentifully manure artichokes and plantains. Continue sowings of hot-weather vegetables.

April.—Begins the dead months; but the first crop of *brinjâls*, cucumbers, &c., should be fruiting, and tomatoes be in full swing. Now is the time for bird-boys and scarecrows, as mangoes, plums, pears, pomegranates, &c., are swelling. Sow millet for the cattle.

May.—Sow maize and millet for the cattle. Plant Jerusalem artichokes and ginger. This is the summer of discontent* in an Indian garden, and the gardener's mind must be given up to watering the plants he has raised.

June.—The same. Keep what you have got as well as you can.

Lawns.—Grass can be grown anywhere with care, if there is a supply of water; therefore, the horrid Indian flower-garden, consisting of mud cart-wheels, divided into contortions by ridiculous little mud paths, should never be countenanced. To secure a good lawn, have the ground manured and levelled; water, level again, and then plaster over with the following composition: Chopped *doob* grass with plenty of roots one part, fresh cow manure one part, earth two parts, mixed into a mortar with water. This never fails with good watering. It is most successful in the rainy months, and least from November to February, when the cold prevents the grass sprouting. If bald patches come on a lawn, manure with liquid manure, and sprinkle with a mixture of sand and *soorki* (red brick dust), or ashes, and water morning and evening with a watering-can. In short, *make the grass grow*. Twice a year top-dress the lawn with leaf mould and fresh manure. Then *flood* with water. When dry, remove the rubbish and make neat. It is also good to loosen the roots once a year with a three-pronged fork. Treated thus, the lawn will be a pride to its owner.

Beds.—To grow good flowers, beds must be like large pots, full of good pot mould, each varying with the flower to be grown in it. They should be raised two inches above the grass, so as just to escape flooding.

Pots.—Pots should be shallow in proportion to their breadth, and are best with three holes, not at the bottom, but close to it on the sides. Lump charcoal is the best substratum. In sowing seeds the earth should previously be well wetted with water, and rubbed up to an even friable state with the hands and put into the pots damp. The pots should not be filled with dry powdery earth and then watered on the top; nor should the pots be quite full of earth. In repotting herbaceous plants, it must be remembered that only those which have *filled* the pot with roots require it; and that repotting should only be done when the plant is beginning its most vigorous growth, the object being to supply it with *more food*. The best soil for pots in India is well enriched leaf mould, garden mould, and well-rotted manure mixed together, and more or less sand added according to the plant for which it is required.

Frames are seldom seen in India, though in the north they are of immense use. The best way to make one is to dig a pit six feet long by three broad and four deep. Fill it with fresh stable manure up to three feet. With large (what are called D. P. W.) bricks* build a low wall round, about seven inches high in front, and a foot at the back. One row of bricks will do, set in mud. Make a movable framework of *bamboo-jâfri*, or lattice-work, and thatch with grass. Water the pit well, and when hot, plunge the pots into the manure, covering with the thatch at night. This will be sufficient to induce vigorous growth to young seedlings, and to bring up cucumbers, &c. The writer once took half the flower prizes at a show by being three weeks in advance of other competitors owing to these simple frames. The bricks can be used over and over again.

Flower Seeds.—Always sow them yourself, and use your common-sense, remembering that most small seeds are better for a glass over them till they germinate, and that they require a very fine, sandy soil. Always date the labels, so that you may know when to expect the seeds to come up. Prick out into small pots as soon as possible, and again transplant into single pots.

As a rule, a seedling is ready to prick into the first pots when it has four leaves, and into the second pots as soon as it looks sturdy. Heartsease are the better for transplantation every ten days. In regard to the special treatment of special flowers, the authors can only refer the reader to a regular manual on gardening. All that is aimed at here is to supply sufficient information to enable some flowers to be grown with a fair chance of success. *Mâli-jee* will tell you that seedlings are as well put straight from the seed pans into the beds, and he certainly tells truth when he says they will not die. Indeed, where the object is simply to have some sort of blossom, his plan answers admirably; but if the desire is to grow blossoms good of their kind, anything likely to check the growth must be avoided. In the quick soil of India, under the vivifying sun, much may be left to nature, but in that case the true gardening instinct remains ungratified, and the grower feels no pride in the perfection of his plants.

The sowing time for English seeds varies immensely with the latitude; but, roughly speaking, it is unwise to begin sowings before August, or to continue them beyond October. Flower seeds are best ordered in a separate box from the vegetable seeds, which require to be opened out earlier.

The following brief calendar may prove useful, especially in Northern India:—

July.—Trial sowings of acclimatised heartsease, gloxinias, and begonias.

August.—Asters, heartsease, and cinerarias; also nasturtiums, Indian pinks, marigolds, and stocks.

September.—First half, trial sowings; second half, regular sowings of most annuals, except larkspur, nemophila, lobelia.

October.—First half, sow every seed you possess.

As a rule, it is best in July and August to give trial sowings only, as much depends on the season.

Always transplant in the evening and shade next day if necessary.

The following annuals and plants grow well without any trouble with good soil and water:—

1. Antirrhinum.	12. Convolvulus major.
2. Alyssum.	13. Calliopsis.
3. Bellis perennis.	14. Delphinums.
4. Calendula.	15. Dianthus.
5. Candytuft.	16. Eschscholtzia.
6. Centaurea.	17. Fever-few.
7. Chrysanthemums, Summer.	18. Forget-me-not.
8. Cineraria.	19. Gaillardia.
9. Clarkia.	20. Godetia.
10. Clianthus.	21. Helichrysum.
11. Coleus.	22. Hollyhock.

23. Ice plant.
24. Linum.
25. Lobelia.
26. Lupins.
27. Mathiola.
28. Mesembryanthemum.
29. Mignonette.
30. Mimulus.
31. Nasturtiums.
32. Nemophila.
33. Pansy.
34. Poppies.
35. Pea, Sweet.
36. Petunia.
37. Phlox.
38. Portulacca.
39. Salpiglossis.
40. Salvia.
41. Scabious.
42. Schizanthus.
43. Stock.
44. Sunflower.
45. Sweet William.
46. Tagetes.
47. Verbena.
48. Wallflower.

Besides most herbaceous plants, such as heliotrope, geraniums, ferns. The cannas do splendidly, especially the new dwarf kinds.

In salt soils it is still possible to have the garden gay with the following plants and annuals that will thrive anywhere: Marigolds, sunflowers, mesembryanthemum, daisies, centaurea, summer chrysanthemums, Indian pinks, ice plant, mathiola, stocks, nasturtiums, poppies, sweet peas, verbenas, wallflower, rose-periwinkles, cannas, &c. &c.

General Remarks on Flowers.—It would take a whole book to give anything like a manual of what ought and ought not to be done. To be brief, the matter resolves itself into this: If you love flowers, you will manage to grow them almost anywhere. If you do not, what use is there in growing them? Nothing makes an Indian house look so home-like and cheerful as a verandah full of blossoming plants, and hung with baskets of ferns. And it is besides an endless amusement and pleasure. All that is required is a little personal supervision, and the recollection that these mute dependents of yours are as liable to starvation, neglect, and consequent death as 'the cattle and the stranger that are within your gates.'* Silent as flowers may be in complaint, they are eloquent in their gratitude, and their blossoming service of praise will make your home a pleasant resting-place for tired eyes. And *how* tired eyes can be of dull, dusty, 'unflowerful ways,'* only those can really know who have spent long years in the monotonous plains of Northern India. There, it seems to the writer, the garden is not merely a convenience or a pleasure, it is a duty.

CHAPTER XII

HINTS ON CAMP LIFE

THE days of real camp life are, it is to be feared, numbered, as, what with railways, district bungalows,* &c., to say nothing of the greater pressure of revenue and other works, most officials, finding they have not time for the leisurely tours of other days, make hurried rushes out to specific places. But there is still sufficient camping left to render a few hints as to the method of doing it comfortably necessary in a book on housekeeping.

First, in regard to tents.

Whether these are supplied by Government or not, it is equally necessary to make them comfortable. The ordinary single pole tent is twice as convenient if it is divided down the centre with a pole and curtains so as to screen off the beds; while, if the inner *kunnât* on the side used as a drawing-room is divided just at the central door and thrown back to the outer *kunnât* (like a bow window), the stove can be placed in the tent, and will thoroughly warm it, whilst in the daytime the bow makes a charming, *light* place for writing or working. All that is wanted to make it perfect, beyond unpicking the join at the door, is a small *durri* to fit the bow, and a roof to match the inner fly of the tent. This is made to lace on with eyelet holes. By having two strips of *kunnât* with perpendicular bamboos, the two bits of verandah on either side can be turned into safe places for the *khitmutgâr*'s table, as by a simple arrangement of tapes and ties no dog can get in. In the same way capital bathrooms can be made on the other side, by closing the verandah in with permanent tight-fitting *kunnâts* on the side nearest the sitting-room, and having curtains on poles and rings at the other. How some people can go on for years and years with the makeshift *purdah*—hung by a string—that jams its horizontal bamboo into the sides of the tent when you desire to pass, and invariably refuses to fill up the space when you desire it to do so, is a mystery. In fact, the first axiom for camp is not to do without comfort, if it does not entail discomfort by increasing the trouble. A comfortable tent is no heavier than an uncomfortable one, and furniture suited to camp life is generally lighter than ordinary furniture. Charming folding tables of bamboo and deodar* can be made for Rs. 2 each, and folding scissors or lazy-jane clothes-racks are to be bought anywhere for a rupee. Add two iron hooks to hang them over the *kunnât*, and you are possessed of hat or clothes pegs. A plain wooden cover for the bath, with three screw-legs to pack inside, gives you an excellent hold-all for boots, &c., and a far better washhand-stand than the usual dreadful gallows construction, which leaves you in doubt whether to put your soap in your pocket or allow it to melt in the basin.

It is another camp axiom that not a single box should be carried that has not a use even when empty. For instance, if thin deal boxes divided into two or three partitions are given to the *khitmutgârs* to pack inside the *kujâwahs* or camel panniers, the china will travel far more safely, and the boxes can be set upon end and used as cupboards.

To begin, however, systematically. The mistress will find it convenient to have a pair of light camel trunks for clothes, books, &c. A charming kind is made exactly like a chest of drawers, the removable fronts being convertible into trestle dressing-tables. It is a great saving of trouble only to have to pull out your drawers instead of uprooting from the bottom of a huge trunk. For stores she will find it best to have a box made and fitted with square tin canisters. A few cane chairs with wadded covers, little tables and tablecloths, and a shelf or two will give a home look to the sitting tent. It will be found also a *great* advantage to have strips of matting for the verandahs. They weigh little and cost a trifle. A square of mackintosh for soap, sponge, &c., is far more useful than a sponge-bag, and it will be found a great saving of trouble to have all these things—towels, basin, &c.—packed in your bath, so that they shall be ready for you on arrival.

If there are children, iron cots will be found the best beds, as by hanging shawls round draughts can be kept off. Bedding may either be rolled up in hold-alls, or, what is perhaps more convenient where folding-beds are not used, left on the bed and covered over with mackintosh sheeting. For comfort in marching in the plains a strong string charpoy is decidedly the best bed, as it rests capitally across a camel's load.

In the cook-room too much ingenuity in devising little conveniences cannot be employed. A pair of string *kujâwars* is the best form of package, and should be ample for all requirements. They should be double-storeyed; that is, with a removable shelf half-way down, and should have wooden covers that lock, and thus allow the *kujâwars* to be used as cupboards. Saucepans should fit in nests, and square tins with lids should be used for all kinds of supplies.

The best oven for camp is a plain round sheet-iron drum, with a lid like a frying-pan. Supported by three bricks, and with dry earth heaped round, it bakes admirably; or an oven can be made thus: Dig a hole of two feet deep and one and a half feet wide in a dry spot. Half fill with sand. When required, fill up with burning sticks and cover over with the top of an ordinary oven. When sufficiently heated, remove the fuel and put in the cake to be baked. The same fire will do for laying on the top of the cover. This oven bakes a three-pound cake in as many hours. Meat safes of mosquito net with iron wire hoops to keep them expanded must not be forgotten. An old umbrella covered with a bag of mosquito net does admirably. Hot water for baths only needs a row of earthen *choolâs* and *ghurras*. The great difficulty is a larder, but a square framework like a folding-bed, consisting of four legs and four bamboos which fit into holes in the legs, will, with a well-fitting cover of mosquito net, be found very useful. Placed on a table, and the net left long enough to draw in with a runner under the top of the table, it makes an absolutely secure milk or meat larder.

The *khitmutgârs* should, as before stated, have thin partitioned boxes for china. Toughened glass will be found an immense comfort. The silver should be carried in baize or flannel hold-alls with flaps, like instrument cases; each spoon and fork fitted into its own band or pocket. Knives in a separate case. In addition to the safety, this enables the *khit* to see at a glance if the tale is complete.

The best lamps for camp are Hitchcock's patent,* because they require neither globe nor chimney, though a shade may be used. Kerosene oil is now to be had in almost every village, therefore it is not necessary to take such elaborate precautions against running out of it as in the old days. The best way of carrying it is in regular tin canisters, such as go with the D. P. W.* lantern. It is a mistake, however, to go into extravagance in the matter of lanterns, since admirable ones, quite hurricane-proof, are to be had in the Delhi bazaar, and it is to be presumed elsewhere, for three rupees.

A regular supply of bread, butter, and vegetables is apt to be a common difficulty; but as a rule the former can be got out from headquarters at intervals, and at the worst bread can be made which is more wholesome, if not quite so spongy, as the baker's efforts. Nor should butter fail, for if you keep cows it is better to let them go into camp with you. If the march is done in the morning it is best to send the cow on half-way immediately after the evening's milking, say, at half-past five. By this means she gets over half the journey at the best time, *i.e.*, when the udder is dry, and rests and eats all night. Next morning at six the cowman should milk her and start off for the remainder of his journey, arriving about nine o'clock, carrying the milk in the pail. Or, if the march is done in the evening, the same plan may be adopted, beginning in the morning. The object in a rest half-way is to give the cow time to chew the cud, which she will never do unless she is at rest; indeed, it is a good plan to make the cowman take a bundle or basket of prepared forage with him, and feed the cow at least once on the road, halting for the purpose for an hour. Treated thus, a cow will not go off her milk at all, and of course it is not often that she will have to march every day. It will be seen, therefore, that it is possible to set half the day's milk for twenty-four hours and half for twelve, even when actually on the march, so there should be no difficulty in making butter; but if the twelve hours' stand does not throw up sufficient cream, it is quite easy to set it for milk butter in a jar. Swung to a camel, the butter will often be found ready made in the jar at the end of the march.

Vegetables are the chief difficulty, unless they can be had regularly from headquarters; nevertheless, they are not absolutely unobtainable anywhere, and they are certainly a necessity of life. Failing other things, country carrots are excellent stewed with gravy, or sliced and served up like beetroot with vinegar and oil. The spinach made from fresh gram leaves or turnip tops is also good; while country turnips, well mashed, the water squeezed from them by means of a cloth-wringer, and fresh milk, butter, salt, and pepper added, lose nearly all their paint-like taste. In addition, white haricot beans and Chollet's compressed vegetables* can always be taken in the store-box.

In regard to other supplies, the difficulty in procuring them depends entirely on your position. The district officials have none, while a mere globe-trotter may starve. It is merely a matter of coercion, for the peasant does not wish to sell, and will *not* sell, if he thinks it polite to refuse. This fact should never be forgotten by the mistress, for it is easy to understand how fearful a weapon for oppression that appalling necessity of camp life, the *tâhseel chuprassi*, or *tâhseel* office orderly, may become.

That he is necessary in the present state of civilisation few will deny; if they feel inclined to doubt it, let them go into a village with a large camp, and see for themselves. They will be exceptionally fortunate if they can get even grass for their horses. As long, therefore, as the present system lasts, one of the chief duties of the mistress in camp is to see, as far as in her lies, that no oppression is committed in her name. How hopeless it is to expect absolute success the authors have learned by long experience; still something can be done, and should be done. Not long ago the *khansâmah* said to one of the authors, 'You make a fuss, *mem sahib*, because three *seers* of milk went into the cook-room this morning; go and look in the *munshi khana*[1]—you will find five *ghurras* full.' And it was true. Some people are content with paying the *chuprassi*, or even the head men; but this is a farce. Insist on an owner being produced, and though in the curiously appropriate idiom of the country it will possibly be a case of '*Mâlik bunwâna*' (Cause an owner to be made), you will at least have done your best to get at the right man. *Du reste;** it is impossible to help those who will not help themselves; and if, when you arrive in a new camp, you send for the shopkeepers and the general supplier and warn them that *you* pay for everything, and that without your order nothing is to be given in camp, the responsibility no longer lies on your shoulders.

In regard to the time of marching, people with children often find it more convenient to march in the afternoon, and in some ways it is easier for the servants. When, however, the breadwinner has outdoor work, as, for instance, in the case of a revenue or canal officer—in fact, of all officers in civil employ—the morning is the best time; for much of his work is sure to lie *en route*, and would necessitate his starting almost in the heat of the day if it is to be done in the afternoon. The great charm of camp, too, the early morning ride, is lost; but in this matter personal convenience has to be consulted. The only difficulty of marching in the morning, viz., the servants' broken rest, is easily reduced to a minimum. One man in turn goes on ahead with one set of *kujâwars*, leaving two men behind to pack up the dinner things and start at daybreak. Or all the equipage can start in charge of one table-servant over night, and the others rise early and

[1] Office tent.

overtake them. But with either camels or carts the native manages to sleep *en route* comfortably enough, especially if he is off duty, and this can easily be managed by putting the servants in charge by turns.

If marching in the morning is the rule, it is an art to leave nothing out except the clothes you are to put on, the bedding, and, in the cook-room, the materials for early morning tea. With children, however, a large kettle and a medicine chest should remain behind.

In regard to stores, it is well to take as few as possible, especially tinned provisions, but do not make yourself uncomfortable for want of things to which you are accustomed.

That is the great secret of camp life.

CHAPTER XIII

HINTS TO MISSIONARIES AND OTHERS LIVING IN CAMP AND JUNGLES

AMONG missionaries, the itinerating mission and the village mission* are now much more resorted to than formerly; while Government is making railways and canals in many directions through sandy wastes and sparsely populated tracts. Thus, in many cases, small parties of our countrymen (and often the solitary bachelor) have to live as best they can at a distance from any station. It is for the benefit of such that this chapter has been written by one of the authors, as a supplement to that on Camp Life.

It is proposed to take account first of the food and drink that is necessary to the proper sustenance of the body, then of lodging as regards living in tents or houses, and lastly, of clothing and bedding, merely as they affect the welfare of the body, and protect it from malaria.

Food is placed first, because practical, experimental knowledge of missionaries leads to a belief that missionaries, as a rule, think it of no consequence—if not worldly or derogatory to their spiritual calling—to give a thought to anything so commonplace. But a regular supply of good and nourishing food is absolutely necessary to repair the wear and tear of tissues involved in their work, and besides acts as a pure prophylactic against malaria and fever. Yet often men and women engaged in severe work, rising early and taking rest late, truly eat the bread of sorrows* in the form of greasy, unpalatable, badly-cooked food, and then are grievously disappointed at being ordered home at once by some doctor who has not the patience to point out that the real root of the disease lay, not in the climate, nor in their work, but in the neglect of the common necessities of our condition, viz., food, rest, sleep. The secret of successful economical work, says an article in the *Civil and Military Gazette*,* should be to work within the limits of repair, as indicated by sound sleep and healthy appetite; and it has been rightly said that food and sleep are as essential to the work of the brain, as fire and water to the progress of the locomotive.

Both also are intimately connected; simple, well-cooked food will produce a clear brain and good general health, and, consequently, sound sleep.

Again, any exertion on an empty stomach has an exhausting effect, and predisposes to fever. Some day you return from your work tired, and perhaps saddened and disheartened; had you started after a simple, comfortable meal, and, after three or four hours' work, returned to find another such awaiting you, the whole aspect of affairs would have been changed. You have been living on the *principal* rather than on the interest of your constitution.

And so food comes first and foremost as essential in keeping brain and body in working order. And the food must be good and nourishing, not a crowd of dishes, sloppy weak soup and tea, hashes and stews warmed up perhaps three or four times, producing biliousness, irritability, and a clogged brain; but a nicely cooked small meal of country produce, which even a missionary, having to live with care as to expense, can procure. For instance, take the case of a person living alone. A native servant cooks the whole fowl or joint at once, and eases his conscience by serving them up again and again. Instead of which a fowl should be halved, one portion used as a stew, the other half will make cutlets or curry, &c., and there need be no warming up. A leg of mutton can be cut into three parts—a nice mock steak from the thick end served up with an onion fried and sliced and placed over it, the centre piece can be baked, the bone taken out and stuffing inserted, and the remaining knuckle end can either be boiled or stewed, whilst from the bone which has been removed sufficient marrow can be obtained to make an appetising snack in the form of marrow toast. When fish is procurable, instead of always frying it, a nice change can be obtained by placing it in a pie-dish with a batter of flour, eggs, and milky seasoning, and then baking it. Eggs are abundant in villages, and very nourishing; but for milk a cow should be purchased; it thrives on the march, gives no trouble, and repays its food by supplying good milk and butter, so necessary to the enjoyment of a cup of tea, a good pudding, a soda-scone, or a slice of cake. Rice flour, wheat, Indian corn, *dâl* (lentils), turnips, and onions are to be found in most villages; fowls, eggs, lambs, kids in many. In the cold season meat, if taken out after the march and hung from the pole of the kitchen tent, quickly dries, and will keep fourteen days. If, therefore, a small sheep or lamb be killed, the head, feet, and bones will make soup for some time; one leg can be corned to imitate salt beef, the suet should be collected for pies and puddings and frying, and the brains, liver, and kidneys utilised to furnish breakfast dishes. Salt beef, if carried in a small wooden tub of pickle with a lid, will keep for weeks. Bread made with baking powder is far more whole-some than the baker's bread—of small stations, at least—when the yeast or bread-sponge, if left thirty-six hours, becomes a sour, almost putrid mass. Ordinary native *chupâtties*, made of good wheat freshly ground and mixed with one-third of *atta* which has been re-ground and sifted, are also very agreeable, a heaped-up tablespoonful mak-ing a good-sized *chupâtti*. With porridge and new milk scones, and fresh butter or home-made jam or treacle, and one or more of the dishes for breakfast, the worker can start on his work refreshed. If he goes some distance, and cannot return for a mid-day meal, many of the dishes recommended can be eaten cold. Savoury omelets cut in slices and laid between pieces of bread and butter, with a seasoning of mustard, pepper, and salt, make excellent sandwiches, and these, with the addition of a little cold rice shape and stewed bazaar fruit, easily carried in a cup, make a simple but sufficient lunch. No excuse then for faintness or headache, 'because, you know, our work did not permit us to think of eating.'

The supply-box already spoken of should contain tea, cocoa, sugar, home-made jam and treacle, biscuits, dried fruits, arrowroot, soap, candles, blacking, &c. &c., which supplement what is obtainable in the villages. Ten minutes spent daily with the cook, arranging for three comfortable meals, between the supply-box, what can be obtained on the spot, and butcher's meat, would be well spent.

Recipes for cooking with things obtainable in the villages will be found in the Cook's Guide. Indian meal makes a change in bak-ing bread, and from its *bhootas* (or seeds) delicious fritter, sweet or savoury, can be made; or the seeds taken off with a fork and boiled, and eaten with salt, pepper, and a little butter, are excellent. Country turnips, so abundant, can be used in various ways; and if two ounces of *dâl* be added to the recipe for mashed turnips in camp life, and all baked together, an excellent substitute for potatoes is obtained. Wheat can be also made use of in various ways, notably in the dish of our ancestors, which consisted of wheat soaked overnight, boiled till it cracks open, and eaten with sugar, honey, milk, or treacle. For breakfast, porridge can be made from wheat, *dulya*, *sujee*, Indian corn (polenta), &c. Oatmeal can be brought out in bulk from England cheaply, if substituted for sawdust in packing glass, bottles, &c., and is a food supplying brain and muscle, heat and force. Rice is a pure food when eaten with *dâl*, milk, or eggs. Milk and eggs are chemically perfect foods. Fresh fruit at breakfast is good, and stewed dried bazaar fruit is easily procured, portable, and wholesome.

Some missionaries prefer doing their own cooking with a portable stove, and this may have its advantages; still it would be an economy of time and strength to keep a respectable servant, as meals prepared by oneself are seldom enjoyed.

Next as to drink. In order to obtain pure drinking water, a portable Syphon Carbon Filter is the simplest; it merely requires to be scraped in order to clean it. After breakfast, two *degchas* of boiled water should be brought, and the filter thrown into each successively. One of the party must draw the tube, and then the water will run clear into bottles, kettles, &c. Village tank water should be avoided. If none other can be had, boil it, add sulphuric acid in the proportion of eight drops to the pint, and then filter it. When the camp marches at night, filtered water for breakfast should always be sent on with it. In warm weather let a common basket filled with wetted grass be fastened to a tree by a rope, place bottles of water, milk, butter-pot, &c., in it, see that it is well covered up and frequently wetted and constantly swung. A delicious coolness will thus be produced. A recipe is given for portable lemonade; but aerated waters are productive of thirst, and give rise to uncomfortable sensations. Plain lime juice and water— barley-water acidulated—tamarind (*Imli*) water occasionally, cold tea, all form good drinks for allaying thirst. Tea, coffee, and cocoa partake of the nature of stimulants; and though it would be hard to forbid what is the greatest refreshment and comfort to water-drinkers, yet it must be borne in mind that they stimulate the brain and nerves, producing over-action, causing a forgetfulness of fatigue, and thus an overtax of the powers, the consequence being perhaps a severe attack of neuralgia, which prostrates us, or, if warnings are neglected, worse disease in the end. *Ghurras* (earthen jars) are a source of trouble in camp. They may be entirely dispensed with, if empty kerosene oil tins are taken instead, with the top neatly cut off and handle attached. Those of the cook-room can be filled on the march with the kitchen odds and ends. Bath water can be heated and brought into the tent in one; the *syces* can soak their gram in another, and use it for a stable bucket. If a few are turned into canisters and provided with hasps and padlocks, they can serve instead of a supply-box.

With regard to utilising a *tâhseel chuprassi* in procuring supplies. Such an official makes the Civil Officer* a terror to the villagers, who look upon his camp as a flight of locusts, as fowls, eggs, ghee, milk, &c., are seized in the Sahib's name, one never knows to what extent. But villagers are not, as a rule, agreeable to strangers, and often do not understand the use of money. A lady in a large Survey camp used to sit and talk kindly with the women, who would often bring her offerings of honey, eggs, &c., while they would barter anything for beads, combs, or looking-glasses.

When a camp halts it may often be feasible to utilise the camel-men and camels in bringing in supplies of wood and grass when these come from any distance.

For others than missionaries it need only be added that if they find their servants slack in providing proper food, it is unwise to make up the deficiency by pegs or tobacco. Far better spend a little time in super-vising the kitchen arrangements and the kitchen servants. The Cook's Guide teems with recipes suitable even for jungle life; and any young man with a gun should be generally able to keep himself supplied with game. It must never be forgotten that if work be hard and food bad, the result is sure to be lassitude and a craving for stimulants.

And next as to lodging. In the chapter on Camp Life almost every-thing necessary to make tents comfortable has been said. All that need be added is, that if a lengthened stay in one place be found necessary, it is a good plan to raise the floor in some way, while a decent fireplace with a chimney-piece can be built in at a trifling cost. It being diffi-cult to know where to place a lamp in a tent so as to be convenient for several persons, it is well to have an iron ring with a hinge and hasp that can be fastened round the tent pole, and from which a strong iron bar ending in a ring projects; into the ring the reservoir of the lamp can be fitted. A wide, white-painted shade above the lamp will throw the light well down.

If a house has to be built, even in a village or a jungle, the dwell-ing-rooms should be large and lofty. This is no luxurious or wrong idea. In India a soldier in barracks is allowed in his dormitory 1800 cubic feet. European hospitals allow 2400 cubic feet to each patient. Missionaries' lives are equally costly and valuable, and they should not have less. It may be a laudable desire to imitate the natives by living in mud huts, but native constitutions and ours are not alike. It will be found no extravagance to have good airy rooms, where work can be carried on and good sleep obtained. Again, houses should be raised at least four or five feet from the ground to avoid damp, to prevent snakes getting in, and to make the house cooler. A good verandah is an indispensable addition.

As to clothing. We should remember that the sun is a good friend to air, and purify, and cheer, but a deadly enemy if met without a shady pith hat and a white umbrella, or with an empty stomach. A doctor who has never once had fever in his family in India recommends white clothing summer and winter during exposure to the sun; common white puttoo* in winter, very light woollens in summer. Be in the open air as much as possible; even plants shut up in the dark get sickly and lose their colour. Fever is invariably brought on by changes of temperature, whether exposure to the sun, or a chill from damp or cold. These must be guarded against either by a pad of chopped corks at the back of the coat to prevent the action of the rays of sun on the back of the neck and spine, or an additional wrap when it becomes chilly.

And lastly as to bedding. A mission lady, of much experience in camping, writes, 'I have a Norwegian reindeer bag for sleeping in at night, which I can recommend as most comfortable, as it does away with all necessity for bedding of any kind, except a sheet and pillow, and in very cold nights a shawl round your shoulders to stop up all air-holes.' The usual bedding is a cotton wadded quilt which serves as a mattress, three striped coloured blankets, two English pillows, a canvas hold-all wrapper and stout cord, and a waterproof sheet.

In conclusion, it is a duty to take some real recreation, and to unstring our bow daily. Of an evening, for instance, all talk of work should be avoided and a real rest taken—not a mere change of leg like the cabman's horse. If several persons are in camp together, a compendium box of games will afford amusement evening after evening; while even a solitary traveller can enjoy variety in healthful reading, a musical instrument, or letter-writing. The annual vacation to the hills should also be regularly taken; not because we are ill, but to keep ourselves well; for though this change may serve to keep off disease, it rarely cures it, and then the only alternative is to give up work and go to England. If the advice given above is followed, life may be spent usefully and happily in this country for many years.

CHAPTER XIV

HINTS ON MANAGEMENT OF YOUNG CHILDREN

ONE of the authors, having had much experience in the bringing up of a large family in India, thinks that this book would be incomplete without a few hints on the management of children during infancy and teething.

One great point to be insisted on is, that all mothers should persevere in nursing* their children. Monthly nurses, to save themselves a little trouble, persuade the young mother that she has not sufficient nourishment and cannot nurse; the doctor tells her that if she has to supplement with a bottle, she had better not nurse at all; gay friends urge that she will be tied down and spoil her figure; and so, distracted amongst them all, she yields the point. As a rule, in the case of every healthy woman, Nature can supply the demand, and the nursing mother retain her usual occupations and amusements in moderation, and enjoy cheerful society and ordinary wholesome food, though stimulants had best be given up. She must not let herself be worried nor imposed upon by the *ayah*, who, whenever she wants to run and have a smoke, will tell her that the child is hungry. The child should be kept to fixed times; two hours at first, gradually increasing to three or four hours, during which the mother can fulfil her outdoor social engagements, and longer than which no woman who loved her home, husband, and child would care to be away. During nursing, should the mother experience a sense of thirst, or what in feminine language is called 'sinking,' there is nothing better than a cup of cocoa or barley-water, cooled with new milk, or in hot weather, milk and soda-water taken when she is in the act of nursing her child; the same to be taken, as she prefers, once or twice during the night if necessary. Another important point is keeping the infant with the mother at night. All doctors will rise in a body to contradict this, and tell melancholy tales of children overlaid or suffocated, which may possibly happen if the mother be intoxicated. The fact, however, remains that better sleep for both mother and child is obtained by this method.

Nature shows that the little life needs warmth and cherishing, and the mother's mind is at rest with her little one close to her. Smartly-trimmed bassinettes, no doubt, look very pretty, and the doctors urge the healthiness and advisability of a child sleeping alone, &c. &c.; but those who follow him, instead of common sense, are up and down half the night, neither mother nor child refreshed by sleep, both chilled, the one from getting up, the other from being taken up. What about a hen and her chickens? Where do they sleep?

Another thing to be remembered regarding feeding an infant, even with plenty of nourishment or with a wet-nurse,* is that the infant should be given the habit of taking at least half a bottle once in twenty-four hours, and this is best given at bedtime in the evening, to allow a little rest to the mother before the night. The Indian climate is too uncertain, and bodily ailments all too sudden, to trust to any one not failing. Should the mother or nurse's supply fail through sickness or accident, the bottle can be continued, and the child's health will not suffer, as has often been the case when the doctor's advice—on no account to mix milks—has been followed. The doctor is and should be the mother's best friend; but he is, after all, a man with chiefly book learning, science, and a knowledge of medicine. He looks on a patient merely in a scientific light, and little common, everyday experiences are not in his Materia Medica.*

The mother should prepare the bottle if possible herself, and the proportions should always be exactly the same, for some months at least. At first there should be one part milk and three parts water; such well-diluted milk being easier to digest, and richer food producing diarrhœa or sickness. Add a very little loaf sugar. The milk and water should be blood-warm, so as to resemble the mother's milk. Should the child be constipated, use raw sugar instead of loaf. The bottle should be washed by the mother, and not left to the *ayah* or *musolchee*, as is sometimes done. Bottles should be rinsed at once if not convenient to wash them at once. Later on they should be scalded, the tube being thoroughly cleaned and examined and put in a window in a fresh draught of air. Milk if kept should be placed in a scrupulously clean vessel, in an airy place, but it is best not left standing; and the time of giving the bottle should be regulated by the time the cows are milked. The milk should be taken from one cow, whose calf is about the same age as the child. A nursing mother should always be relieved of the child when he wakes, which is generally about 5 A.M.; then she should have her *chota hâzree* and go to sleep for an hour or so, when she will get up refreshed. The *ayah*, having had an undisturbed night's rest in her house, should be always ready at this hour to take the child.

For weaning: every mother who has brought up a family has some particular food she weans by; it would therefore be better for obvious reasons not to dictate or lay down the law as to any particular food. Chavasse gives a list of foods in his 'Advice to a Mother,'* which contains on the whole some good advice. The only point to be urged is that in India, certainly, where diarrhœa and dysentery prevail so much amongst children, the author's experience is that till the first set of teeth are through no broth whatever should be given. After nine months a farinaceous food may be given once a day with the spoon, the evening bottle of milk being still continued. At this stage, too, a crust or biscuit may be allowed, and gradually, month by month, the farinaceous food may be increased. Wean the child as soon after the year as possible. This gradual weaning saves much trouble, for the mother can wean the child herself in a night with perhaps one fit of crying, or perhaps not even that. After the child is weaned no bottle or food whatever should be given *during the night*. The child will sleep till early morning. If it be proved beyond a doubt that the mother cannot nurse, a *dhaee* or wet-nurse should be procured.

The bottle is unsatisfactory without constant supervision. As wet-nurses, none are better than the Cashmiri women at Amritsar,* although the Agra* *dhaees* have got a great name. The former are very amiable, get very fond of their charges, are simple in their ideas and unsophisticated, and not so grasping in their expectations. It is a great mistake to change the *dhaee's* habits beyond insisting on personal cleanliness and frequent change of clothes. The simpler and more familiar the food she gets, the better she will digest it, and the better will be her nourishment for the child. To bring a very poor woman into one's house, feed her with baker's bread and meat, tea and milk *ad libitum*, whilst taking the toil off her hands, will bring on indigestion, and consequently green motions in the babe. Within limits she should be allowed to see her friends, and she should not be treated as if she were merely an animated bottle. Four complete suits of clothing are necessary for her, which consist of trousers, petticoat, *chuddar*, and coat. Of these last, however, there should be some extra, so as to allow a clean coat on every morning after her bath.

In addition, a warm loose coat to be worn over her other, or, as some prefer, two warm flannel ones, which can be worn under the cotton one, and washed every week, and a native *lohee* or shawl for a wrap is required. She will also need a *ruzâee* (wadded quilt), a blanket and bolster pillow, and a string *charpoy*, which is cleaner to sleep on than the floor. When the child has to be nursed at night, it should, when taken from its mother, be wrapped in a shawl or blanket, and care should be taken that it takes all it wants before going off to sleep again. Native women suckle their children constantly; the *dhaee* will need to be taught only to nurse the child at regular intervals. Three plates or vessels are also provided, a large round plate on which her ordinary rice and *dâl*, &c., are placed when cooked, and shown to the mistress, a basin about the size of an ordinary slop basin, and a *lota* which has a spout, in which her drinking water, tea, &c., are kept. All these are of copper, and should be tinned regularly. She generally has one good meal about twelve o'clock, and in the evening and morning a basin of milk and tea with half a loaf of bread or *chupâtties*. If she smokes, let her continue to do so; it would be hard on any one to take away what has become second nature.

The mother should bathe her infant herself the first year. The tub should have a stand made to fit it, for the fatigue of stooping is unnecessary. The present writer bathes her own infants when fifteen days old, the tub being placed on her bed and the clothes all laid ready. It is stooping that makes it an exertion, and it does not take ten minutes when all is placed in readiness, and the articles of clothing in the order they are to be put on. By this means a mother knows that her babe is well and thriving. For any chafing or excoriations a little salad oil is preferable to violet powder,* which often irritates, especially if too plentifully applied. If any white specks appear on the mouth and lips, this is called thrush. Great cleanliness is necessary, besides smearing with borax and honey. A disgusting Indian habit, which should be put down by all mothers, is for the *ayah* to keep the baby's soiled napkins in the bathroom for at least twenty-four hours, after which she has a grand wash, wasting no end of soap, and throwing out the water in the bathroom. Each napkin when taken off should be placed in a vessel provided for the purpose, which should be at once filled up with water and removed by the sweeper. The latter, in a suitable place outside, should have a little tub and a line hung up. He should at once do the necessary washing, and then hang the napkin out to dry; not, as is the case, in the room, and so cause an unhealthy smell. After which the *dhobi* should iron them, and the *ayah* bring back every evening all that have been used during the day. An extra rupee may be given to the man for his amiability in setting aside *dustoor*, which will be well spent both for sanitary reasons and in order to keep the *ayah* to other duties.

As to infants' clothing. In India most mothers put too much clothing on their children, which is a fruitful source of colds, croup, &c. So is also the *ayah*'s habit of sitting into the fire in the cold weather whilst holding the child. All that is necessary is a knitted belt and vest—preferable to flannel, which gets hard and tight—a flannel petticoat, and in the cold weather a knitted well-fitting jacket, fastening at the back and with long sleeves, *under* the usual cotton monthly gown. Woollen frocks for infants are objectionable, for the reason that they cannot be changed as frequently as the cotton ones can. The Indian fashion of opening all garments down the back is an abominable one, the poor child being consequently often exposed to cold in its most delicate parts. The author has taken young infants of a month or six weeks old into camp in December and January, clothed as she has described—only adding a warm pelisse on first issuing from the night tent and during the march, but which was discarded during the day—and they never got cold. But they slept with their mother. Head-squares, woollen gowns, and too many shawls and wraps, added to the *ayah* sitting into the fire in a room hermetically shut up, are productive of croup and cold.

Vaccination is much better performed at the expiration of the first month if the babe be healthy and the weather cold or cool. Ask your doctor to send the vaccinator, with a healthy child to take the lymph from, and have it done before you. There is no occasion (as is the custom) to do it on both arms, nor on the arm at all, if you fear future disfigurement, though in the case of a boy it may not signify. A child of the author's, when about six weeks old, being met by the Civil Surgeon on the Mall at Simla, was there and then vaccinated by him on the *knee*, after he had vaccinated another child on the ankle. Four or five punctures are quite sufficient, if properly effected. Hold the part vaccinated close to the fire or in the sun till perfectly dry, after which there is no need to make any fuss, or to tie up the sleeve, or to take it out, as will doubtless be suggested. When the scab forms and the arm is very red for two or three days, put the cotton gown next to the arm and the jacket outside. The author's first child nearly died from bronchitis brought on by the absurd advice referred to; and as vaccination is usually performed in the cold weather, it is well to make a note of this.

Dosing a child perpetually is a bad custom, and for this reason don't be sending for the doctor every day. Remember that a child's motions depend on the action of the liver and digestion, which is often not quite right; and as long as its motions are kept under control, there is nothing to be uneasy about if the child looks well, and is bright and thriving in other respects. A few simple powders of rhubarb and soda, or magnesia, or rhubarb and bismuth,* given in dill water, will probably be all that is necessary. The nursing mother, without being fidgety, should be careful to keep to wholesome and simple food, and this principle should be followed in the case of the *dhaee*, and even of the cow, for the sudden change from *bhoosa* to green wheat will affect the cow, and the child through her. Should diarrhœa set in, give a teaspoonful of castor oil in warm dill water to clear out irritating matter, and then give just a little rhubarb and aromatic chalk only. Powders can be given in dill water and sweetened slightly. Few medicines in a nursery are best, and every mother should understand exactly how to act, though she can leave what is outside her understanding to her doctor. Diarrhœa sometimes precedes dysentery. Dysenteric stools may be accompanied by bile and substance: this is a favourable symptom, and a grain of ipecacuanha* added to the rhubarb and soda may suffice. Sometimes there is no bile and no substance present, merely great straining, while very little is passed, and that mucus or blood, or mucus only. The passing of mucus and pain point to dangerous symptoms, and it will be well to consult the doctor, who will give ipecacuanha combined with soda, or if fever be present, Dover's Powder* probably, ipecacuanha being the great specific for dysentery, and the Dover's Powder containing opium. It is well to remember in dysentery as well as in diarrhœa to give the digestion as little to do as possible. When the disease has been got under, then the child can be fed up, and if old enough a tonic can be added. Milk alone, even if diluted, is sufficient to support a child. Diluted milk is therefore the best food, given very little at a time, perfectly fresh, with a little loaf-sugar and a very little lime-water perhaps, and neither hot nor cold. After giving ipecacuanha, the child should be kept quite still, and no food should be given for at least a quarter of an hour before or after, as the ipecacuanha produces great nausea and incites vomiting. Most careful watching day and night is necessary. Each stool should be carefully inspected by the mother, who should keep paper and pencil by her, and note down the time it was passed and its nature, as also times of giving medicine and food. The doctor will then be able to follow the case, the effect of the powders, &c.; for dysentery and diarrhœa, like many diseases, should be carefully watched, the symptoms followed, and medicine regulated accordingly, and not by a hard-and-fast rule. Should the gums be stretched tightly over a tooth, so that the latter is visible beneath, take a small, sharp penknife, have the child's head between your knees and the child's body held firmly by another person; then with a steady hand cut the gum through to the tooth. This affords great relief. Besides diarrhœa and dysentery, there is sometimes great sickness. In such cases, when the stomach is very irritable, a mustard leaf protected by muslin can be put at the pit of the stomach before giving food, which should be very weak chicken broth or Liebig's Extract,* if the milk be persistently thrown up. The following mixture, one teaspoonful three times a day, may be given for a child from one to two years old: 25 grains carbonate magnesia, 2 drops peppermint oil, 1 oz. distilled water. Shake the bottle. Or 2 grains carbonate soda and 2 drops of essence of peppermint in a teaspoonful of water three times a day. If the child seems very weak, add a drop of sal volatile to each meal of chicken broth, and rub its limbs well with cod-liver oil, and put pieces of sponge soaked in the oil under its armpits and knees. Nutritive enemas are excellent in such cases.

Sometimes during teething an eruption appears, spreading all over the body. On no account check this. Keep the child scrupulously clean with carbolic soap, and dress night and morning with old cambric or linen steeped in a mild solution of carbolic oil. Fever is very common in India, and in its simple form can be controlled. But should there seem no abatement after administering a diaphoretic,* send for the doctor. The child's temperature must be taken, to reduce which it may be necessary to give a cold bath and wrap in cold wet sheets. In ordinary cases, stop the morning bath, giving instead a warm one at night. Wrap the child in a well warmed blanket afterwards, and lay in bed, give a dose of diaphoretic, which should be repeated every third hour till a free action of the skin sets in and perspiration takes place. If the head and hands be very hot, sponge with vinegar and water, and leave a thin muslin rag over the forehead to be wetted from time to time. Bowels can be acted on by Gregory's Mixture* if constipated, or red mixture if there be diarrhœa. If the child be over four, a grain of calomel* may be added to the Gregory's Powder with advantage. Diet must be light and fluid so as to encourage perspiration. Tamarind water (*Imli*), made from tamarinds obtained from the bazaar, is very agreeable, and has laxative properties. After free perspiration has taken place, and in the absence of fever, quinine in hydrobromic acid* should be given three times a day. The hydrobromic acid prevents tightness and other head symptoms. Convulsions very often accompany fever, or sometimes twitchings; if the latter are taken in time, convulsions may be warded off. In such cases nothing is better than a hot bath, cold applications to the head, and a dose of Gregory's Powder. The diet must be light and nourishing. Barley or oatmeal water, or rice water cooled with milk, are all good drinks.

Croup is a very alarming illness, but it should be remembered that if taken at once it is seldom fatal. It is when the doctor is sent for too late that it has got beyond him, having reached the lungs. A mother should always keep a small bottle of best fresh ipecacuanha wine by her. Give a dose of two teaspoonfuls every five minutes till free vomiting sets in. Repeat the emetic if necessary every hour, finishing off with small doses. This is for a child of three years old. Less in proportion must be given to a younger child. A hot sponge or a mustard leaf may be applied to the throat, and a hot bath given if necessary. But this is a risk in a tent or draughty cold room. Rubbing back and chest well before a fire with hot mustard oil till the skin is red is a good substitute for the hot bath.

In sore throats, the throat should be touched inside with solution of concentrated alum, 3 drachms to 1 oz. of water, or nitrate of silver solution, strength 10 grs. to 1 oz. distilled water. Gargles for children of hot milk, milk and alum, or alum 1 drachm to 8 oz. water, should be used if possible. If not, try compressed tablets of chlorate of potash and borax, which can be placed in the child's mouth, or the mouth and throat can be cleansed by a powder of chlorate of potash placed on the tongue. Mustard leaves protected by muslin, linseed poultices, with or without mustard sprinkled on them, are all beneficial.

Coughs and colds should be attended to *at once*. Give the cough mixture recommended three times a day, rub back and chest at night with hot mustard oil, give small pieces of ipecacuanha lozenges at night to suck, and linseed and black currant tea, hot, going to bed.

Bronchitis needs a doctor, as it is very fatal to young children. It needs great care and watching, as the child's strength must be kept up to battle with the disease. The author's own experience points gratefully to Brand's Essence of Beef.* Food in some form, *e.g.* cream, chicken broth, raw-meat juice, Brand's Essence, or even stimulants when ordered, must be given every half-hour, and, as before stated, it is always advisable to keep paper and pencil to mark down all that has passed and been given since the doctor's last visit. The room must be kept night and day at an equable temperature: a thermometer should be hung up away from window or fireplace; either fire or lamps used to keep up the temperature. A boiling kettle should be placed opposite the patient so as to moisten the atmosphere. A flannel sprinkled with the turpentine and camphor liniment should be fastened round lungs, back, and chest, and small doses of ipecacuanha given in the absence of any special prescription from the doctor.

Such are some of the common ailments of children; but it would take a large book to describe all, for every mother knows she never comes to the end of her experience, and that each child differs from those that have come before. An old-fashioned doctor gives three things necessary for a child, which the author heartily endorses—plenty of milk, plenty of air, plenty of flannel. Where there is a child, it is a *sine quâ non* a cow should be kept. It should be well looked after and carefully fed, the milk-pans and pail being inspected daily. Plenty of air is a grand thing; and if the child be protected from the sun with a good umbrella or pith hat, and kept under a tree during the heat, it can be almost out all day. But a word of caution is necessary about sending out children in the very early morning in the cold weather with native servants, who invariably sit down to have a chat, thus exposing their charges to extremes of heat and cold. Flannel, thick or thin, should invariably clothe a child all the year round. The author remembers some sensibly dressed children who wore *one* under-garment, neatly fitting, which combined vest, chemise, body, and petticoat in one. To this a band was attached underneath to which the child's drawers were buttoned. Nothing but the frock or pinafore was worn over this. A child should never be burdened with clothing, and flannel does away with a number and variety of garments. Merino socks and stockings can be worn all the year round.

When a mother's careful, loving eye is over her nursery, not fidgeting and worrying, but with common-sense and sound judgment, the little ones should rarely require a doctor among them. Still, one word of advice. Make your doctor's acquaintance during health, look upon him as your best friend, and never hesitate to send for him when *your* work ends, and *his* begins.

The following are a few simple prescriptions for the mother:—

Red Mixture (*for diarrhœa, green motions, to be followed up with doses of aromatic chalk. Good in fever*).—Rhubarb, 12 grains; calcined magnesia, 2 scruples; oil of aniseed, 6 drops; sugar, 1 drachm; compound tincture of lavender, ½ drachm; sal volatile, ½ drachm; water, 1½ oz. One teaspoonful three times a day.

Powders (*for infants in green motions caused by indigestion*).—Carbonate of soda, 24 grains; rhubarb, 12 grains; bismuth, 6 grains. Make twelve powders. One every third hour. In dysentery (simple) add ipecacuanha according to age.

Diaphoretic Mixture.—Sweet spirits of nitre, 1 drachm; nitrate of potash, 1 scruple; liquor of acetate of ammonia, 4 drachms; camphor water, 4 drachms; water, 1½ oz. A teaspoonful every third hour for a child from two to four years old.

Quinine Mixture.—Sulphate quinine, 5 grains; hydrobromic acid, ½ drachm; water, 1 oz. One teaspoonful three times a day in absence of fever for a child two to four years old.

Cough Mixture.—Bicarbonate potash, 1 scruple; syrup of squills,* 2 drachms; ipecacuanha wine, 1 drachm; sweet spirits of nitre, ½ drachm; compound tincture camphor, 1 drachm; mixture of acacia (liquid gum),* 2 drachms; anise water, 2 oz. Shake the bottle. One teaspoonful every three hours, not after or before food.

Dysentery Powders (*if fever be present*).—Powdered ipecacuanha, 3 grains; carbonate of soda, 5 grains; Dover's Powder, 2 grains; grey powder,* 5 grains; compound kino powder,* 4 grains. Make six powders. One powder every two hours if necessary. Child two to four years.

Bronchitis Liniment (*poison*).—Compound camphor liniment, 2½ oz.; turpentine liniment, 2½ oz. Shake the bottle well and keep corked, and sprinkle on new flannel as required. Keep away from fire or candle.

CHAPTER XV

SIMPLE HINTS ON THE PRESERVATION OF HEALTH, AND SIMPLE REMEDIES

MUCH fuss is, as a rule, made about the unhealthiness of India, but, as a matter of fact, if due attention is paid to the novel conditions of life, and the same precautions which are, as a matter of course, taken against the damps and chills of England be taken against the sun of India, there is no reason at all why the health should suffer. It is not only heat which the sun brings with it. That heat in its turn, combined with the intermittent and copious rain, is favourable to the development of malaria and countless bacilli* of all sorts. Thus, necessarily, the risks to be run from the malarial type of disease is greater than in England. At the same time, the better class of Europeans should have immunity from a thousand dangers which have to be run at home from infection, cold, bad ventilation, and unscientific drainage. For it must be remembered that if the water-system drainage be not *perfect*, it is simply a death-trap.

That India itself has little to do with the mortality charged against it may be seen from the fact that while the civilian European popula-tion has a death-rate of only 20 per mille (or the same as London), soldiers in barracks have one of 69.* That is the result of crowding, errors of diet, intemperance, exposure, immorality, and the imperfect ventilation and sanitation inseparable from large numbers, joined to a want, during the hot weather, of rational exertion, mental and bodily. These various evils have therefore to be guarded against in India even more strenuously than in England.

In regard to the sun, it must not be forgotten that it is a *friend* as well as an enemy. Half the cases of neuræsthenia* and anæmia among English ladies, and their general inability to stand the hot weather, arises from the fact that they live virtually in the dark. They feel 'too languid' to go out early. 'It doesn't suit them to go out before break-fast,' &c. &c. Then it is too hot to leave the cool house before sun-setting. So, as the house, for the sake of what is called comfort, is kept shut up and in semi-darkness all day, it often happens that the sun is never *seen* or *felt*. The writer believes that the forced inertia caused by living without *light* is responsible for many moral and physical evils among European ladies in the Tropics.* In the chapter 'In the Plains' more is said on the subject of making the sun your *friend*.

Let us now think of him as an enemy, in reference, first, to clothing. On this point, also, details will be found in another chapter, that on Outfits. Flannel next the skin day and night is, of course, the shibboleth of doctors, and doubtless they are right. The writer, however, never wore it day or night, and she never once went to the hills unless on leave with her husband, which means that two hot weathers out of every three were spent entirely in the plains. She wore *silk*, discarded stays, &c., and, as a rule, had her dresses of nuns-veiling or thin serge.* And during the hot weather she used a thin white Rampore chuddar* or shawl instead of a sheet. The aim and object is, however, to avoid chills and heats. To effect this, sound good sense and the energy which does not mind a little trouble are all that is necessary; unless, indeed, the claims of fashion are allowed to overbear those of comfort and health.

Food and drink should be, as in other parts of the world, simple and digestible. Alcohol is certainly not required; at the same time, its moderate use seems no more hurtful than it is in England. Some people complain of great thirst in India. Cold tea, without milk, and with lemon juice added to it, quenches thirst, but it is not a very wholesome drink, especially if tea is taken at other times. Barley water poured while boiling on shred lemons is better. This can also be made with citric acid, or cream of tartar (see recipe for Imperial). Ice should not be taken on trust and put into drinks unless it is known to be made in a machine from pure water. Food in the Tropics, doctors say, should be very nutritious and very abundant. They also recommend early dinners. The writer's sole advice on this subject is to use common-sense. If you wake with a chippy mouth, and feel as if the whole world was hollow, and your doll stuffed with sawdust, you may be *sure* your liver is out of order; in which case don't blame Providence and fly to a podophyllin pill,* but think over yesterday, from morn till eve, and find out whether it was that greasy side-dish at dinner, or the delay in changing to a warmer dress when you began to feel chilly, which is responsible.

In regard to bathing, few people can stand cold water in the Tropics, unless in a swimming bath.

Malaria is briefly an earth-and-water-born poison produced in soils not fully occupied in healthy work, and may be taken into the body through the skin, the lungs, and the stomach. In the first case it generally enters by inoculation from the bite of some insect which has been previously feeding on malarial poison. Mosquitoes are great offenders in this matter, especially near stagnant water, where they breed. It is well, therefore, to keep covers on all water jars near the house, and to adopt the plan of closing the house at dawn which is recommended elsewhere. Dew falling on the body through malarial air will introduce it by saturation. In the second case the poison is in the air. This malarial air clings to the surface of the earth, and cannot be produced at an elevation of 3000 feet. It is denser before sunrise and after sunset, when evaporation is at its height. Sunshine disperses it, and places known to be malarious may be safe by day and deadly by night. Owing to these facts, it is safer during malarial seasons to sleep on the roof or in an upper room. Those who have to work in malarial districts will find a charcoal respirator* a great safe-guard, also double-walled tents and camp fires. A belt of trees round a house protects it. Two to three grains of quinine should be taken morning and evening, and the greatest attention paid to the general health. No one should ever go out of tent or house in the morning till some *food* has been taken. In the third case of malaria poison-ing (by the stomach), milk is a great offender. This, especially when bought in the bazaar, should be boiled before using. If the taste of the 'boil' is objectionable, a regular steriliser should be made or bought. It is, briefly, a *bain-marie* pan, with thick glass hermetically stoppered bottles, in which the milk is placed and brought to boiling-point. This milk will keep—in its stoppered bottle—for a week or more, and has no taste. Tubercular germs are also largely disseminated by milk, and it is responsible for many cases of decline and phthisis.*

Where the great heat of the sun has to be braved, a large pith hat should be worn, a real mushroom, that will protect the nape of the neck. A cork protector, made by quilting shredded cork down the middle of a sleeveless jacket, should be worn over the spine. An umbrella covered with white and dipped occasionally in water will make a hot, dangerous walk less dangerous.

In regard to exercise, especially in hot weather, men are apt to err in taking too much, women too little. A languid stroll from your drawing-room to your carriage and back again is *not* sufficient to keep your organism going. It will soon begin to stroll also from sheer lack of stimulus. At the same time, all excessive fatigue leaves you a prey to the bacilli which compass you round about, seeking whom they may devour.

With these few remarks we proceed to detail the following simple, useful, and nearly always obtainable remedies, for the common complaints and accidents likely to occur in India, when medical assistance is not at hand.

A mistress will find the following limited stock of medicines meet most cases coming under her care:—

1. Powdered ipecacuanha. This keeps much better than the wine, and is therefore safer for emergencies. In croup, a child's life may be lost from using a medicine that has become inert.
2. Kâla dâna purgative powder. Recipe No. 1.
3. Sulphate of quinine.
4. Chlorodyne.
5. Pure carbolic acid.
6. Castor oil.
7. Eno's fruit salt.
8. One bottle each of McKesson and Robbin's compound podophyllin;* ipec: comp: pulv:; and aloes and myrrh pills.
9. Stick of nitrate of silver.
10. Cholera pills.
11. Iodine.
12. Tabloids of antipyrin.*
13. Do.   phenacetin.*
14. Salicylate of soda.*
15. Boracic acid.
16. Some kind of cough lozenge.
17. Tabloids of grey powder.
18. Kaye's essence of linseed.*

These, and the medicines to be bought in any bazaar, of which the following is a list, are the only ones used in the following outline of treatment of the usual ills which come under the eye of the Indian house-mother. The doses given are for adults:—

Aconite (*Atees*).—Care required in selection of roots. Should have a white starchy fracture, and should not numb the tongue when chewed. Dose, 5 to 10 grs. In fever.

Borax (*Sohâga*).—If impure, dissolve 1 lb. in 3 pints of water, add 1 dr. quicklime, and evaporate in the sun. Chiefly as external application, ½ oz. to 8 oz. of water. Dose, 20 to 40 grs.

Butea Gum (*Palas ki gond*).—Astringent in diarrhœa. Dose, 10 to 30 grs.

Camphor (*Kafoor*).

Catechu (*Kât*).—Astringent, 10 to 15 grs.

Chiretta (*Chereyetah*).—Excellent tonic. Bruised chiretta, 1 oz.; hot water, 1 pint. Infuse six hours, and strain. Dose, 2 to 3 oz. daily.

Copper, Sulphate of (*Neela Tootiâ*).—Solution for external use, 2 to 10 grs. to the oz. of water. As emetic, in emergencies, 5 grs. in a pint of tepid water, gulped down at one draught.

Galls (*Mâi-phul*).—Wash or gargle. Boil 1½ oz. bruised galls in 1 pint of water. Also used in dysentery. Dose, 1½ oz. daily. Ointment, 1½ drs. galls to 1 oz. ghee.

Hemidesmus [*Country Sarsaparilla*] (*Jungli chambeli*).—1 oz. to ½ pint boiling water. Infuse 1 hour, strain. Dose, 2 oz. daily.

Iron, Sulphate of (*Kussees*).—¼ gr. to 2 grs. Valuable tonic in anæmia.

Kâla dâna.—Aperient, 30 to 50 grs. For adults only.

Kumâla (*Kumela*).—In tape-worm, for adults only, 2 to 3 drs. in honey.

Lemon-grass Oil (*Ukya-ghâs-kâ-itr*).—Three to 6 drops on sugar in flatulent colic or cholera spasms. Rubbed externally for rheumatism.

Myrobalans (*Hur, Reelee-hur*).—Aperient for adults. Six nuts bruised, 1 dr. cloves. Boil in water, 4 oz., for ten minutes.

Nim (*Neem*).—The bark as astringent tonic, 1 dr. three or four times a day. A poultice of neem leaves is good for indolent ulcers.

Papaw Tree (*Pupaiyâh*).—The milky juice. In lumbricus or round worm, a tablespoonful, followed by castor oil. In ringworm, the unripe fruit shred and rubbed on the spot; also the milky juice of the unripe fruit in large spleen and liver, a teaspoonful every day.

Plantago (*Ispaghool*).—Demulcent, 2½ drs. of the seeds mixed whole with a little pounded sugar, in diarrhœa of long standing. Or in bladder troubles, 2 to 4 oz. of decoction made by boiling 2 drs. of the seeds in 1 pint water for ten minutes.

Pomegranate (*Anâr*).—The rind in diarrhœa, &c. In decoction. Boil 2 oz. of rind and 2 drs. cinnamon in 1 pint of water for fifteen minutes. Dose, 1½ oz. three times a day. Or as a gargle with 1 dr. alum.

The root bark in tape-worm. Take 2 oz., water 2 pints; boil to 1 pint. Dose, 2 oz., followed by castor oil.

Omum Seeds (*Ujwain*).—Distil 3 lbs. seeds to 4 quarts water. Dose, 1 to 2 oz. Valuable as anti-spasmodic and diffusible stimulant in colic, hysteria, cholera.

Sal-ammoniac (*Nowsâder*).—Should be dissolved, strained, and evaporated. For external application, 2 drs. sal-ammoniac, 1 oz. spirit, 1 pint rose-water. Or 15 to 20 grs. in rheumatism, bilious nervous headache. Or in chronic coughs, 1 dr. in 6 oz. honey and water. Dose, 1 oz. six times a day. In liver complaints and chronic dysentery, 20 grs. twice a day.

Tylophera [*Country Ipecacuanha*] (*Untâ-mool*).—Dried leaves as emetic, 40 grs. Expectorant, 4 to 8 grs. In dysentry 15 grs. three times a day.

A large number of these medicines are quite as efficacious as their more expensive imported congeners, and missionaries would do well to use them more than they do at present. In fact, with Waring's book, 'Bazaar Medicines,'* in the hand, the doctor is practically independent of many drugs now imported at a heavy charge to the funds.

The following is a list of the more common ailments and their treatment:—

Abscesses or Boils.—Try iodine and hot fomentation to disperse them. If this fails, try rice poultices or a plaster of equal weights brown sugar and English bar-soap. Give a dose or two of Eno, and if the constitution is disturbed, recipe No. 2.

Asthma.—No cure; but strong black coffee will sometimes cut short an attack. The fumes of blotting-paper which has been steeped in very strong solution of saltpetre and dried, gives relief. So, *used with caution*, will twenty grains of dried datura leaf* smoked with the ordinary tobacco.

Bites of Wasps, Scorpions, &c.—A paste of ipecacuanha and water applied at once over the bite generally acts as a charm. Stimulants if severe symptoms follow.

Of Mad, or even Doubtful Dogs.—Cut with a lancet or pen-knife down to the very bottom of the wound, and again across, so as to let it gape and bleed. Then cauterise remorselessly with nitrate of silver, or carbolic acid, or actual hot iron. The object is to destroy the bitten tissue, so see that you get to the *bottom*.

Of a Snake.—If in a toe, finger, or end of a limb, apply a ligature with the first thing handy. Whipcord is best, but take the first ligature that comes to hand. Twist with a stick, or any lever, as tight as you can. Apply two or more nearer the heart, at intervals of a few inches. Meanwhile, if you have help, get some one else to cut out the flesh round the fang-marks, and let it bleed freely. If the snake is known to be deadly, amputate the finger or toe at the next joint; or if you cannot do this, run the knife right round the bone, dividing the flesh completely. Let the bitten person suck the wound till you can burn it with anything at hand—carbolic, nitric acid, nitrate of silver, or actual hot iron. Give one ounce of brandy in a little water. The great object is to prevent the poison getting through the blood to the heart, so every additional pulse-beat before the ligatures are on is a danger. If symptoms of poisoning set in, give more stimulants; put mustard plasters over the heart; rub the limbs; treat, in fact, as for drowning, even to artificial respiration.

Bleeding from Internal Organs without Fever.—Keep absolutely quiet. Apply cold effusions.* Drink lemonade or alum whey, recipe No. 3. A little opium may be given. When there is fever, give fever mixture, recipe No. 4. **From the Nose.**—It will generally cease if a teaspoon of salt and water is poured down the nostril. If not, try alum and water, twenty grains to one ounce, or turpentine.

Burns and Scalds.—Keep out the air at once, by oil, butter, or flour, the first thing handy. Then beat up equal parts of limewater and any kind of sweet oil; soak a cloth and lay over the whole burnt part. Bandage lightly. Do not touch again for thirty-six hours, but pour more lime and oil over the cloth. If the surface burnt is very large, give a liberal diet.

Colds, Catarrhs.—May be almost entirely prevented by small doses of opium. The best remedy is fifteen drops of chlorodyne at bedtime on the first symptoms, repeated next night if necessary. Quinine in small doses is also good. For children, small doses of compound ipecacuanha powder is best. The fumes of burning camphor or turmeric in the room relieve the stuffing in the nose effectually. Kaye's essence at night is good for adults.

Cholera.—In cholera seasons check all premonitory diarrhœa with twenty drops of chlorodyne in some *ujwain* water, No. 5. It is easy to give an antibilious pill after if the diarrhœa turns out to be bilious. The treatment of pronounced cholera is a disputed point, and what is best in one epidemic often fails in the next, but the acid treatment on the whole seems most successful if commenced in time. One tablespoon of vinegar and one teaspoon of Worcester sauce has long been a fairly successful treatment amongst tea coolies, and of late the merits of twenty drops of diluted acetic acid and ten drops of sweet spirits of nitre in a wineglass of water has been greatly extolled. The famous Austrian remedy was diluted sulphuric acid, three drachms; nitric acid, two drachms; syrup, six drachms; water, to make the whole to ten ounces. One tablespoonful in very cold water, and repeated in half-an-hour. Even if collapse sets in, and apparent death, hope should not be given up. Every effort to keep up circulation should be continued, many people having literally been brought back to life by devoted nursing. Hand-rubbing, hot bottles, mustard, turpentine, everything should be tried; stimulants and opium avoided, and ice given liberally; and also beef-tea iced to a solid. If the patient fancies any remedy, try it at once, as the '*saffron bag worn at the pit of the stomach*,' as Mr. Caxton says,* is of more use in this disease than any other. Pluck and a determination to pull through are ever so many points in the patient's favour. In fact, at present, the best doctor in the world can do little more in cholera than assist nature to get rid of the poison by keeping the circulation going.

During an epidemic be as clean and careful as possible in personal and household matters; keep a separate *mushk* for the *bheesti* to bring drinking water in. See the water is boiled and filtered before using, and that the water for kettles and water for soup and cooking is taken from the filter. The filter itself will need cleaning out and renewal from time to time. Visit your cook-house and *khitmutgâr*'s washing-up places daily. Provide a *ghurra* of whitewash, and have it used frequently about drains, &c. This applies to bathrooms also. Avoid exposure to sun, chills, and fatigue, raw vegetables, melons and unripe fruit, coffee, and spirituous liquors. Wine, if taken at all, take sparingly. A few drops of Rubini's camphor* can be taken occasionally on sugar. Have by you a bottle of sulphureous acid mixture. (*See* Simple Remedies.) If choleraic symptoms set in, it must be given at once, and the doctor sent for. Have Brand's Essence of Beef or Chicken in the house, and give it in the intervals of vomiting, whether retained or not, as some may be absorbed. Have jugged chicken or beef soup got in readiness at once, and give teaspoonfuls of it in intervals of five minutes, whether vomiting goes on or not. Have a few bottles of champagne in readiness for an emergency. Cleanliness, ventilation, and temperance in all things must be borne in mind, and every endeavour should be made to limit the possibility of contagion as much as possible. Washing should be scrupulously done at home, and a careful eye kept on food supplies. It may be mentioned that quite recently a new treatment by a salt called *salol** has, in the writer's personal experience, proved most successful. The inoculation system is as yet on its trial.*

Colic or Violent Pain in the Bowels.—If there is no fever, it is most likely wind. Give a dose of *omum* or *ujwain* water, No. 5, or a teaspoon of ground ginger and a little sugar mixed with a tumbler of hot water. A few drops of chlorodyne may be added. Give a dose of castor oil when the pain has abated. If there is fever and constipation with great tenderness, put on a linseed poultice, give a full dose of opium, and send for a doctor sharp.

Constipation.—Give *kâla dâna* mixture, or, to children, castor oil. For habitual constipation give aloes. In obstinate constipation try repeated enemas of soap and water.

Convulsions.—Put at once in a hot bath, give castor oil, and if the child is teething, lance the gums. In adults, put cold water to the head, mustard plasters to the calves of the legs, and give a strong purgative, or, if unable to swallow, give the medicine by enema.

Coughs, Bronchitis, &c.—Put on linseed and mustard poultices, and give quarter or half-grain doses of ipecacuanha mixed with a little sugar. Or give recipe No. 6. Inhale hot water to which vinegar has been added, and if the breathing is difficult, apply turpentine stupes.*

Croup.—Give emetic doses of ipecacuanha, and put the patient in a hot bath; but keep the head cool, and do not stifle the child with heat.

Diarrhœa.—Give No. 5, with a few drops of chlorodyne. Then castor oil. In chronic cases, diet and mild remedies, such as *bael* sherbet and pomegranate bark, are best.

Dysentery.—Give the compound ipecacuanha pills at night, and a full dose of castor oil with thirty drops of chlorodyne next morning. If the symptoms increase, give twenty grains of ipecacuanha powder in five-grain pills, to be taken in jelly. *No fluids* for at least one hour before and after. This is effectual, but terribly nauseating; and it is well to try first the effects of a rice poultice on the stomach sprinkled with one or two teaspoons of ipecacuanha powder. Milk diet.

Earache.—Equal parts of opium and any sweet oil. Rub up together, soak a bit of cotton-wool in it, and insert *not too far down* the ears.

Eyes, Sore.—Alum solution, six grains to the ounce. If severe, nitrate of silver solution, two to four grains to the ounce; or sulphate of copper, No. 7. To relieve pain, poppy-head poultice.

Fever (*Ordinary, Intermittent with Ague*).—Give hot lime-juice and water, with a little ginger in it to relieve the cold stage. Cold water on the head in the hot, and as soon as the sweating begins, fifteen drops of chlorodyne and six grains of quinine. In long-continued hot stages, give fever mixtures. Arsenic often succeeds in breaking the fever when quinine fails. *Dose.*—Five drops of Fowler's solution* twice a day. Care should be taken with this medicine, as it is an accumulative poison. It is well to intermit a few days after, say, a fortnight's use. *In simple continued fever* give small doses of quinine and ipecacuanha, and fever mixtures, or antipyrin; for the debility after fevers, give chiretta infusion, No. 8. Arsenic must not be given to children.

Headache.—Give an aperient. If nervous, try a mustard plaster at the pit of the stomach and strong coffee. Eno's fruit salt is good. Phenacetin is an immediate and almost certain cure. For the headache of overwork bromide of potass tabloids are very useful.

Indigestion (*Acute*).—During the fit, *ujwain* water with twenty grains carbonate of soda.

For Dyspepsia or Habitual Indigestion.—Chiretta infusion. A teacup full of boiling hot water taken as hot as possible quarter of an hour before meals sometimes has an excellent effect in nervous dyspepsia. Mother Seigel's Syrup* is worth a trial, the best treatment being diet and exercise.

Hiccough.—Hold the right ear with the left forefinger and thumb, bringing the elbow as far across the chest as possible. An unreasonable but absolutely effective cure.

Hysteria.—Whisky and water with a little chlorodyne and a little wholesome neglect. This applies to hysterics at the time; but a nervous hysterical state generally points to functional disorders, needing active treatment.

Itch.—Sulphur ointment, No. 9.

Liver, Chronic.—Podophyllin pills, dry rubbing with mustard over the liver, or if there is tenderness, turpentine stupes. In violent pain and feverishness, hot-water fomentation, fever mixture, and leeches.

Lungs.—In threatened inflammation, linseed poultices and ipecacuanha, in half-grain doses. With natives begin stimulants at once. A bran jacket, as described later on, is useful, as it is less troublesome than poultices, and the natives are more likely to use it.

Neuralgia.—Try quinine and iron pills. Ginger poultices over the part. But no two people are relieved by the same medicine.

Piles.—Sulphur, a small teaspoon every morning; or equal parts of sulphur, cream of tartar, and treacle, a large teaspoon every morning. For local application use gall ointment, No. 10.

Poisoning by Narcotics, such as Opium, Datura, &c.—Empty the stomach with the first emetic at hand—salt and water, if there is nothing else to be had; give strong coffee, some stimulant, and rouse the patient with smelling salts, cold water, and flicking the legs and body with wet towels. If possible, give a decoction of galls* (*maiphul*) made with two ounces of galls to a pint of water. Four or five tablespoons every ten minutes for one hour.

Poisoning by Acids.—Give milk, soap and water, whites of eggs, any kind of sweet oil, rice-water, and any kind of mucilaginous drinks *at once*.

Poisoning by Minerals, such as Arsenic, Copper.—Give an emetic, then treat as for acids. Sugar is worth a trial; but copious draughts of any mucilaginous mixture that will protect the coats of the stomach from the irritant poison is what is required.

Prickly Heat.—Try lemon-juice or sandal-wood dust, or coal tar soap; a very weak solution of carbolic and water, applied with a sponge.

Rheumatism.—Use liniment No. 11. Drink lime-juice, and take small doses of quinine. Salicylate of soda three times a day, in 15 grain doses.

Sunstroke.—Cold water to the head by pouring cold water in a small stream from a *ghurra* over head, spine, and chest from a height of three feet. Hold the patient in a sitting posture. Put mustard plasters on the calves. The object is to lower the temperature of the body, so use ice, evaporating lotions, and get the room as cool as possible. If insensibility continues, try artificial respiration.

Spleen.—Give sulphate of iron two grains, black pepper three grains, made into a pill. Take one twice a day, and avoid all acids. Take a *kâla dâna* purgative once a week, and rub the spleen or ague cake with turpentine or capsicum water till the skin is red; or try iodine painted over the spleen.

Swallowing Foreign Substances.—Children will sometimes swallow buttons, &c., when playing with them. Beat the whites of three eggs with a little water and give it at once; it may be sweetened and flavoured; five minutes after give a *full* dose of ipecacuanha. The white of egg coagulates in the stomach, and will often close round the foreign matter and bring it away *en masse*.

Sprains.—Hot fomentations at once. Then rub with embrocation No. 11, and bandage.

Toothache.—Forty drops carbolic acid, sixty drops eau-de-cologne, a tiny piece of gum mastic* (*mustiqa*). Dissolve. One drop on cotton-wool to the hollow. Eau-de-Suez* used regularly certainly prevents teeth from aching.

Wounds.—Dress with *boiled* water or carbolic oil, No. 12.

The following is a list of prescriptions mentioned in the above, or otherwise useful:—

1. **Kâla Dâna Mixture.**—Powdered *kâla dâna* seeds, one ounce; cream of tartar, two ounces; powdered ginger, two drachms. Mix and sift through muslin. Put away in a wide-mouthed stoppered bottle. *Dose.*—Thirty to sixty grains.

2. **Sarsaparilla Infusion.**—Hemidesmus root or *jungli chambeli*; two ounces of the bruised roots in half a pint of boiling water. Let stand for an hour, then strain. *Dose.*—Two tablespoonsful three times a day. Useful in all skin diseases, also in debility.

3. **Alum Whey.**—Two teaspoons of alum powdered, boiled with two tumblers of milk. Strain. Two tablespoons of the whey three times a day in any kind of excessive or unnatural hæmorrhage.

4. **Fever Mixture.**—Two drachms of nitre dissolved in one quart of barley water; add lemon juice, and sugar to taste. Drink in the course of twenty-four hours. Or, nitre, ten grains; camphor spirit, ten drops; water, one tumbler; Eno's fruit salt, one teaspoon. A little lime-juice may be added, and the camphor omitted.

5. **Ujwain or Omum Water.**—Can be bought in the bazaar, or may be distilled from one pound of *ujwain* seeds to two quart bottles of water. This should make about one and a half bottles of distilled water. *Dose.*—Two to three tablespoons.

6. **Cough Mixture.**—Water, one pint; fresh bruised *mulâthi* roots, two ounces; honey (or sugar), six ounces; gum, half an ounce. Boil the roots and gum for half-an-hour in water, add the honey, and strain. For one dose take a dessertspoon of this, add two of water, two grains of sal-ammoniac, and half a grain of ipecacuanha. Five or six times a day.

7. **Eye Lotion.**—Two grains of sulphate of copper dissolved in two ounces of water. A drop or two in the eye.

8. **Tonic Infusion.**—Chiretta, one ounce; boiling water, one pint. Infuse for two hours. *Dose.*—Four tablespoons three times a day. *Or*, chiretta, five ounces; rectified spirit, one quart. Macerate for fourteen days,

and strain. *Dose.*—One tablespoonful. *Or,* sherry, one bottle; chiretta, two ounces. Macerate for a week. From half to a whole wineglassful before breakfast and dinner.

9. **Sulphur Ointment.**—One part of pounded sulphur to six of any kind of fat. Good fresh butter is as good as anything, or a simple ointment prepared from one part wax, one part suet, and two parts sweet oil melted.

10. **Gall Ointment.**—One drachm of powdered galls (*maiphul*); half drachm opium; one ounce simple ointment.

11. **Embrocation.**—Quarter ounce spirits of wine beaten up with quarter ounce camphor, add half a pint of vinegar, one ounce turpentine. Shake all together in a bottle. Excellent for sprains.

12. **Carbolic Oil for dressing Sores.**—One drop carbolic in thirty drops sweet oil.

13. **Ginger or any Spice Cordial.**—Steep six ounces of ginger in a quart of spirit (gin, brandy, or whisky) for nine days; or cardamom, cinnamon, allspice, carraway; or a mixture of any may be used. Loaf sugar also may be added.

14. **Gargle.**—Alum as much as will lie on a four-anna bit; as much of red pepper, and a teaspoon of bruised sage leaves. Pour half a tumbler boiling water over pepper and sage, and let it stand half-an-hour. Strain. Add the alum, and, if liked, a glass of port-wine and some sugar. Gargle with half this mixture and half water.

15. **Gargle.**—Salt and water, then paint the back of the throat with sage oil.

16. **Lime Water.**—One ounce of slaked lime, shaken up with three quart bottles of distilled or filtered water, allowed to stand for at least twelve hours. Then decant the clear portion.

17. **Neuralgia Mixture.**—Chloride of ammonia, four drachms; compound mixture of cardamoms, six drachms; syrup of orange bitters, six drachms; infusion of gentian, six ounces. Twelve marks on bottle. One mark every four hours.

18. **Hair Lotion.**—Olive oil, two drachms; oil of mace, one drachm; solution of ammonia, one and a half drachms; spirit of rosemary, half ounce; rose water, three ounces.

The following are recipes made entirely from drugs procurable in the bazaar. Doses for an adult.

1. **Fever Powder.**—Aconite* (*atees*), 5 grains; sal-ammoniac (*nousâda*), 15 grains. One three times a day.

2. **Fever Mixture during Hot Stage.**—Barley water or any demulcent* drink, 1 oz.; sal-ammoniac (*nousâda*), 10 grains. Three times a day.

3. **Mixture for Enlarged Spleen.**—Sulphate of iron (*heera-kusees*), 2 grains; *atees*, 5 grains. Twice a day.

4. **Cholera Pill.**—Opium, ½ grain; red pepper, 1 grain; assafoetida (*hing*), 2 grains. One pill.

5. **Dysentery or Diarrhœa Powder.**—Alum (*phitkurri*), 2 grains; kino (*kumarkus*) powder, 5 grains. Three times a day.

6. **Mixture for Indigestion.**—Chiretta (*charaiytah*), ½ drachm; aniseed (*somf*), 1 drachm; cardamoms (*ilâi chi*), 1 drachm; water, 6 ounces. Infuse two ounces twice a day.

7. **Pill for Anæmia.**—Sulphate of iron (*heera-kusees*), 1 grain; confection of roses (*gool kund*), 4 grains. Twice a day.

8. **Powder for Piles.**—Black pepper, 10 grains; sulphur (*gunduk*), 10 grains.

9. **Bronchitis or Cough Mixture.**—Cardamoms (*ilâi chi*), 10 grains; aniseed (*somf*), 10 grains; tea, 10 grains; dried violets (*bunufsha gool*), 1 drachm; sugar, 1 drachm; liquorice (*mullathi*), 10 grains; water, 2 ounces. Infuse. When the cough is troublesome.

10. **Liniment for Rheumatism.**—Camphor (*kafoor*), 20 grains; oil, 2 ounces.

11. **Lotion for Eyes in Ophthalmia.**—Alum (*phitkurri*), 4 grains; rose water, 1 ounce. Drop in eye.

12. **Cough Mixture.**—Poppy-heads (*posth*), 1 middle-sized; raw sugar (*goor*), 4 drachms; milk, 8 ounces. Boil together. Take at bedtime as a posset in severe influenza colds. Not to be given to children.

13. **Toothache Drops.**—Catechu* (*kâth*), 10 grains; opium, 1 grain; country spirit, 2 drachms; gum mastic (*mustika*), a small piece. Infuse, decant, and use a drop on a piece of cotton-wool in the cavity.

14. **Fever Draught in the Hot Stage.**—Nitre (*shora*), 2 drachms; rice-water (*kunji*), 1 pint; lemonade, half-pint. Daily as a drink.

The following are useful recipes for the sick-room:—

1. **Imperial.**—One full teaspoon cream of tartar, one sliced lemon, sugar, two tablespoons, one quart boiling water or barley water. Stand till cold, then use. In fevers, &c., use as a drink.

2. **Chicken Tea.**—Mince one medium chicken, bones and all. Put in a basin, and just cover with cold water. Stand for two hours. Put all together in a jar, lute* the cover on with *atta*, and bake or boil for an hour. Should give nearly a breakfast-cup of the strongest soup. Can be made with any kind of meat.

3. **Cannibal Broth.**—One pound good lean beef, minced raw: place in a basin and sprinkle over it two tablespoons water mixed with ten drops dilute hydrochloric acid. Macerate, after careful mixing, for half-an-hour. Put in a clean cloth and extract the juice. The residuum should be quite pale and stringy. Season the meat essence with salt, and for captious patients disguise the colour with a spoonful of cream, or a trifle of burnt-sugar water. A dessertspoon at a time in extreme debility and typhoid.

4. **Barley Water.**—Two ounces pearl barley boiled for half-an-hour in one quart of water. Strain. If acids are inadmissible, it may be made palatable with lemon essence.

5. **Raw Meat Sandwiches.**—Take a slice of fresh raw beef and scrape it to a pulp with a knife; season with pepper and salt; add to each two tablespoons of pulp one of Devonshire cream, and use to make very thin sandwiches.

6. **Champagne Jelly.**—Dissolve four annas-weight of pure gelatine in half a teacup of champagne, by placing the cup in hot water and stirring the gelatine; add another half cup of champagne, and ice. Most useful in excessive vomiting.

7. **Convalescent Quenelles.**—Pound half the white meat of a young chicken and rub through a sieve. Add enough milk to make it the consistency of a custard, and if allowed, one tablespoon whipped cream. Flavour with salt only, and steam in a teacup for half-an-hour. Break down the bones and other meat of the chicken, make into half a teacup of strong tea, and pour round.

8. **Savoury Custard.**—A teacup of strong beef-tea, half a teaspoon cornflour, the yolk of one egg. Boil the beef-tea and cornflour well, stir in

the egg with a seasoning of salt, and steam for a quarter of an hour in a buttered mould. Should be quite firm.

9. **Barley Custard.**—As above, only boiling one dessert spoon of barley with the beef or chicken tea for an hour, then adding the egg.

10. **Brandy Mixture.**—Four tablespoons of brandy and four of water. One full dessertspoon of sugar, and the yolk of two eggs. Beat yolk and sugar, then add the brandy and water. Stimulant and restorative in two tablespoon doses.

11. **One Egg Pudding.**—Half a teacup bread-crumbs, three-quarter teacup boiling milk, one egg. Pour the milk over the bread-crumbs, and beat with a fork; add the yolk well beaten, and half a teaspoonful of sugar. Steam in a buttered teacup, with oiled paper tied over it. Serve with a little lemon syrup.

12. **Linseed Tea.**—One ounce whole linseed, one ounce white sugar, half ounce *malathi*, or real liquorice, four tablespoons or less lemon-juice. Pour over one quart boiling water and macerate for three hours. Strain, and use as barley water. In India the *bhindi* or lady's finger may be used as a demulcent drink, or the *isphagul* seeds.

13. **Beef Tea.**—1 pound finely minced beef, 1 pint water. Boil hard for half-an-hour. Strain. Pound the meat in a mortar, add the fluid, and rub through a very fine hair sieve.

14. **Soup, when the Digestion is poor.**—Add half a teaspoon of curry powder to half-pint strong chicken soup. Boil, strain. Should be quite clear.

15. **Castor Oil Emulsion.**—Castor oil is often a difficulty. The following is at least better than most methods of taking it: Beat the oil up with the yolk of an egg, add a teaspoon of ginger cordial and a claret glass of hot water. Put into a bottle and shake violently; drink at once. Or put plain water with a good deal of salt, and three drops tobasco sauce.*

16. **Mustard Plasters.**—Are best spread on paper and the edges folded in to the depth of half an inch. Soften with flour and linseed, and strengthen with ginger and red pepper.

17. **Poultices, Emollient.**—One of the best poultices for the servants is a thick *chupâtti* made rather wet and baked on one side only. Tear off the skin on the uncooked side and apply. It can be re-heated by placing on the girdle again, and may be moistened with linseed oil, or dusted with mustard.

18. **Linseed Poultices.**—Are best put into muslin bags and tied up. If the bag is large enough, this will not affect the shape, while it prevents messiness.

19. **Bran Jacket.**—Take two strips common coarse muslin or cheese cloth, wide enough to go round the body. Place together. Then fold in half. At the fold and the rough end shape for arm-holes and shoulders. Run the two strips together, and join shoulder on the folded side. Quilt loosely with bran. On the joined side and shoulder put tapes. Dip in scalding water, wring out in a towel as dry as possible. Slip on over one arm, and tie on opposite side and shoulder.

20. **To keep Ice handy.**—Tie a piece of flannel loosely over a basin or tumbler. Break the ice into convenient-sized bits with a needle, and put in the strainer formed by the flannel. As the ice melts the moisture will drain away. Cover the tumbler with a *sola* or wadded cover.

21. **To Raise a Weak Patient.**—Take 1¼ yards stout canvas or calico. Sew a runner at each end. Slip this under the patient; run a stout bamboo in each runner. Then with a person on each side the patient can be raised easily. By making this the full length of the bed, slipping it under like a draw sheet, and then putting stout poles into the runners, a most efficient and comfortable litter is made. It is a refinement in the former to cut two semicircles on each side of the cloth before hemming the runners, so as to leave hand-holes for the nurse to get a good grip on the bamboo.

22. **Doses.**—The doses given above are for adults. The following formula for children's doses is useful: Add 12 to the age, and divide by the age. Thus 2 years old + 12 = 14. This divided by 2 = 7, one-seventh of an adult dose. Four years + 12 = 16÷4, gives one-fourth as the dose. Never give poisonous medicines to children without advice. They are very intolerant of opium, and the smallest dose is sometimes followed by unpleasant results.

CHAPTER XVI

ON THE HILLS

WHEN are you going to the hills? becomes the stereotyped question when April draws near, and people who have hitherto told you that they love heat begin to wonder what it will be like when it gets warmer. In India we launch from winter into summer, and the first experience of heat is a trying one.

And here a word about the advantage of going to the hills. One of the authors recommends it as a preventative measure, the yearly visit materially assisting in the maintenance of good health: her own experience of its benefits was that, having brought up a large family during a residence of twenty years in India, she was never once invalided, and only went to England twice during that period, and then in the company of her husband and children. Many wives, no doubt, cannot make up their minds to break up their homes and separate from their husbands, but if the choice lies between a few months' absence from home yearly and visits to England lasting several years, surely the former is preferable. And a good wife can do much to keep her husband's home in the plains comfortable during her annual visit to the hills: she can make wise arrangements before leaving, and can even send him weekly bills of fare, lists of servants' wages, &c.

But what makes such a change generally a necessity? When a woman cannot sleep at night her nervous system suffers, and failure to obtain a good night's rest is one of the great drawbacks of a hot weather in the plains. The days, with their varied occupations, may speed happily along, but the house is not sufficiently cool at night to enable us to sleep with any comfort, and sleepless nights in India predispose the system to disease, especially of a malarious kind. And the constant talking about the heat is so depressing, that the mere thought of being able to get cool by a trip to the hills makes us better able to endure it while it lasts, taking away, as it does, the feeling of hopelessness which generally sets in about July or August.

When the choice of a hill station has been made, there is much to be thought of. After all, it is either for the protection or the improvement of health that the home is broken up: the selection of a suitable house is therefore all-important. Too often houses are taken for us which are antagonistic to healthy conditions. There are houses on ridges, houses on banks, houses in valleys, houses by the roadside. Houses that bear sweet names, such as 'Moss Grange' and 'Ivy Glen,' awaken early poetical memories; our spirit soars as we read of the 'Eagle's Nest,' 'The Crags,' or 'The Highlands,' whilst 'Sunny Bank' and 'The Dovecote' open out a vista of quiet restfulness. But old stagers know that there is nothing for it but to go up and see for oneself, and trust to no one. As a rule, we do not recommend ridges. Cholera (please do not start!) often dwells in the clouds which float over our Hill Capuas,* and may just rest on the ridge, to say nothing of its being enveloped in damp clouds, and at the mercy of the violence of the storm. Banks should be avoided, especially if the walls of the back rooms are built up against them without any space between. One of the authors speaks feelingly on this point, having had a providential escape from being buried alive in a landslip, by which, though life was saved, valuable property was lost. A house in a valley is too shut in; good air is a necessity. Nor, unless you wish all the community to see your rooms being turned out, should you choose a wayside cottage. Go into every room, and avoid houses with dark inner rooms. Windows and doors should be large enough to allow a free range of sun and air from floor to ceiling. You require shelter, and you require pure air. Rooms in the hills are naturally smaller than those in the plains, and to compensate for this disadvantage more attention must be paid to our surroundings, or we shall lose the benefit which we have come so far to seek.

It is also well to remember that hill houses have very scant accommodation for native servants: the usual allowance is one servant's house for every Rs. 100 paid as the annual rent; so inquire, when securing your house, as to the number of servants' houses, and stalls for ponies and cows, and limit the number of your followers as far as possible.

Do not be alarmed at the dirty state of the house at the beginning of the season—it is English people's dirt, not entirely natives'—and arises simply from the fact that at the close of the previous season the fair occupier could not or would not take the trouble to leave the house in decent order before descending to the plains. The house should therefore at once be thoroughly cleansed, chimneys swept, floors

scrubbed, and all carpets and hangings put out in the air. Throw open
all doors and windows, examine them for broken panes of glass, and
light blazing fires. The tapes* should be taken off the bedsteads and
washed; sanitary arrangements should be minutely inspected. Next,
go round your house outside, and have all rank vegetation cut down;
it harbours dirt, and emits injurious gases, which taint the air. In a
cholera epidemic the neglect of such precautions may prove fatal; for
it has been well said, 'Cholera is a dirt disease, carried by dirty people
to dirty places from dirty places.'*

Why is it that sickness so often supervenes on first arrival at a hill
station? Often from the neglect of such precautions as the above; the
death of a child from bronchitis once resulted from some broken
panes having been overlooked. Nor should suitable food and suitable
clothing be forgotten. Food should be plain and sufficient. Supplies
are generally more difficult to be obtained than in the plains, and not
so good. Vegetables bought in the bazaar, perhaps having been washed
in dirty or scanty water, are dangerous. A *dâli* or basket from a garden two or three times a week is preferable, though, of course, more
expensive. Sometimes a little garden can be made if *jhampannis* are
amiable, and the lady and children do a little work in it: one of the
authors had in this way a capital garden, which supplied her and often
her friends with potatoes and vegetables, to say nothing of flowers.
Watering before the rains is a difficulty, but bath-water should be
made to go as far as possible. If you do not keep cows, the next best
thing is to hire them: they will then be brought morning and evening
to be milked before you and into your own milk-can. Of course a good
deal more has to be paid for milk obtained in this way than for that
bought in the bazaar, but it is the only safe course to adopt. Next to
food comes pure water, and if water cannot be obtained from a spring,
it should be boiled and filtered in the way described in another part
of this work.

And then as to suitable clothing. It must be remembered that on
the hills the sun's rays are very powerful, and the changes of temperature great. Children should not be allowed to go in the sun
without some protection from its rays, and should always be in
the house shortly after sunset, and this especially during the damp
weather of the rainy season. It is a pity that more mothers do not go
out with their children early in the morning; those who do this look
healthy, while the others sleep heavily and get up feeling as sleepy

as ever. The children are better looked after, and on her return the mistress will probably have time before breakfast to see that the house has been well swept out, and to take the cook's account. We blame India for all our ailments, forgetting to accommodate our habits to its climate. Instead of taking exercise, we drink hot tea on an empty stomach, and follow this by a hot bath, which relaxes the muscles and enfeebles our nervous system, and then we try to remedy this with beer or wine, which only irritate the nerves more!

Pardon this digression. The rains, which commence about the end of June, too often bring in their train diarrhœa, dysentery, colds, and chills; special precautions are needed to guard against these. It will be necessary to light fires, not for heat, but to keep everything dry and to dispel mustiness. An incessant downpour lasting nearly three months naturally renders maintenance of health a difficulty; but man possesses capacity for living in all climates, and by adapting ourselves to the conditions of the rains we can get accustomed to them. The hardihood of hill races is proverbial. Look at the stalwart *jhampannis*; they do not fear the rains; but then they do not go about in cotton clothing. Light woollen clothing, even on days when the sun shines brightly, is always safest; above all, wear thin woollen stockings and be well shod. We all know the valuable properties of flannel worn next the skin; warm in structure, and possessed of water-absorbing property, it is the very protection we need to ward off the evils of excessive damp and changes of temperature. For children, night and day, it is indispensable.

Other disagreeables inseparable from the rainy season must be cheerfully met by wise forethought. Woeful is the delay in the washing of clothes; but pity the *dhobi* a little; his wits are sorely taxed to accomplish his task at all. And be careful to air everything he brings. Now is the time to give out warm coats to the servants and blankets to the cowman and the stablemen, who are much exposed to the weather in their avocations. The *jhampannis* are dressed as their mistress's taste dictates; but be merciful in the display of it. Choose good sensible material and trimming that will stand a good soaking; remember that the wearers never use soap, and that a wetting in the rain is their only experience of water.

Put away ostrich feathers and delicate gauzes: they cannot bear the rains. Look to your boots and shoes and articles of leather; all such, as well as books, need constant airing and rubbing. The piano should occasionally have an *angethi* filled with charcoal[1] placed under it, and there should be a fire frequently in the room in which it stands. At the beginning of the rains look well to the roof; otherwise at the first downpour you may have to spend the night trying to save bedding, carpets, and furniture from destruction, or dragging your bed about the room to avoid sleeping under an umbrella. Chilly work! Whenever the sun comes out, call in your servants and have a grand turn-out. The rank vegetation which you had cut down on first coming up will also need seeing to again.

In the hills a *dandy* or *jhampan*, and, if you have children, a *dooly*, are *de rigueur*, even though you prefer, as the authors do, a pony or your own feet. For church, or parties, or state visits, nothing is so convenient as a *dandy*: it is a canoe-shaped chair, which is carried on men's shoulders. From two to four men are required, who should be engaged in a team, all of the same height, and, if possible, of the same build. They will carry you, when they please, about four miles an hour, are generally good-humoured and chatty, and will scramble up or down hill to pick ferns or flowers. They should bring in a bundle of wood or grass daily, which should be inspected, as they are up to all sorts of tricks; and they should appear before you by twelve o'clock. They should be ready to clean windows, or help in the garden, or go messages in the interval between bringing in the wood or grass and carrying you out. Each hill station has its scale of wages for these men, and it is usual also to buy tickets for permission to cut wood and grass in the forests. Hatchets, or sickles, and ropes must be served out. The bearer should be supplied with a padlock, and should lock up the wood, but it must be dried; and it is well on first arrival to lay in a small supply of dry wood in order to eke out the daily bundles. The *dandy* and *dooly* will require a top and curtains of some kind, or a hood; and one or two waterproof sheets are most necessary to spread over the *dandy* or over your saddle when you dismount. A few country-made umbrellas (canework frames covered with leaves) will be a boon to the servants (especially to the *ayah*) on their journeys between their houses and yours. A covered way from the kitchen to the house is a great convenience, and preference should be given to a house with such.

---

[1] A saucer full of unslaked lime placed inside answers the purpose as well.

Preparations for the hills must be carefully thought out—what to take and what to leave behind for the master of the house. It is well when you have selected a house to make a rough plan of it, showing doors and windows and sizes of rooms; so do not forget paper, pencil, and measuring tape. Carpets for the sitting-rooms and all curtains must usually be taken, piano, small tables, comfortable chairs, nick-nacks, ornaments (many of these latter packed in among your dresses), chair backs, tablecovers, something to cover the mantelpiece, and possibly a few pictures. You might also, without being accused of vanity, just see what your landlord provides in the way of looking-glasses. They are marvellous sometimes, and it is best to take one's own; unscrewed from its stand, it can be packed amongst the house linen, whilst stand and supports can be stowed away inside the bundle of carpets, blankets, and rugs. Lamps, some crockery, house linen, and plate must be taken, also kitchen and pantry gear. Books must not be forgotten; and it will be well to inquire from people with local experience whether any stores, wine, &c., should be taken up from the plains. The furniture provided in hill houses being of the scanti-est, and wardrobes a luxury, a hanging wardrobe can be conveniently made out of a plank about three feet long and nine inches wide, down the middle of which insert some six hooks in a row; bore two holes at each end, through which pass strong cords, and fasten the ends of each to hooks in the roof. Tack cretonne round the board a little full, and cross the ends in front. Towel-rails can be extemporised by fas-tening bamboos by strings at either end to hooks in the wall.

Some hill stations possess fair roads, in which case everything can travel all the way in country carts, while others are approached only by tracks fit for camels and mules. Packing arrangements must depend on the kind of carriage available. Excellent camel and mule trunks are often procurable, which are very roomy, and are useful for storing house linen and such like. Chests of drawers made in two parts are very useful to take. They can be packed full of things, and travel well on a camel, and on arrival add much to one's comfort. They should be sewn up in sacking and roped, old rags being put under the ropes and at the corners. It is well to take your head servant into your con-fidence, and to talk over the state of the roads, the kinds of carriage available, &c., with him. Your servants will do all the packing and sewing up, under your superintendence, quickly and cheerfully. When all is packed, sewn up in bundles, and labelled, it is well to make out a list of the articles, and to give a copy to the servants, together with a plan of the house, showing for what purpose each room has been allotted. When the time comes for loading up, retire gracefully. As has been said, 'The servants then become very active, the bullock-drivers being passive, except perhaps to remark, as each box or load is placed, that their bullock will certainly die.'

The following is a list showing the way in which the property of a family, consisting of a lady, three or four children, and an English nurse, might be packed and loaded:—

1st camel load: Two large trunks and two smaller ones with clothing.

2nd camel load: One large trunk containing children's clothing, plate chest, three bags, and one bonnet-box.

3rd camel load: Three boxes of books, one box containing folding chairs, light tin box with clothing.

4th camel load: Four cases of stores, four cane chairs, saddle-stand, mackintosh sheets.

5th camel load: One chest of drawers, two iron cots, tea-table, pans for washing up.

6th camel load: Second chest of drawers, screen, lamps,[1] lanterns, hanging wardrobes.

7th camel load: Two boxes containing house linen, two casks containing ornaments,[1] ice-pails, *angethis*, door-mats.

8th camel load: Three casks of crockery, another cask containing ornaments, filter, pardah bamboos, tennis-poles.

9th camel load: Hot-case, milk-safe, baby's tub and stand, sewing-machine, fender and irons, water-cans, pitchers.

10th camel load: Three boxes containing saddlery, kitchen utensils, carpets.

11th camel load: Two boxes containing drawing-room sundries, servants' coats, iron bath, cheval glass, plate basket.

Or the above articles could be loaded on four country carts, each with three or four bullocks for the up hill journey and two or three for the descent.

Camels travel at the rate of three miles an hour, and bullock-carts more slowly still, so time must be allowed, and personal luggage must be carried by mules or coolies.

---

[1] Breakables are preferably carried on mules; camels are not patient—except in poetry.

A piano, where carts can be used, requires a cart to itself, and should be swung to avoid being injured by jolting. If the road is only a camel-road, the piano must be carried by coolies, of whom fourteen or sixteen will be needed.

Servants are best left to make their own arrangements for themselves and their goods and chattels; but a stand should be made against mill-stones and bedsteads, and extra special conveyance should as a rule be refused. They will perch on carts, camels, and mules, much as birds of the air do; and they will quarrel among themselves. But it is best to be inexorable when appealed to.

When a march is made by stages, and one's own cows accompany, these latter should start, after being milked, the night before the family; at the first halting-place the milk should be left ready for the family on arrival. The last day of the march the morning's milk should be taken on in bottles to be made into butter on arrival, and the cows should reach their destination in time to be milked there that evening.

Then as to the journey of oneself and family. This can now be accomplished with comparative comfort and even in luxury. Railways now so often run to the foot of the hills, and carriages to the door of one's house on the hill-top, that the miseries of the *dâk gâri* and *dooly* are almost a thing of the past. Oh! those *dâk gâri!*—boxes on wheels, with windows which have to be opened with a bang, and doors which are shut with difficulty, only to slide open again! Then the start—the wheels pushed from behind, a rope fastened round the horse's leg pulled, and off you go at full gallop, the servants flying along and clambering up behind! The maxim must be borne in mind, 'It is not well to stop a *dâk gâri*, for it is always uncertain when you can start again.' If you have to travel some hours in one of these vehicles, it should be packed with whatever may be required *en route*. In England the smaller amount of luggage you have the greater your peace, but in India it is just the contrary, and happiness consists in carrying all kinds of creature comforts, and being able to get at them easily. Servants love *guthris*, those indescribable bundles, which, do what you will, they will bring with them, and which often turn out as useful as the lucky-bag in the 'Swiss Family Robinson.'* Next to a *dâk gâri* for misery comes a *dooly*. It is a box on a pole or poles, carried by four men—with two or four more to change at intervals—scantily clothed, and redolent of saturated humanity and *ghee*. They pile their dirty clothes and shoes on the top of the *dooly*, smoke the *hubble-bubble* with rank tobacco, and clamour for *buksheesh* at the end of each stage. Make an agreement with them, and advance the *buksheesh*. The *dooly* can also be packed like the *dâk gâri*. The *tonga* is now pretty generally in use, and is an advance in civilisation; it is a low, two-wheeled cart, drawn by two or three horses, which will carry three (or sometimes five) people, besides the driver, and perhaps a few children also. It has a canvas top. The best seat is that beside the driver. With a crack of the whip and many ejaculations, off you go, rattling and jolting at a grand pace!

Going to the hills is not quite as simple a matter as going to the seaside in England, but then there are the delightfully hairbreadth risks and miraculous escapes as a pleasant excitement, and there is always something new and wonderful. Globe-trotters miss all these when they take good care to return home at the end of the cold season, to tell their friends that India has a most delightful climate. But it is almost worth going to India to experience the pleasures of getting to the hills; especially when one has undergone a captivity in a shut-up house, the slightest fall in the temperature being only 'mitigated misery,' the night a series of moanings and tossings, the only relief an evening drive in the scorching blast of a furnace, with a parched earth below and a sky of brass above. To leave all this behind, and to be hurried along past murmuring streams, green grass, lovely flowers, and shady trees is indeed refreshing. The life-giving breeze fans the wan and hollow eyed children, and our physical and mental energies are awakened. We feel our hearts bound at the sight of the distant snows, and the sweet smell of the pines and wild flowers; and they re-echo a glad alleluia: 'I will lift up mine eyes unto the hills, from whence cometh my help'*—and health! Yes, whether you can get away for six weeks or six months, there is an escape from the furnace of the fiery plains, and well for those who can take advantage of it!

CHAPTER XVII

IN THE PLAINS

THIS is the other side of the shield of truth, and the reader of this and the preceding chapter can—as the showman said to the inquirer as to which was Wellington and which was Blucher in the panorama*—pay his penny and take his choice. The writer spent fourteen whole hot weathers in the plains, and proposes to give her experience of how it can be done comfortably and healthfully, premising always that the decision to set the claims of the husband above those of the children is a wise one.

That very young children can be kept in the plains successfully is undeniable. Indeed babies, if nursed by the mother, thrive better there, and as a rule, they do not suffer until the age when the necessity for keeping in the house all day becomes irksome. In these times of depreciated currency* many parents cannot afford to send their children home, and in that case the usual arrangement is that the mother should go to the hills with all the children. In some cases this is inevitable, but the writer's private opinion is, that in many more the proper course is to send the elder children away under a responsible nurse or governess, or to school, and for the mother to stay down with her husband for as long as she can. His risks, his discomforts, are infinitely greater than those run by the chicks in a healthy climate, and most mothers at home have to send their children to school. It is, however, a question on which stereotyped advice is useless; but that, *per se*, an Englishwoman cannot stand the hot weather as well, and perhaps better than a man, the writer strenuously denies.

Let us suppose then that the reader has nerved herself to give this most unusual reply to the question with which the last chapter opens: 'I am not going to the hills unless my husband gets leave.' In this case she must look ahead deliberately and count the cost. That it is an ordeal none will deny; the more so, because so few face it, and she may be, as the writer has often been, the only lady in the station for months.

Naturally, her aim will be to make this ordeal as light as possible, and the first step towards this is to keep her house as cool as possible.

In Northern India,* the writer strongly advocates thermantidotes. These are machines like the old-fashioned winnowing machines— briefly described, a box with a revolving fan, turned either with handle or treadle by a coolie outside. In the sides of the box are *khus khus* grass screens, which are kept constantly wetted. By this means the air sent into the room by the revolving fan is sometimes 10 degrees cooler than that outside. During a dust-storm the thermometer placed in the mouth of the thermantidote often falls to 70 degrees, though outside it may be 100 degrees or more. Never buy a cheap, ramshackle thermantidote. Money expended in a good Johnson's self-watering machine* will never be regretted. The author once had three of these going in a very large house day and night. And that house was a haven of refuge for every one in the station, since, during a stifling hot weather, its temperature never rose above 85 degrees. In regard to punkahs, in the writer's opinion they are comparatively of little use except to keep away mosquitoes, or when sleeping on the roof. At mealtimes they are a necessity. But they are too intermittent a palliative to be satisfactory. The presence of a punkah rope in a coolie's hand seems positively to have a soporific effect on him, whereas the handle or treadle of a thermantidote acquires an impetus of its own, and asserts its intention of going round, will-he nill-he.* Finally, owing to the thermantidote being built into the wall or door, there is less temptation to burst out on the offender and slay him on the spot, since to do this you must go round deliberately by another door. Even if this homicidal mania does not seize on you, a thermantidote prevents the possibility of spoiling your boots and shoes by throwing them at the coolie's head. It must be admitted that many people consider thermantidotes unwholesome, and provocative of climatic disease. The writer's experience, however, is that they virtually stopped the intermittent fever which year after year attacked one of her household. After adopting them he never had a bad attack, though the current of damp air in which he sat by day and slept by night ought, in the opinion of most doctors, to have aggravated his complaint. Care must, of course, be taken to avoid chills; but the increase of comfort and the refreshing sleep enjoyed are well worth some trouble.

Punkahs are generally put up in Northern India about the beginning of April. The cloth-covered frames supplied by the landlord of the house are usually whitewashed, and after several coats the lime is sure to come off in flakes and get into your eyes. This is an evil only to be mitigated by having the frames well scraped. The Bombay and Bengal punkahs* consist often of a bar of polished wood, from which the fringe hangs. This is prettier and cleaner, but it hardly gives so much wind as the broad, flat frame. Sometimes you meet with wooden panelled frames. These are best; but failing this, and if the whitewash nuisance be great, it will be found wiser to re-cover the frames with cotton dyed to match your room. The frill can be made pretty in a thousand ways. It will not cost much. There is nothing more difficult than to judge the height at which a punkah should be hung. Strictly speaking, it is always too high or too low; in other words, it either scrapes your head or leaves you perspiring. In fact, at its best it is an instrument of torture. On the other hand, it appears to please the coolie who pulls it. The squeaking of a punkah at night is very distracting, but can generally be cured by black lead or oil. The latter, however, is apt to smell. Leather thongs for pulling are dearer to begin with, but more satisfactory than ropes; nothing is more maddening than to have to get up and splice the latter in the middle of the night. A towel pinned on at night to the punkah fringe makes its sweep greater. After punkahs and thermantidotes, the next luxury is an ice-box. In this, again, stinting is *no* economy. In the mere waste of provisions which a good one avoids there lies a saving. A real, large refrigerator is better than a doctor, but it requires scrupulous cleanliness, and the personal attention of the mistress. Meat put into it should be wiped over with a solution of boracic acid, and a pan of charcoal kept in the refrigerator. The usual plan of putting first ice, wrapped in blankets, into a tin-lined box, and then stuffing the box with indiscriminate provisions wrapped in dirty dusters, is *not* sanitary. Milk should never be put in with meat. It is far better to boil it, put it into a tightly-corked bottle, and set it *on* the ice, which should be in a different compartment. But scalded milk will keep a day in the hottest weather if properly treated.

The next important point is the opening and closing of the house. With a thermantidote it need never be opened, as a fresh supply of air is constantly being pumped into it. With punkahs, common-sense and care is needed, and an almost daily order; otherwise the bearer will disregard whirlwinds, dust-storms, in fact, all natural phenomena and seasons, in favour of an implicit obedience to mere time, which is as unusual as it is irritating. If the doors are open all night they should invariably be closed half-an-hour before sunrise and for the half-hour after sun-setting. This is *mosquito time*, to say nothing of malaria time. Attention to this detail will keep your house comparatively free of both. Draperies should be removed for the hot weather, and everything likely to harbour insects put aside; but it is a mistake to strip your rooms and make yourself uncomfortable.

It is an enormous mistake to darken your rooms too much. You may succeed in keeping them a degree cooler, but, as has been said elsewhere, the sun is your friend, and you cannot shut him out altogether from your life with impunity. The enforced idleness of a dark room is worse for your body and soul in the future than many degrees of present heat. In fact, the writer looks back gratefully to certain artistic leanings which, in her early Indian days, made the lack of light impossible. To it she owes much of her freedom from the usual effects of India on womankind, which are generally set down to the climate. In regard to getting up early. People say they cannot; that it does not suit them to go out before breakfast. Now, early and late are purely relative terms, and breakfast is a movable feast. If you go to bed two hours earlier, five o'clock becomes as late as seven o'clock was when you retired to rest two hours later; while it is always possible to invert the sentence and have breakfast before you go out! The object being to gain, out of doors, an hour or two during which you can walk, and ride, and play tennis with comfort, a time when the sun can shine on you undimmed by the gases and vapours he draws from the heat-stricken world. Sleep in the day, by all means, if necessary; in this case go to bed deliberately. Do not simply *lie down* in your day clothes. It isn't half so refreshing as a real sleep on a real bed. Get out into the garden as soon after five o'clock as it is possible, and don't look at the thermometer half-a-dozen times a day. The constant friction between your desires and the actual facts tends to make your temper, at any rate, rise considerably. The writer's idea of a healthy, comfortable, hot-weather day is as follows: Rise at five o'clock, or half-past, after a night spent under a thermantidote, or on the roof with a punkah. Take tea and toast. Then, on some pretence or another—if possible with an object—stay out of doors riding, driving, or walking till half-past seven or eight o'clock. Take some porridge and milk, or some other light refreshment, remembering that in the hot weather it is a mistake either to feel empty or to take a *full* meal. Then bathe, either in a swimming-bath or in a tub full of really *hot* water.

Look after the housekeeping, &c., either before or after your bath. Not later than ten o'clock, breakfast, and work steadily at something till noon. From twelve till two lie down and read, or sleep. It is a horrible mistake to sleep *after* a heavy luncheon; you wake unfit even for your own society. Lunch at two, or half-past. Work till four, bathe, dress, and go out. So, as Pepys says, dinner at eight, and to bed about half-past ten.* For children the same routine may be adopted, except that they should sleep from half-past eleven to half-past three, if possible. That is to say, there should be two nights in every twenty-four hours. Even if they cannot sleep, they should be dressed in their flannel night-gowns and kept as quiet as possible, in a cool, darkened room. So much for *entourage*.

In regard to housekeeping cares, the effort to get good digestible food must be constant. Meat must, without an ice-box, be eaten the day it is killed, and thus it is almost invariably tough. But any stringy stuff may be improved by being minced, beaten, and pulped through a coarse sieve. It can then be formed into cutlets and grilled. This is a very different thing from the *khânsamah*'s *melange* of meat, spices, onions, and sauces, which goes by the same name. Quails are a great stand-by; so are eggs, fowls, and fish. The hot-weather vegetables have a bad name, but that is largely the fault of the cooks. Properly dressed, they are quite palatable. Good butter can always be made from milk, and the writer was never without cream to her tea during the whole two-and-twenty years she lived in India. This is mentioned to show that the heat need not dislocate the whole articulations of life, unless we choose to have it so. The fact is, that many people make the climate of India into a Frankenstein monster,* and straightway become alarmed at their own creation. It is often necessary to engage another *bheestie* for watering the thermantidotes during the hottest months, and in view of epidemics an extra sweeper is a desideratum. When the rains set in, a covered shelter on the roof will be found a great comfort. As a rule, you will be able to sleep there soundly, if a punkah be rigged up to keep away mosquitoes. Failing a permanent erection, the upper part of a tent does well. Some people say that once the rains set in, thermantidotes are no use. This is not the case. They always give a purer, freer current of air than the punkah can do.

In regard to drinks, iced milk and soda-water is as good as anything, but the writer believes largely in not drinking whenever you feel thirsty. The habit of only drinking at certain times is easily acquired, and is far more wholesome. There is a certain somewhat vulgar story about a cure for sea-sickness effected by the captain of a merchant vessel, which ends with this piece of advice, 'Don't give in to your stomach, and your stomach will give in to you.'* That is true of all things; and so when all has been said that can be said about the hot weather and the way to endure it, the gist of the whole lies in this—*Don't give in to it, and it will give in to you.* Keep your house cool and light, your mind employed, and your muscles in reasonable training. Then there remains nothing out of your control save prickly heat (*lichen orientalis*). This attacks some skins more than others, and, as a rule, has to be endured. But sandal-wood dust used as powder is one palliative. The other is, that those who suffer most from prickly heat, are, as a rule, free from more serious ailments.

As to clothing, a woman who wishes to live up to the climate must dress down to it. Frills, furbelows, ribbons, laces, are so much off that sum-total of comfort which it is your aim to increase. The writer found one silk under-dress (a sort of combination chemise and dual garment) and light woollen tea-gowns best for morning wear. For tennis, &c., a silk petticoat, silk combination, pretty nuns-veiling or serge costume, with a blouse bodice. For riding, her usual heavy skirt with a white shirt, and very light coat matching the skirt exactly in colour. It must be remembered that these remarks 'In the Plains' apply entirely to Northern India, or any climate where summer and winter temperatures vary considerably. In Madras and parts of Lower Bengal,* life runs much on the same lines all the year round. One word as to insects and snakes. Phenyle is good for keeping away mosquitoes—a weak solution washed over the floor. Shutting up doors and windows (during your absence from the house), and burning red pepper and sulphur, is a heroic measure apt to be disagreeable even on your return, but effectual. For snakes, constant care, the raising *daily* of the edges of the matting, and snake-proof nettings at the bathroom water-drain will do much. When doors are open at night, a sprinkling of carbolic powder right across the lintel will prevent them crossing it; for carbolic acid kills snakes. The keeping round about the house of fowls and ducks reduces insect life immensely, but their house should not be too near, as snakes are very fond of eggs. *Milk*, however, is the great attraction, and where it is kept snakes should always be

guarded against. In sleeping out in snaky places, it is a good plan
to put the legs of the bed into saucers filled with carbolic powder.
No one should ever go about at night without a light of some sort.
And in the storeroom or linen cupboard, or any place where there
is peace and quiet, the hand should never be poked carelessly into
corners. It may be mentioned, however, that the writer was fourteen
years in India before she saw a live snake in her house.

During very dry weather it is a good plan to place a saucer of water
in the piano, while during the rains one of quick-lime will help to
absorb excessive moisture. Clothes will require constant airing
during the damp season, and, damp or dry, white ants will attack
anything and everything within reach; so furniture, boxes, &c., must
be constantly moved.

CHAPTER XVIII

TABLE OF WAGES, WEIGHTS, ETC.

Showing the Amount for One or more Days at the rate of One to Ten Rupees per Month of Thirty-one Days

Rupees.	1	2	3	4	5	6	7	8	9	10
Days.	Rs. a. p.	Rs. a. p.	Rs. a. p.	Rs. a. p.	Rs. a. p.	Rs. a. p.	Rs. a. p.	Rs. a. p.	Rs. a. p.	Rs. a. p.
1	0 0 6	0 1 0	0 1 6	0 2 0	0 2 0	0 3 1	0 3 7	0 4 1	0 4 7	0 5 1
2	0 1 0	0 2 0	0 3 1	0 4 1	0 5 1	0 6 2	0 7 2	0 8 3	0 9 3	0 10 3
3	0 1 6	0 3 1	0 4 7	0 6 2	0 7 8	0 9 3	0 10 10	0 12 4	0 13 11	0 15 5
4	0 2 0	0 4 1	0 6 2	0 8 3	0 10 3	0 12 4	0 14 5	1 0 6	1 2 6	1 4 7
5	0 2 6	0 5 1	0 7 8	0 10 3	0 12 10	0 15 5	1 2 0	1 4 7	1 7 2	1 9 9
6	0 3 1	0 6 2	0 9 3	0 12 4	0 15 5	1 2 6	1 5 8	1 8 9	1 11 10	1 14 11
7	0 3 7	0 7 2	0 10 10	1 0 6	1 2 0	1 5 8	1 9 3	1 12 10	2 0 6	2 4 1
8	0 4 1	0 8 3	0 12 4	1 0 6	1 4 7	1 8 9	1 12 10	2 1 0	2 5 1	2 9 3
9	0 4 7	0 9 3	0 13 11	1 2 6	1 7 2	1 11 10	2 0 6	2 5 1	2 9 9	2 14 5
10	0 5 1	0 10 3	0 15 5	1 4 7	1 9 9	1 14 11	2 4 1	2 9 3	2 14 5	3 3 7
11	0 5 8	0 11 4	1 1 0	1 6 8	1 12 4	2 2 0	2 7 8	2 13 4	3 3 1	3 9 9
12	0 6 2	0 12 5	1 2 6	1 8 9	1 14 11	2 5 8	2 11 4	3 1 6	3 7 8	3 13 11
13	0 6 8	0 13 5	1 4 1	1 10 10	2 1 6	2 8 3	2 14 11	3 5 8	3 12 4	4 3 1
14	0 7 2	0 14 5	1 5 8	1 12 10	2 4 1	2 11 4	3 2 6	3 9 9	4 1 0	4 8 3
15	0 7 8	0 15 6	1 7 2	1 14 11	2 6 8	2 14 5	3 6 2	3 13 11	4 5 8	4 13 4
16	0 8 3	1 0 6	1 8 9	2 1 0	2 9 3	3 1 6	3 9 9	4 2 0	4 10 3	5 2 6
17	0 8 9	1 1 6	1 10 3	2 3 1	2 11 10	3 4 7	3 13 4	4 6 2	4 14 11	5 7 8
18	0 9 3	1 2 6	1 11 10	2 5 1	2 14 5	3 7 8	4 1 0	4 10 3	5 3 7	5 12 10
19	0 9 9	1 3 7	1 13 4	2 7 2	3 1 0	3 10 10	4 4 7	4 14 5	5 8 3	6 2 0
20	0 10 3	1 4 7	1 14 11	2 9 3	3 3 7	3 13 4	4 8 3	5 2 6	5 12 10	6 7 2
21	0 10 9	1 5 8	2 0 6	2 11 4	3 6 2	4 1 0	4 11 10	5 6 8	6 1 6	6 12 4
22	0 11 4	1 6 8	2 2 0	2 13 4	3 8 9	4 4 1	4 15 5	5 10 10	6 6 2	7 1 6
23	0 11 10	1 7 8	2 3 7	2 15 5	3 11 4	4 7 2	5 3 1	5 14 11	6 10 10	7 6 8
24	0 12 4	1 8 9	2 5 1	3 1 6	3 13 11	4 10 3	5 6 8	6 3 1	6 15 5	7 11 10
25	0 12 10	1 9 9	2 6 2	3 3 7	4 0 6	4 13 4	5 10 3	6 7 2	7 4 1	8 1 0
26	0 13 4	1 10 10	2 8 3	3 5 8	4 3 0	5 0 6	5 13 11	6 11 4	7 8 9	8 6 2
27	0 13 11	1 11 10	2 9 9	3 7 8	4 5 8	5 3 7	6 1 6	6 15 5	7 13 4	8 11 4
28	0 14 5	1 12 10	2 11 4	3 9 9	4 8 3	5 6 8	6 5 1	7 3 7	8 2 0	9 0 6
29	0 14 11	1 13 11	2 12 10	3 11 10	4 10 10	5 9 9	6 8 9	7 7 8	8 6 8	9 5 8
30	0 15 5	1 14 11	2 14 5	3 13 11	4 13 4	5 12 10	6 12 4	7 11 10	8 11 4	9 10 10
31	1 0 0	2 0 0	3 0 0	4 0 0	5 0 0	6 0 0	7 0 0	8 0 0	9 0 0	10 0 0

TABLE I.—*Showing the price of any number of Seers or Articles from 1 to 100 at rates varying from Rs. 2 each to 9 per Rupee*

No. per Rupee	½	1	2	3	4	5	6	7	8	9
No. of Articles	Rs. a. p.	Rs. a. p.	Rs. a. p.	Rs. a. p.	Rs. a. p.	Rs. a. p.	Rs. a. p.	Rs. a. p.	Rs. a. p.	Rs. a. p.
1	2 0 0	1 0 0	0 8 0	0 5 4	0 4 0	0 3 2	0 2 8	0 2 3	0 2 0	0 1 9
2	4 0 0	2 0 0	1 0 0	0 10 8	0 8 0	0 6 5	0 5 4	0 4 7	0 4 0	0 3 7
3	6 0 0	3 0 0	1 8 0	1 0 0	0 12 0	0 9 7	0 8 0	0 6 10	0 6 0	0 5 4
4	8 0 0	4 0 0	2 0 0	1 5 4	1 0 0	0 12 10	0 10 8	0 9 2	0 8 0	0 7 1
5	10 0 0	5 0 0	2 0 0	1 10 8	1 4 0	1 0 0	0 13 4	0 11 4	0 10 0	0 8 11
6	12 0 0	6 0 0	3 0 0	2 0 0	1 8 0	1 3 2	1 0 0	0 13 8	0 12 0	0 10 8
7	14 0 0	7 0 0	3 8 0	2 5 4	1 12 0	1 6 4	1 2 8	1 0 0	0 14 0	0 12 5
8	16 0 0	8 0 0	4 0 0	2 10 8	2 0 0	1 9 8	1 5 4	1 2 4	1 0 0	0 14 2
9	18 0 0	9 0 0	4 8 0	2 0 0	2 4 0	1 12 10	1 8 0	1 4 6	1 2 0	1 10 0
10	20 0 0	10 0 0	5 0 0	3 5 4	2 8 0	2 0 0	1 10 8	1 6 10	1 4 0	1 1 9
20	40 0 0	20 0 0	10 0 0	6 10 8	5 0 0	4 0 0	3 5 4	2 13 8	2 8 0	2 3 1
30	60 0 0	30 0 0	15 0 0	10 0 0	7 8 0	6 0 0	5 0 0	4 4 6	3 12 0	3 5 6
40	80 0 0	40 0 0	20 0 0	13 5 4	10 0 0	8 0 0	6 10 8	5 12 5	5 0 0	4 7 3
50	100 0 0	50 0 0	25 0 0	16 10 8	12 8 0	10 0 0	8 5 4	7 1 3	6 4 0	5 8 10
60	120 0 0	60 0 0	30 0 0	20 0 0	15 0 0	12 0 0	10 0 0	8 9 1	7 8 0	6 10 7
70	140 0 0	70 0 0	35 0 0	23 5 4	17 8 0	14 0 0	11 10 8	10 0 0	8 12 0	7 12 5
80	160 0 0	80 0 0	40 0 0	26 10 8	20 0 0	16 0 0	13 5 4	11 6 11	10 0 0	8 14 2
90	180 0 0	90 0 0	45 0 0	30 0 0	22 8 0	18 0 0	15 0 0	12 13 8	11 4 0	9 15 11
100	200 0 0	100 0 0	50 0 0	33 5 4	25 0 0	20 0 0	16 10 8	14 4 6	12 8 0	11 1 9

Examples.—Wanted the price of 9 Rolls, at 18 to the Rupee. Look at Table 2, and it will be found in the column headed 18 and opposite 9=Rs. 0-7-11.

Wanted the price of 96 seers of charcoal, at 27 to the Rupee. Look for the price of 90 in Table 3, Rs. 3-5-3, and that of 6 in same Table, Rs. 0-3-6. Add these two sums together, which gives Rs. 3-8-9 as the price of 96 at 27 to the Rupee.

TABLE II.—*Same at 10 to 19 per Rupee*

No. per Rupee	10	11	12	13	14	15	16	17	18	19
No. of Articles	Rs. a. p.	Rs. a. p.	Rs. a. p.	Rs. a. p.	Rs. a. p.	Rs. a. p.	Rs. a. p.	Rs. a. p.	Rs. a. p.	Rs. a. p.
1	0 1 7	0 1 5	0 1 4	0 1 3	0 1 2	0 1 1	0 1 0	0 0 11	0 0 10	0 0 10
2	0 3 2	0 2 11	0 2 8	0 2 5	0 2 3	0 2 1	0 2 0	0 1 11	0 1 9	0 1 8
3	0 4 10	0 4 4	0 4 0	0 3 8	0 3 5	0 3 2	0 3 0	0 2 10	0 2 8	0 2 6
4	0 6 5	0 5 10	0 5 4	0 4 11	0 4 7	0 4 3	0 4 0	0 3 9	0 3 6	0 3 4
5	0 8 0	0 7 3	0 6 8	0 6 2	0 5 9	0 5 3	0 5 0	0 4 9	0 4 5	0 4 3
6	0 9 8	0 8 8	0 8 0	0 7 4	0 6 10	0 6 4	0 6 0	0 5 8	0 5 4	0 5 0
7	0 11 3	0 10 1	0 9 4	0 8 7	0 8 0	0 7 6	0 7 0	0 6 7	0 6 2	0 5 10
8	0 12 10	0 11 8	0 10 8	0 9 10	0 9 2	0 8 6	0 8 0	0 7 6	0 7 0	0 6 8
9	0 14 5	0 13 1	0 12 0	0 11 1	0 10 4	0 9 6	0 9 0	0 8 6	0 7 11	0 7 7
10	1 0 0	0 14 6	0 13 4	0 12 4	0 11 6	0 10 6	0 10 0	0 9 6	0 8 10	0 8 6

TABLE II.—*Same at* 10 *to* 19 *per Rupee (Cont.)*

No. per Rupee	10	11	12	13	14	15	16	17	18	19
No. of Articles	Rs. a. p.	Rs. a. p.	Rs. a. p.	Rs. a. p.	Rs. a. p.	Rs. a. p.	Rs. a. p.	Rs. a. p.	Rs. a. p.	Rs. a. p.
20	2 0 0	1 13 1	1 10 8	1 8 7	1 6 10	1 5 4	1 4 0	1 2 9	1 1 9	1 0 10
30	3 0 0	2 11 7	2 8 0	2 4 11	2 2 3	2 0 0	1 14 0	1 12 2	1 10 8	1 9 3
40	4 0 0	3 10 2	3 5 4	3 1 2	2 13 8	2 10 8	2 8 0	2 5 7	2 3 6	2 1 8
50	5 0 0	4 8 8	4 2 8	3 13 6	3 9 1	3 5 4	3 2 0	2 15 0	2 12 4	2 10 1
60	6 0 0	5 7 3	5 0 0	4 9 10	4 4 6	4 0 0	3 12 0	3 8 5	3 5 4	3 2 6
70	7 0 0	6 5 9	6 10 4	5 6 1	4 15 11	4 10 8	4 6 0	4 1 10	3 14 2	3 10 11
80	8 0 0	7 4 4	6 13 8	6 2 5	5 11 4	5 5 4	5 0 0	4 11 3	4 7 1	4 3 4
90	9 0 0	8 2 10	7 8 0	6 14 9	6 6 9	6 0 0	5 10 0	5 4 8	5 0 0	4 11 9
100	10 0 0	9 1 5	8 5 4	7 11 0	7 2 3	6 10 8	6 4 0	5 14 1	5 8 11	5 4 2

TABLE III.—*Same at* 20 *to* 29 *per Rupee*

No. per Rupee	20	21	22	23	24	25	26	27	28	29
No. of Articles	Rs. a. p.	Rs. a. p.	Rs. a. p.	Rs. a. p.	Rs. a. p.	Rs. a. p.	Rs. a. p.	Rs. a. p.	Rs. a. p.	Rs. a. p.
1	0 0 10	0 0 9	0 0 8	0 0 8	0 0 8	0 0 7	0 0 7	0 0 7	0 0 6	0 0 6
2	0 1 7	0 1 6	0 1 5	0 1 4	0 1 4	0 1 3	0 1 2	0 1 2	0 1 1	0 1 1
3	0 2 5	0 2 3	0 2 2	0 2 0	0 2 0	0 1 10	0 1 9	0 1 9	0 1 8	0 1 7
4	0 3 2	0 3 0	0 2 10	0 2 9	0 2 8	0 2 6	0 2 5	0 2 4	0 2 3	0 2 2
5	0 4 0	0 3 9	0 3 7	0 3 5	0 3 4	0 3 2	0 3 0	0 2 11	0 2 10	0 2 9
6	0 4 10	0 4 6	0 4 4	0 4 1	0 4 0	0 3 9	0 3 7	0 3 6	0 3 4	0 3 3
7	0 5 7	0 5 3	0 5 0	0 4 10	0 4 8	0 4 5	0 4 3	0 4 1	0 3 11	0 3 10
8	0 6 5	0 6 0	0 5 9	0 5 6	0 5 4	0 5 0	0 4 10	0 4 8	0 4 6	0 4 4
9	0 7 2	0 6 9	0 6 6	0 6 2	0 6 0	0 5 8	0 5 5	0 5 3	0 5 1	0 4 11
10	0 8 0	0 7 7	0 7 3	0 6 11	0 6 8	0 6 4	0 6 1	0 5 11	0 5 8	0 5 6
20	1 0 0	0 15 2	0 14 6	0 13 10	0 13 4	0 12 9	0 12 3	0 11 10	0 11 5	0 11 0
30	1 8 0	1 6 10	1 5 6	1 4 10	1 4 0	1 3 2	1 2 5	1 1 9	1 1 1	1 0 6
40	2 0 0	1 14 5	1 13 0	1 11 9	1 10 8	1 9 7	1 8 7	1 7 8	1 6 10	1 6 0
50	2 8 0	2 6 1	2 4 4	2 2 9	2 1 4	2 0 0	1 14 9	1 13 7	1 12 6	1 11 7
60	3 0 0	2 13 8	2 11 7	2 9 8	2 8 0	2 6 4	2 4 10	2 3 6	2 2 3	2 1 1
70	3 8 0	3 5 3	3 2 10	3 0 7	2 14 8	2 12 9	2 11 0	2 9 5	2 7 11	2 6 7
80	4 0 0	3 12 11	3 10 1	3 7 7	3 5 4	3 3 2	3 1 2	2 15 4	2 13 8	2 12 1
90	4 8 0	4 4 6	4 1 4	3 14 6	3 12 0	3 9 7	3 7 4	3 5 3	3 3 4	3 1 7
100	5 0 0	4 12 2	4 8 8	4 5 6	4 2 8	4 0 0	3 13 6	3 11 3	3 9 1	3 7 2

TABLE IV.—*Same at 30 to 39 to the Rupee*

No. per Rupee	30	31	32	33	34	35	36	37	38	39
No. of Articles	Rs. a. p.	Rs. a. p.	Rs. a. p.	Rs. a. p.	Rs. a. p.	Rs. a. p.	Rs. a. p.	Rs. a. p.	Rs. a. p.	Rs. a. p.
1	0 0 6	0 0 6	0 0 6	0 0 5	0 0 5	0 0 5	0 0 5	0 0 5	0 0 5	0 0 4
2	0 1 0	0 1 0	0 1 0	0 0 11	0 0 11	0 0 10	0 0 10	0 0 10	0 0 10	0 0 9
3	0 1 7	0 1 6	0 1 6	0 1 5	0 1 4	0 1 4	0 1 3	0 1 3	0 1 3	0 1 2
4	0 2 1	0 2 0	0 2 0	0 1 11	0 1 10	0 1 9	0 1 9	0 1 8	0 1 8	0 1 7
5	0 2 8	0 2 6	0 2 6	0 2 5	0 2 4	0 2 3	0 2 2	0 2 1	0 2 1	0 2 0
6	0 3 2	0 3 0	0 3 0	0 2 10	0 2 9	0 2 8	0 2 7	0 2 6	0 2 6	0 2 5
7	0 3 8	0 3 6	0 3 6	0 3 4	0 3 3	0 3 1	0 3 1	0 2 11	0 2 11	0 2 10
8	0 4 3	0 4 0	0 4 0	0 3 10	0 3 8	0 3 7	0 3 6	0 3 4	0 3 4	0 3 3
9	0 4 9	0 4 6	0 4 6	0 4 4	0 4 2	0 4 0	0 3 11	0 3 9	0 3 9	0 3 8
10	0 5 4	0 5 1	0 5 0	0 4 10	0 4 8	0 4 6	0 4 5	0 4 3	0 4 2	0 4 1
20	0 10 8	0 10 3	0 10 0	0 9 8	0 9 4	0 9 1	0 8 10	0 8 7	0 8 5	0 8 2
30	1 0 0	0 15 5	0 15 0	0 14 6	0 14 1	0 13 8	0 13 3	0 12 11	0 12 7	0 12 3
40	1 5 4	1 4 7	1 4 0	1 3 4	1 2 9	1 2 3	1 1 9	1 1 3	1 0 10	1 0 4
50	1 10 8	1 9 9	1 9 0	1 8 2	1 7 6	1 6 10	1 6 2	1 5 7	1 5 0	1 4 6
60	2 0 0	1 14 11	1 14 0	1 13 0	1 12 2	1 11 4	1 10 7	1 9 10	1 9 3	1 8 7
70	2 5 4	2 4 1	2 3 0	2 1 10	2 0 10	1 15 11	1 15 1	1 14 2	1 13 5	1 12 8
80	2 10 8	2 9 3	2 8 0	2 6 8	2 5 6	2 4 6	2 3 6	2 2 6	2 1 8	2 0 9
90	3 0 0	2 14 5	2 13 0	2 11 6	2 10 3	2 9 1	2 7 11	2 6 10	2 5 10	2 4 10
100	3 5 4	3 3 7	3 2 0	3 0 5	2 15 0	2 13 8	2 12 5	2 11 2	2 10 1	2 9 0

TABLE V.—*Rough equivalents of Weights and Measures*

LIQUID

English.	In Spoonfuls.	Indian.
60 minims (η) = 1 drachm ($\mathfrak{Z}$).	1 teaspoon.	4 mashas.
8 drachms ($\mathfrak{Z}$) = 1 ounce ($\mathfrak{Z}$).	2 tablespoons.	½ chittack.
5 ounces ($\mathfrak{Z}$) = 1 gill.	10 tablespoons or 1 teacup.	2½ chittacks.
4 gills = 1 pint (O).	40 tablespoons or two tumblers.	10 chittacks.
2 pints (O) = 1 quart (Oij).	80 tablespoons or 4 tumblers.	20 chittacks.
4 quarts (Oij) = 1 gallon (C.).	16 tumblers.	5 seers.

SOLID

English.	In Spoonfuls.	Indian.
1 drachm (dr.).	1 teaspoon.	4 mashas.
8 drachms (dr.) = 1 ounce (oz.).	1 tablespoon.	½ chittack.
16 ounces (oz.) = 1 pound (lb.).	32 tablespoons.	8 chittacks.
28 pounds (lb.) = 1 quarter (qr.).	......	16 seers.
4 quarters (qrs.) = 1 hundred-weight (cwt.).	......	1 maund 24 seers.
20 hundredweight (cwt.) = 1 ton.	......	32 maunds.

TABLE VI.—*Indian Weights*
There are no recognized Liquid Measures

12 mashas = 1 tola (1 sikka rupee).
5 tolas = 1 chittack.
16 chittacks = 1 seer of 80 sikka rupees.
40 seers = 1 maund.

TABLE VII.—*To find the Value of 1 Seer from the Price per Maund of anything*

Count each rupee of price as 8 units and each anna as ½ a unit. Five units equal 1 paisa or ¼ of an anna.

Example.—One maund costs Rs. 5.10; 5 × 8 = 40 units; and 10 ÷ ½ = 5 units. Total, 45 units ÷ 5 = 9 paisas or 2¼ annas.

CHAPTER XIX

HINTS ON OUTFITS, ETC.

THE following chapter has been added by request, and the constant queries on this subject in the *Queen** and other ladies' newspapers incline the authors to believe that it will be very generally acceptable.

Their first duty, however, is to remind their readers that India is not what it was when an order from England could not be given and executed under nine months. Six weeks is now sufficient; and those who have recently gone out to India generally have plenty of kindly eyes watching them, and kindly hearts only too glad of an opportunity of doing something for those who in most ways have gone beyond the reach of practical sympathy. Therefore, as a rule, there is little difficulty in ordering things to be sent out to meet requirements as they arise. This point is not sufficiently considered in the preparation of most outfits, and it is no uncommon thing to find boxes and boxes full of unworn clothing in a lady's wardrobe. It is easy to understand what a ghastly mistake this may be in a country like India, which teems with insect life at all seasons, and with damp fungoid growths during one-half of the year, and dry rot at the other! In addition, clothes have a fatal habit of disappearing every time they are unpacked for airing unless their owners keep an eagle eye upon them. The authors therefore strongly advise the utmost moderation, not only in dresses, but in underclothing. In regard to this, it must not be forgotten that the increased necessity for constant change is almost counterbalanced by the corresponding facility in getting things rapidly washed.

It is, of course, manifestly impossible to give a hard-and-fast list of underclothing necessary, as this must vary largely; but, roughly speaking, it may safely be said that no one needs more than a dozen all round of whatever under-garments may be worn. It is a mistake to employ fine lawn or cambric for underclothing, as the perspiration soaks into them, and they get wispy and stringy. Nothing is cooler or more wholesome during the Indian hot weather than soft washing silk, and its use does away with the necessity for flannel, which is so

irritating to some skins. The great secret of coolness and comfort, however, lies in wearing one well-fitting, absorbent under-garment, and
one only. For this purpose nothing can be better than a combination
garment of silk or cellular flannel, with the lower part made loose
and roomy, without any knickerbocker frills and furbelows. With this,
a pair of open net stays, on to the lower edge of which a fine white
petticoat buttons, and a spun-silk jersey bodice as a stay protector,
and a lady will find the discomforts of clothing in a temperature over
98° reduced to the minimum compatible with European ideas.

There can be no doubt, however, that where the climate ranges
between such extremes of cold and heat, as it does in many parts of
India, it becomes necessary to yield to it in the matter of dress, unless
fashion is to be set before health and comfort. And there is really no
reason why the Englishwoman in India should burden herself with
the same number of petticoats, shifts, bodices, and what not, that her
great-grandmother wore in temperate climes. We do not advocate
any sloppiness in dress; on the contrary, we would inveigh against
any yielding to the lassitude and indifference which comes over the
most energetic in tropical heat, but we would have people as comfortable as they can be under the circumstances. And any multiplicity in
under-garments, no matter how thin they may be, keeps in
perspiration and conduces fatally to prickly heat. For hot-weather
nightgowns nothing is pleasanter to wear than fine nuns-veiling.
To have them with short, open sleeves and low at the throat sounds
cooler than it is in reality, and gives mosquitoes and sandflies a larger
area for exploration.

The fewer frills the better for Indian underclothing, as the *dhobi*
is relentless; and it is a great saving of bother to do away with
buttons altogether, and substitute studs in their place. For trimming,
torchon lace* is incomparably the best, but even here it is well to
choose a strong, rather coarse-threaded, but closely-woven lace. Where
decoration is liked, hand embroidery on the cloth and coral stitches
may be employed, but any attempt to combine the Indian *dhobi*'s
prejudices with fine Madeira edgings* will be disastrous to the latter.

In regard to the quantity of each article, we have already remarked
that a round dozen should suffice. In the matter of stockings,
however, much will depend on the number of dresses, since it is
always nicer to have them to match. It is also advisable to buy a cheap
quality, as the colour goes with the strong sunlight. If double-woven

heels are not bought, it is best to run the heels with spun silk of the same colour. The gritty sand of India gets into the shoe and acts as a regular sandpaper on the heels of one's stockings. It is a good plan never to wear stockings more than once without making the *ayah* rinse the feet out in lukewarm water. This removes the grit. *Dirzies*, too, are very bad darners, and the effort to make expensive stockings last a reasonable time is greater than the result warrants. For print dresses, tan stockings and shoes are infinitely the best, as they do not show the dust. Whilst on the subject of stockings, a word of warning may be given as to open-work decoration: *mosquitoes are very prevalent in most parts of India*. At least four pairs of stays (if worn) should be taken, as in hot weather they get sodden and require drying and airing.

From the above remarks it will be seen that the question of under-clothing differs little in its bearings from its English aspect, save in regard to the difference in stuff and the quantity worn during the hot weather. In the cold season the clothing necessary for an English spring is suitable.

Dresses, both in number and style, vary according to the station and the individual. For morning wear, in the cold season, a light, or heavy, tailor-made tweed is best, the warmth depending on the destination of the wearer. But whether in Madras the material is beige, or in the Punjab a Harris tweed,* the style is much the same. In the hot weather print or *mousseline de laine* tea-gowns,* *without trains*, are invaluable. The great feature of Indian society is, of course, the daily tennis party, where, in large stations, costumes suitable for garden fêtes are worn, and even in small ones a dowdy dress is the exception. For those who play tennis, at least two really smart costumes are necessary, and in addition two white flannel skirts to be worn with various bodices. Indeed, for young girls nothing is so becoming for tennis as the plain skirt and loose bodice, smocked perhaps with some dainty colour, with a broad sash to match. Here, again, the Indian *dhobi*'s fatal facility for washing out even ingrain colours must be remembered. For those who do not play tennis we recommend in the hot weather pongee silks* or *mousseline de laines*. The latter wash most beautifully, and last clean much longer than any cotton fabric. In the cold season cashmeres, vicunas,* and all kinds of fancy cloths are suitable. In regard to all day costumes, it is a good plan to bring out, unmade, sufficient stuff, buttons, &c., to make a *replica in style*, but not necessarily in colour or texture, for the *dirzies* will copy a dress without much fear of failure. Thus when the original dress is put aside for morning wear, you can appear in a new one in the afternoon. A *few*, and for small stations, *very few*, good evening dresses should be brought out, if only for the reason that on the occasions on which they have to be worn you naturally want to appear well and fashionably dressed. This you cannot hope to do, unless you are a millionaire, if you get more than one good dress at a time, since they will go hopelessly out of fashion before you have a chance of wearing them. On the other hand, there is a vast amount of friendly entertainment in India, where pretty demi-toilette* is required. For this the married lady will find tea-gowns very suitable, while girls are the better for at least two simple but nicely-made dresses of nuns-veiling or pongee silk. Ball dresses are a necessity, and *one* should always be ready for an occasion. On the other hand, nothing suffers more from the voyage, and for girls especially it is better to have at least two silk bodices and slips, one white or cream, and to take out net, lace, ribbons, flowers, &c., for various trimmings and skirts. In addition, a black lace dress should be in every outfit.

A habit* is a necessity, and it should be made by a good tailor of moderately thick cloth. For camp work and, indeed, for all real work, hop-sacking* is best. Tweeds are at present fashionable, but they need to be very dark and of an even mixture, or they look speckly. Breeches and topboots* are far preferable to trousers, especially for rough work. In the morning rides in camp, when a wife accompanies her husband, she may like to dismount and walk with him. Thorns, sand, and snakes make topboots a great comfort in such cases. For the hot weather a lighter tweed habit may be taken; but one of the authors, who, during her twenty-two years in India, rode every march up to thirty miles in summer and winter, found that she was far more comfortable in the saddle in her thick cloth habit skirt with a stockingette habit body to match made *without any lining*, and worn over a white spun-silk vest. Light cloth habits, even if made by Wölmershausen,* are apt to ride up with the best riders, and only those who have spent hours in the saddle know the annoyance of wrinkles. Whilst on this subject a word of warning must be given as to the fitting of habits. To ensure a fashionable cut, the armholes are often so tight that any unusual exertion, such as pulling in a runaway, results in numbness and temporary paralysis of the muscle. As this may mean life or death when the country is nasty, we warn ladies to see that they have plenty of room across the chest, and that the sleeves are not too tight. The loose-fronted jacket with a waistcoat or shirt is far the best country habit.

Again, to ensure what is technically called 'a skirt like a board,' it is often ten minutes' work to get the various gussets and gores over their respective pummels. Now, if a lady cannot reach her saddle, settle herself into it, gather up her reins, and be off almost as quickly as a man, there is something amiss with her riding *or her habit*. Generally it is the latter. They are too tight for real honest work. One of the authors holds that if a lady is not able to mount herself anywhere and everywhere—provided, of course, that her horse be suitable for a lady's riding—she ought not to ride across country. Again, it may be fashionable to show one's boots under a short habit, but it is very cold work on a winter's morning, even in India. For station riding a billy-cock hat is usually worn, and for country work a double *terai*.* Shade for the eyes is imperative if you ride far on into the day.

In the matter of boots, your choice will depend on whether you are going to keep up your English habits of walking occasionally. We believe that the sudden giving up of an exercise to which most girls are accustomed has much to say to the ill-health of India. But, except for shooting work in camp, boots need to be lighter than is necessary in England. Tan leather tennis shoes with a strap across are the neatest for Indian wear.

Before going on to consider the question of boxes and dresses on the voyage out, the authors give a few hints applicable to the various Presidencies, which have been obtained from reliable sources, beginning with the Punjab and North-West. This is compiled from the author's own experience.

PUNJAB AND NORTH-WEST

Owing to the extreme variations in climate, two outfits are required if the hot weather is to be braved. If not, an ordinary English outfit is all that is required, with the addition of a sun hat, a white umbrella cover, and a few more underclothes. It must be remembered that in the cold weather many people have fires in their bedrooms, and that a double blanket is necessary. In the hills again, it rains on end for two months. Between these extremes lies a glorious, sunny, bracing climate, in which neat, bright, summer costumes show at their best, and life goes on much as in England when the clerk of the weather deigns to supply sunshine. The least supply for a residence during the whole year in the plains is, for a station where there is society:—

6	Calico nightgowns.	2	Winter afternoon dresses.
6	Silk or wool „	2	„ tennis „
	(For hot weather.)	?	Evening dresses (to taste).
6	Calico combinations.*	6	Summer tea gowns.
6	Silk or wool „	4	„ tennis gowns.
6	Merino vests.	2	„ afternoon gowns.
6	Spun silk „	1	Riding-habit, with lighter
6	Calico slip bodices.		jacket.
6	Trimmed muslin bodices.	1	Ulster.
12	Pairs tan stockings.	1	Handsome wrap.
12	„ Lisle thread stockings.	1	Umbrella.
6	Strong white petticoats.	2	Sunshades.
6	Trimmed petticoats.	1	Evening wrap.
2	Warm „	1	Mackintosh.
4	Flannel „	2	Pairs walking shoes.
36	Pocket-handkerchiefs.	2	„ boots.
4	Pairs stays.	1	„ tennis shoes.
4	Fine calico trimmed	?	Evening shoes.
	combinations for evening.	4	Pairs house shoes.
2	Winter morning dresses.	2	„ strong house shoes.

The present style of blouses can be confidently recommended. A goodly assortment of them to a serge skirt or two is really all that is needed for tennis. Evening dress should always be really smart and good, even when it is demi-toilette, as people dress more in India than they do at home.

The best cholera belt for night wear is an ordinary silk or woollen *pugree* wound several times round the body outside the nightdress. For day, shaped knitted ones. Many people never use them, except during epidemics. They are only a precaution against chill.

Finally, a few hints as to the dresses, &c., may be given. The ulster* should be smart and warm. In railway travelling, which in India lasts for days on end, it will be found invaluable. The travelling cap should match. The jacket should be fur-trimmed and warm, as it will be used chiefly for putting on after tennis or dancing. Sunset brings a distinct

chill with it, except during the very hot weather. Even then a white
flannel tennis coat or a light shawl is advisable. For early morning
drives, too, a warm cloak of some kind is comfortable, and in most
parts of India a sealskin or fur cloak will be found most useful. It
is only in the extreme north of India that either jacket or cloak is
needed during the calling hours (from twelve till two o'clock). Therefore, except for church, which is often chilly, a smart *confection** is
not required, and the costume should be complete in itself. In regard
to the minor accessories of the toilette, it must be remembered that
lace, ribbons, gloves, &c., though not to be had in great choice or of
the most novel description, may always be procured at very reasonable prices at the great Calcutta houses, such as Whiteaway, Laid-
law & Company.* It is also quite easy to arrange for a proper supply
from home, while nothing is more annoying to a reasonable woman
than to be obliged to wear out old and yet unworn things because she
has been foolish enough to buy them on the chance of their being
wanted. A large supply of haberdashery should be taken out, and also
all work materials, colours, paint-boxes, &c., as these are not to be
procured at a pinch. Perhaps the best advice the authors can give to
any one going out to India is this—Life is uncertain. More uncertain,
if not as to duration, at any rate as to circumstance, in India than
elsewhere. Therefore look six months ahead, *and no more*. Have an
official document transferring you and your dresses to *Ultima Thule**
in your mind's eye whenever you look at a shop window, and think,
'How would that lovely costume look folded up with camphor in an
air-tight tin box?' Such reflections take the gilt off the gingerbread
very efficiently. On the other hand, if life *is* certain for six months,
dress becomingly during that period, and never, even in the wilds,
exist without one civilised evening and morning dress. That important envelope with the big red seal may come any day, and you may
find yourself in the paradise of a big station yet unable to appear from
want of clothes!

CEYLON

The climate being as a rule warm and damp, a large supply of
under-linen is required. It is a good plan, however, to take out only a
dozen of everything made up, as they can be copied most admirably
by the tailors if material be also brought out. This should be fine India

long-cloth* and torchon lace. The nightdress should not have short sleeves or low neck, and everything should be plain to stand the rough usage. The following list is given as sufficient:—

1 doz. night-dresses.	4 pair silk stockings.
1 „ combinations.	4 pair stays.
8 white petticoats.	1 doz. petticoat bodies.
4 coloured „ thin.	3 „ pocket handkerchiefs.
4 flannel „ thin.	3 pairs house shoes.
1 dozen Indian gauze vests.	3 „ walking shoes.
	1 doz. Lisle thread stockings.

Stockings should not be open-work, nor black in colour. Tan is as good a colour as any. Dresses should be of washing material, and of the sort requiring little starch, on account of the damp. Summer cashmere, washing silks, and delaines* are suitable. For the colder hills, serge and tweeds, with one or two really warm dresses. Avoid gauze and tulle for evening wear. The damp soon makes it drop to pieces. Native tailors will always make a dress for Rs. 5, therefore take materials. Not many flowers, gloves, ribbons, &c., as they spot quickly. Gloves should be rolled up in pairs in flannel, and put into prune bottles kept tightly closed, or in air-tight cases of any sort. Camphor should be put with all clothes, except uniforms, as it tarnishes gold lace. Leather goods must be constantly wiped and dresses aired. Needles sealed up in court plaster.* Light wraps are better than regular mantles, and light tea-gowns are useful for home dinners. Also morning robes. A very small supply of thin walking and house shoes, as these are best sent out by post as required. A good light waterproof is required. For plantation work blouses and thin woollen skirts, nuns-veiling, or India tweed are most useful. Also nankeen coats and skirts.* For the hills, furs and English dress. In Colombo ladies go in for dressing; for out-station work, however, one or two evening dresses will be sufficient. But two riding-habits are necessary, unless a skirt, blouses or shirts, and jacket is worn. The life is quite a country one on the plantations, and dress must be suitable to country pursuits.

MADRAS

The under-linen should be of India cloth, and in number much the same as for Ceylon. In regard to dresses, thin woollen ones are useful in Madras itself for walking on the beach. Ostrich feathers are taken out of curl at once by the sea breeze, and starch for the same reason soon ceases to deserve its name. Most people go to Ootacamund in the summer, where the climate is that of an English summer. The Madras embroideries are famous, so in bringing out material for washing dresses, it may be remembered that trimming can be got cheaper and better on the spot. As in all parts of India, a certain smartness of costume is desirable, as the afternoons are very generally spent at what is to all intents and purposes a garden party. Nothing that spots easily should be brought out. Light woollen or silk nightgowns are safer than cotton. Sunshades should be large, or they are of *no* use.

CALCUTTA AND BENGAL

People generally bring out two dozen of the different kinds of underclothing. The authors think this excessive. It is, however, no use bringing out material to make more things if wanted, as tailors charge high. The outfit mentioned for Ceylon would be a very suitable one for Bengal. But in Calcutta itself it must not be forgotten that the life is a *town* life to all intents and purposes; also, that most things can be got almost as cheap in the large shops. In fact, people going to Calcutta should take a very few thoroughly stylish dresses. Riding-habits should be of thin cloth, and as little padding as possible put in the bodice.

RANGOON

The same remarks apply to Burmah, only more so, since the climate is warmer and damper. Briefly, an outfit for Rangoon may be drawn up on the Ceylon lines, bearing in mind that everything must be of the thinnest, and yet stand bad washing. Riding is a great amusement in Rangoon, and two habits are a necessity. One should certainly be of a light serge that will not easily show dirt. They should be made of the *best shrunk cloth*, as they will have to stand *washing*, owing to the mud. Saddles should be brought out, and they must be made to fit ponies under thirteen hands. Waterproof covers should be brought out for saddles, and a chamois leather cover is also a good thing. Mosquitoes being a perfect curse, all dress should aim at leaving no portion of the body exposed that *can* be protected. Mosquito net in large quantities is also useful.

BOMBAY—*Same as Madras*

Finally, a few general remarks may be made about clothing suitable to warm climates. Dark colours absorb the sun's rays, and are consequently hotter than light ones. White reflects all the rays, and is therefore coolest.

The thinnest materials are not the coolest in direct exposure to the sun's rays. The Arab in the desert throws the loose end of his bernous* over the shoulder on which the sun falls most. Thus a white coat, padded over the spine and other sensitive parts, is the best clothing in which to brave a tropical sun.

The head-dress should be light in colour and weight, and admit of free air passing to the scalp. The neck should always be loosely clothed, especially in hot weather. In fact, a general easiness of clothing conduces greatly to comfort. But do not bring out shoes a size too large for you, on the advice of friends. The feet do not swell as a rule.

In regard to boxes, the best boxes are tin ones—either the American round-topped ones, or the overland case in wooden covers. One of the authors has invariably travelled to and fro with ordinary dress baskets, and has not had to complain of any injury. For the cabin, however, she certainly recommends a low tin case of regulation size. Every one is so eager to have the port open that, sooner or later, a sea is almost sure to come in and set things floating. The fewer things you can take into your cabin, the greater your comfort will be. It is an excellent plan, however, to have a second small box for the voyage marked *cabin*, which, of course, will be left on deck till your arrival, when a word to the baggage officer will generally secure its being placed in a get-at-able place in the hold, whence on baggage days you will have no trouble in unearthing it. The journey, however, occupies so short a time nowadays that elaborate preparations are not so much needed. No one with any liking for comfort will inflict on themselves the punishment of changing costume on board ship oftener than is absolutely required.

A tweed costume for what is called the 'Homi-cide,' and two dark nuns-veiling or cambric dresses for the 'Suez-cide,' should, with two demi-toilettes for dinner, be sufficient. Indeed, one skirt with a few coloured bodices looks as well as anything, while for dinner nothing looks better than pongee silk. Two tea-gowns, one warm and one cool, are absolutely necessary to those who rightly object to play hide-and-seek for an hour every morning before breakfast in the effort to get a bath. Robed in these, the wearer can sit and read, or work, in the saloon, watching her opportunity, instead of stewing in the anteroom, or diving backwards and forwards from her cabin with indecent haste. There is, perhaps, nothing more mysterious in Nature than the harsh line of decency and indecency which most ladies draw between a tea-gown and a dressing-gown. Attired in one they will face a crowd with complacency; in the other, they will fly from a steward. Yet we suspect that, to the ordinary male comprehension, there is no tangible difference between the two.

It is a great art to keep your cabin tidy, and to arrange times and seasons with your fellow-sufferers. At best, life in a space 6 by 6 is confined, but some amelioration may be effected by method. A chintz bag for soiled linen, a holdall for hanging on the wall with more pockets than fittings, are useful. The best holdalls have a hem top and bottom, into which two flat sticks are run, and into which you can screw little hooks for hanging up trifles. If you can get old underlinen, it is advisable to use it on board, throwing it away when soiled. Books are a necessity of life, and so are work and a plentiful supply of writing materials. Deck shoes with indiarubber soles are advisable, and a cloud* or muffler for windy days. In the Red Sea the wind is generally strong, fore or aft. At such times a white gauze veil, long enough to tie round the hat and under the chin, helps tidiness. A light, shady straw hat and a travelling cap are indispensable, and so is a wrap for wearing on deck after dinner.

The deck chair is best of wicker, and if a pretty one is chosen, it comes in usefully for the drawing-room afterwards.

A pound or two of tea should be taken, and those who dislike sugar in their tea should provide themselves with some of the new brands of unsweetened, desiccated, or reduced milk.

Those who have to travel up-country should bring a feather chintz-covered pillow and an Austrian blanket* or two with them. They will then be able to sleep comfortably in the train. If possible, it is wise to arrange in Bombay or Karachi* for a supply of food which will render them independent of refreshment rooms. It is not well to have one's first impressions of India marred by starvation or indigestion. This is especially needful on the Karachi line, where on one occasion the writer was twenty-four hours without the possibility of procuring anything but whisky and soda and a biscuit.

A basket containing a spirit lamp and kettle, a bottle of essence of coffee,* tea, preserved milk, bread, potted meat, Bovril,* biscuits, &c., is invaluable. The best tinned meat is a Paysandu ox tongue.* A few limes for making lemon squash during the heat of the day increase comfort. A bottle of chlorodyne and some good whisky or brandy should not be forgotten. Even if a provision basket is not carried, it is well to have a tin of biscuits and a breakfast cup or tumbler into which the tea purchased at the refreshment rooms can be poured. This is especially convenient in the railway journey across France or Italy.

In these later days, a bicycle dress* is as much a necessity in India as in England; indeed, even more so, since the Indian roads, level, smooth, and springy, seem made for the scorcher, the only drawbacks being dust and buffaloes. As, even with the lessening of fatigue caused by the perfection of track, bicycling is hardly the exercise for very hot weather, the usual English outfit is all that is required. It must be remembered, moreover, that the pneumatic tyres are very liable to burst unless the machine is carefully protected from the sun.

CHAPTER XX

PRELIMINARY REMARKS ON COOKING

THE number of ladies with a practical knowledge of cooking is few, despite schools of cookery and a general but ill-defined feeling that modern education is wanting in what was undoubtedly the first duty of women. Even when some amount of training is gone through, it is apt to take the form of learning how to make boned larks with truffles, or ice pudding and nougâts—dishes admirable in themselves, but not of much use as food staples; whereas the knowledge really required by a mistress is of that half-practical, half-theoretical and wholly didactic description, which will enable her to find reasonable fault with her servant. We have all laughed at the young bride who said tentatively, 'And if you please, cook, you needn't put the lumps in the butter sauce another time, for your master doesn't care for them'; but numbers of the laughers would be puzzled to tell how the evil was to be prevented, or how the lumps came. In the same way most people like clear, golden-brown, well-flavoured soup, and creamy rice puddings; but unless their cook knows how to send these to table they cannot tell what is lacking. Finally, they know too little of the dangers besetting a dainty dinner to be able to weigh out blame accurately, and their eye is equal for a curdled sauce and a greasy cutlet. Whereas the former may occur to Francatelli* himself, and the latter is simply inexcusable even in a coolie. It is this art of just appraisal and dispassionate judgment that the mistress must cultivate, and to aid her in the task we enumerate a few of the most common causes for the most glaring faults.

1. Dull, cloudy soup is caused by failure to skim and too rapid boiling, by which the flakes of albumen—which any one who has had a cup of beef-tea must have seen—are broken up so fine that straining will not rid the soup of them. The remedy is to put in more albumen, which, coagulating with heat, closes round and imprisons the floating atoms in larger flakes. White of egg, or raw, lean meat, finely minced, whipped up with a teacup of cold water, will clear any soup. The stock must first be allowed to cool a little, and after the albumen is added it must be quickly stirred until the boiling point, so as to ensure it being well mixed.

2. Greasiness in frying comes from the medium being below the frittering or boiling point when the things to be fried are put in. Instead of hardening the outside in a moment, the grease sinks in.

3. A bad colour comes from faulty egging and crumbing, over or under cooking, and dirty fat.

4. Lumps in sauces come from laziness in stirring in the flour. This must either be mixed to a paste with the butter, or mixed with a little cold stock or milk, and then strained to the boiling sauce.

5. Hardness in boiled meat comes from rapid boiling at first; soddenness and stringiness from being put on in cold water.

6. Want of crispness in roast meat from being done in a close *degchi*, as a rule, two hours before it need see the fire. Greasy, watery gravy from pouring hot water over the joint instead of warmed-up gravy from a previous roasting.

7. Waxy potatoes, when not the fault of the kind, come from skinning before boiling, and not pouring off the water and setting to dry beside the fire.

8. Curdled sauces will constantly occur unless a *bain-marie* is used, as any approach to boiling point will coagulate eggs, and there is nothing so hard to manage as custard sauces and soups without proper appliances.

9. Heavy pastry comes from too much handling, slack firing, and failure to have butter and paste of *exactly the same consistency*. Heavy puddings from bad mixing.

10. Sodden vegetables are produced by allowing them to stand in the water in which they have been cooked.

The recipes in the following chapters have all been practically tested; and if the directions are implicitly carried out, it is believed that the mistress will not require more hints for faultfinding than have been given above. Incidentally, it may be mentioned—for the benefit of total abstainers—that most of the recipes given in the following chapters in which wine is used can be made without it, if alcohol in any form is considered objectionable.

Finally, as to weights and measures. After long cogitation the authors have decided on purely proportional measurements as being the easiest to handle in all circumstances. The unit employed therefore throughout this book, wherever possible, is a tablespoon filled, pressed down lightly by the hand for solids, and as full as it can be in fluids; that is to say, approximately one ounce, if that measure be preferred. This gives a result suitable in size for two or three people. Therefore, in working by this book, the unit is practically one ounce for things which cannot be measured in a tablespoon, such as unminced meat. It follows, however, that any other unit of measurement, either bigger or smaller, may be used, provided *it is used throughout*. An English egg is held in this book to be two units—one of white, one of yolk. Two units is thus one egg. In India, however, an allowance of one-third has to be made on account of the smallness of the Indian egg. For convenience an equivalent table from 1 to 10 units is given here:—

In Recipe.		In Indian Eggs.	In Recipe.		In Indian Eggs.
1 unit	=	1	6 units	=	8
2 „	=	3	7 „	=	10
3 „	=	4	8 „	=	11
4 „	=	6	9 „	=	12
5 „	=	7	10 „	=	14

For convenience sake also a proportional table is here inserted, giving the ratios required in what may be called foundational cooking in order to secure a good result. With the help of this a fairly intelligent woman will be able to vary her dishes to any extent, and lose nothing for want of knowing how to employ it:—

TABLE OF PROPORTIONS

1. Batter	Baked or boiled, 4 units flour, 8 eggs, 16 milk. Frying batter, 1 unit flour, 2 liquid, 2 egg, ¼ oil. Soufflée batter, 1 unit flour, 1 water, ¼ butter, 2 egg. (This has to be boiled before frying.)
2. Cakes	A standard cake, 16 units self-raising flour, 12 sugar, 8 butter, 10 eggs.
3. Custards	Baked, 6 units egg to 20 milk; boiled, 8 to 20.
4. Gelatine Jellies and Creams	2 units chip or 1 unit ground gelatine to 20 liquid; cream, 2 or 1 to 24.
5. Farinaceous Shapes	Cornflour, 1½ unit to 20 of liquid; rice, 8 to 20; sago, 4 to 20; ground rice, 6 to 20; semolina, 4 to 20; arrowroot, 1 to 20; tapioca, 3 to 20.
6. Meat Moulds	Raw meat, 1 unit to 2 milk or stock; cooked meat, 2 units meat, 1 panade,* 1 milk, 1 egg.
7. Milk Puddings	Cornflour, 1 unit to 20 of liquid; arrowroot, 1 to 20; rice, 3 to 20; sago, semolina, and tapioca, 2 to 20; macaroni and vermicelli, 4 (solid) to 20.
8. Pastry	Puff, 4 units butter to 4 flour; medium, 3 butter, 4 flour; family, 2 butter, 4 flour; short, 2 butter, 4 flour, 1 sugar; suet, 5 suet, 8 flour.
9. Stock	*Ordinary*, 16 units meat or fish (solid) to 44 liquid. Add 8 meat for best *consommé*.
10. Thickening	Soups, ½ to 1 unit flour to 44 liquid; ordinary sauces, 1 unit flour, 1 butter to 15 liquid; thick do., to 12; thin do., to 20.

CHAPTER XXI

ADVICE TO THE COOK[1]

————◆————

MOST likely you belong to a family of *khansâmahs*, cooks, and *khitmutgârs*; so, of course, it is likely you know a good deal about your business, but it is also certain that you do not know everything. Now it is no disgrace not to know what you have not been taught, but it is a disgrace not to try to learn. There are always new dishes being invented, and every year clever men are finding out the cause of this disease and that disease. Now, as half the illness in the world comes from the stomach, for which it is your business to provide, it stands to reason that a cook ought to do his best to do everything in the best possible way. And it lends to the comfort of the whole house; for if the dinner is badly cooked, your mistress will be angry, the master will have an indigestion, and be cross; everything will go wrong, and whose fault will it be? *Yours.*

All Indian people have a great respect for custom, and like to do as their fathers and grandfathers did. This is right enough, but it does not do to carry it to extremes. For instance, you all use matches. Did your fathers use them? No, because they had never seen them. Did they use kerosene oil? No, because even in England it had not been discovered. Therefore, the first thing a cook should learn is not to be distrustful of new ways. Many of them save an immense deal of trouble. Supposing, therefore, you are really willing to be cleverer than your fathers were, the first thing you have to learn is to be a great deal *cleaner* than they thought it necessary to be.

The doctors have found out that some of the worst kinds of fevers come from dirty milk and bad water. So, if you keep your milk close to a dirty-smelling kitchen drain, and use water from a *ghurra* that has been standing in a dirty puddle of that drain, amongst the refuse of vegetables, chickens' entrails, and Heaven knows what, you may poison your master or your master's child, as surely as if you had put arsenic in their food. Cleanliness, then, is no mere fanciful fad on the *sahib-logue*'s part. It may be a matter of *life* or *death*. Never forget this.

[1] This may be had, translated into Roman Urdu,* in a separate pamphlet.

It is not difficult to be clean even in the poor cook-rooms you generally have. First of all, at least once every six months ask leave to have your cook-room thoroughly whitewashed, and on such occasions make a general clearance of everything. If the floor is of mud, beg your mistress to have it laid down in broad flat bricks, nicely joined with mortar. See that the tank or sink where you empty slops has a high rim, and beg some empty kerosene tins of your mistress, cut the lids off, and have a bit of iron wire put across as handles. Three or four of these, kept full of water on one side of the sink, will be much more convenient than *ghurras*, especially if you keep a tin dipper by them. Then if you want water in a hurry, you have not to let go of everything, and lift up a heavy *ghurra* with both hands.

Water to be *used in the cooking*, as for soups, tea, boiling vegetables, &c., should be kept by a *ghurra* filter outside. Insist on the *bheesti* keeping this full; do not hesitate to report him to your mistress if he gives trouble.

Paper your *almirahs* (cupboards), and have a separate nail in the wall for every saucepan. If you make a point of two things—never hanging up a dirty saucepan, never going to bed till every saucepan *is* hung up—do you know what will be the result? You will have learned almost everything about cleanliness we want to teach you.

Because—

1. Every morning all your saucepans will be clean.
2. Therefore you cannot have left soup, milk, stews, &c., in the saucepan all night.
3. You will have put all the remains of eatables away in their proper place.

And if you would only add to this habit that of keeping the cook-room doors and windows open all night, you would positively have nothing more to learn. For this would mean—

1. That the meat was in its proper place in the safe.
2. That the potatoes were not in a heap in the corner amongst charcoal ashes and old feathers.
3. That the charcoal was not loose on the floor.
4. That your favourite *hukka* was not lying about.
5. That you were not sleeping in the cook-room.

Because—

1. If the doors were open, you would not care to sleep in the cold cook-room.
2. If thieves could get in, you would never have your favourite *hukka* lying about, to say nothing of other things.
3. If dogs could roam in and out, you would not care to feed them on the meat.

Now, as a matter of fact, you cannot always leave the doors open, but the windows should never be shut at night; and if your mistress would give you *chick* doors, which could be locked and yet let the air in, your cook-room will always be sweet, clean, and healthy. Take a pride in keeping it so. It is your first duty.

The next point is to keep yourself clean. Cooks must use their hands a great deal. Some things are better done with the hand than with spoon or fork, but not with *dirty* hands; so keep a piece of soap and a towel handy by the sink for constant use, and don't use your hands unnecessarily. Don't, for instance, stir eggs into a pudding with your fingers. *They do it very badly.* Do not cook in woollen clothes. Do not keep spices, &c., in screws of paper. There are always plenty of tins and bottles.

Remember that if you have a place for everything, everything will be in its place.* Keep your charcoal in a locked box, and take out your day's supply every morning in a separate open box. Your fellow-servants are not always honest. Why should you be accused of extravagance by your mistress for their fault?

Do not throw away refuse out of the door, but insist on the sweeper sweeping out the cook-house every day. The day's work should be done with method and order. First of all, call both sweeper and *bheesti*. Remove yesterday's ashes, sweep the cooking platform, and let *bheesti* with *mussack* and sweeper with broom wash out the floor and the sink. Make the former bring fresh water and the latter empty the tub, which should always be placed outside to receive the slops. Light one *chula* (charcoal fire) only, and put on the kettle. Then is the time for marketing. Arrange in your own mind a suitable dinner, so that you may have some suggestions to give your mistress, and make sure that nothing which can be reasonably wanted is forgotten. Breakfast will, of course, have been ordered the night before, and does not, as a rule, require lengthy cooking; but in the three hours before it is served much can be done. The stock-pot will, of course, be simmering away on its appointed *chula*. Jellies and creams for dinner and most cold puddings may be made and set aside. Meat in pickle may be rubbed, and that in the safe carefully looked at, and, if necessary, treated. Where cows are kept, the skim milk required for daily use may be boiled and put into a cooler.

Breakfast over, you should at once attend for orders with your accounts. With regard to the last, remember the words of the Koran, and do not disobey your religion for the sake of a few pice.

Do not stand mum-chance* before your mistress, but suggest what *you* have thought over. If she says leg of mutton, don't say '*acchchi bât*' (a good word), when you know it is as tough as tough can be, and ought to hang two days longer; especially if there is a sirloin of beef looking a little doubtful in the safe.

Ask for everything you can want that day, and if you can write, put down your orders on a slate, then there will be no mistakes. Take the orders for breakfast also; and if there is to be a dinner-party next day, settle the outlines, so that you may be prepared. Try your best to help your mistress in making a pleasing variety in the food. She will be pleased if, when she is racking her brains for a pudding, you say, 'There was extra skim milk to-day, so I made a caramel custard,' or, 'The rice at breakfast was not eaten, and the *khit* says some of the dessert apples are going, so we can have a nice apple *meringue* if you like.' Instead of which, Indian cooks too often say, '*Jo huzoor ke hukm*' (As your honour orders), just as if it were the name of a new dish.

Immediately after breakfast is the best time for you to eat your food and smoke, if you must smoke. The *chulas* should then be allowed to go out, except two, one for the kettle, which should always be ready, and the other for the stock-pot. About an hour and a half before luncheon the cook's real work begins, and does not end till dinner is served.

Advice as to the best way of boiling, baking, roasting, stewing, frying, will be found under these heads and in all recipes; any common mistakes and bad habits have been pointed out, so no more need be said here, except to assure you that the *easiest recipes* have been given; and if you try half the plan given and half your own, you are *quite sure* to come to grief.

Serving the meals is, perhaps, the cook's busiest time, and without method you are sure to fail. At breakfast all the dishes should be sent in at once; at luncheon there are seldom but two courses. With dinner it is different, but if you make a proper use of your hot case there need be no delay. If your mistress has not given you one, it is better for you to get one made out of an old box and kerosene tins than to be hurried and bothered by doing without it; so for keeping sauces hot, if you have not a regular water bath, or *bain-marie*, use an old kerosene tin cut down to six or eight inches. Put this over the fire with hot water in it, plunge your little saucepans in it, and there you are.

A cook that wants to cook well will always manage to do so.

If you take an interest in your work, it will interest you.

A cook who really cares to be a *chef* will do as an old cook of one of the authors used to do. After a dinner-party, when the guests had gone, if it was twelve or one o'clock at night, Imam Khan used to appear in clean clothing, and ask if all had gone well; and one day, before his mistress could say a word, he said—

'I know it, *Mem Sahib*; I know it. The wild duck *was* underdone. *Tobah! tobah!*' (My fault, my fault.)

It is the fashion nowadays for cooks to say they cannot make nice dishes unless they are allowed truffles and cream, and butter and champagne, and goodness knows what. By saying this they confess their own ignorance, since any fool can make nice dishes out of nice things; it is only a real *cordon bleu** who can make the commonest food delicious. There is but one ingredient without which it is impossible to send up a palatable dinner, and that is care.

CHAPTER XXII

ADVICE ON BOILING, FRYING, ROASTING, STEWING, AND BAKING

BOILING, if the water in which meat is boiled is not fully made use of, is a very extravagant way of cooking, because all the best part of the meat dissolves into the water. To avoid this as much as possible, meat that is to be eaten should never be put in until the water boils furiously. It should continue to do so for at least five minutes; the reason of this being that meat contains a substance like the white of an egg, which hardens at once with great heat. Thus the outside of the meat becoming hard prevents the juices of the inner part from escaping into the water. After the five minutes, if you continue to boil furiously, *all* the white-of-egg-like stuff will harden, and your meat will be uneatably tough; so let the fire be slack, and keep the water just simmering.

Fish, on the other hand, should never be put into very hot water, or the skin will break. Vinegar and salt should always be put in the water; and if you want your fish to be very good, you should previously make a boiling-liquor for it with water, vinegar, claret, onions, carrots, and a faggot of herbs boiled together and allowed to get cold. Then strain and use the liquor for boiling your fish.

Vegetables are not to be boiled in the soup, or all together in one saucepan, as is too often done by Indian cooks. In some of the best houses the authors have seen specks of carrot amongst the cauliflowers. How did they come there? You might as well boil the fish, the beef, and the plum-pudding in the same saucepan. Vegetables should not be washed until they are about to be cooked, and they should be plunged into boiling water to which one dessertspoon of salt has been added for every forty tablespoons or one quart of water. The saucepan should be uncovered, and they should boil furiously. Peas and beans require a teaspoon of sugar in addition to the salt. Potatoes, however, should always be put on in cold water, only just sufficient to cover them, and after the first boil they cannot simmer too slowly. Then they require at least an hour to dry after the water has been drained off. Yet Indian cooks seldom begin to boil potatoes till just before dinner.

Puddings require to be boiled very fast. Quarter an hour for every 16 oz. should be allowed for boiling meat.

FRYING

Frying does not consist in cooking anyhow in a frying-pan. It means cooking in boiling fat; and many fried things, such as fritters, rissoles, croquettes, must be fried in a small saucepan. The first requisite is plenty of fat; the second is the right sort of fat.

Most Indian cooks say at once, 'Oh, if I am to use all that fat, you must allow me ever so much more in the month.'

This is a mistake; for if you use little fat it becomes so dirty, and is so impregnated with the taste of what is cooked in it, that it has to be thrown away; whereas a saucepan full of fat can be used dozens of times. All that is required is to have three separate vessels for your frying grease—one for fish, one for meat, one for sweet things; and invariably to use the whole quantity for your frying, carefully straining it back to its vessel when the work is done, and at least once a week clarifying it in salt and water with the addition of new fat to make up waste.

Oil is the best frying medium. Dripping and the fat from boiled meat is the next. Beef and mutton suet carefully prepared is the third. Butter and *ghee* are the worst, as they are apt to fry of an ugly black brown. A good cook will seldom require *ghee* for frying, except for some sweet dishes. He will save every bit of fat, even the trimming of chops, the kidney suet from loins and saddles, the under fat of sirloins, and boil it all up in a very large saucepan with salt and water. When everything is thoroughly melted he will set the whole aside to cool. Next morning the clarified fat can be removed in a cake, which will keep good for months. If necessary, he will clarify it a second time; and unless the meat used in the house is very poor, or very small in quantity, he will feel thoroughly ashamed of himself if he has to charge his mistress with fat for frying.

The fat must be boiling before you *begin* to use it. The best test of this is dipping a bit of bread into the fat. If it *instantly* fritters a pale brown, the fat is ready. The things to be fried should be completely immersed in the fat, and they should be done of a light golden brown.

Now if you go into any Indian bazaar, at the first cook-shop you will find all these conditions fulfilled; that is to say, the pan will be full of boiling grease, and the fried things will come out crisp and of a beautiful colour. Why, then, do Indian *cooks* seldom fry well? The reason is hard to find.

After removing fried things from the pan they should be set to drain on a sieve in the hot case. Frying-pans should never be washed with water, but be scoured clean with sand, and then wiped out.

When cutlets, &c., have to be egged and crumbed for frying, beat the egg thoroughly first, and do not smear it over the cutlets with your finger, but dip them into it, first one side, then the other, and at once lay them, first one side and then the other, in stale bread crumbs—not bread toasted to a brick-like consistency in the oven and then pounded to a powder in a mortar, but stale bread *grated* into distinct crumbs. Most Indian cooks use the former, which is one reason why their fried things seldom have the proper rough, dry, crisp, golden-brown surface they ought to have.

ROASTING

Try and get your mistress to give you a regular roaster, which may be bought at the Roorki workshops. It is a sort of open grate, holding a thin layer of charcoal, and having a dripping-pan, spit, and jack complete. Without something of this sort you cannot save the dripping, which is so useful to you; with only the old spit, all the fat falls into the fire, and the good gravy too, which is so useful for sauces. Again, to roast meat well it must be basted well, and how can that be done when the fat puts out the fire?

The great secret of roasting is to put your meat down to a sharp fire, and then reduce the heat when the outside is set. Flour should always be dredged over it to absorb the gravy and prevent more oozing out; and it is simply impossible to baste too much. As a rule, quarter of an hour for every 16 oz. of meat is sufficient time for cooking with a roaster, but with the old spit Indian cooks will put down a saddle of mutton at three o'clock for an eight o'clock dinner, and then wonder why the mistress complains of the meat being sodden. In a family where economy is necessary, it is a good plan to bone meat before roasting, as the bones will make far better soup when uncooked, and the meat will also cut less to waste. Game requires very light yet quick roasting, and cannot be properly done in a *degchi* or oven. It takes even more fat for basting than butchers' meat, and if wanted very good may be basted with equal parts of claret and cream.

STEWING

Is by far the most economical method of cooking meat, but it requires time and patience. A stew made in an hour will be meat badly boiled, and if cooked too fast will be a mass of strings. The Indian cook, however, has no excuse for not stewing well, as he has the best fire in the world for it, viz., a charcoal one.

It is also the easiest method of cooking, because it can be done at leisure, and the stew will not spoil in the least if the time of serving is delayed. It also has the advantage of enabling the cook to give otherwise tasteless meat an appetising flavour, by the addition of various vegetables and spices. In spite of all this, many an Indian cook's stews are simply appalling. Lumps of hard meat floating in a greasy, dark gravy, with a few underdone onions and potatoes swimming round! This is called *brun-estew*,* and is served up with complacency by men who have a pocketful of *chits* as high-class *khansâmahs*. A really good stew is perhaps the most savoury of all dishes, but it must be made to recipe, and have both time and care in the preparation.

If the meat used in stews be at all fat, it is absolutely necessary that, when three parts done, the stew should be allowed to cool, when the fat can be easily removed from the surface. The cooking can then proceed. Nothing is more disgusting than *grease* to the European, and the cook should remember this peculiarity of his master's. He should also remember that hashes, *salmis*, and *rechauffés** are not stews, and that they are ruined if treated as such. They are simply meat warmed up in a previously prepared rich gravy.

BAKING

Almost every kind of cake and pudding requires a particular kind of baking, and cooks in India invariably forget this. But if the only oven be a *tezâl*, that fact should be held to cover a multitude of sins. True, one of the authors once had a cook who produced triumphs in the baking art out of a mere hole in the ground, but he was a baker by trade, and had a curious, intuitive knowledge of when it was time to unearth that hole and dig up the cake.

Baking is a very economical way of dressing food, and some joints of meat eat better baked than roasted, notably rolled ribs of beef. A baked ham, too, is delicious. For cakes, especially ones with fruit in them, a rather fierce heat at first is necessary. A slack oven at first is the common Indian fault, and the cook should remember that in nine cases out of ten a cool oven does more harm than a fast one. Another fault is constant opening of the oven. If it is heated as experience teaches, there is no reason why the process of baking should be watched at all.

All cakes and puddings with soda in them require a hot oven; shortbread, biscuits, milky puddings, &c., a slow one.

As a rule, if a little flour sprinkled on the baking-sheet browns rapidly, the oven is hot enough for cakes.

It is a golden rule never to mix either cake or pudding till the oven be hot enough to cook it. Delays are fatal.

CHAPTER XXIII

SOUPS

In India the *khansâmah* invariably makes soup of beef-bones. Now you can no more make all soups from one thing than you can make all kinds of puddings. The first lessons, then, for the Indian cook to learn are briefly these:—

1. *All soups cannot be made from beef-bones.*
2. *All soups should not taste strongly of meat.*
3. *The strength of a soup is not shown by its jellying when cold.*
4. *Bones should not be bought; if they are wanted, those of the roast meat may be used.*

Soups may be divided into five classes: Clear soups, or *consommé*; plain stock soup, or *bouillon*; thick vegetable soup, or *purée*; thickened soups; and soups without meat. Each of these classes must be treated separately.

The first, that of clear soup, is capable of many variations, according to the flavouring and quality of the stock, and the different things, vegetables, macaroni, quenelles, eggs, &c., added to it. The foundation is good clear stock, a supply of which should always be ready, as it is not only necessary for soups, but also in almost every sauce and made dish. In India, where guests come unexpectedly, a tin of Bovril or Extract of Beef should always be within reach. With its aid, any soup for two can be made soup for four. The following recipe is sufficient for all requirements:—

Strong Clear Stock.—To every unit[1] of meat take 2 units of water. Supposing this unit to be two pounds (32 oz.), the smallest worth handling for stock, then the seasoning will be one onion stuck with three cloves, one carrot, one turnip, savoury herbs, one teaspoon sugar, one teaspoon salt. The meat should be cut into dice as for curry. Place the stock-pot on the fire, rub the bottom with a little fat or butter, lay in

---

[1] The unit is either one tablespoon or one ounce.

the meat neatly, and add eight tablespoons cold water. Boil down till the bottom of the pot is covered with a jelly-glaze, then add the rest of the water, cold, add the flavouring. Do not let it *boil*, but simmer for six hours. If made properly, and skimmed carefully, this stock will *never* require clearing. If it does, the white of an egg may be used, or what is better, save a portion of the meat, mince fine, just cover with water, and let it stand till the stock has been made. Let the stock cool, add the fresh meat, and put on the fire again, stirring till it boils. Let it cool a little and strain carefully. White of egg is used the same way. The secret of clearness lies in diligent stirring till the boil, and not letting the boil continue. The bones of the roast meat should always be added to the stock-pot. They should be broken up in a mortar, put in a muslin bag kept for the purpose, and added with the water to the stock. This stock is the foundation of all clear soups, and should be of a clear, light-brown colour. Water must, of course, be added to make up the quantity that boils away. Good stock cannot be made unless the lid of the pot fits tight; but in India one often sees the soup being made in an *open degchi!* If the stock is required stronger, it can be reduced a little, and during this process various flavourings can be added. Half the soups with fine names are made by putting prettily decorated *croutons* or timbals* in each soup-plate and pouring boiling *consommé* on them.

CLEAR SOUPS

1. **Brunoise.**—The same as Julienne, but add Brussels sprouts and crusts of bread dried in the oven. Bread and vegetables to be cut into dice or shapes with a cutter.

2. **D'Esclignac.**—With savoury boiled custard cut into squares and placed in the tureen with French beans cut small. The custard must be made firm.

3. **Julienne.**—Carrots, turnips, celery, lettuce leaves shredded fine and lightly fried in butter. Add to the stock, with a little more sugar and a few drops of tarragon vinegar.

4. **Mulligatawny** (*clear*).—Flavoured strongly with curry powder, and served with rice quenelles poached separately. A little lemon juice.

5. **Quenelle Soup.**—With quenelles made in a teaspoon. If made of various colours they look very pretty.

6. **Wyvern Soup.***—A neatly poached egg slipped into each soup-plate and just covered by a very brilliant strong *consommé*.

STOCK SOUPS OR BOUILLONS

They do not require to be so strong, and the colour should be of a very light golden brown. As extreme clearness is not necessary, they are suitable for everyday use.

1. **Bouillon or Pot-au-feu.**—One unit of beef cut into thin slices, 2 units of water. For 2 pound unit add a whole carrot, turnip, and onion, savoury herbs, and a little sugar. Lightly fry the slices of meat in a little butter, add a quarter of the water, and boil quickly to a glaze. Add the rest of the water, and simmer for four hours. Half-an-hour before serving add some sliced lettuce leaves and celery. Toast a slice of bread, cut into strips, pour the soup over it, meat and all, and serve.

2. **Camp Soup** (*made in an hour*).—Mince 1 unit of meat, put to it 2 units of cold water, and let it stand for half-an-hour. Put on the fire and boil briskly for another half-hour with such seasoning as may be procurable. This is an excellent, clear, almost colourless stock, and may be varied as opportunity affords. A handful of Chollet's vegetables, a poached egg, or a leason of flour and butter, with a few tinned oysters, will, on an emergency, provide a good tureen of soup.

3. **Friar's Chicken.**—A medium fowl trussed as for boiling, half an onion, a slice of green ginger, salt, pepper, 60 tablespoons of cold water. Set to simmer slowly till the fowl is fully done. Remove the white meat and replace the remainder. Just before serving, strain and add a spoonful of chopped parsley, the white meat cut into neat slices, and 2 tablespoons of the yolk of eggs. They must be mixed with a cupful of the broth in a basin first, or they will curdle.

4. **Prince of Wales Soup.**—Cut four or five large turnips into rounds with a cutter. Boil until quite tender and the liquor no longer covers them. Take 10 units of this and add to 40 of strong brown stock, which should taste strongly of the turnip. A little sugar may be added.

5. **Scotch Broth.**—Take 32 units of neck of mutton and joint it. Parboil 2 units of pearl barley in 80 units of water. Add the meat, 6 units of turnips cut into dice, 2 units onions sliced, a good handful of kale, and some parsley. Season with salt and pepper, and simmer gently for four hours. In this broth the meat remains palatable, and should be eaten with the broth. It is very useful for children, and may be made of beef also.

6. **Spring Soup.**—Take 40 units of ordinary stock made from any meat. Shred one onion, one lettuce, and a little parsley; boil these with

6 units of green peas and 1 unit butter in 10 of water. When about to serve, strain the vegetables and add them to the stock. Beat 2 units of yolk of egg to the liquor strained from the vegetables, give it a heat over the fire, add to the soup, and serve with fried sippets.*

Purées or Vegetable Soups

The stock for these should never be strong, or the flavour of the meat will overpower the more delicate flavour of the vegetable, and the result will be a meat soup thickened. The consistency should never be *thicker than that of twelve hours' raw cream*. It is a common fault to make these soups too thick.

Almost every vegetable can be made into a *purée*, and fried *croutons* should invariably be handed round with these soups. The stock is almost invariably the better for a slight flavouring of bacon or ham. In all cases the vegetables should be gently stewed in a little butter and water, and then passed through a sieve until quite smooth. The stock should then be added until all is of proper consistency. The addition of a plentiful amount of cream renders most of these *purées* delicious. In fact, with vegetables, eggs, and cream, very little stock is required even for a dinner-party. The following are among the most common kinds of *purées*:—

1. **Bonne femme**.—Any kind of beans, lettuce, onion, carrot, cucumber, cream, and a leason of eggs.* It should have shredded leaves of spinach in it.

2. **German**.—Cabbage, with strong flavour of bacon.

3. **Italian**.—Tomatoes, one carrot, two onions, flavouring of celery and thyme, a little wine, and anchovy sauce.

4. **Palestine**.—Jerusalem artichokes, with sufficient cream to whiten it.

5. **Russian**.—One cabbage, two turnips, one onion, two leeks, four units peas. Add small strips fried bacon and slices of sausage.

Thickened Soups

The stock for soups that are to be thickened with meat should invariably be made partially of that meat, and those to be thickened with farinaceous substances should be made of clear pale stock. In these soups, therefore, the *khansâmah*'s favourite beef bone is nowhere.

1. **À la Reine.**—Boil 8 units of rice in 20 units of light stock for an hour. Take the white meat of a roast chicken; pound it in a mortar with a little stock and the rice; moisten with 40 units of light stock, and rub through a sieve; add 6 units or more of cream, and serve with fried *croutons*. Celery is the only flavour permissible, and almonds *must not* be put in.

2. **Giblet Soup and Kidney Soup** are made with strong beef stock poured over lightly fried giblets. Stew for an hour. Thicken, season, and add wine.

3. **Hare Soup.**—Skin the hare, saving all the blood in a basin. Cut it into joints, add the blood mixed to a smooth cream with 1 unit of flour and 60 units of water. Flavour with 1 onion stuck with cloves. *Stir continually* till it boils. If properly stirred the blood will not curdle at all afterwards. Boil for three hours, add a little port wine before serving. It can also be made clear without the blood.

4. **Mock Turtle.**—This can be fairly made with a sheep's head. The head must not be skinned, but the hair scalded off. It must be split, first parboiled in water, and then boiled to a perfect jelly for hours in good strong stock, fully seasoned with ham, onions, cloves, celery, herbs, &c. The head should then be removed and allowed to cool under a weight, and the stock set aside. Shortly before serving remove every particle of grease, thicken with flour and butter, add some sherry, some force-meat balls, a little glaze or Bovril, and the most gelatinous portions of the head cut into squares, and serve.

5. **Mulligatawny Soup.***—Slice three onions and fry them without colouring in 1 unit of butter. Add one apple, cut into slices, and let it dissolve over a slow fire. Then mix in 1 unit of curry powder and flour, add 40 of medium stock, and simmer for an hour. Pass through a sieve, and serve with any remains of cold poultry cut into slices and warmed in the soup. Rice, and lemons in slices, to be handed with it.

6. **Oxtail Soup.**—The stock for this should be made of the tail, and requires careful clearing. If wanted very good, stock must be used instead of water, in the usual proportion. The joints of tail should be removed when cooked, and the soup finished by clearing with white of eggs. A little wine, some cut carrots, turnips, button onions, and celery (previously boiled) should be added, and finally the ox-tail.

SOUPS WITHOUT MEAT

1. **Bisque.**—Make a good stock by boiling 1 unit of good fresh river fish with 1 unit of water. Add a sufficient flavouring of onion, carrot, celery,

parsley, thyme, and a suspicion of garlic. Fry these with a little butter, add the stock, and let all simmer. Take some of the liquor and meat of a tin of lobster and pound in a mortar, add to the stock, and give one boil. Pass through a sieve, and season with sherry, some Harvey* and anchovy sauce, cayenne, or lemon juice. Pour over little bits of lobster, and serve. This may be made with prawns also.

2. **Bisque à l'Indienne.**—As for mulligatawny, but made with fish and the addition of a little anchovy.

3. **Bouillabaisse** (*original Provençal recipe*).—This dish cannot be made by rule. All that can be said is this: Take one, two, or three onions, according to the quantity required, a clove of garlic, and a handful of parsley, some pepper, lemon peel, salt, spice, and saffron. For every consumer 10 units of water and 2 of oil. Add as many different kinds of fish as you can lay hold of, in equal proportion to the water, cut into slices, put over a *fierce fire*, and the *bouillabaisse* is done in a quarter of an hour. It is either a magnificent success or an ignominious failure. Add saffron if liked.

4. **Oyster Soup.**—Take 2 units of the liquor from a tin of oysters, add 2 units of milk; thicken with sufficient white *roux* to make it the consistence of cream. Add 1 unit of cream, season with salt, nutmeg, cayenne, and the squeeze of a lemon. Pour over some oysters, cut in halves, and serve.

5. **Vegetable Soups.**—All the *purées* can be made without stock by using milk instead, but in this case increase the quantity of butter. These milk soups are very good for children.

Before leaving the subject of soups, we give a few hints as to their thickening, clearing, and colouring, although a good cook will seldom require to perform the two latter operations.

In this country thickening must be made in very small quantities. For brown thickening take 4 units of butter and melt it, then dredge in 6 units of flour, stir it over a slow fire until it becomes of an even light brown, and put it in a jar for use. White thickening is made the same way, but not allowed to take any colour. One unit should be enough for 40 of stock or more.

In regard to clarifying soups, it is only by negligence in skimming and over-boiling that it becomes necessary. In such cases refer to p. 220.

Colouring for soups should never be used. A decent cook will be able to vary his stock to every shade of brown by the length of time he allows the meat to 'sweat' in the pan before filling up with water.

Burnt onions and sugar are the refuge of the negligent. It is now the fashion to serve (separately) elaborate *croutons* or rolls or other garnishes with soup, which in this case is a clear, bright *consommé* flavoured to suit.

The following soup maxims should be committed to memory:—

> Keep the lid tight.
> Do not boil.
> Do not strain through a duster.
> Do not leave the soup to cool in copper *degchies*.

CHAPTER XXIV

FISH

THERE are many good Indian fishes, so it is a mistake to despise them, and use English tinned fish on all occasions. Many of these Indian fish are doubtless full of bones; but if you cut them into slices cross-ways, instead of lengthways, you can remove most of the worst ones. Stale fish is perhaps the most dangerous of all foods, therefore a cook must take the greatest care to ascertain that it is fresh. Even if his mistress has ordered fish, he will disappoint her rather than bring *rank poison* into the house.

Very few cooks clean their fish really well. It requires a *great deal of water*, and it should finally be rinsed in salt, vinegar, and water. If there is any fear of its tasting muddy, let it stand in strong salt and water for half-an-hour.

White carp is the best fish. It is the *rohu* which has white silvery scales, not red. It has no barbels. *Rohu* or red carp is also good. *Mâhseer* is by some liked the best. *Singhâra* has only one bone, and is very rich. *Sahul*, only one bone. Both these last require wine in the sauce and careful dressing. *Tingan* is a remarkably good fish in the North-West.

1. **Aspic of Fish.**—This may be made of any cold fish, and is an excellent way of dressing tinned fish. It requires a very *clear* jelly, which is best made with either gelatine or the fish bones, as any taste of meat is fatal. The jelly should only be flavoured with salt, pepper, and vinegar. A pretty aspic is made by making fish quenelles and embedding them in jelly, or by making one big quenelle mould, then slicing it, and putting alternate layers of differently tinted jelly. It should be served with mayonnaise or mousse sauce. Aspic of fish may also be made by poaching cutlet-shaped pieces of fish, as in the recipe for sautéed fish, and when cold setting them in jelly.

2. **Baked Chilwas.***—Take the largest chilwas you can get (they are to be had the size of smelts), or small mango fish.* Spread a pie-dish with butter, and strew well with bread-crumbs, minced parsley, onions, pepper, and salt. Lay the fish on this in a row. Moisten with a mixture of equal parts Harvey sauce, anchovy, and white wine. Repeat more butter, seasoning and

crumbs, moistening with melted butter last of all. Bake for quarter of an hour. Excellent for breakfast.

3. **Baked Fish.**—Scale the fish whole and cut open as little as possible in cleaning. Stuff with a good forcemeat made of fish, anchovies, hard-boiled eggs, parsley, bread-crumbs, and butter. Sew up securely. Place in an S form in a baking dish; rub over with egg, sprinkle with bread crumbs, and drop a good quantity of oiled butter over it. After it has been in the oven quarter of an hour add a cup of stock and one of red wine, and baste the fish constantly with this. When done use the liquor to make some Aurora sauce,* and serve round. If the dish is to be put on the table, it is best to sprinkle more bread-crumbs and butter over the fish about ten minutes before taking it out of the oven to ensure a good appearance.

4. **Creams, Fish.**—Eight units pounded fish passed through a sieve, 6 of panada, 1 of butter, 3 of thick cream whipped, 2 of *Béchamel* sauce, 4 of eggs, whites and yolks beaten separately and added last. Mix and pass through a sieve. Steam in any kind of shape. Both these and quenelles can be varied a thousand ways by the shapes and the sauce. The centres of these creams may be filled with oyster ragout or prawns. A little ingenuity and a French dictionary will supply an intelligent cook with many new dishes.

5. **Curry, Fish.**—Fish curries may be made like other curries, but ginger is never put in, and many people use mustard oil for them. Where this is disliked, use olive oil or butter, and a larger quantity of cocoanut milk. Fish is best half boiled before currying. The following is a good proportion for the spices: 1 unit of salt, 3 of ground onions, 1 of turmeric, ½ of chillies, 12 cloves, 16 cardamoms, 2 sticks cinnamon. The milk of a cocoanut and some lemon-grass.

6. **Dublin Lawyer.**—One tin of lobster, 2 units butter, 5 of sherry, red pepper, and salt to taste, and a squeeze of a lemon. Heat all together in a silver dish over a spirit lamp. Excellent for breakfast.

7. **Fillets of Fish au Citron.**—Cut your fish into thinnish cutlets and draw out all the bones you can; sprinkle with pepper, salt, and taste of a lemon. Butter a stewpan, put in your fillets; let them fry for five minutes, then moisten with fish stock (made from the coarser parts). When nearly reduced, add the juice of a lemon to the sauce, and dish your fillets round some finely mashed potatoes.

8. **Fillets of Fish, farced.**—Cut long thin fillets of fish, beat them to an even thickness, trim, and mask over with any fish or lobster farce.* Fold in two or roll. Put in a shallow buttered pan, cover with buttered paper, and

bake for fifteen minutes, basting well. Serve very hot on a potato bed, with suitable sauce. The fillets may be brushed over with glaze and decorated, or sprinkled with grated cheese. The centre may be filled with any ragout, or with saffron-coloured *pilau* made of fish.

9. **Fillets of Fish with Tomatoes.**—Fillet your fish, then set them in a pickle of onion juice, red pepper, mango chutney, salt, and salad oil. Prepare a thin *purée* of tomatoes, in which there should be more than a suspicion of garlic and some butter; add to it sufficient bread-crumbs fried in butter to make it thick. Grill your cutlets over a sharp fire, and dish them on the tomato *purée*. Or they may be put in a shallow dish, covered with the *purée*, strewn over with crumbs, baked. When this is ready, rub your fillets with butter, grill over a sharp fire, and serve with the tomato sauce under and around. The sauce should be quite thick, and should, of course, be seasoned with sugar as well as salt.

10. **Fritters of Fish.**—Take any kind of cold fish and add to a *very* stiff *béchamel* sauce, made with cornflour. Pour into a soup-plate, and let it set. Cut into dice; roll lightly in flour; then dip in beaten eggs, and again in flour; fry in boiling fat.

11. **Fish Jelly.**—Take the head and bones of a large fish, and to every unit allow three-fourths of a unit of water; add salt and a few peppercorns. Boil over a quick fire for about fifteen minutes, or until the fish is about three parts done. If boiled beyond this, the jelly will *never* set. By this time the liquor should be reduced by one-third. Clear with white of egg, and, if necessary, add a little gelatine. The jelly should be *quite* colourless and *very* strong. The bones and head, if large, should be broken up a little.

12. **Kidgeree of Fish.**—Take 6 units of boiled rice and flaked fish, some pepper, salt, and 2 units hard-boiled eggs chopped fine. Heat together over the fire, moistening slightly with a little butter or cream, or a little raw egg.

13. **Kippered Fish** (*author's recipe, excellent*).—Take your fish, split it clear down one side of the backbone from the inside until it lies flat. Do not remove the skin, but scale. For every 32 units of fish allow 2 of coarse sugar and ¼ unit of ground black pepper. Rub in thoroughly back and front; after twelve hours rub the pickle in again, and leave for another twelve hours. Then add ½ a unit of salt to each 32 of fish if for immediate use; twice that if for long keeping. Rub in salt and pickle for a quarter of an hour at least, and leave for a third twelve hours. Give a final rubbing, drain from the pickle, fold in two, and put aside for use. It may be smoked with green wood or coated like Findon haddocks* with burnt sugar. Cook by grilling thin slices, cut across the fish, on a quick fire. White carp done this way is most excellent for breakfast.

14. **Papers, Fish in.**—Place boned fillets of fish in a pie-dish with a little butter, anchovy, Harvey sauce, and sherry. Bake in the oven. When done, remove and add to the liquor some parsley, chopped mushrooms, or truffle, the squeeze of a lemon, and some nutmeg, pepper, and salt. Bind with the yolks of eggs till quite thick. Lay the fillets on oval oiled papers, mask with the preparation, and fold in cutlet shape by turning in the edges of the paper. Broil over a slow fire and serve on a napkin.

15. **Pie, Fish.**—Make a good béchamel sauce with 15 units milk or fish stock, 2 of flour, 2 of butter, 1 of yolk of egg, and some lemon juice and chopped parsley. It should be rather stiff. Place a layer of this in a pie-dish, lay on this some of the flaked fish, and some thin slices of hard-boiled eggs. So on, in alternate layers, till the dish is full. Cover with mashed potatoes, bake and serve. Oysters or anchovies may be added to vary the flavour, and tomatoes or cold sliced potatoes give a welcome change to this universally liked dish. It may be covered with fried bread-crumbs.

16. **Quenelles, Fish.**—Six units pounded fish, raw or cooked, 2 units bread panada, 4 of eggs. Incorporate thoroughly, adding a seasoning either of parsley and lemon juice or anchovy to taste, and poach carefully. Serve with Ravigotte sauce.*

17. **Scalloped Fish.**—Flake some cold fish. Make a good white sauce in the usual proportions. Add a little anchovy sauce, chopped parsley, lemon juice, and yolk of egg. Stir in the flaked fish gently. Fill the scallop shells, cover with fried bread-crumbs, and bake for five minutes. Oysters, lobsters, and any kind of fish can be scalloped in this way.

18. **Skewered Fish.**—Cut your fish into pieces as for *kabobs*, only larger; pickle them in oil, pepper, parsley, salt, and lemon juice. Skewer them in rows with a very thin slice of mango pickle between each bit of fish, egg and crumb, or dip in batter and fry. Serve with Ravigotte sauce or Aurora sauce, which are the best for all kinds of fresh-water fish.

19. **Smoked Fish.**—Take a large fish, split it down the back, remove the skin, and place it on two crossed sticks over an earthen dish of water. Pile on the fish as much as will lie on it of the following mixture: Common brown sugar, 8 units; salt, 4; pepper, 2. In three hours remove, wash, and smoke over a charcoal fire deadened with bran and sugar.

20. **Soufflées of Fish.**—One unit butter, 1 flour, 5 of milk, 2 of yolk of egg. Stir over the fire till it nearly boils. Mix in 3 units raw pounded fish, seasoning, and 3 units of white of eggs, well beaten. Either steam or bake.

SAUCE is not simply a mixture of gravy, flour, and burnt sugar, or milk, cornflour, and butter. There are hundreds of different kinds of sauces, all giving a distinct flavour to the dish with which they are served. For ordinary, plain, and good cooking, however, the following recipes will be found sufficient; but no one should presume to call himself a cook till he has these by heart.

Sauces should always be prepared at leisure, long before the dinner-hour, and may be kept hot, without spoiling, in a *bain-marie* or water bath. One of these can be made for a rupee, by cutting down a kerosene tin for the bath, and having handles fixed to suitably sized jam or fruit tins. These make excellent little saucepans for this work, as they have never to be put on the fire, but only in the hot-water bath. It must be remembered that the making of sauces is exact work, and cannot be done by guess. If a certain proportion is ordered and you use another, you will completely spoil your sauce. At the same time, if the general proportion of all sauces be remembered—that is, 15 units of liquid to 1 of flour or ½ of cornflour, and from 1 to 2 of butter—many sauces may be invented, since most have the same foundation, and only differ in the flavouring. To save trouble, therefore, the recipes are given in groups.

FIRST GROUP

Founded on White Sauce made with Milk or—

Béchamel.—Flavour 15 units of milk with 1 carrot, 1 onion, some parsley, thyme, nutmeg, pepper, and salt. Melt 2 units of butter in a saucepan, stir in 1 unit of flour; strain the hot milk to it, and boil till thick enough. If wanted cold, to mask chickens, &c., use ½ unit or more of cornflour, as it sets better. The following are varieties of béchamel.

Cream Béchamel.—Add 2 units cream and 2 sliced and cooked mushrooms.

Allemande.—Add 8 units yolk of egg and 1 lemon juice.

Aurora.—Add 3 units yolk of egg, 1 unit each of tomato sauce, Harvey sauce, and grated cheese, ½ unit each tarragon vinegar and anchovy sauce.

Maître d'Hotel.—Add 2 units more butter, 2 chopped parsley, 1 lemon juice.

Ravigotte.—Add 1 unit butter, ½ unit tarragon, and Chili vinegar, Harvey sauce, and ¼ anchovy sauce.

Soubise.—Equal parts béchamel and *purée* of onions, thickened with yolk of egg.

Shrimp, Lobster, Oyster.—Béchamel or velouté made with fish stock, to which is added either of these three whole, chopped, or passed through a sieve.

SECOND GROUP

Founded on White Sauce made with Stock or—

Velouté.—Flavour 15 units good white stock to suit the dish with which it is to be served, making it, if possible, from the same sort of meat. Melt 1 unit of butter in a saucepan, stir in 1 unit of flour, add the stock, boil till thick enough.

The following are some varieties of velouté. Their name is legion:—

Green Sauce.—Boil a handful of parsley till tender, pound, rub through a sieve; add to the velouté.

Poulette.—Three units yolk of egg, 3 of mushrooms.

Angel Sauce.—Boil 15 units stock with 3 units sliced mushrooms and 3 sliced onions and some herbs. Pass through a sieve; thicken as above, and add 3 units cream.

Matlotte.—Add 2 units oysters, whole, 2 units mushrooms, 2 units small button onions, 2 units yolk of egg.

Mona Sauce.—Add 1 unit sherry, 1 hock, to 13 of fish stock, flavour with onion, thicken as above, add 1 unit chopped mushrooms, and 2 cream.

Mousseline.—Four units white of egg, 4 yolk of egg, 2 velouté sauce, 5 fish or oyster liquor. Whip over boiling water till spongy. Add 4 units chopped oysters or prawns or lobster, salt, pepper.

Mushroom.—Make the velouté half strong chicken stock, half mushroom liquor. Flavour with lean ham; add 1 unit sherry, 4 thick cream, 4 chopped mushroom.

Vin Blanc.—Make the velouté half fish stock, half hock; add 4 units cream, 2 chopped truffles, 2 ham, 2 hard boiled whites of egg.

THIRD GROUP

Founded on Brown Sauce made with Stock or—

Espagnol.—Fifteen units good brown stock strongly flavoured with ham and herbs. One unit sherry, thicken as before with 1 unit butter, 1 unit flour. There are endless sauces with this as their foundation. The following are some:—

Brown Mushroom.—Add 4 units mushrooms.

Brown Caper.—Add ¼ unit anchovy sauce, 1 unit Harvey, and sufficient capers.

Fins herbes.—Add 2 units mixed chopped herbs, 2 lumps sugar, 1 unit lemon juice.

Italian.—Add 2 units tomato pulp, 1 salad oil, 2 units onion pulp.

Orange.—Add 4 units orange juice, 2 units pulp, 2 units peel shred as for marmalade and boiled, a little sugar.

Polish.—Add 2 units claret, ½ red currant jelly, 1 sliced mushroom, 1 horse radish, 1 onion, 1 tomato pulp. Pass through the sieve.

FOURTH GROUP

Founded on a Sauce made of Egg and Butter only, or
Custard Sauces, as—

Bearnaise Sauce.—Four units butter melted in a basin over boiling water, add by degrees 4 units yolk of egg. Whisk till stiff. Flavour with 4 units chopped onions boiled in 4 units vinegar and pulped through a sieve; salt, pepper.

Cream.—Three units yolk of egg, 1 butter, 3 cream, 1 unit chopped herbs, 1 unit béchamel.

Dutch.—Four units yolk, 2 units butter, 2 milk, pepper, salt, ½ unit tarragon vinegar. Make as custard.

Tartar.—Four units yolk, 2 cream, 2 salad oil, ¼ anchovy, ½ Chili vinegar, 2 units chopped, boiled, or pickled onions or capers.

All these sauces are very apt to curdle. A spoonful or two of béchamel will mend matters somewhat.

FIFTH GROUP

Sauces without special foundation.

Bread Sauce.—Soak 6 units bread-crumbs in 6 of thin white stock for an hour. Heat over the fire until like panada, then thin with good béchamel. (N.B.—Remember that bread sauce is not a poultice!)

Hare.—One unit port wine, 2 red currant jelly, 6 strong gravy.

Rich.—Twelve units strong fish stock, 1 unit sherry, 2 units claret, 6 whole Norwegian anchovies, 1 unit sliced onion, 1 unit lemon juice. Boil, strain. Thicken with 2 units butter, 1 unit cornflour. Add 2 units tomato pulp, 2 units whipped cream.

Robert.—Two units chopped onions, 2 units butter. Fry. Dredge in 1 unit flour; fry a light brown. Add 14 units stock or milk and 1 of vinegar. This can be made thicker.

Poivrade.—Two units chopped lean ham, 2 units chopped carrot, onion, celery. Fry in 1 unit butter. Add 2 units vinegar, boil, tanny.* Add 10 units Espagnol sauce* and 2 of sherry.

Wild Duck.—Two units port wine, 1 lemon juice, 1 Harvey sauce, ½ onion juice, 2 gravy, pepper, salt.

SIXTH GROUP

Cold Sauces, foundation Mayonnaise.

Albert.—Six whole Norwegian anchovies rubbed through a sieve, 5 units thick mayonnaise, 5 units whipped cream, 4 units chopped prawns.

Mayonnaise (*English, very excellent*).—The yolks of 2 raw eggs, 3 tablespoons of salad oil, 2 tablespoons vinegar, 3 tablespoons of cream whipped, a seasoning of pepper and salt. Stir the oil and vinegar to the eggs alternately drop by drop. When well mixed and *quite thick* add the cream. This sauce may be flavoured a dozen ways; with anchovies for fish, with tarragon vinegar, with onion juice, a little Harvey sauce, &c. &c. A more economical sauce, very useful for masking cold chickens, &c., may be made by substituting cornflour mixed with milk for cream. And at any time, should mayonnaise or tartar sauce curdle, a spoonful of white sauce will generally mend matters.

Mayonnaise Sauce (*French*).—Three raw yolks of eggs, a little pepper and salt. Place in a basin and work in gradually 6 tablespoons of salad oil and 2 of tarragon vinegar. It is a good plan to work in oil and vinegar by alternate quantities, a few drops at a time. There is less risk of curdling.

Mousseline Mayonnaise.—Melt 5 units aspic jelly. Whisk till nearly cold and frothy like lemon sponge. Add 5 units mayonnaise and 5 units whipped cream. This may be made any colour or flavouring.

Tarragon Cream.—Three units butter, add slowly 3 units yolk of egg, 1 tarragon vinegar, 2 chopped tarragon. Whisk before the fire till quite smooth, then let it cool.

SEVENTH GROUP

Store Sauces

Tomato Sauce (*for keeping*).—To every 40 units of tomato pulp allow 20 units of vinegar, 2 of salt, 1 of garlic, ½ of red chillies, ¼ powdered ginger, the juice of three lemons. Boil, rub through a sieve, and reduce till it is thick. It will keep for years. Or add 8 units sugar, a seasoning of mixed spices, and boil till quite a paste. Spread out to dry on plates in the sun, cut up into strips, roll them up, and place in tins in a dry place. (*Excellent for camp work.*)

Store Sauce (*imitation Harvey*).—Forty units green walnut juice, 120 units vinegar, 1 unit cayenne, 1 unit garlic, 20 units port wine, and 20 soy. Pound the garlic and cayenne to a paste, mix with the other ingredients, let it stand for a fortnight, and decant into bottles. The soy, if not procurable, may be made as follows: Treacle 40, salt 20, mushroom ketchup 5, bruised wheat 20, port wine 5. Heat over a very slow fire, stirring constantly. Let it stand a week, and decant the clear portion as soy.

Superlative Store Sauce.—Walnut pickle 80 units, port wine 40, soy 20, anchovy sauce 4, fresh lemon peel 2 units, garlic, allspice, black pepper, and curry powder, of each 1 unit; mix and let stand for a fortnight. Strain and bottle.

Tapp Sauce.—Twenty units sliced green mangoes, 10 units ground raisins, 2 of sugar, 4 of salt, 2 of garlic, 1 of ground chillies, 2 of ginger. Mix with 40 units vinegar and 5 of lime juice. Set in the sun for fifteen days. Strain, give one boil, and bottle.

EIGHTH GROUP

Sweet Sauces, Cold and Hot

Almond Sauce.—One unit ground almonds, 1 unit water, 4 units white sugar; pound. Put in a basin over boiling water with 5 units thin cream and 2 units yolk of egg. Whisk till it is a hot froth.

Mousse Sauce.—Four units castor or pounded white sugar, 4 units yolk of egg, 2 white of egg, 4 brandy, 2 lemon juice. Whip as above.

Mousseline (*hot*).—Two units yolk, 1 unit white of egg, 2 units castor sugar, 3 any liqueur. Whisk as above.

Mousseline (*cold*).—Boil 2 units water with 4 of sugar. Stir to it 3 units yolk of egg, 1 unit cherry-brandy, 5 of banana pulp, a few drops of cochineal. Whisk. Add 5 units whipped cream when cold.

Orange Sauce (*cold*).—Five units water, 4 units sugar; add a 4-anna weight of gelatine. When half cold add 5 units orange pulp, 2 brandy or Maraschino, and some yellow colouring. Mix in 5 units whipped cream and some boiled shredded peel.

Plum Pudding Sauce.—Eight units butter, 4 units coarsely pounded sugar, 5 units Curaçoa or brandy, 2 units yolk of egg. Cream the butter, add the sugar and egg, and stir in the brandy. It can be made without the eggs.

Plantain Sauce.—Five units plantain pulp, 5 orange pulp, 2 units sugar, 8 units water; boil, pass through sieve; add 2 units noyeau and a few shredded almonds.

Purée Sauces.—Made of any fruit or jam passed through a sieve and thinned with water.

Sweet Sauce.—One unit cornflour, 2 of sugar, 5 of sherry, 1 of lemon juice, 1 of butter or more; add 10 of water.

Syrup Sauces.—Six units of sugar to 3 of water, any flavouring or colour. Chocolate sauce is made by adding 1 unit of cocoatina to this.

CHAPTER XXVI

PLAIN ENTRÉES

———◆———

By plain *entrées* is meant those inexpensive and easily prepared dishes which are suitable for everyday cooking.

1. **Boudins** may be made of any cold meat, either pounded or minced, and bound with eggs and thick sauce. They may be poached or steamed in a mould, or used to fill up the centre of a chartreuse, that is, a mould lined with vegetables. The only thing to remember is that a chartreuse mould must always be lined first with buttered paper. The proportions are invariably: 5 units of pounded cooked meat, 2 of panard* (see Miscellaneous), 1 thick brown sauce, ½ butter, 2 eggs.

2. **Brains au Gratin.**—Parboil, cut into slices, toss up with *allemande* or *maitre d'hotel* sauce. Fill some paper cases with the mixture, strew fried bread-crumbs over, and, if liked, a rasp of cheese. Bake for five minutes.

3. **Brain Cutlets.**—Blanch the brains in cold water for half-an-hour and remove the skin. Boil slowly in a little vinegar and water with seasonings. When cold, cut into cutlets, dip them in butter or egg, and crumb. Fry in sufficient boiling fat to let them swim. Drain and serve with tomato or Robert sauce.*

4. **Bubble and Squeak.**—Place small thin slices of cold salt beef in a frying-pan, taking care to have plenty of fat bits. Just fry through without drying. Set the meat aside, and in the same pan put a sufficiency of boiled and chopped cabbage. Fry sharply; add the meat; save a few bits for garnishing. Let the whole bubble and squeak well. Serve very hot, arranged in a pyramid, and garnished with the bits of meat set aside.

5. **Chicken, Fricassée.**—This is generally made from cold chicken, when it consists of meat warmed up in a white velouté sauce. When, however, it is made from a raw chicken, it will be found best to parboil the bird whole in milk and then joint it. This prevents the meat shrinking, and makes it far more juicy. Indian cooks put ground almonds in the sauce. This is a mistake. The milk in which the bird has been boiled will of course make the sauce.

6. **Chicken Rolls.**—Bone a chicken, opening it from the back. Trim to an even square, and use the trimmings to make a forcemeat

with bread-crumbs, parsley, chopped bacon, &c. Spread lightly over the chicken, roll up in an even roll, and skewer or sew together. Stew very gently in stock or milk. When done cut in rounds about half an inch thick, and dip each piece in reduced velouté sauce. Serve with any garnishing in the centre. Or you may use brown sauce as a variety. The same method is excellent, served cold with mayonnaise sauce and salad of tomatoes and cucumbers in the hot weather.

7. **China Hash.**—Forty units raw minced mutton, 20 of shred lettuces, 10 of peas, 10 of carrots and turnips minced, 5 of water, 2 of butter, some salt, pepper. Put all together, stir till hot, then cover and simmer for two hours. Serve with rice. A teaspoon of curry powder is an improvement.

8. **Cold Meat, Glacé.**—Cut the meat in ovals about ½ inch thick. Lay in a stewpan with some butter, fry lightly on either side, add some good gravy, and stew for ten minutes. Thicken the sauce to a glaze, and pour over the meat. Dress the collops neatly round any garnishing, and pour a brown or white sauce round. Tomatoes in the centre and spinach sauce looks well.

9. **Croquets.**—These may be made of anything and everything, and may be seasoned with anything and everything. The foundation is minced meat or fish. This should be put into a saucepan with enough white velouté sauce to moisten it. When hot, add the strained yolks of eggs. When nearly set, pour out on a dish to cool, and when firm cut into pieces the size of a cork. These must be rolled to some uniform shape in bread-crumbs, dipped in beaten eggs, smoothed again in bread-crumbs, and plunged into boiling fat. The great art in croquets is to have the outside properly hardened by the boiling fat before the inside has time to melt; in this way the croquets will be full of delicious gravy. Croquets are excellent made of macaroni and cold tongue, and are most economical, as a very small portion of meat suffices to make them. One of the prettiest shapes for croquets is that of a pear. They should be dished standing upright, with a green stick of parsley as a stalk in each. The general proportion for croquets is 10 units of minced meat, 4 of gravy or sauce. They may be made with panade. The only point is to have them firm enough to handle.

10. **Croustades, Croutons, and Patties.**—These are useful for using up any cold meat or fish. In economical houses, patties will only be made from the trimmings of puff paste used for tarts, &c., but croutons are always easily made. Take a stale loaf; what is called a *chuppur* or close-grained loaf is best. Cut into slices 2 inches thick, and from these punch out circles 2 inches across. Stamp or mark out an inner circle, remove it carefully as

a lid, and scoop out the crumb inside, leaving a thick enough wall. If the
crouton is merely to be baked in the oven till crisp, a thin wall will hold; if it
is to be fried in butter, one slightly thicker will do; but for croutons which
are to be soaked in custard and fried, at least a ¼ inch must be left. The
latter way is very excellent, especially if the custard be made with a little
broth. The cut-out croutons should only be soaked for a minute or two,
then fried at once. With sweet custard flavoured with essences many pretty
and delicate puddings may be made with croutons. Croustades are made
of short paste, and can therefore be easily made also. The tin croustade
moulds, which are rather like dariol moulds,* and of various shapes, are
lined as for cheesecakes with the paste, baked with raw rice inside them.
The croustades can then be filled and decorated according to taste. All that
is required is a good sauce, either sweet or savoury, and the remains of
some other dish. Even custard pudding cut into dice, with jam and a little
whipped cream, will fill a croustade.

11. **Cutlets (*Plain*) of Fresh Meat.**—The great fault of Indian cooks
in regard to cutlets is over-handling. They beat, chop, and season the meat
out of all distinctive taste. Now, a plain cutlet should simply be *cut* and
trimmed, dipped in the yolks of eggs, bread-crumbed, and fried a light
golden brown. One great mistake is also bread-crumbing with crumbs
made by drying the bread in the oven, and beating into a *powder* in a
mortar. Things crumbed in this way have no *grain*, and will not take the
fry. This is the reason of half the black, greasy cutlets in India, which look
so different from the crisp, rough golden grain of English cutlets. Bread
should be allowed to get stale, and be *grated*, not pounded. Plain cutlets
may be served with any sauce and round any garnishing. They are, perhaps,
the most *uncommon* dish in India at present, for the ordinary cook always
marinades his cutlets, even if he does not mince them.

12. **Cutlets of Cooked Meat.**—Twenty units of pounded meat, 5 of
pounded bacon or ham, ¼ unit minced onion; pound with 1 unit Espagnol
sauce and 1 of lemon juice; add 1 unit fresh bread crumbs and 2 whole
anchovies. Put through the sieve, and 1 unit yolk of egg. Mix intimately,
adding flavouring of pepper and salt. Form the farce into cutlets, egg,
crumb, and fry. This is an excellent way of using cold meats.

13. **Fillets of Beef** (*Italian fashion*).—Take a good fillet from the under
cut, slice it crossways into pieces about ½ inch thick. Lay in salad oil for
two or three hours, or in cold weather for six. Broil lightly over a very
clear fire, and dish up round a pile of fried potato chips, placing a piece of
mâitre d'hotel butter on each fillet. The ways of dressing fillets of beef are
three—braised, broiled, fried; the method of decorating and serving them
endless; also the names by which these decorations are called.

14. **Haricot** may be made of any part of the meat, but is usually made from the breast of mutton. Divide and trim the cutlets; fry a pale brown with the fat trimmings. Remove, and in the same fat fry lightly equal quantities of shaped carrots and turnips, and about half quantity silver pickled onions. Place meat and vegetables in a stewpan, and cover with boiling water. Give one boil, and set to simmer. When nearly done, set aside to cool. Remove every particle of fat, and heat up again. The seasoning should be varied to taste; sometimes three cloves stuck in an onion, sometimes lemon peel, or a faggot of herbs. The sauce may be thickened with browned flour and butter, but it should be more of a glaze than a thick sauce. Dish with the vegetables piled up in the middle and the cutlets round.

15. **Hashed Mutton** is not thin shavings of meat, sodden, yet hard, in a thin gravy. Cut the mutton into thick slices, and again into pieces about two inches long. Flour and season with pepper and salt. Put some good broth, one lump of sugar, one onion, and the squeeze of a lemon into a saucepan; boil and thicken with flour and butter; add a taste of wine or sauce; put in the mutton, warm through, and serve. Hashes of all kinds must never be cooked, but only warmed through, and the meat should be put into the gravy when it is nearly cold, and then warmed up.

16. **Kidneys au fins herbes.**—Cut the kidney with a sharp knife from the outside rounded part, making the incision deep but not too broad, and fill with chopped herbs. Skin them and broil over a clear fire in a frying-pan, with just enough butter to prevent them burning. When done, add ½ a unit of catsup and 1 of gravy to the glaze, lay the kidneys on rounds of fried toast, pour the gravy over, and serve very hot.

17. **Kidneys, Stewed.**—Six kidneys skinned and halved, ½ unit of flour, minced parsley, and onion, 1 unit of butter. Fry the kidneys lightly in the butter, dredge in the flour and seasoning, add a ¼ of a unit of lemon juice and any store sauce, and 3 units each of sherry and gravy. Serve very hot in a rice border. The wine may be omitted.

18. **Mince Collops.**—Twenty units minced raw meat; season with pepper and salt; add one unit of water, and stir gently over a slow fire, taking care that the mince does not get lumpy. Serve in a wall of mashed potato with poached eggs on the top.

19. **Quenelle of Brains.**—Skin the brain and beat with a fork, mixing in some oyster liquor and a few pounded oysters. Butter a china mould, fill and steam for half-an-hour. Use more liquor and oysters to flavour a thick white sauce, and pour round. As only a small quantity of oysters are required, this is a good recipe for utilising the remainder of a tin.

20. **Rissoles.**—These are made of minced or croquet meat variously prepared and rolled in puff or potato paste, then fried in boiling fat. They are simply an offshoot of croquets, given above. Rissoles should invariably be crisp, and if possible be sprinkled with broken vermicelli to increase their crispness. They look best cut out with a fluted tin cutter. They are dished on a napkin, with branches of fried parsley served in the middle. Potato rissoles are made by inserting a tablespoonful of mince, mixed with good white or brown sauce, in a ball of mashed potato. This should then be egged, dipped in broken vermicelli—the native sort does well—and fried in boiling fat, in which the ball will float. These are best made a few minutes before dinner and placed in the oven to dry, as the paste takes so short a time to fry that the inside is apt to be cold. Rice rissoles are made the same way, with rice boiled in thin stock or water to a paste.

21. **Sheep's Head Fritters.**—Boil a blanched, not skinned, sheep's head till tender. Bone. Make a farce of the trimmings, with ham seasoning, onions, &c., varying it to taste. Spread over the head, roll up, tie with string, or in a cloth like a roly-poly pudding. Braise in good stock. When cold cut in slices, dip in batter, and fry. Garnish with any *piquante* sauce.

22. **Sheep's Trotters.**—Clean and wash in several waters, parboil for two hours in water with salt, a sliced onion, two carrots, and some herbs. The addition of a lump of suet is an improvement. Remove, and carefully bone. The trotters are now ready for dressing, and may be stewed or done with white sauce as follows: Let the trotters get tender by stewing gently in a little stock, with proper seasonings, and a pinch of flour. When done, add 2 units yolk of egg, 1 of butter, and the squeeze of a lemon. Serve with croutons or fried potatoes. Sheep's trotters make an excellent curry, but all dishes of trotters are improved by bacon as a seasoning.

23. **Toad in the Hole.**—Sixteen units (solid) of rump steak and an ox kidney. Scald the kidney, skin, and cut the steak into collops. Season with pepper and salt, and fry brown over a sharp fire. Add a little water to the glaze in the frying-pan, or a little stock, and ½ a unit of catsup. Lay the kidney and collops in a pie-dish, and pour the gravy over. Make a batter of 20 units of milk, 3 of flour, and 4 of eggs. Beat well for at least ten minutes to make it light, season with salt and nutmeg, pour it over the collops, and bake.

24. **Veal or Chicken Flädeln.**—Take some cold chicken, mince and season highly. At least six hours before they are wanted make some small, rather thick, pancakes, which must be cooked only on one side. Just before dinner cut those into neat squares or rounds about the size of a small saucer. Fill with mince, as in turnovers. Egg, crumb, and fry. This is

a German variety of kromeskys. It can be varied many ways by making the flädeln with sauces, or by egging and crumbing these and then frying in boiling fat. For instance, cut two heart-shaped pieces of pancake, dust over with grated cheese, make into a sandwich with a mince of chicken made with cream, egg, crumb, and fry. Brush a little liquid glaze over one side, dip in grated ham; the other in grated yolk of egg.

CHAPTER XXVII

HIGH-CLASS ENTRÉES AND GARNISHES

—————◆—————

In no other branch of cookery is a French dictionary and a vivid imagination more necessary than in the preparation of what are called high-class *entrées*. Their name is legion already, and yet an ordinarily intelligent cook might increase their number indefinitely. Just as there are only four kinds of pudding—a boiled pudding, a baked pudding, a fried pudding, and a pastry pudding—so all *entrées* group themselves under a few heads. Fully one-half of the new side-dishes are simply varieties of the quenelle-custard-cream genus, while the other half belong to the patty-croustade-croquet-kromesky family. Some are served with one sauce, some with another; in some the whites of the eggs are used, in some they are not; but when all is said and done, a cook who can make a *Turban à la something* can put the same mixture into a different shape, and call it *Little Chickens à la something else*; the something else being a variable quantity also. So the following recipes must be taken as indications of what may be attempted rather than as a complete collection of what has been done. In regard to decoration, a protest has been entered elsewhere against over-colouring and the plastic art. There *can* be no reason why one-half of a dish should be coloured pink with a tasteless, useless drug, and the other half green. But it is quite allowable to decorate with ham, truffle, eggs, chopped parsley, glaze, &c. With these few remarks we pass on to the recipes.

1. **Chicken Quenelles.**—One unit flour, 1 unit butter, 5 of cream. Make into a thick sauce. Sixteen units white meat pounded in a mortar, flavour to taste, and incorporate with the sauce. Add 2 units of yolk of eggs. Shape with tablespoons, or put into buttered quenelle moulds and poach for three minutes in boiling water. Another equally good recipe is as follows: Take 12 units raw chicken pounded and rubbed through a sieve, 3 of butter, 4 of panada, made by steeping the crumb of a loaf in warm water, wringing out in a cloth, and heating over the fire with a little butter and salt until it leaves the sides of the pan and is a compact, smooth paste. Pound all together, add gradually 4 units of eggs, 1 of thick white sauce, and 1 of yolk of egg. Season to taste. Poach in boiling water, in buttered moulds. Each

quenelle should be decorated with truffle or ham. In poaching quenelles, the water should be boiling when the moulds are set in it. It should then be allowed to come to the boil again, when the pan should be put where it can just simmer. Fast boiling makes the quenelles hard and curdy.

2. **Compôte of Pigeons**.—Lay some slices of bacon in a stew-pan with a little butter. Fry and place your pigeons on the bacon, turning them round till set all over. Then cut the pigeons in two, lay round the stewpan, and cover with strong stock, and add a carrot and onion or two and a faggot of herbs. Simmer gently for an hour. Strain the gravy, thicken with flour, 1 unit to 15, and pour over the pigeons, which should be dressed on a masked potato border with a ragout of mushrooms or any other suitable garnishings.

3. **Creams**.—A number of pretty cold *entrées* can be made with whipped cream, adding to it pounded lobster or chicken. As an instance of what a little thought can produce, we give the following charming dish for hot weather: Take eight tomatoes exactly the same size and shape, cut off the tops about one-fourth of the depth of the fruit, and carefully scoop out the seeds. Take some Barataria prawns,* cut into smallish bits, and mix with a cream mayonnaïse sauce. Sprinkle the inside of the tomatoes with salt, pepper, oil, vinegar, and half fill with the prawns. Pound the rest of the prawns to a paste, and moisten with the *red* pulp of the tomatoes. Mix sufficient whipped cream to make it pale pink and stiff. With more cream mix salt, a drop of pepper, sauce, and a spoonful of pounded pistachio nuts. If not green enough, add a little spinach juice. Take a slice off a large cucumber, cut it with a round fluted cutter, and stick it upright in the centre of the tomato; fill one side with pink cream and the other with green. Dish up round a mould of very clear aspic jelly containing prawn quenelles. The foundation of all these cold side-dishes is the same, the variant is ingenuity and care.

4. **Custards**.—Beat the meat of a raw chicken or rabbit, pheasant, or mutton, or beef to a pulp and rub it through a sieve several times. To every unit of pulp add 2 units of pure milk or thin cream. Mix thoroughly, and rub through the sieve again. Butter small moulds and steam the custards. This is simply a perfect recipe, and practically does away with all need for panade sauce, butter, and eggs. Any sauce may be poured round the custards; they may be made any shape, and flavoured in a thousand ways.

5. **Cutlets, Braised**.—Do not use a chopper to cut with, but a *saw* and a very sharp knife. Do not pound or mince the cutlets, simply cut them into shape and trim the bones. The spine bone should be sawn off and the rib bones sawn across before the cutlets are divided. When neatly

trimmed, lay the cutlets in any kind of seasoning for an hour. Then place in a stewpan with some butter or fat. Fry brown on both sides; sprinkle over a little flour, fry for a minute or two, then add sufficient stock to cover and braise for half-an-hour. Cutlets done this way are the foundation of many dishes called by different names according to the garniture and sauce with which they are served.

6. **Fillets of Mutton or Lamb or Beef.**—Remove nearly all fat from the fillet of mutton or lamb, and divide it into suitable pieces. Cut these lengthwise. Lard them with bacon, and set to pickle in vinegar and seasonings. Spread some butter on the bottom of a deep baking-dish or pie-dish, lay the fillets neatly on this with a wineglassful of the pickle. Bake in a quick oven for a quarter of an hour. When done, glaze them in a thick brown glaze, and serve with a sharp brown sauce or with any garnish suitable. Scallops of mutton or lamb are made the same way, but the fillets are cut across like beef fillets, in thin round slices, and are not larded. In fact, scallops, epigrams,* and fillets of mutton are all one. Like cutlets they can be braised, fried, or sautéed, or dressed.

7. **Fritots.**—These are simply fritters, or kromeskys without the bacon. The meat, sheep's head or trotters, has to be braised first with plenty of seasoning, then cut into shapes, dipped in batter, and fried. They should be wrapped in pork caul, but this is not to be had in India; a very thin pancake can be used for sloppy fritots of mince and *purée*.

8. **Kidneys with Champagne.**—Skin the kidneys and slice in rounds. Dust over with flour, and lay in a stewpan with a unit of fresh butter, some pepper, salt, chopped parsley or thyme, and the squeeze of a lemon. When brown, add 5 units of champagne, and stew till the sauce adheres to the kidneys. Serve in patties, or in a large crouton, or as a ragout round a macédoine of vegetables.

9. **Kromeskys** are simply croquets made of meat, tongue, ham, macaroni, truffles, rice, bound with a rich sauce. After shaping each croquet like a cork, wrap round in a thin slice of bacon, dip in frying batter, and fry in a basket. The distinctive mark is the bacon, otherwise anything will make a kromesky.

10. **Ox Palates à la Florentine.**—Soak the palates in salt and water for several hours and rub well. Then parboil until the horny skin will rub off. When clean put in a stewpan with water, or stock, and the usual garnishings, and boil gently for three hours, or till quite tender. Put between two dishes to press. When cold stamp out with oval or round tin cutters, and warm up in a thick brown glaze. The trimmings may be minced up

with ham, a little grated cheese, chopped macaroni, and white sauce to a good croquet forcemeat, which should also be set to cool and be stamped out, dipped in batter, and fried. Dish on rice and tomatoes, and pour Italian sauce* round.

11. **Olives of Pigeon.**—Bone your pigeons by opening them down the back. Divide in two, and trim the edges. Use these trimmings to make a forcemeat with chopped olives and pounded pistachios. Season the pigeons, and roll up each bit with some of the forcemeat. Take trouble to shape the rolls properly into the shape of large olives or small eggs. Then braise, taking care to stew very gently, and serve with macaroni kromeskys.

12. **Patties.**—These are generally made of puff-paste and filled with ragouts of sorts. But made of potato-paste in shallow patty-pans they are useful for dishing up fillets of beef, mutton, in fact, anything. By half filling the little dish, as it were, of potato with a *purée* of peas or tomatoes, laying the fillet on it and garnishing with mushrooms, &c., both meat and vegetables are helped at once.

13. **Sheep's Tongues à la Milanese.**—Braise eight tongues, after larding them carefully so as to show the lards in two rows, down the front of the tongue. The lards may be of bacon, or truffle. When braised, make an incision down the middle of the tongue, between the lards, and fill with white quenelle forcemeat. Sprinkle with fried bread-crumbs and cheese, and moisten with melted butter. Push the tongues into the oven, or salamander them.* Then glaze the tongues, and serve upright, the thick ends to the middle, on a border of Milanese rice. This *entrée* is very pretty if neatly made, as the centre of the tongues can be filled in with reduced celery *purée* or tomato custard, and the tongues glazed white or brown.

14. **Soufflées, Cold.**—Are made by adding chopped and seasoned game, ham, chicken, lobster, fish, &c., to liquid aspic jelly, adding cream, and whipping till it is cold. They may also be made of vegetable *purée*.

15. **Soufflées, Hot**—Any kind of pounded meat well seasoned 4 units, eggs 4 units, panade 1 unit. Mix intimately, reserving the white of egg till the last. Add well whisked. Soufflées can be steamed or baked, or first steamed then egg-crumbed and fried.

16. **Timbales** are made of pipe macaroni or macaroni paste. The latter is seldom seen in India. Boil some pipe macaroni, not too soft, cut into half-inch lengths. Butter a mould, preferably a pudding basin, very thick with butter. Stick the macaroni upright, beginning with the middle and working to the sides, until the whole sides are covered. Then carefully press in some well-seasoned quenelle forcemeat, and steam for half-an-hour.

It should turn out quite evenly, showing all the holes of the macaroni. Serve with allemande sauce.*

17. **Vol-au-vents**.—The *vol-au-vent* itself comes under the head of puff-paste, and its beauty entirely depends on the cook's capacity for pastry. It is simply an oval of paste about two inches thick when it goes into the oven, and with an inner oval marked *deep* with the knife. It should rise at least three times its original height. The top should then be removed and the inside scraped out. The contents may be anything, but are chiefly teaspoon quenelles, cockscombs,* truffles, chicken in dice, &c., in white cream sauce or a brown glaze. It is, in fact, a large patty. *Vol-au-vents* are generally beyond the Indian cook, who seldom arrives at the necessary perfection in pastry.

CHAPTER XXVIII

GARNISHES

—————⟫◆⟪—————

1. **Chartreuse.**—Prepare vegetables in a mould as for a moulded macédoine, but fill the inside with braised cabbage or dressed spinach.

2. **Egg Garnish, White.**—Two units white of egg, ½ unit thick cream, some salt. Mix. Poach till firm. Cut to shapes. **Yellow.**—Two units yolk, 1 unit cream; as before. Any flavouring. For soups, &c., or the whites may be whipped very stiff and dropped through a forcing-pipe into boiling milk, then used.

3. **Milanese Macaroni.**—Cut in small pieces about one inch long, and the same width, a little cooked macaroni, ham, or tongue, mushrooms, cold chicken, or game. Put them in a saucepan with sufficient good thick white sauce to make them cohere; add grated Parmesan cheese to taste, and pepper, salt, and nutmeg. Heat, and use as required.

4. **Provençale.**—Chop six large onions and stew very gently with 2 units of butter, nutmeg, pepper, salt, and the juice of a lemon. Do not let the onions brown, but cook till quite soft, then add the 4 units yolk of egg, and stir till the whole is a thick paste. Use this to mask fillets or cutlets, and then sprinkle with fried bread-crumbs and Parmesan cheese.

5. **Potato Croquets.**—Take a sufficiency of well-mashed potatoes, add some yolk of egg and some cream; form into any shape, egg and crumb, or roll in broken vermicelli. Fry a golden brown. A variation is made by cutting the paste with a cutter like shortbread, egging-over, and baking. A little nutmeg should be dusted over after egging.

6. **Reform Garnish.***—Shredded ham, whites of egg pickled, gherkins, mushrooms, and truffles; warm up in brown *piquante* sauce.

7. **Rice Borders** (*Plain*).—Two units rice, 20 units thin stock. Boil, add seasoning, 1 unit of butter and 2 egg. The rice must be very dry. Press into a buttered mould, stand it in a baking tin of water, and bake 20 minutes. Turn out and use as a border for ragouts, hashes. *Red.*—With ½ tomato *purée* and ½ stock. *Green.*—With spinach. This last is good made with Indian corn meal or semolina. Cheese may be added.

CHAPTER XXIX

SAVOURIES

HALF the battle with savouries is that the hot ones should be hot, the cold ones cold. Toasts also should never be flabby or greasy. By far the best way of preparing them is to put the bread ready cut to shape and lightly buttered on both sides into the oven till brown.

1. **Adelaide Sandwiches.**—Take 2 units of cooked chicken in dice and 1 unit of ham in same form. To ½ unit curry spices or paste add 2 of good brown sauce; and if spices are used, a little tomato conserve or chutney. Add the chicken and ham as soon as the spices are cooked, first by frying in a little butter, then by boiling with the sauce. Have ready rounds of fried bread about one-eighth of an inch thick and three inches across. Make into sandwiches with the mixture, arrange on a baking sheet, and on the top of each place a ball the size of a walnut of grated cheese and butter in equal parts kneaded together. Bake in a sharp oven for five minutes, and serve on a napkin.

2. **Canapées** are simply croutons dried in the oven, or dipped in milk, and then dried. They are filled with various kinds of mixtures—chopped eggs, anchovies, cress, cucumbers, &c., mixed with vinegar, salad oil, or tartar sauce. Or game in dice, celery, aspic jelly, mayonnaise sauce, decorated with anchovies, &c. Almost anything and everything may be utilised to make a pretty appetising dish.

3. **Cassolettes or Croustades.**—These are made of short paste baked in patty-pans of various shapes. Line the moulds thinly, and fill up with uncooked rice in order to keep the shape. These cases when cold can be filled to taste with various *hors d'œuvres*, creams, *purées*, &c., and served cold or hot. The paste can be varied by adding cheese, or pounded anchovies, or mushroom powder. The cassolettes can be decorated any way. A pretty form is to brush when cold with white of egg, and sprinkle with chopped parsley or lobster spawn.

4. **Cheese Straws.**—Three units flour, 1 unit grated breadcrumbs, 2 units butter, and 2 units cheese. Mix; add a little more butter if too stiff. Season with red pepper, roll out to quarter of an inch, cut into strips quarter-inch wide and about five inches long. Bake in a slow oven.

5. **Cheese, Stewed.**—Take some very thin slices of toast, spread with thick cream, dust over with a thick layer of grated cheese. Make these into sandwiches and cut in strips, which place in a silver dish, in the bottom of which equal parts of grated cheese, thin cream, and beer, or white wine have been mixed. Push into oven until the cheese is melted.

6. **Creams.**—Quite a variety of creams can be made for cold savouries by taking any quantity of whipped cream, mixing to taste with *purée* of anchovy, game, sardines, prawns, &c., and piling up on croustades decorated with tomatoes, cucumber, &c.

7. **Fried Custards.**—One unit cheese mixed with 4 units of eggs and 3 units of cream. Butter some little bomb moulds very well, pour in the mixture, set in a baking tin in boiling water half-way up the moulds, and bake in a very moderate oven for ten minutes. When cold remove from moulds, egg, crumb, and fry. These custards may be made of many things. They are excellent with half anchovy *purée* and half cream, or with tomatoes.

8. **Macaroni** is almost invariably ruined in India by being dressed with eggs. The following is the Italian recipe: Boil 16 units of macaroni in 120 units of boiling water with 1 unit of oil, some salt, and a clove of garlic stuck with two cloves. It will take three-quarters of an hour to boil. Drain and put in a saucepan with 5 units of grated cheese, 5 units of cream or milk, and 2 of oil or butter. Shake over the fire till the cheese strings, pile on a dish, and serve. Macaroni as usually sent to table is *au gratin*; that is, sprinkled over with fried bread-crumbs and grated cheese. A welcome change may be made by substituting weak broth for the milk or cream, and a favourite Italian dish is made with the addition of 2 units of tomato conserve.

9. **Mushroom Soufflé.**—One unit of butter, 1 unit flour, 5 of thin cream. Mix the flour with the butter, add the cream, and boil till thick, stir in 4 units yolk of egg well beaten, and five large mushrooms finely minced. Add 5 units well-beaten white of egg, season with salt and pepper, and bake in a soufflé case. If fresh mushrooms are not to be had, mince half a tin of mushrooms, and with the other half make a *purée* with the cream. This is necessary, because tinned mushrooms will not soften and give out their flavour. The best substitute for fresh mushrooms is mushroom powder. Made with this, mushroom soufflé is delicious.

10. **Pâte de Foie Gras en Aspic.**—Is simply a *pâté* set in clear aspic jelly, and though scarcely a savoury, can be used as one in hot weather. A very good imitation of *foie gras* is made by baking 16 units of calf's or

lamb's liver with 8 units of bacon in a closed vessel. Pound together, add mushrooms, and season highly. It is excellent for pies, &c.

11. **Savoury Jellies.**—The foundation of all these is aspic jelly, which is easiest made with gelatine and weak, clear stock in the proportion of 2 units of Swinbourne's opaque gelatine,* or 1 of the powdered gelatine (which will be found most convenient for measuring), to every 20 units of stock, either game, chicken, fish, or meat. Liebig's essence or Bovril* and water may be used on emergency. The jelly must be highly flavoured with Chili and tarragon vinegar or celery essence, and must be cleared with white of egg. (See Sweet Jelly, where a recipe for making aspic without gelatine is also given.) It may be set in border or dariol moulds, with prawns, quenelles, cremes, *pâté de foie*,* &c. Serve with mousseline or mayonnaise sauce and assorted salads.

12. **Soufflées.**—These can be made of cheese, dried haddocks, &c., and are simply cream or milk thickened with a little flour, to which grated cheese, &c., and whisked eggs are added in a proportion of 4 units eggs to 4 of cream and 1 of grated cheese, &c. Haddock and anchovy *soufflées* are really a sort of savoury custard, and are best made by pounding the fish raw and adding a sufficiency of cream and an egg or two to make the whole set. They may be poached or baked in little cases.

13. **Toasts** are legion, the prime considerations being that the toasts themselves should be crisp and of a pale golden brown, and the various compositions with which they are covered should be boiling hot. Decorations are delightful, of course, but are dear at the price of lukewarmness. A Laodicean toast* is horrible. But there is no more economical savoury than a toast, for the veriest remnant can be made into a palatable morsel and given a fine name.

CHAPTER XXX

DRESSED VEGETABLES

INDIAN vegetables are often called insipid, but the fault lies chiefly in the disgraceful way in which they are cooked. It is no uncommon thing to find them all boiling in one saucepan, or even in the soup, the result being one confused want of flavour. This habit should be sternly reproved, and the cook taught that it is better to have one vegetable decently cooked than half-a-dozen which are not worth eating. All vegetables should be well washed and picked, and the water should be boiling furiously before they are put into it, otherwise all the goodness and flavour pass into the water. Salt should never be omitted, and a little soda may be added to green vegetables.

In hot weather few things are more wholesome and appetising than dressed vegetables, and yet, except in curries, it is rare to see them at Indian tables. Most of the following recipes would, with a thick soup to begin with, form a light and tempting luncheon when heavier meat dishes could not be touched.

1. **Artichokes à l'Italienne.**—Pare the artichokes to the quick of the leaves with a very sharp knife, halve and remove the choke, and put in water at once, or the colour will change. Parboil in salt and water for five minutes. Then melt 1 unit of fresh butter, or put 1 unit of olive oil in a stewpan, range your artichokes neatly round the stewpan, and give one fritter; add 10 units good stock, ¼ of vinegar, some salt, pepper, and a clove of garlic. Stew gently for three-quarters of an hour. Dish, thicken the sauce with a little flour, and pour round.

2. **Artichoke (*Jerusalem*) Soufflées.**—Make a *purée* of artichokes as for soup. To every 6 units of this allow 6 units thin cream, 2 units yolk of egg, 1½ of flour, 1 of butter. Stir these over the fire with seasoning of pepper and salt till they boil. Add the *purée* and 3 units white of egg well whipped. Bake in a soufflé dish with a sprinkling of brown bread-crumbs on the top. Turnips can also be cooked this way.

3. **Asparagus, with Cream.**—Make a rather thick sauce of melted butter, with a seasoning of chopped green onion and parsley; add cream,

some yolk of egg, a little sugar, salt and pepper. Cut the asparagus into peas,* warm in the sauce, and serve in a crouton.

4. **Baingans, Brinjals, or Egg Plant au Gratin.**—Boil the baingans, cut in half, and mix the pulp with ½ unit of whipped cream to each *baingan*, and a little salt, pepper, and nutmeg. Fill the skins, sprinkle with bread-crumbs, moisten with a little oiled butter, and bake.

5. **Bhindies.**—*Bhindies, okra,* or lady's fingers are excellent in many ways, the only thing to remember being to remove their clammy mucilage by parboiling in salt and water, and then wiping each pod. They may then be sliced, fried with onions, or made into fritters. The seeds may be taken out, and mixed with a good cream sauce, in which a dash of lemon juice has been added, then used for a crouton ragout, either with or without the yolk of an egg.

6. **Broad Beans, with Cream.**—Boil with parsley and salt. Put into a pan with 2 units butter, chopped parsley, pepper, salt, and nutmeg. Heat, then add gradually 3 units yolk of egg and a squeeze of lemon. Serve with croutons.

7. **Cauliflower au Beurre.**—Break the cauliflower to branches, put in a stewpan with 1 unit butter, 1 unit milk, the juice of a lemon, salt and pepper, and when three parts done remove. When quite cold, dip in a thin batter and fry. Serve with a sauce made by adding milk and flour to the butter, &c.

8. **Carrots, Curried.**—Choose good red carrots. Boil, cut in shapes with a cutter, and curry, using mango or tomato chutney to give acidity to the curry sauce.

9. **Cabbage, Braised.**—Cut the cabbage to quarters, scald it, cover the bottom of a stewpan with thin slices of bacon, place your cabbage and moisten with stock, add green onions, parsley, whole peppers, but no salt. Stew with closed cover. When done, reduce the sauce, remove the bacon, and thicken with a little flour and butter.

10. **Celery, Braised.**—Cut six inches long and parboil in water, braise in stock and a little butter for an hour. Then drain and serve, dished round a centre crouton filled with white celery *purée* made of the remainder of the celery, and pour a *piquante* glaze sauce round the celery.

11. **Cucumber Fritters.**—Cut into pieces about two inches long. Scoop out seeds. Boil in salt and water till nearly done. Set upright on a floured plate. Pour into the centre of each a thickened ragout of ham, chicken, or game that will set when cold. Dust over with Parmesan cheese

or curry powder. Egg, crumb, or dip in batter, and fry in boiling fat. Serve on a round of fried toast spread with flavouring to suit.

12. **Endive or Lettuce with Cream.**—Wash in several waters, plunge in boiling salt and water, and when quite tender drain in a colander, carefully squeezing out the moisture. Chop and pass through a coarse wire sieve. Put in a stewpan with 1 unit butter, a little nutmeg and salt. After ten minutes' slow boiling add ¼ unit of sugar, 3 units of cream, and 1 of thick white sauce. Reduce to a thick *purée*, and serve like spinach with croutons.

13. **French Beans Maître d'Hotel.**—Boil the beans. Put 3 units of white sauce in a stewpan, 1 of butter, 1 of chopped parsley, a little nutmeg, pepper and salt, and the juice of half a lemon. Stir, add the beans, and warm thoroughly, and serve with sippets of fried bread. *Lobeas, toorees*, and many of the hot-weather squashes and gourds, which are cooked as French beans, are good done in this way.

14. **Onions, Stuffed.**—Choose large onions, and scoop out the inside so as to make little cases. Braise these in good stock. Then fill with various ragouts of vegetables or meat, cover with brown bread-crumbs or rasped ham or grated cheese; pour a suitable sauce round, push into the oven, and serve either on a crouton or together on a dish. They are particularly good with ham and cheese.

15. **Peas, Stewed.**—Put 24 units of peas in a stewpan with 1 unit butter. Fill up with water, and then, with the hands, rub the butter into the peas. Pour off the water, add a large cabbage lettuce shredded small, 2 whole green onions, and some parsley, salt, and ½ unit of sugar. Stew with the lid on for half-an-hour. Reduce if there is too much liquor, remove parsley and onions, and add a little light glaze and flour to thicken. The lettuce may be omitted.

16. **Potatoes au Gratin.**—Make a crouton of fried bread, slice cold boiled potatoes, and arrange in rows in the crouton with the following mixture between each row: Two units white sauce, 2 of butter, 4 of yolk of egg, 2 of grated cheese, nutmeg, pepper, salt, lemon juice, and 2 units of cream. Sprinkle with fried bread-crumbs, and serve.

17. **Spinach à l'Italienne.**—Boil in plenty of water, pass through a fine sieve, add 1 unit of cream, 1 of butter, some nutmeg and salt to every 15 of spinach, reduce till a stiff *purée*, and serve with croutons. The delicacy of this dish depends on the smoothness of the *purée*.

18. **Turnips, Blanquette of.**—Boil white turnips. When cold, slice, and lay in a soup-plate with thick scalded cream between each layer; season with pepper and salt, and just *heat through*. Any *cooking* is disastrous.

19. **Tomatoes au Gratin** (*original recipe*).—Slice off the stalk ends of large ripe tomatoes, and scoop out the seeds and pulp with a spoon, taking care not to remove too much. To 1 unit of pulp add 1 of bread crumbs, ½ of chopped hard-boiled egg, 1 of whipped cream, a suspicion of onion, salt, and pepper; mix to a rather liquid farce, fill the tomatoes, and cover with fried breadcrumbs and a grate of cheese. Bake till done, and serve with the remainder of the pulp made into a thin *purée* with ordinary stock.

20. **Vegetable Oysters**.—Boil native *brinjals* till three parts done; cut in slices, and punch into rounds the size of an oyster. Pickle for five minutes in vinegar. Beat 2 units yolk of egg with 1 of cream and 1 of milk; add plenty of black pepper and salt, and a *taste* of nutmeg. Pour over the sliced *brinjals*, which should be drained from the vinegar, stir gently, put into scallop shells, and strew fried bread-crumbs on the top. It is hardly to be distinguished from scalloped oysters.

CHAPTER XXXI

SALADS

———◆———

'THANK you, I never eat salads, except at my own house,' was the inadvertent reply of a *gourmet** to his hostess. In India, at any rate, the habit is a safe one; for anything more appalling than the usual mess of flabby shreds mixed with mustard and vinegar, and decorated lavishly with hard-boiled eggs and beetroot, cannot be imagined. Yet nothing is more simple than salad-making. First, the gardener should have orders *not* to wash the lettuce. A washed lettuce is a spoiled lettuce. Secondly, lettuces should never be eaten the day they are cut, but the next. On being brought in from the garden, they should be cut with a sharp knife about one-fourth of their length from the top, so as to cut across the leaves, and just expose the white heart. They should then be stood upright, roots up, cut leaves down, in about one inch of water. The leaves will suck up the water, and become wonderfully crisp and juicy. The great Soyer* never used a lettuce until it had stood two days in this fashion, and his salads were the wonder of all who ate them.

Half-an-hour before they are to be eaten, the lettuces should be pulled to pieces with the hands, dirt removed with a damp cloth, and each leaf broken into three or four. A leaf that will not break is not worth eating. Next, rub a clove of garlic round the bowl, pour in 3 units of salad oil. Add the lettuce and shake well. Then add 1 unit of vinegar—tarragon if possible—salt, pepper, and sugar, about ½ unit each, 1 unit of chopped chervil, and 1 of the green part of young onions. Mix by putting a plate on the top of the bowl and shaking. Salads may be treated with mayonnaise sauces, but the plain dressing is more wholesome.

The following salad maxims were given to the writer by a pupil of Soyer: Never let water touch the lettuce. Never let a knife touch it. Never touch it till half-an-hour before it is to be eaten. Never put mustard in a salad sauce. Never mix different kinds of salad stuffs. Never decorate your salads.

1. **English Salads.**—These are for the most part served as an accompaniment to cold meat, and the sauce, as a rule, seems compounded of mustard, vinegar, and the yolks of hard-boiled eggs. Yet few, who have once tasted a really well-dressed salad, do not prefer it to the ordinary sort of pickle. Great care must be used in the selection of the oil, as any suspicion of rancidity in it completely destroys a salad. Half the oil which comes out to India is in reality cotton-seed oil, which has been expressed in, and exported from Italy.

2. **Italian Salads.**—These are really cold macédoines of vegetables, and may be made of any kind, mixed with endive or lettuce. Three or four kinds are enough, of which one should be cold-boiled potatoes. Add a little shredded ham or game, anchovies, olives, &c. Dress with tartar sauce, and serve in an aspic border.

3. **German Salads.**—Celery, beetroot, white chicken meat, and hard-boiled eggs, dressed with cream mayonnaise. Serve in a vegetable border.

4. **Russian Salads.**—Beetroots, carrots, cucumber, lobster or prawns, seasoned with mayonnaise. Serve in an aspic set with balls of caviare, or fillets of preserved herrings or smoked haddock.

5. **Spanish Salads.**—Ripe tomatoes, boiled, sliced onions, French beans sauced with vinegaret, or ordinary salad dressing. Arrange round endive mayonnaise, dressed with anchovy and olives.

6. **Vegetable Salads** are endless. They can be dressed with tartar, vinegaret, or mayonnaise, and served in aspics with prawns, lobsters, quenelles, &c. &c. They are always served as a second course.

CHAPTER XXXII

GAME

THE Indian cook does not in the least understand the treatment of
game. When it goes into the kitchen, it is either left lying in a heap
on the ground, or hung up in a bunch, most likely by the legs. At
the first moment of leisure the cook-boy is set to work to pluck and
disembowel the whole game larder, which is then either put to dry in
a strong winter wind, or laid out carefully as a fly-trap. When ordered
to prepare any for the table, the cook invariably chooses the freshest-
looking, and thereafter comes to say, with clasped hands and a smirk,
'The rest, by the blessing of God, has gone bad.'

A sportsman, therefore, who desires to eat of the sweat of his brow
without making experiments on his teeth and his stomach, will, when
in camp, have regular *shikar* sticks* for each day of the week, and
strict orders should be issued that the birds are not to be touched
without a reference to supreme government. It stands to reason that
if a bird is plucked and clean, it will dry to a chip; while if it is hung
up by the legs, the parts most liable to go bad are forced into the
breast, and are likely to taint it. If it is necessary to draw the birds,
this should be done without plucking them, and a bit of charcoal may
be put inside the bird with advantage. All game birds, except snipe,
should before dressing be thoroughly washed out with scalding hot
water to which some charcoal has been added. Great care should be
observed in plucking, and the feathers of wild duck and geese carefully put aside in bags kept for the purpose. It is no uncommon sight
to see a man who has killed hundreds of wild duck still sleeping on
flock pillows,* and, what is more, sometimes complaining of their
hardness.

1. **Wild Duck.**—These birds will not keep long, and are best the second
or third day. Those who like this bird should have a little silver saucepan
made with a spirit-lamp stand to keep the sauce quite hot, or to make it
possible to prepare it for oneself at the dinner-table. It is sometimes difficult
to know what to do with wild duck, but they make excellent custards (see
High-Class Entreés), and are as good as any other bird in a game pie.

2. **Florican*** requires to be kept, and is, in the author's opinion, best eaten cold. Like all game, it requires constant basting and roasting, not *baking*.

3. **Game Pie** may be a perfect *olla podrida;** but the lines are the same throughout. The fillets should be removed from the birds, and if it is necessary to use the legs, the bones should be removed. All the bones should be broken up (save duck-bones, which give a fishy taste) and put on to boil for jelly. A sheep's trotter or two may be added if it is not likely to be stiff enough. The seasoning should be heavier than usual for aspic jellies. Lay the fillets in a large pie-dish, season with pepper, salt, sliced onions, a very little spice, and some mixed herbs and a few slices of bacon. Fill the dish, and cover with a plain flour-and-water crust. Bake for half-an-hour. When cold, use the contents to dress the pie in this fashion. A layer of fillets, some mushrooms (if handy), liver forcemeat, hard-boiled eggs, the interstices filled with jelly. Then a layer of game custard made by recipe in High-Class Entreés, but reducing the quantity of milk or cream. Then more fillets, jelly, &c., seasoning throughout highly with pepper and salt. Cover with a good crust and bake. When it comes out of the oven, fill to the brim (with a funnel through the central hole always left in meat pies) with stiff melted jelly highly seasoned with salt, pepper, and wine. All kinds of game may be used. The custards or quenelles should be very firm, made with the pounded raw meat, and just a little milk or stock, and cooked in a big mould, then sliced.

4. **Hare.**—Indian hare is apt to be tasteless, especially when roasted plain in the English fashion. The practice, too, of *hulal*, or cutting the throat, in deference to religious customs, makes it almost impossible to get good hare soup in India, as little, if any, blood remains in the body. Hare, however, makes most excellent quenelles, soufflées, and custards. These should be decorated with red currant jelly, and served with a strong unthickened *consommé* sauce made of the bones.

5. **Kulang** is a coarse bird, but makes an excellent game *purée* soup, and is also very good in custard or quenelles. Boned, stuffed, rolled, and dressed like a galantine, it is very good cold.

6. **Partridge.**—Black partridge, if carefully hung, and carefully roasted, is almost as good as the English partridge. Indian cooks invariably truss them wrong, sticking their legs and wings in unholy positions. They should be trussed like chickens, but the legs should not be cut off, only the feet. The breast should be well plumped by bringing the legs far up, and *no string* should be used anywhere, only skewers. When trussed, if the bird looks the

least dry, poach for half a minute by plunging into boiling water. Then roast before the fire, basting steadily, and when nearly done, dredge flour over it. Serve on toast with brown gravy round and bread sauce in a tureen. A partridge will only take twenty minutes to roast. Partridges may be cooked in all the ways given for chickens, pigeons, &c., but are best with cabbage.

7. **Quails** are best roasted plain, but should invariably be poached for one minute in boiling water. They may be wrapped in vine leaves afterwards or stuffed with green chillies, but onions or any highly flavoured seasoning ruin the delicate taste of the quail, which is really neither fish, flesh, nor fowl, but something peculiar to itself. Quails are, however, excellent *au gratin*, as for snipe, and they go well with pistachio nut forcemeat.

8. **Snipe** should be eaten fresh. They should be roasted—not done in a *degchi*—and served up on toast. The best way is when half done, that is to say, in a minute or two—for a *gourmet* has been known to say that a snipe is best cooked by carrying it twice round the kitchen table—to place the bird on a bit of toast, and finish cooking, taking care to baste with butter or good *ghee*. This prevents any of the trail* being lost. Or if the trail *au naturel* is objected to, let the cook remove it carefully when the bird is half done, and pound it in a mortar, with a drop of onion juice, pepper, salt, and a pat of butter. The gizzard must not be used. Spread over the toast. Where snipe are plentiful, it is a good plan to use the trail of another snipe for the toast also, the carcass going to make soup or *entrées*.

9. **Sand Grouse.**—An excellent bird if kept long enough. It is better to risk over-keeping, or even to remove the legs and back, which are the first to taint, than cook an under-kept sand grouse. Well hung, it should be treated as grouse, and served on buttered toast with gravy round, and fried bread-crumbs in one sauce-boat and bread sauce in another. Like all roast game, sand grouse should be constantly basted and well frothed with flour and butter before sending to table.

10. **Tickle Gummy.**—Into an *all-blaze* pan—that is to say, an enamelled iron stewpan with two handles and a cover—place as many game bones as it will contain, 8 units of lean bacon, 2 cloves of garlic, a bunch of herbs, half a lemon in slices, 3 units sugar, and a high seasoning of spices. Fill up with a bottle of claret and 1 of good stock. Stew for hours as for stock. Strain, salt to taste, and use as the foundation sauce of a general stew, or *olla podrida* of all kinds of game. Every day some new addition should be made to it; and if no vegetables are put in, and the stew is heated up every day, it will keep good for a month. It is very useful in camp, as it may be eaten cold or hot. Tomato conserve is a great improvement.

11. **Venison** is tasteless as a rule, and the chops are the best part. The only way to hang venison in India is to envelop it in an *atta* paste to prevent it drying up; but in this case the paste must be changed at first every two, afterwards every day. It is best baked in an oven in a closed dish, with slices of suet laid over it. Deer's liver is much liked by some, but it is too strong for most people. It can, however, be used in moderation for flavouring forcemeat for pies. Fillet of venison done like the hare (No. 4) is excellent. So are cutlets of venison made like cutlets of beef.

CHAPTER XXXIII

HOT PUDDINGS

BEFORE turning to the sweet course, the authors wish to touch on a criticism which has been very generally made, viz., that the following recipes err on the side of simplicity, in that a certain knowledge of cookery is assumed. That is true. It is sheer waste of time to repeat again and again 'Butter a mould,' for pudding moulds are made to be buttered, just as jelly moulds are made to be steeped in cold water before using. To facilitate matters, therefore, a few general maxims for each class of pudding have been compiled, and a reference to these will settle doubts. There are really only a very few types of puddings, and only these are given. It is sheer waste of time to reiterate the same recipe again and again with only some trivial difference.

BOILED PUDDINGS

A pudding must not be mixed and then set to stand before being cooked. The lightest ones will become sodden with such treatment. Flour must be dried and sifted. Butter beaten to a cream with a wooden spoon. Whites and yolks of eggs beaten separately, except when otherwise directed. Whites of egg and flavourings added last of all. Moulds must be well buttered, and water boiling when the mould is set in it. Suet finely chopped and rubbed into the flour. All puddings are the better for a pinch of salt.

1. **Albert Pudding.**—Four units flour, 4 butter, 2 sugar, 2 minced peel, 1 of sliced almond, 2½ of brandy, 4 of eggs. Beat the butter to a cream, add the sugar and yolks of eggs. Whisk till quite white. Dredge in the flour, and add the fruit, almonds, and brandy, last of all the whites whipped firm. If wanted very good, two units of whipped cream and liqueur instead of brandy may be used. Boil for at least two hours in a covered mould. This pudding can be varied many ways. It is the foundation of all steamed cake-puddings.

2. **Batter Pudding** is most difficult to make well, and the success depends entirely on the vigour with which it is beaten. Six units eggs, 3 of flour, 1 of butter, a pinch of salt, ¼ of sugar, 11 of milk. Mix flour and milk

very smoothly, pour in the butter melted, then the yolks well beaten, finally the whites, beat for a quarter of an hour, and boil in a very tightly-closed mould for an hour and a half, taking care to shake the mould about for the first ten minutes in order to prevent the flour settling to the bottom. Batter made by this recipe may be poured into a buttered basin in which fresh fruit has been placed, and sprinkled with sugar. When baked, the whole will turn out together and form a very wholesome pudding for children.

3. **Caramel Custard.**—Twelve units of milk, flavour with vanilla and a little sugar, add either 6 units yolk of egg or 4 units yolk and 2 of white. Strain through a hair sieve several times. Line the bottom of a mould with rather burnt caramel, let it set, then pour in the custard, and steam slowly. If the water once *boils* furiously, there will be holes in the custard. This recipe, if properly made, is like a blancmange in consistency. It is good made with coffee beans boiled in the milk. The easiest way to make the caramel is to put 2 units of pounded sugar in the mould, which should be a plain oval one, and let it melt till it is brown; then turn the hot mould about till properly lined. All steam puddings can be cooked in caramel moulds.

4. **Cannella Pudding.**—Ten units milk, a zest of lemon, some cinnamon, 3 units castor sugar. Boil. Add 4 units ground rice, and when boiled set to cool. Add 8 units of eggs, 1 unit crystallised cherries, ½ angelica, ½ shred almonds, some vanilla essence. Line a plain mould with buttered paper, sprinkle it with fine strips candied peel, and steam for 1½ hour. Turn out and serve with sweet orange sauce.

5. **Plum Pudding.**—Mrs. Beeton's recipe* is by far the best if modified a little: Twelve units *manukka* raisins, 14 of currants, 8 of sultanas, 16 of sugar, 16 of bread-crumbs, 16 of suet, 8 of candied peel, 4 of ground almonds, and 20 units eggs. Spices to taste, as some people cannot bear them. Have the fruit and flour perfectly dry, beat the eggs well, and last of all stir in from a claret glass to a teacup of brandy. Tie the mixture in a new pudding cloth prepared in the following fashion: Stretch the cloth over a large sieve or basin, and pour over some melted suet. Let it nearly cool, then sprinkle well with flour. This will ensure the pudding being of a rich brown colour. Boil the above quantity for six hours. In India it is the fashion to put ginger preserve, marmalade, &c., into plum pudding, but to English tastes they spoil it.

BAKED PUDDINGS

Most baked puddings, if to be turned out, are the better for having a very well-buttered mould thickly covered with bread-crumbs. Those in a pie-dish should have the rim decorated with pastry.

1. **Apricot Pudding.**—Take 2 units of dried apricots (*koumani*), soak, and boil with sugar to a preserve. Roll in pounded sugar and set to dry. Take 4 units butter, 4 of sugar, 4 of eggs, and beat for quarter of an hour till quite frothy. Add 4 units flour, a little lemon peel and cinnamon, the apricots shredded, and ¼ unit of baking-powder last of all. Bake in a mould with a pipe in the middle, and well covered with browned crumbs. Turn out, fill the centre with a *purée* of apricots, and sprinkle with chopped pistachios and almonds.

2. **Bread and Butter Pudding.**—Fill a pie-dish with thin slices of bread and butter. To 20 units milk allow 2 units egg. Boil the milk, stir-to the egg. Pour the custard over the bread and butter at least two hours before baking. If the bread soaks up all the custard more must be added. Bake.

3. **Brown Bread German Pudding.**—Eight units brown bread-crumbs, 4 of sugar, 10 of whipped cream, 8 of eggs. Mix in a basin, previously beating the whites of the eggs to a froth. Butter a round mould, strew with crumbs, and fill the mould with alternate layers of the mixture, and any kind of fruit that is not very acid. Bake and turn out. Serve hot or cold. Cherries are the fruit in the German recipe, but stoned *lichees* will do, or sliced peaches. Failing fresh fruit, jam may be used. The mixture should be flavoured to suit the fruit.

4. **Cassel Puddings.**—Four units of flour, eggs, butter, and sugar. Beat the butter to a cream, add sugar and the yokes of the eggs, whisk till white, dredge in the flour, add the beaten whites, and bake in small upright moulds called dariol pans. If half-patent flour (see Bread and Cakes) be used, the puddings will be super-excellent. Serve turned out with raspberry or any fruit syrup round. They can be varied in a number of ways, with chopped preserved ginger, almonds, cherries, &c., or the mixture may be baked in one large tin, soaked with liqueurs, and decorated with cherries, &c. Each of these puddings has a different name, but the mixture is the same. It is the foundation of all baked cake puddings.

5. **Milky Puddings** are generally very badly made in India, while the number of eggs used is frightful. The old English milky rice pudding is made by putting 5 units of washed rice into 44 of milk and pushing it into the oven. When three parts done, withdraw it, and let it get cold to cream. It may either be warmed up when wanted *plain*, or an egg or two may be mixed in it. All milky puddings should be begun by letting the farinaceous part swell gradually in the milk in the oven, except, of course, cornflour and arrowroot puddings. The proportions for puddings are given in the preliminary proportion table. The recipe for sago pudding shows the procedure to be followed in making plain milky puddings.

6. **Soufflées** are the hardest puddings to make. Indian soufflées are really only omelette soufflées, while a French soufflée is an extremely light pudding. The following will answer if accurately followed, not otherwise. It is sufficient for four persons: Six units eggs, 5 of milk, 1 of cornflour, ½ of butter, 2 of white sugar. Beat the yolks with the sugar till white, and add vanilla, lemon, or almond essence. Boil the milk, reserving a spoonful to wet the cornflour. When *boiling*, stir-to the wetted cornflour, add the butter, and stir for half a minute. Pour on the beaten yolks and sugar, and stir again. When a little cool add the whites of the eggs whisked to the stiffest possible froth, and bake in a *slow* oven for half-an-hour, and send to table *at once*, or it will fall. Chocolate soufflées may be made by adding one tablespoon of Van Houten's Cocoatina,* mixed to a thin paste with milk to the above.

FRIED PUDDINGS

1. **Apple or any Fruit Fritters.**—Fritters can be made of any fruit sliced thin, dipped in batter, and fried. The batter is best made as follows: To 1 unit of flour allow ¼ salad oil, 2 units egg, 1 of water, and 1 of brandy. Mix all, save the white of the egg, and beat hard for ten minutes, set aside, then add the white well beaten, and use at once. The brandy may be omitted, and milk, or plain water, or beer substituted.

2. **Crême Frite.**—Two units flour or ½ of cornflour, 10 units of milk, 2 of sugar, 1 of butter, a few crushed ratafias or cake-crumbs, 3 of yolk of egg, and 1 of white. Mix flour and sugar with the whole egg, add the milk and butter and ratafias and boil, add the strained yolks of four eggs, and cook gently till the mixture is as thick as cornflour for a shape. Pour out on a dish and let it cool. Cut into lozenges, egg, crumb, and fry in boiling fat. This is the original of what is called Bombay pudding, and is much nicer. The ratafias may be omitted, and the custard flavoured with vanilla. Bombay pudding is generally made of *soojee* boiled in water till thick.

3. **French Pancakes.**—Ten units of thick cream, 10 units eggs, 3 of flour, 2 of white sugar. Stir the yolks of the eggs to the flour and sugar, beat till white. Whip the cream stiff, also the whites separately. Mix with the other ingredients, and bake at once in little round tins or saucers about one inch deep. The mixture should be about half an inch deep in each, and the tins well buttered. Dish in a pile with preserves between each, and garnish with preserve and whipped cream. The native cook generally makes excellent plain pancakes.

4. **Mônch-kappe.**—Beat 1 unit yolk of egg with 5 of milk, ¼ of sugar, and a taste of lemon. Cut slices of close-grained bread two inches thick and

two inches broad—in fact, into two-inch cubes. Then divide each cube lengthwise into two pieces, and soak in the custard for a few minutes. Dip in beaten egg, and flour or crumb. Fry a light golden brown, and serve with the following sauce: Three units white wine, 1 lemon juice, 2 of sugar, 5 of water, 3 of yolk of egg. Make a custard with the water, sugar, and yolks, add the wine and lemon juice.

5. **Profitrolles.**—Two units butter, 2 sugar, 4 rose water, 3 ground rice, 5 of milk. Mix. Boil for 5 minutes; let it cool. Add 6 units eggs, unbeaten, and 4 units chopped almonds. Fry in small oblong bits in boiling fat. Some chocolate or cocoatina added to this makes a change.

CHAPTER XXXIV

COLD SWEETS

—◆—

COLD sweets are legion, but they may be roughly divided into five classes—shapes, &c., made with farinaceous substances, those made with cream, those stiffened with gelatine, clear jellies, and miscellaneous sweets of the cake and pudding description. For the sake of convenience we give a few recipes in each class, with the remark that these may be varied, by flavouring and decoration, to an almost endless extent.

FARINACEOUS SHAPES

1. **Cornflour Blancmange.**—Indian cooks never boil this enough. They use too much flour, and leave it with a raw taste. The proportions should be 20 units of milk to 1 of cornflour. Boil the milk, reserving half a cupful to wet the cornflour. Add any flavouring desired and 1 unit of white sugar to the milk, and then pour on to the wetted cornflour, stirring it well. Boil till it leaves the side of the pan. Stir in a pat of butter, and pour at once into a mould that has been steeped in water. Cornflour should be boiled for *at least* ten minutes. Almonds may be pounded and put to the milk, or the milk may be boiled and poured on to rasped cocoanut for ten minutes, then strained. Cream may be used instead of milk. Egg spoils it.

2. **Fruit Shapes.**—All kinds of syrup and fresh-pulped fruits make into nice shapes with arrowroot or cornflour. A little more than 1 unit cornflour to 20 of liquid is enough. In fact, *with care*, cornflour will, for everyday use, take the place of gelatine. The shapes may be coloured green or pink or yellow. The butterman will always supply you with *annatto*,* if it is wanted, for yellowing, or saffron may be used.

3. **Rice Cream.**—Twenty units milk, 10 of whipped cream, 2 of white sugar, 1 of rice, 1 of arrowroot, vanilla or lemon. Boil the rice in 10 units milk till quite soft, and put aside. Boil the other 10 units of milk with the sugar, and stir to the arrowroot. Boil till very stiff, stir in the rice and milk, and boil again if too thin. Add the whipped cream and the flavouring, and set in a mould. This is delicious iced, and should be served up with apricot jam.

4. **Sago and Tapioca Jelly.**—Five units of sago well washed. Boil to a jelly in 25 units of water. Add 5 units of raspberry vinegar, and 1 unit of red currant jelly, colour with cochineal, and pour into a mould, or use 20 units of water and 3 each of sugar, lime juice, and sherry. Tapioca can be used the same way; about 3 units are sufficient. Arrowroot or cornflour also make good jellies; the proportion will be rather more than 1 unit to 20 of liquid.

CREAMS

Require 2 units chip or 1 unit ground gelatine to 25 units cream.

1. **Creams, Plain.**—Creams (or *Crèmes à l'Anglaise*, as they are called by French cooks) are simply whipped cream rendered firm by adding melted gelatine. The amount of gelatine necessary varies with the temperature. But in ordinary cold weather, 3 units of chip or 1½ of ground gelatine is enough for the ordinary pint and half mould, if made as follows: Twenty units cream whipped to a stiff froth, 8 units of water. Soak the gelatine in the water, and add 4 units white sugar, and melt over the fire. Stir to the whipped cream, and add some essence. These creams may also be flavoured with curaçoa, noyeau,* or any liqueur, always remembering that with sweet liqueurs little sugar is required, and that the total liquid must not exceed one and a half pint. The mould should be oiled.

2. **Decorative Creams** are ingenious elaborations of all the old methods. Clear jelly is used in layers, and various-coloured creams are cut into shapes and embedded in others; but the taste is the same. Given cream, gelatine, liqueurs, comfits, preserved fruits, &c. &c., and the result is sure to be good to eat! To explain the decorative part in detail is not the object of a Cookery Book.

3. **Fruit Creams** are made with the pulp of ripe fruit in the proportion of half pulp and half whipped cream, or with jam rubbed through a sieve after being moistened with water, or with syrup. To make strawberry or raspberry cream from jam take 2 units of chip or 1 of powdered gelatine, and dissolve in 5 units water. Whip 10 units of cream, add 5 of syrup or pulped jam, and the dissolved gelatine. Colour with cochineal. Peach or apricot, or any other fruit cream can be made by pulping the fresh fruit with sugar to taste, and adding to every 10 units of pulp 10 units of cream whipped and a little more than the above proportion of gelatine dissolved in 5 units of water.

GELATINE SHAPES

Require 3 or 4 units chip or 1½ to 2 units of ground gelatine to the pint and a half mould. The jelly tablets now sold in nearly all flavourings are an immense saving of trouble. By dissolving them in less water than directed and making up the amount with custard, or cream, or pulped fruit, a thousand different shapes may be made. A recipe is given for one.

1. **Bavaroise** (*made with Tablet Jelly*).—One pint lemon tablet dissolved in 9 units of water. Add 9 of plantain,* pulped with a little sugar, 1 of apricot jam, and 4 of Maraschino. Whip till cold and spongy. Or 1 pint tablet, 8 units water, 8 units fruit pulp, 6 whipped cream or thick custard. Decorate the shape prettily with preserved apricots.

2. **Bavaroise** (*with Gelatine*).—Five units any fruit pulp properly sweetened, 5 units whipped cream, liqueurs to taste, added to a custard made with 4 units eggs and 10 units milk, in which 2 units chip or 1 ground gelatine have been dissolved. Stir till cold, or whip and set in ice.

3. **Blancmange.**—Three units chip or 1¼ ground gelatine, 20 units milk, 10 cream, 4 of white sugar, 2 almonds. Pound the almonds, mix with the milk, set to stand for an hour. Strain. Dissolve gelatine and sugar in the milk, add the cream and a few drops of bitter almonds. French blancmange is made entirely with milk of almonds—about 3 units to 20 of water, as for orgeat.*

4. **Flummery.**—Three units of chip or 1½ of ground gelatine, 6 of loaf or white sugar, 10 of sherry, 10 of water, 3 of lemon juice, 3 milk punch, 4 of yolk of egg. Mix everything, save gelatine and water, together. Then add the latter dissolved, and boil for one minute. Strain into an oiled mould. Another flummery is made by letting the custard thicken but not boil, and then setting it in the mould *without* straining. Lemon shape is made without the wine, and with more lemon juice and sugar.

5. **Fruit Shapes** can be made of mangoes, peaches, plums, raspberries, or any kinds of fruit, by adding 3 to 4 units of chips or 1½ to 2 units of ground gelatine dissolved in 10 units of water to every 20 units of pulp sweetened to taste. The amount of gelatine depends on the weather. With ice the smaller quantity does well at any season.

JELLIES

1. **Calf's Foot or Gelatine Jelly.**—It is an immense saving of trouble to make jellies with gelatine, especially as real calves' feet are seldom to be had in India, and cow-heel is always considered a little rank. Sheep's head and trotters make excellent jelly, but require care. But whatever the material used, the first operation is to boil whatever is used in water, until, when cold, it sets as a firm jelly. Forty units of water for each foot, boiled

for four hours and reduced to half, will be found correct (or, as has been said several times, 2 units of chip or 1 of ground gelatine to 20 units of water).

When the former is set firm, remove every bit of fat (a cloth dipped in hot water is the best way), and put the jelly in a scrupulously clean saucepan with 6 units of sugar, the rind of 1 lemon, 1 unit of juice, and quarter a stick of cinnamon. Let the jelly dissolve, but not get warm, and then stir in 1 unit white of egg and the shell. Crush the shell and beat with the white to a froth before mixing. Put over a clear fire, and boil *fiercely* for about two minutes, and set aside to settle. The whites of eggs only clear the jelly *mechanically*, that is, by imprisoning the atoms which give the cloudy look in a coating of albumen, which, *setting* firm with the heat (as white of egg always does), leaves the liquid clear. The yolks of eggs are *oily*, not albuminous, therefore they spoil jellies, though Indian cooks often put them in. The secret of clear jelly is to mix the whites of eggs so thoroughly with the liquid that when the boiling hardens them they act on every *drop of it*. And, therefore, the whole should be *stirred rapidly*, almost whisked, until boiling commences, or the white of egg, being heavier than water, may sink to the bottom and leave the top partly cloudy. Boiling should only continue half a minute. Then set aside to cool.

A jelly bag is a mistake. It is awkward, and difficult to clean. The best strainer is a square of the best thick-felted flannel (called bath coating), stretched tightly by the corners over a four-legged stand. A chair turned upside down answers the purpose, but a rough four-legged frame can be made even of branches for two annas. A basin should be put underneath, and the jelly, after standing to settle, should be poured gently on to the flannel, not from a height, but with the edge of the saucepan on the edge of the flannel. Take care not to break the scum, which should be thick on the top, or stir, or do anything to *break* the little bits of albumen. Jelly may also be cleared with pounded raw beef, as it contains a great deal of albumen. As a rule, if the above instructions are attended to, the jelly need only be run through once; if a second time is necessary, pour it back *very* gently, so as not to disturb the sediment. Now add the wine or liqueur to taste, also colouring if necessary; but do not pour into moulds till cool. The flavouring of jelly requires tasting, and should therefore always be referred to the mistress. Aspic jelly is made exactly the same way, except that the stock is flavoured with salt, ham, vegetables, pepper, &c. Any clear stock that jellies does for aspic; but the taste of meat will not do for sweet jellies.

2. **Decorative Jellies** are made by colouring jelly and flavouring it with various flavours, or by embedding groups of fruit in them. This is done by putting a mould in ice or cold water, and keeping the basin with the jelly in warm water. Begin by setting a layer of jelly in the mould, arrange the

fruit to pattern, and put in another layer of jelly. When that is set, continue the fruit, and so on; and in this way groups of fruit may be arranged with angelica stalks and leaves which, seen through clear jelly, have a pretty effect. Orange skins emptied carefully of their contents through a round hole large enough to admit a teaspoon, and then filled with alternate layers of jellies and creams, afterwards cut into quarters, and arranged in a dish, look well. Indian cooks are fond of treating egg-shells the same way, but the blancmange so moulded has a horrid, hard-boiled look. What Ruskin says of general ornamentation is true in cooking, '*Imitation is false art.*'*

3. **Fruit Jellies** are made with fruit syrups and gelatine, and are served with fruit embedded in them. The following is a typical recipe: One tin of pineapple, or a fresh pine. Cut into slices after peeling and carefully cutting out the eyes. Make a syrup with 20 units of water and 8 of sugar, the juice of two lemons, and pour over the slices. Boil for a few minutes, and strain, add 3 units of chip or 1½ of ground gelatine soaked in 5 units of water to the syrup, and clear with 2 units white and shell of egg. Take a border mould, and fill about one inch deep with jelly, let it set; then arrange the pineapple round, as you would cutlets in a side-dish, and fill the mould up with the jelly. If possible, fruit jellies should be iced; in this case reduce the amount of gelatine, and increase the sugar by at least a quarter. To ice, set the mould for half-an-hour before serving in rough ice and salt. Any fruit may be used, remembering that the jelly must be flavoured with the same fruit syrup. These fruit jellies are made to perfection with the tablet jellies.

4. **Liqueur Jellies** must have the amount of sugar reduced, and the lemon juice also, except in rum jelly, where the lemon may be used in a larger quantity. Maraschino should be a light fawn jelly, curaçoa darker, and noyeau *almost* white.

Miscellaneous Sweets

1. **Strata Pudding.**—Put a layer of jam in a pie-dish, and pour over it the following mixture: Five units of bread or cake crumbs, 2 units or more of yolk of egg, 10 units of milk, 1 of butter, 2 of sugar, ¼ of lemon juice, and six drops of lemon essence. Bake in a very slow oven, so as just to set the eggs. Let it cool a little. Then pour over an icing made of 2 or more units white of egg, 8 of ground white sugar, and 1 of lemon juice. Make in the morning, if wanted for dinner. The icing should be *set* on the top, but still creamy inside. Decorate with strips of jelly, &c.

CHAPTER XXXV

PASTES AND PASTRY

IF you want to have good pastry, give up using *soojee*, and take to good kiln-dried flour from any of the new mills.* *Soojee* is antiquated, and more trouble than it is worth.

1. **Best Feuilletage.***—Take 16 units flour and mix it to a stiff paste with water, 2 units egg, some salt, and ½ unit lemon juice. The amount of water cannot be given, as it varies both with the flour and the butter. The rule is, lay paste and butter before you, press each with the forefinger, using the same force. The dent should be the same depth—that is, paste and butter should be the same consistency. Form the paste into a ball, and press it out with the knuckles to a circle, thicker in the middle than the sides. Take 16 units of butter free from water, and as *firm* as possible; make it into a ball, roll it in flour, and put it in the centre of the circle of dough. Fold the edges on it, taking care to cover the butter well. Turn the whole upside down on a floured pasteboard, and *press* out with the knuckles carefully to an oblong. Give one roll, and again turn upside down. Fold in three. Shift it on the board, so that the folded edges are to your right and left hand, and roll out carefully to three-quarters of an inch thick, and about eighteen inches long. Fold again in three, and set aside for ten minutes in a cool place. Shift as before, and give two more rolls and turns. Set it aside again, and finish with three turns, or seven in all. The great art is not to let the butter break through the paste. To prevent this—

1. The butter must be solid.
2. It must be of like consistency with the dough.
3. It must be *well worked*, and not grainy in texture.

It may be made easier to the beginner by dividing the flour and water paste into two equal portions, and rolling each out like a platter to exactly the same size. Spread the butter on one, lay the other over as for a sandwich, pinch the edges, and proceed.

This paste, well made, cannot be surpassed. It can be made equally well with suet brayed* in a mortar till of the consistency of butter, or with half butter and half suet. Proportions, 12 units to 16 of flour. It requires an even oven with a good top heat. In hot weather ice is a necessity to cool both dough and butter. Margarine makes excellent pastry. Proportions, 12 to 16.

2. **Short Crusts for Sweet Tarts.**—Sixteen units of flour, 8 of butter, 4 of sugar, 2 of yolk of egg, 5 of milk and water: mix all together to a paste.

3. **Suet Crust.**—For dumplings, &c. Sixteen units prepared patent flour (see Bread), 10 of finely chopped suet. Mix with milk to a paste not too stiff. *Unsurpassed* for roly-polys, meat puddings, and all things requiring a light suet paste. It can be boiled or baked. In the former case always use a tin mould with a cover instead of a basin and cloth; even roly-polys are best made so by lining the mould with the paste, then filling with alternate layers jam and paste.

4. **Vol-au-vents** require extra care. After the first four turns, let the paste remain twenty minutes cooling. Roll it out one foot long, brush it over on the top with lemon juice; fold. Roll to as near the shape of the *vol-au-vent* as possible, and brush again with lemon juice, and fold again. Roll it to the shape of the *vol-au-vent*. Brush again with white of egg, and place on the top a thin cake of plain paste made with a little flour, water, and butter. Then turn the whole upside down, thus making a tough foundation for the *vol-au-vent*. The whole should be about one and a half inches thick. Cut with a fluted or plain cutter, or trim with a knife, and mark a lid inside. A *vol-au-vent* will, if well made, rise three times its own height in the oven. The secret is to *roll* evenly and cook evenly, so that it may rise evenly. A *vol-au-vent*, therefore, is best made out of the middle of a large quantity of pastry, as the folds are always even in the centre.

5. **Pastry Creams, or Custards.**—These are of various kinds, and they are used for filling open tarts, covering *flans*, and decorating all kinds of pastry and puddings.

Frangipane.—Ten units milk, 3 of yolk of egg, ½ of butter, 1 of sugar, ½ of pounded almonds, 1 of grated green citron preserve, and cornflour. Mix the milk, cornflour, and sugar, boil till thick, add the butter and eggs, let the latter set, stir in the almonds and citron, and use for pastry.

Chocolate Cream.—Ten units milk, 1 of cocoatina, 2 of sugar, ½ of cornflour, 2 of yolk of egg, some vanilla. Mix and prepare as above, and use as required.

Lemon.—Ten units milk, ½ of cornflour, 2 of yolk of egg, 2 of sugar, 1 of lemon juice, some essence of lemon, 1 of butter.

Ratafia.—As above, omitting the lemon juice, and stirring in 2 units crushed ratafia. All these may be made with cream instead of milk.

6. **Tourtes**, or open tarts, are made in a variety of ways, and filled with, for instance, a layer of pounded almonds and sugar, then apricot jam,

then some pastry cream, and decorated. A variety of dishes may be made this way.

7. **Cheese-cakes, Mirletons, &c.**—These are all made in patty-pans lined with the trimmings of puff paste, and filled with various mixtures, a few of which are given below.

Mirletons.—Four units eggs, 3 of sugar, 1½ of cake crumbs or ratafias, 1 of butter, a little salt, and some orange-flower water. Whip the whole together for quarter of an hour. Put a layer of jam at the bottom of each patty-pan, and a spoonful of the mixture on the top.

Plain Cheese-cakes.—Four units *koya* or curd, 1 of ratafias, 3 of sugar, 1 of butter, 4 of yolk of egg, some nutmeg, and the grated rind of half a lemon. Pound the curd and ratafias, and mix in the other ingredients; decorate with slices of green citron.

8. **Petites-bouchées.**—These '*small mouthfuls*' may be made of any trimmings of puff or short paste, and give the cook an opportunity for an almost endless display of his ingenuity and skill. They may be made of any shape; and be filled, covered, or glazed with any kind of cream, preserve, fruit, or icing. Chopped or whole almonds and pistachios may be embedded in them; indeed, there is scarcely any limit to their variety, and they will be found most useful as a second sweet, when one is required, at a small dinner. One pretty method is the *pompadour*, that is, short paste rolled very thin and then folded round the outside of little tin cylinders, which must be very well buttered. When cooked, slip the cylinder out and fill the *pompadour* to taste with cream, custard, or preserve.

CHAPTER XXXVI

BREAD, CAKES, AND BISCUITS

FERMENTED bread is hard to make in India, owing to the difficulty in keeping yeast in small quantities, especially in warm weather. The following recipe, however, answers capitally in small quantities:—

1. **Bread, to make.**—Half fill a small bottle with sultana raisins well washed in *cold boiled* water. Fill up the bottle with cold boiled water, and cork loosely. The raisins will ferment in from one to four days, according to the temperature. They may then be used for making bread in the following manner: Take 4 units *atta* or flour, mix with 2 units of the ferment (raisins and all), and 5 of warm water. Set aside in a warm place, with a wet cloth over the basin, for twelve hours. When the sponge has well risen, knead in 8 units more flour with enough warm salt and water to make it into an ordinary dough. Knead well, picking out the raisins as they show. Place in a tin, and set to rise. When double its original height, bake. For camp work, if the sponge is set in the morning after arriving, it will be ready for kneading at night, and the loaf can then be carried in its tin to the next halting-place, when it will be found ready for baking. The ferment must be made fresh and fresh, as it only lasts good a short time. In cold weather care must be taken to keep the dough warm.

2. **Baking Powder** is not wanted if patent flour is always kept ready, as it should be; but the following recipe is a very good one: Take 6 units soda, 6 of cornflour, and 12 of cream of tartar. Dry separately, grind very fine, and mix intimately.

3. **Crumpets.**—Mix 2 units patent flour with sufficient milk to make a thin batter, and bake in muffin tins well buttered or floured. About 2 units of batter go to each mould.

4. **Griddle Cakes.**—Mix 8 units flour to a stiff paste with water and a little salt. Roll it out to quarter of an inch thick. Spread it thinly with butter. Fold in three, and roll out again. Do this four times, each time spreading with butter. Cut into thin round cakes and bake on a girdle or *tawa*. Eat hot with jam. About 3 units of butter will be sufficient for 8 units flour.

5. **Oat Cakes.**—It is impossible to give exact quantities, as oatmeal varies in its power of taking up water. Take about 16 units oatmeal. In 20

units of hot water put 1 of butter, or dripping, and ¼ teaspoon of salt. Mix the oatmeal with this to a medium paste, roll out very thin, cut into rounds with a peg tumbler, and bake a fawn colour on the *tawa*. If the paste dries and crumbles, add more hot water. A little experience will produce crisp, even cakes. If the meal is very coarse it must be reground. The best oatcakes are made with the grease from fried bacon.

6. **Patent Flour.**—To every 64 units of flour, best kiln-dried if possible, add 2 of cream of tartar, dried, ground, and sifted. Mix, sift. Then mix in 1 unit carbonate of soda, 1 of salt, 1 of sugar, each separately dried, ground, and mixed. Sift once or twice thoroughly, and put in a tin for use. *Invaluable* for all cakes, bread, &c. *Keep dry*. For larger quantities the proportion is 2 teaspoons cream of tartar, 1 of soda, sugar, and salt to each pound of flour.

7. **Brown Bread.**—Take 16 units coarse *atta* or whole flour, ¼ carbonate of soda, ¼ salt, ½ cream of tartar, 20 of water, or milk and water. Mix the soda and salt intimately with the flour, sifting through a sieve twice. Dissolve the cream of tartar in the water, and mix rapidly but thoroughly. Bake in a floured tin in a sharp oven for one hour. White bread may be made the same way, or with the patent flour just mixed with milk and water. To get real whole wheat flour, buy one rupee worth of finest hard red wheat and have it ground and sifted in the compound. About one-eighth will sift out as bran, and may be used for the fowls and horses.

8. **Rice Muffins.**—Five units rice, 4 of flour, 4 of eggs, enough milk to make a thin batter, ¼ of salt, 1 of melted butter. Mix, and bake in a brick oven, in small muffin moulds.

9. **Scones.**—Five units patent flour, about 10 of milk. Mix very quickly as for rolls, but the dough is a little firmer, and should be cut in three-cornered shapes, and baked on a *tawa* or native *chupâtti* girdle, first on one side, then on the other.

10. **Tea Cakes.**—Eight units patent flour, 2 of butter, 4 of eggs, 10 of milk, 1 of sugar. Beat the yolks, add to the milk. Put the butter and sugar in the flour, mix, add the beaten whites, and bake at once. Slice, toast, butter, and serve hot.

CAKES AND BISCUITS

1. **Almond Wafers.**—Eight units almonds chopped fine, 4 of sifted white sugar, 1 of flour, 4 of eggs, some candied orange flower. Mix all together without previously beating the eggs, and spread the mixture on a baking tin which has been well lined by warming the tin, and then rubbing

it over with white wax. Push into the oven, and when half done cut into squares or circles. When of a light fawn, remove one by one, rolling them outside-in, into cornucopias* or rolls. If they cool, they become brittle and unmanageable. Serve with a little whipped cream, or any pastry custard, in each, or plain.

2. **Chocolate Cake.**—Four units flour, 4 units sugar, ⅛ of carbonate of soda, 1 unit cocoatina, 6 units eggs, 6 units of *quite sour* cream. Add this last of all, and bake.

3. **Diet Loaf or Scotch Seed Cake.**—Four units butter and 8 of flour, 8 of eggs, 3 of shred almonds and citron, ¼ carraway seeds, 3 units brandy. Decorate on the top with 'carways' or carraway comfits.* Bake in a *square* tin, not too deep.

4. **Ferozepore Cake.**—Sixteen units patent flour, 10 of butter, 4 of sugar, ¼ of salt, 8 units eggs and 4 units yolk of egg, 4 units pounded almonds, 4 of baked pistachios, 3 of green citron, 10 of thin cream. Beat butter, yolks, and sugar. Set the almonds to steep in the cream, strain to the mixture, add the whites, and pour the whole over the flour, stirring rapidly. Add citron and pistachios, and bake at once in a sharp oven. Eat warm for afternoon tea.

5. **Fruit Biscuits.**—Take any sort of fruit, and put in an earthen vessel. Place in a saucepan of water on the fire. Pulp through a sieve. To every 16 units of fruit pulp allow 16 of white sugar sifted through muslin. Add 6 units white of egg. Whisk till firm. Then form into biscuits like meringues, and bake in a slow oven.

6. **Genoese Cakes.**—Two units butter, sugar, flour, and eggs. Beat the yolks with the sugar and butter till quite white, dredge in the flour, using half-patent flour. Add a little brandy and any flavouring desired. Bake in shallow tins or paper cases. Slice, and spread sandwich-fashion with jam, then ice over with any kind of icing. Chocolate with an arabesque* in white and pink pearls looks well. Or steep in liqueur, and glaze, or cut in small rounds, place a layer of preserved apricot on the top, and cover with almond icing, then glaze. Or brush with white of egg when half done, and pile with shred almonds. The varieties are endless. In making these niceties of the cook's art, it is necessary to have proper utensils, biscuit forcers, &c., especially a wire-drainer on which to dry the variously iced cakes. A pair of sugar-tongs will be useful for holding the cakes, but in default of other arrangements, it will be found a good plan to prepare your cakes first by sticking bits of bamboo skewerwise into them. You can then dip them swiftly into the icing, and set to drain by sticking the other end of the skewer into a box filled with clean wet sand.

7. **Plain Biscuits.**—Sixteen units plain flour, salt, 1 unit yolk of egg, milk sufficient to knead the whole into a stiff paste. Beat with the rolling pin for ten minutes, roll out very thin, cut into biscuits, and bake; or as follows: Sixteen units flour, 2 of butter, 10 of milk and water mixed; as before, pricking with a fork neatly. The secret of water-and-milk biscuit is beating the dough well and making it stiff.

8. **Plum Cake.**—The usual Christmas cake in India is very rich, and consists of 4 units sugar, raisins, currants, ground almonds, and preserved peel, 6 units butter, and 10 units eggs, 3 units of flour, and 1 of *soojee*. Add spices and brandy.

9. **Rice Cake.**—Eight units rice flour, 4 of loaf sugar, 8 of eggs, 2 of butter, 20 drops lemon essence. Beat yolks, sugar, and butter together, add flour, then whites. Bake in a slow oven.

10. **Short Bread.**—Eight units flour, 6 of sugar, 6 of butter. Mix all together, without creaming the butter, to a stiff paste; add 1 unit of yolk of egg if too stiff, or some milk. Roll out, cut with a saucepan lid in rounds six inches across, pinch the edges, decorate with white carraway comfits and citron peel.

11. **Sponge Cake.**—Eight units eggs, 8 of white sugar, 4 of flour. Break the eggs *whole* on the sugar, and beat steadily for half-an-hour by the clock with a *spoon*, sift in the flour, and beat for ten minutes. (*Unrivalled.*)

CHAPTER XXXVII

CONFECTIONERY

—————◆◇◆—————

1. **White Icing.**—Sixteen units ground white sugar sifted through fine muslin, 4 units white of egg, and ½ unit of lemon-juice. Put the whites and sugar in a bowl, and beat with a wooden spoon till white; add the lemon-juice by degrees. For ornamentation 1 unit of arrowroot may be added, and the sugar may be slightly increased. If icing is put on when the cake comes out of the oven, it will be firm when it is cold.

2. **Almond Icing.**—Eight units almonds, 8 units white sugar, 2 units white of egg, orange-flower water. Pound, but be careful not to oil. Put on with a knife dipped in water.

3. **Butter Icing.**—Take 8 units of very good fresh butter, beat to a cream, and dredge in enough finely-powdered white sugar to make it quite a stiff paste. Add any flavouring liked, and colour if desired. Allow it to set a little, then with a biscuit-forcer cover your cake with it in fancy designs. It will never get quite hard, and must be kept in a cool place.

4. **Chocolate Creams.**—Mix 2 units arrowroot smoothly with 8 of cold water, add 12 of powdered sugar, and boil rapidly from eight to ten minutes, stirring continually. Remove from the fire, and stir till a little cool. Flavour with vanilla or rose. Continue stirring till it creams, then roll it into little balls. Melt some chocolate over steam, adding no water; and when the cream balls are cold, roll them in it one by one, and lay them on a buttered slab to cool. The creams may be varied by dividing the creams into three parts, adding grated cocoanut to one, chopped almonds to another, and pistachios to the third. By decreasing the water slightly and adding a little melted butter, this makes a good icing for cakes.

5. **Cream Toffee.**—10 units white sugar and 5 of cream; boil till the bottom of the pan shows distinctly in the stirring. Time depends on the thickness of the cream. Add vanilla, and pour on an oiled tin. When cold, cut into squares.

6. **Fondants.**—Take any quantity sufficient of loaf sugar, and boil to the blow (see No. 10); add essence to taste, and a little rectified spirits of wine. Pour it on to a slab or iron plate. As soon as it is fairly cool, rub it with a knife till it sets, when it should be of the consistence of very thick

whipped cream. Fill into small shapes (which are specially made) by putting the fondant mixture into a small jug or a cup with a spout or lip, and warming over the fire; it must not boil. These are delicious, and, as their name implies, melt in the mouth directly. If you want to make fancy devices for ornamenting dishes of dessert, you should get as follows: An oblong box or tray three inches deep. Fill it with arrowroot, dry whisked, to make it light. Also a straight piece of wood for smoothing down. Have some shapes made as desired. The original French ones are of plaster-of-Paris, but could be made of other material. With them make impressions in the starch in rows as far as the box or tray will allow of. Fill these impressions by means of a funnel with the fondant mixture, and sift some of the starch powder over them. Place in the oven till next day.

7. **Glacé Icing.**—To every 2 units of white sugar put 1 of water. Boil for one minute, and set to cool, stirring vigorously. Add any flavour desired. The syrup will soon begin to get cloudy, then opaque. Seize the intermediate state, when it is fairly cloudy but still liquid, and use it to mask cakes, brioches, Genoese pastry, &c. Curaçoa, rum, noyeau, &c., may be used as flavouring. If lemon is desired, take for, say, an icing of 8 units of sugar as much tartaric or citric acid as will lie on a two-anna bit. Wet it with a drop or two of water and lemon essence, and stir the whole to the syrup when it begins to get cloudy, *not before*. The syrup will never harden if it is not stirred, but the above proportions cannot fail with one minute's boiling.

8. **Greengage* and Cherry Rings.**—Take 8 units green mango pulp and 8 units sugar. Mix. Colour half with cochineal, leave the other green, and set out in layers one-eighth of an inch thick on dishes in the sun. As soon as it dries, cut into strips and twist into knots, or stamp with a cutter to fancy shapes. Dust with sugar, and put away. The pulp, if thin, may be evaporated to dryness in an enamelled pan over the fire.

9. **Massepains.***—Eight units almonds pounded with 1 unit white of egg till it is absolutely smooth, mix with 8 units of apricot marmalade, or any preserve of similar consistency, or any jam reduced to that consistency, and freed from seeds, &c. Put the whole into an enamelled saucepan, dust with finely-powdered white sugar, and stir till dry enough to roll out or press into sugared moulds. This, variously coloured and flavoured, is the foundation of many French bonbons.

10. **Sugar, to Boil.**—For confectionery purposes, sugar must be of the best. If necessary, the syrup must be cleared with white of egg, and strained. When boiled until small pearl-like bubbles show on the surface, it is called *pearl sugar*. This is also what is called a 'syrup of twenty-eight

degrees,' and can be made accurately by 2 units of sugar to 1 of water, boiled *furiously* for one and a half minutes. The next degree is *thread sugar*, when a drop can be drawn out into a thread between the wetted forefinger and thumb. After this comes *blow sugar*, when by blowing through the holes of a skimmer dipped in the syrup, little bladders form on the reverse side. The next is *feather sugar*, or when the syrup flies off in feathery scraps when the skimmer is given a sudden flirt. Then comes *crackle sugar*, when a portion of the syrup put into cold water does not melt, but becomes brittle. The last is *caramel*. This is simply melted sugar, whence *all* the water has been driven by boiling. It is impossible to say how long it takes for sugar to pass from one degree to another. All depends on the fire.

CHAPTER XXXVIII

JAMS, PRESERVES, PICKLES, CHUTNIES, AND LIQUEURS

MOST of the Indian fruits require different treatment to English fruits in making jam, owing to the wateriness of the pulp and its tasteless quality. For this reason it is always advisable to boil the fruit down well before adding the sugar, the evaporation making the juice heavier and of better flavour. The sweetness again necessitates long boiling, as sugar put into the full orthodox quantity, viz. equal weight, makes Indian jams dead sweet, while the addition of lemon-juice impairs the flavour peculiar to each fruit.

1. **Apricot or Peach Chutni.**—These and many other kinds of chutnies are made by boiling fruit pulp with sugar till it is thick, then adding vinegar, salt, raisins, and spices. The proportions are generally 16 units of fruit pulp, 12 of vinegar, 8 of sugar and raisins, and from 2 to 4 each of salt, ginger, chillies, and garlic according to fancy.

2. **Cherry Brandy.**—Half fill some bottles with crushed hill cherries, and then fill up to the neck with white sugar, No. 1. Pour in as much rum, brandy, or whisky as the bottles will hold. Stand for a month. Then strain and filter till clear. Or six bottles of brandy and six of cherries, each cherry pricked with needles. Allow them to macerate for a fortnight with two bruised bitter almonds in each bottle. Strain, add 32 units of loaf-sugar. Put a few of the cherries into clean bottles, fill up with the strained liqueur, and cork.

3. **Fruits, to bottle.**—Apricots, peaches, and plums skinned, halved, or sliced, may be bottled by packing the raw fruit in bottles and filling up with a syrup of twenty-eight degrees. This is made by 2 units of pounded sugar to 1 unit of water, boiled together for one minute and a half. Wrap each bottle with straw, and pack standing in a large *degchi*. Fill the *degchi* up to the neck of the bottle, and boil for ten minutes. Cork down while still hot, and wax over with bottle wax. A plug of cotton wool dipped in oil is as good as a cork if it is really tight.

4. **Ginger Preserve.**—Scrape and boil the ginger in two or three waters till soft. Then carefully look over and cut out all the knots. Fill

wide-mouthed jars half full with ginger, and pour over a boiling syrup made of No. 3 Shahjehanpore sugar, 2 units to 1 of water. Strain away next day, and boil up. Repeat this till the syrup remains thick and the ginger has become quite clear. Some people add lime-juice to the syrup.

5. **Kasoundé.**—Slice fifty green mangoes, and lay, as for chutni, in the sun for a day sprinkled with salt. Then pack in wide-mouthed bottles in layers, sprinkling between each a mixture made of 4 units each of chillies, mustard-seed, salt, ginger, and garlic, and 16 units of fresh tamarinds. Cover with mustard oil. Next day boil up the whole for a quarter of an hour and bottle, taking care that there is sufficient oil to cover the fruit.

6. **Lime Pickle.**—Put fifty ripe limes into wide-mouthed bottles, cover with salt, and let them stand for a week. Shake out and wipe each lime, replace in the bottles, and fill up with vinegar. Next day pour off the vinegar, and add to it 4 units sliced green ginger, 2 of ground green chillies, and mustard-seed, and 1 of turmeric. Bring to the boil, pour over the limes, cork, and set in the sun for a few days.

7. **Mango Chutni.**—Sixty-four units (solid) green mangoes sliced, sprinkled with salt, and set in the sun for twenty-four hours. Then drain, and boil with 20 units of vinegar till tender. Boil 20 more units of vinegar with 16 of sugar, and stir into it 16 of pulped dried apricots, 8 each of almonds and ground green ginger, and 4 each of garlic, red chillies, and mustard-seed, all ground. Add to the mangoes, bottle, and set in the sun. If put in glazed jars, the acid will eat into the glaze, and the chutni become unwholesome. Glass bottles are best.

8. **Mango Pickle.**—Peel and half split 50 unripe mangoes. Remove the stones; fill, and cover with salt. In two days wipe dry with a cloth. Fill with the following mixture: Green ginger, 16 units (solid). Salt, garlic, of each 6 units. Chillies and mustard seed, each 2 units. Cardamoms, ½ unit. Boil 70 units of vinegar with 32 of sugar, 1 of ginger, and ½ of pounded saffron. When cold pour over the mangoes and bottle.

9. **Melon Preserve.**—Take unripe melons and grate the outer rind off with a bit of glass. Stand the melons for twenty-four hours in a basin of cold sugared water. Then cut a piece off one end, scrape out the seeds, and simmer the melons with half their weight of sugar, and enough of the water they have stood in to cover them. While the syrup boils, stand the pan by the fire, and cover with vine leaves for two hours. Then strain, and boil the syrup up with 4 units (solid) of green ginger to each two melons. Put the melons in a jar, cover with vine leaves, and pour the boiling syrup over; repeat for three days.

10. **Milk Punch** (*West Indian Recipe*).—Six bottles of rum, three of brandy. Steep the rinds of fifty small limes in the spirit with twenty cloves, ten coriander seeds, half a nutmeg, and two sticks of cinnamon. Macerate for two days, add two bottles lemon juice, two of green tea made very strong, and 96 units (solid) of sugar. If liked, add a tin of preserved pineapple or a fresh pine sliced. Let all stand for six hours, then add six bottles of boiling milk. Strain carefully; it should make sixteen bottles. By reducing the green tea by one bottle and the milk by two, the product is very strong and good. It is a good plan to let the punch stand for a fortnight and then decant into fresh bottles.

11. **Mixed Pickles.**—These may be made of any kind of vegetable or seed pod. The method is the same in all. If wanted for immediate use, the vegetable is parboiled and dried, and the spiced vinegar poured over hot. If not, the vegetables are strained with salt, set to stand for two days, then covered with spiced vinegar, and set in the sun. A good proportion for spices is: To 44 units vinegar allow two cloves of garlic, two onions, 1 unit of mustard seed, salt, and bruised ginger, ½ unit of black pepper, cardamoms, and turmeric, and ¼ unit red pepper and allspice.

12. **Orange or Lemon Marmalade.**—Boil any number of oranges, lemons, or *kuttas* (Seville oranges) in salt and water till a pin's head will run into them; remove the skins, pare out the inside white, and slice very fine. Slice the pulp also, taking care to remove every scrap of skin or string. Boil the whole with equal units (solid) of fruit and sugar if the oranges are sour; if sweet, boil pulp and juice first till a little reduced, then add sugar to taste (not less than ½ units), finally the chips. Another, and often a better way, is to boil the oranges whole as above, after steeping them in water for a day. Set aside to drain, then slice without removing the skins. Pick out pips and stringy part and proceed as above.

13. **Peach, Apricot, or Plum Jam.**—Boil any quantity of sugar to the pearl. This may be done by putting 1 unit of water to 2 units of sugar and boiling for two minutes. Then throw in equal units of sliced fruit to the sugar, and boil till the whole jellies when poured on a plate.

14. **Preserved and Candied Fruits** are difficult to make, but the process is the same in all, viz., the pouring on of boiling hot syrup at the pearl to the fruit, either raw, or parboiled and dried. Finally, if they are to be candied, dipping the fruits in sugar boiled to the candy point, and setting in the sun to dry. On a small scale candying is very expensive, as so much sugar is wasted in the numerous processes.

15. **Raspberry Whisky.**—Fill bottles with equal measures of whisky and hill raspberries. After three days pour off the whisky into bottles half

full of fresh raspberries. Let them stand for three days, then add 5 units (solid) of loaf sugar to every bottle.

16. **St. Bartholomew.**—Peel fourteen pomeloes* *very fine*—just the yellow rind—and macerate for two days in ten bottles of best gin; add a syrup made of two bottles of water and 64 units (solid) sugar, and filter. If one bottle of spirit is digested with spinach or parsley leaves for five days, the whole product will be as green as Chartreuse. This makes one dozen.

17. **Tapp Sauce.**—Green mangoes, salt, and raisins, each 8 units, red chillies and garlic 4, green ginger 6. All these units are solid. Vinegar 130 units, lime juice 22 units, sugar 4 units. Pound and macerate together for a month in the sun. Strain through muslin and bottle.

18. **Tipparee,* Guava, Crab, Plum, or Mango Jelly.**—Put the fruit into a copper preserving pan with enough water to cover it, and let it pulp by the fire. Put into a jelly strainer, and let the clear portion run away without pressure. Place the juice in a clean preserving pan, and boil down to about one-half; then add white sugar in equal units, and boil till it jellies, as a rule five minutes. Some idea of the immense amount of boiling some of the juices require may be gained from the fact that an excellent recipe allows 10 units of sugar to 80 of unboiled guava juice. It is quite impossible to give the absolute number of hours or minutes, as so much depends on the fire; but the later the sugar can be put in, the better for economy.

CHAPTER XXXIX

EGGS

———————

1. **Â la Byculla.***—Poach eggs in separate cups so as to be quite round. Have as many circles of fried toast soaked in gravy, to which some curry powder has been added. Dish the eggs on them with a boned anchovy curled on each.

2. **Au Miroir.**—Break the eggs carefully on to an enamelled iron dish, sprinkle salt and pepper over, and on the top break little bits of butter. Place over a slow fire till the whites just set, and serve very hot. Little oval dishes with handles are made on purpose for this dish. By adding ½ unit cream to every egg instead of the butter, and then covering with fried bread-crumbs, another excellent variation can be made.

3. **Au Vin.**—Melt 1 unit butter in a small stewpan, add one dozen small onions, fry. Then add 10 units of red wine, some salt, pepper, and enough flour to thicken slightly, about ½ a unit. Boil till the onions are tender; remove, then poach four eggs in the sauce, place on the onions, pour the sauce round, and serve.

4. **Omelet au Naturel.**—To every 2 units of egg add 1 of milk, some pepper, salt, seasoning herbs, onion. Do not whisk, but stir till fairly mixed. Put ½ a unit of butter into the omelet pan, place over a very clear, sharp fire, and when it is *quite hot* and smoking pour on the mixture. If it does not immediately sputter and rise in large bubbles, the fire and butter are not hot enough, and your omelet will probably stick to the pan. With the spoon or fork with which you mixed your omelet stir it slowly, or rather loosen the edges, which set first and let the uncooked portion get close to the heat. When still a little liquid at the top remove and hold in front of the fire to rise. This is a difficulty in India which in France is met by a salamander.* The best way to overcome it is either to have one '*chula*' (charcoal hole) made wide enough to let the omelet pan be held under the grating (and, of course, the fire) for a second or two, or to have a top to the omelet pan on which live coals can be put. When cooked loosen with a knife and roll. Serve with a strong, brown gravy. This recipe is for real French omelet, not for the greasy leather which goes by that name in India. Omelets require a special pan, which should be *used for nothing else*. You can vary your omelet a thousand ways by folding up ragouts and garnishings inside.

CHAPTER XL

ICES

ICES require a little practice on the part of the cook in freezing properly; and as there is no possibility of the mistress giving personal supervision at the time, it is distinctly advisable to practise the cook daily *en famille* till he is perfect. The best freezer by far is the new American tub freezer. It consists of a very small wooden tub with a zinc mould inside connected with a ratchet wheel on the principle of an egg whisker. The ice, salt, &c., is packed between the zinc mould and the tub, and the former is then turned rapidly round by means of the wheel and handle, while a spatula inside the mould is also kept in motion. The risk of salt getting in is infinitely less than in the 'heels-over-head' freezer, where it was always with a forlorn hope that the progress of the ice was examined, since the complete closing of every crevice was more good luck than good management, at least in the servant's hands. Here the only opening is above the ice and salt, whilst the machine is nearly, if not quite, as economical.

The best freezing mixture will be seen by the following formulæ:—

Ice	2 parts	}	Thermometer sinks to 5°
Salt	1 part		below zero.
Ice	5 parts	}	
Salt	2 parts		„ „ 12°
Sal ammoniac	1 part		
Ice	12 parts	}	
Salt	5 parts		„ „ 25°
Nitrate of ammonia	5 parts		

As a rule, far too much ice and too little salt is used. Water ices take longer to freeze than cream ices, and an excess of sugar will render it extremely difficult to set the ice properly. In India, at private houses, ice is generally only congealed milk or custard, having a *hard* consistency and a regular *crystal fracture*, instead of being almost like butter. This is owing to the deficient working of the mixture when freezing. It should be scraped from the sides and vigorously mixed several times with a regular ice spatula in order to break the crystals. It must be remembered that cold reduces the sweetness of everything, so that ices must, if anything, be oversweet to taste before freezing. In the absence of cream, it will be found that the native preparation of milk called *koya** will, if carefully rubbed up with fresh milk, answer the purpose almost as well. Swiss milk* also does very well.

1. **Fruit Cream Ices.**—Equal units of fruit which has been pulped with sugar to taste and a good custard. Add half the units of whipped cream. In India it is sometimes difficult to get cream; in such cases it will be found a good plan to make the custard with tinned milk, using a larger proportion to the mixing water than usual. It gives a creamy flavour to the custard. Melon ice, with the juice of a lime added and twenty drops of vanilla, is delicious. So is bottled gooseberry ice. It should be coloured green.

2. **Mille Fruits.**—Make a rich custard with 20 units of milk, 6 units yolk of egg, and 4 of sugar, freeze, then add meringue paste made with 2 units white of egg and 4 units sugar. Then 5 units of curaçoa. Finally, 1 each of pistachio, orange peel, chocolate, comfits, cherries, and citron, and 5 of whipped cream. This makes a good ice pudding.

3. **Nesselrode Pudding.**—Make a custard with 20 units of milk, 6 or more of yolk of egg, and 1 of cornflour. When hot, stir in a bit of butter as big as a walnut, add 5 units of pineapple syrup, in which a little additional sugar has been melted. When the custard is quite thick, rub through a sieve, and freeze. Then stir in 10 units of thick whipped cream, and the following fruits, which should have been steeped for some hours in a teacupful of Maraschino: 2 units citron peel and sultanas, 1 of currants, angelica (if possible), and cherries. The variety of fruits may be omitted and any other preserve put instead, as preserved green mangoes for angelica. When thoroughly set and worked smooth, mould into an ice mould, and set in rough ice and salt till wanted.

4. **Sorbets or Granitos.**—Steep the rind of two oranges in 10 units of syrup made with 6 units of sugar. Add the juice of six oranges and 30 units of water. Then put it to one bottle of good claret and freeze. Serve in a jug in a semi-liquid state. Any kind of wine may be used if the flavouring be varied. Sherry requires lemon, and hock, peach syrup. Pineapple syrup, half a bottle of Moselle, and 3 units of Maraschino makes an excellent granito. Where wine is an objection, plain orange or lemonade iced to a semi-liquid state, and drunk out of small tumblers, will be much appreciated.

Sorbets are really strongly iced cup. They are excellent as a drink if half a bottle of soda water is poured over say 2 units of Sorbet, just before drinking.

5. **Water Ices.**—Twenty units water, 24 of sugar, add 20 of any fruit juice. This is as near as possible the recipe for all water ices. Of course, where the fruit juice is very strong, as in lemon juice, it must be diluted with water. Some fruits, as melons, peaches, apricots, and pineapple, are best pulped and rubbed through a sieve. Mango ice is also good made this way, and the addition of a unit or two of liqueur will improve many Indian fruits. In pomegranate ice it is best to make the syrup with the juice only, as it is so watery that it will not stand dilution.

CHAPTER XLI

SANDWICHES, SUPPER DISHES, ETC.

1. **Anchovy Sandwiches.**—Take three boned anchovies, pound in a mortar, mix with 2 units fresh butter, and six minced olives. Spread on thin slices of bread, cover with another slice well buttered, and cut into oblongs. Or, bone six anchovies, and cut into small fillets. Pound 5 units hard-boiled egg with cayenne and ½ unit vinegar. Spread the egg mixture on buttered bread, sprinkle over the finely-minced whites, then lay on the filleted anchovies, and cover with chopped mustard and cress, and another slice of buttered bread.

2. **Caviare Sandwiches.**—Toast some thin slices of bread, and when still warm split and butter on the inside. Take 1 unit of caviare and 1 of butter; mix intimately with a silver knife, adding lime-juice, cayenne, and if needful, a little salt. Spread on the inner sides of the toast when cold, press together, and cut into squares.

3. **Egg Sandwiches.**—Pound 5 units yolk hard-boiled egg, with 2 of butter, ½ of tarragon vinegar, salt, and cayenne to taste. Mix in the finely-minced whites of the hard-boiled eggs, and use the mixture for sandwiches. Pickles may be added, and the sandwiches cut into shapes with a paste-cutter.

4. **Lobster or Chicken Sandwiches.**—Shred chicken or lobster, mix with a *very* thick mayonnaise sauce. Spread on buttered bread with a layer of lettuce or watercress leaves.

5. **Nasturtium Sandwiches.**—Spread the bread with anchovy butter, made with 1 unit of anchovy paste to 4 of butter; lay nasturtium leaves over.

6. **Supper Dainties.**—Excellent little mouthfuls for light refreshment suppers may be made by using pastry made as for bread-and-butter pastry,* made into sandwiches with finely-shredded chicken, covered with mayonnaise or other sauces, or with slices of stiff aspics of game or *pâte de foie*. Rounds of short crust can also be made the foundation for many appetising morsels, and round captains' biscuits, daintily decorated with anchovy or maitre d'hotel butters, olives, &c., &c., are much liked.

GENERAL REMARKS

Almost anything can be made into sandwiches, so it is unnecessary to give more recipes. It may be taken as an axiom, however, that, even for solid sandwiches, the meat should be pounded and moistened with gravy and properly seasoned. What can be more appalling than a bite at the usual sandwich, which either lands you with no meat at all, or leaves two disconsolate pieces of mustard-patched bread to lament the slice of tough beef which you are struggling to conceal from your neighbour! To most tastes, also, sandwiches are the better for a leaf of lettuce, some cress, or some chopped celery, as an *entre deux.* A nice change in sandwiches to those who often have to lunch off them, is a breakfast roll or scone hollowed out and filled with a savoury mince.

CHAPTER XLII

NATIVE DISHES

THE following native dishes have been added by request. It may be mentioned incidentally that most native recipes are inordinately greasy and sweet, and that your native cooks invariably know how to make them fairly well.

1. **Burtas.**—Burtas are macedoines* of vegetables, and are useful for using up the remains. They are constantly served at breakfast. Potato burta is mashed potato mixed with fried onions, and well seasoned. An excellent variation is cabbage and potato. Brinjal *burta* is a great favourite. The brinjals are roasted in the ashes and the skins removed. The pulp is then mashed, fried with a little butter and seasonings, including lime-juice.

2. **Chitchkee Curry.**—This is a vegetable curry. Slice some fresh onions, fry them in plenty of butter, mix the curry powder to a paste with a little gravy. Add to the butter, fry slightly, then put in an *olla podrida* of vegetables—the greater variety the better—and simmer the whole till done. Serve with rice.

3. **Dâl.**—Lentils stewed. Fry 4 onions in 1 unit butter or fat till brown, add also ¼ unit curry powder, then 5 units of washed lentils and 5 of thin stock. Stew till tender, adding more stock if required. It should be the consistency of porridge. Serve with rice kidgeree.

4. **Dâl Pooree.**—Five units of *dâl* washed. Boil till tender. Add 1 unit ground onions, ¼ of ground chillies, ¼ of ginger and turmeric mixed, a clove of garlic, and ¼ unit salt. Brown 6 onions in 2 units butter and stir to the *dâl*. Make a flour-and-water paste as for water biscuits. Take a piece of this the size of a walnut and hollow into a saucer, put into this sufficient quantity of the prepared *dâl*. Lay on another similar saucer, lute the edges, and roll out as thin as possible. When the size of a dinner plate fry in boiling *ghee*. Or the *dâl* can be made into puffs or rissoles with ordinary puff paste.

5. **Dumpoke.**—One boned chicken. Make a forcemeat with boiled rice as for pilau, and fresh herbs, and onions, and hard-boiled eggs. Stuff the chicken with this and braise it gently.

6. **Kulleah Yekhanee.**—Slice 32 units solid of lean mutton into a stewpan with enough water to cover it, add four onions, ¼ unit each of ginger and cloves, 1 unit sugar, 2 of lime juice, and ¼ unit curry powder, and salt to taste. Stew till tender.

7. **Kidgeree.**—Into 4 units of boiling *ghee* fry 4 units sliced onions, cut lengthways. Remove, add 4 units of well-washed rice, and 4 units *dâl*. Fry till the butter is absorbed. Add some slices of green ginger, peppercorns, salt, cloves, and cardamoms to taste, and a stick or two of cinnamon. Just cover with water and simmer in a covered pan till almost quite *dry*. Care is required not to let the contents burn. They should be shaken up occasionally and stirred with a wooden spoon. Serve with the fried onions scattered over the top.

8. **Pilau.**—Slice six large onions, and two green mangoes, and fry in two units butter, and set aside. Truss a chicken as for boiling. Fry it in 2 units butter, and put into the stewpan. Cover with water and stew gently. When half done, remove and finish the cooking in a *degchi* as for a roast chicken. Wash 4 units of rice and boil in the chicken stock. When done, drain away the surplus stock, add a little butter, some raisins and almonds, cloves, &c., and let it dry. Serve round and over the chicken with the stock reduced as a gravy and a decoration of hard-boiled eggs.

CHAPTER XLIII

MISCELLANEOUS

⟡

1. **Batter.**—One unit flour, 2 units eggs, 6 units milk. Beat well.

2. **Breakfast Brawn.**—Take a sheep's head and trotters, both with the skin on, and stew till quite soft in lots of water garnished with herbs and a piece of fat bacon. When almost dissolved, remove the meat and bones, strain the liquor, and reduce, adding a little vinegar, black pepper, salt, onions, &c. Cut the gelatinous portions of the head in dice, also the meaty parts and the bacon, fill a round mould, decorating it with hard-boiled eggs, &c., press tight, and fill with the very much reduced liquor. It should cut quite firm when cold, and the jelly and meat should not look separate. To ensure this, fill the mould well with the meat, and keep pressed down with a weight on the top.

3. **Curry Powder, Madras.**—Coriander (*dhunnia*); turmeric (*huldi*); and cummin (*iira*), of each 8 units. Pepper (*mirch*) and dry ginger (*sonth*), of each 4 units. Fenugreek (*mêthi*); cardamoms (*ilâchii*); chillies (*lâl mirch*); and mace (*jowtri*), of each 2 units. Mustard seed (*surson*); cloves (*lông*); and poppy seed (*khus*), of each 1 unit (excellent).

4. **Curry Powder, Malay.**—Turmeric, 24 units; dry ginger, 16 units; chillies, 4 units; cardamoms, 8 units; cinnamon and cloves, 1 unit. Pound and mix. Malay curries are invariably made with cocoanut milk prepared by grating a cocoanut and steeping in boiling water. Strain after a quarter of an hour with pressure. Garlic must be used, and the cloves and cinnamon increased if a spice flavour is desired.

5. **Farce.**—Equal units of meat, panade, and butter. Add a unit or two of egg.

6. **Hunter's Beef.**—Salt in pickle for three days, then rub with mixed spices as follows: One unit each of cloves, cinnamon, cardamoms, allspice, mace, and 2 of black pepper. Continue rubbing morning and evening for eight days. Wash off the spices, lay in a flat earthen dish with suet in thin slices under and over, cover with a flour and water crust, and bake.

7. **Hams, to Boil.**—An English ham is worth a little trouble in boiling it properly. As usual, it is simply boiled, and nothing more. If fresh, it is not

necessary to soak a ham more than one hour, just to remove dirt, &c. Let it be well washed and rubbed all over with vinegar and pepper, then washed again. Put one bottle country vinegar, half-bottle white wine, four carrots, six onions, some thyme, peppercorns, mace, and half-pound beef suet into enough warm water to cover the ham, boil for ten minutes, put the ham in it, and let it cool. Then boil about half-an-hour for each pound of ham, and let the whole get cold together. Hams are also excellent baked like Hunter's beef, with half-bottle wine added to the suet.

8. **Mango Chips.**—Peel any quantity of unripe mangoes, and cut them in rings after removing the stone. Thread them on strings, and hang to dry in the sun. They will keep like apple chips.

9. **Panade.**—Five units water, ½ unit butter, salt, pepper, onion-juice. Boil. Stir in 2 units flour until all is a thick smooth paste. May be made with milk.

10. **Paper Cases.**—Take an oblong sheet of paper (say half-a-sheet of notepaper), and fold exactly in three, as for an envelope. Turn the top ply back to the outside edge, and fold exactly in two. Then the next ply to its outer edge. The paper will then consist of one broad central ply and two narrow ones. Double back, to have a division in the centre. Let the two upper narrow plies stand up in the centre, and fold in the corners of the broad ply, so as to touch the middle crease of the upper plies. The bits turned in will be exact triangles. Then fold the upper plies to match, and press quite flat. The paper will now be as it was before, but the ends will be pointed. Fold these two pointed ends in, so as to make the paper square or oblong. Then raise up the side-flaps, pinch the corners, and a neat little square box will be the result. They can be made any size, and used for anything.

11. **Vinegars.**—Vinegars are very useful for cooking, and may be made by steeping herbs, mint, &c., in vinegar for several days. The proportion is 3 units of leaves to 20 of vinegar. The following is excellent: In 30 units of vinegar steep for fourteen days 5 cloves, 2 cloves of garlick, 1 lime in slices (the thick-skinned kind), a small handful of thyme and savoury, also, if possible, tarragon, and 1 green chillie. Decant and bottle.

12. **Yeast.**—One handful hops gently stewed in 60 units water for two hours. Strain. When cool, stir in 4 units flour and 1 brown sugar. Fill bottles half full of the mixture. Cork, and tie down with string. Shake three times a day for two or three days, according to heat of weather. It should open with a pop, and foam. This has to be kept up in apostolic succession*—a little of the old yeast added to the new decoction hastening fermentation.

In cold weather this yeast remains good for ten days, but its goodness is easily gauged by the way it opens. One bottle of this yeast is amply sufficient for three pounds of flour, which should make a quartern loaf. It must be mixed over night in proportions of 1 unit of yeast, one of flour, 2 of lukewarm water, about ⅛ of brown sugar, and salt to taste, to a batter as thick as cream. Cover to keep out dust, and set in a warm place. Next morning it should be like a sponge. Add flour till it is too stiff to work with a spoon. Knead well, then put back to the basin. Cover and keep warm. In about two hours it should have risen enough. Make into cottage loaves and bake.

EXPLANATORY NOTES

In preparing these Notes we are particularly indebted to the following standard reference works: *New Oxford English Dictionary* (2nd edn., 1989) and the *OED Online*; the *Encyclopaedia Britannica* (11th edn., 1911) and *Britannica Online*; *Brewer's Dictionary of Phrase and Fable* (17th edn., 2005); and the Bible (King James Version). Geographical information provided is historical rather than contemporary.

5 *Upper India*: the North-Western Provinces and Oudh and the Punjab.

  poor rate: a property tax levied on a parish to provide poor relief to the parish poor; it was usually paid by the tenant rather than the owner of the property.

7 *The age of the Nabobs*: Nabobs were Anglo-Indians who made rapid fortunes in India, often through private trading and corrupt administration, and aspired to gentility at home; the term became common currency following Samuel Foote's play *The Nabob* (first performed 1772). The age of the Nabobs is most commonly applied to the period from the battle of Plassey in 1756, after which large areas of India came under Company control, to the beginning of Lord Cornwallis's administration in 1786 when reforms imposed on the East India Company by the British Government prevented Company officials from engaging in private trading.

  the Pagoda tree: a phrase used, particularly in England, to describe the opportunities for making rapid fortunes that at one time existed in India.

  'Europe stores': stores such as Fortnum and Mason and Harrods famous for the variety and high quality of their food products which could be ordered from India at a price.

8 *Board Schools*: schools under the management of elected School Boards, as established by the Elementary Education Act of 1870.

11 *the careworn Martha*: an active or busy woman, usually one occupied with domestic affairs. In Christian allegory Martha is a symbol of the active life (as opposed to the contemplative life typified by her sister, Mary). See Luke 10: 38–41.

  a den in St. Giles: a dwelling unfit for human habitation; historically, St Giles was one of the worst slums in London.

12 *Mary Jane*: a common generic name for a female domestic servant in nineteenth-century Britain; John Thomas was the most common male equivalent.

  Hindustani: a mixture of Hindi and Urdu used across much of northern India and favoured by the Anglo-Indians.

12 *The laws of the household should be those of the Medes and Persians*: the Medes
were an ancient Indo-European people who established the Median Empire
south-west of the Caspian Sea and including most of Persia (now Iran), in
the seventh century BC, which was supplanted by a unified Median and
Persian Empire under the rule of Cyrus the Great in the fifth century BC.
The laws of the Medes and Persians, once promulgated, could not be altered.
See, for example, Daniel 6: 15: 'Then these men assembled unto the king,
and said unto the king, Know, O king, that the law of the Medes and Persians
is, That no decree nor statute which the king establisheth may be changed.'

13 *the upper servants*: the bearer, cook, and *khitmutgar*.

14 *bazaar*: here, the 'native' quarter of a town in India; also a market or street
of shops or stalls.

caravanserai: a building (serai) for the accommodation of travellers and
their pack animals (caravans).

cantonments: sites where troops were encamped on a permanent basis;
military stations.

15 *written certificates to character*: (a chit) an employment certificate given to a
servant.

Officials: those having official duties as a representative of the government
or administration, civil or military.

16 *the seven cardinal virtues*: (also the seven heavenly virtues) the four
cardinal virtues, justice, prudence, temperance, and fortitude, together
with the three theological virtues of faith, hope, and charity.

livery coats: distinctive, uniform style of clothing provided to servants.

Broadcloth: traditionally, a dense, woollen cloth.

serge . . . Elgin Mills: *serge* is a durable twilled cloth or worsted; the *Elgin
Mills* was the first cotton mill established in Cawnpore (Kanpur) in 1864 as
a subsidiary of the British Indian Corporation.

the warm season: April to September.

a whited sepulchre: something that is attractive on the outside, but conceals
horrors within. An allusion to Matthew 23: 27: 'Woe unto you, scribes and
Pharisees, hypocrites! for ye are like unto whited sepulchres, which indeed
appear beautiful outward, but are within full of dead men's bones, and of
all uncleanness.'

George Eliot: [Mary Ann Evans] (1819–80) Victorian novelist whose works
include *Mill on the Floss* (1860) and *Middlemarch* (1871–2). By eulogizing
Eliot, a controversial figure who lived openly with a married man for over
twenty years until his death, as the greatest of modern women, Steel and
Gardiner show a characteristic lack of concern for conventionality.

'nothing offends her more . . . from ordinary household duties': not traced; the
sentiment is commonplace in biographical writing about Eliot.

18 *the back purlieus*: the fringe areas of the household; here, the haunts of the
servants, the pantry, scullery, and kitchen.

19 *Brookes' soap*: Brooke's Soap Monkey Brand was a popular cleaning product in the late nineteenth century, used for cleaning pots and pans, brassware, crockery, and other things.

20 *the dignity which doth hedge about*: an allusion to Shakespeare's *Hamlet*: 'There's such divinity doth hedge a king' (IV. V. 122).

22 *Snowflake American*: brand of flour established in the Cape Colony (now part of South Africa) in 1877.

23 *the Italian wine merchants, Acerboni & Co., Calcutta*: located at 14 Grants Lane in the Bow Bazaar district of Calcutta.

Lax: cured salmon fillet.

Californian fruits in tins: the canning industry in California was in its infancy in the last quarter of the nineteenth century.

24 MISCELLANEOUS: some of the less familiar articles include:

Cocoatina: Schweitzer's Cocoatina, a brand of instant cocoa beverage sold in tins, was advertised as 'The Queen of Cocoas'.

Rutz pommade: (correctly Putz Pomade) a metal polish in paste form.

Browning: in cookery, a preparation for imparting a brown colour to gravy.

Knife-powder: polish, in powder form, for cleaning and polishing cutlery.

Plate-powder: a product for cleaning and polishing silver-plated metal without removing the thin layer of silver-plate; the first such product to be marketed was Goddard's Non-Mercurial Plate Powder in 1839.

Blacking: a preparation, such as shoe polish or stove polish, used to impart a black colour.

DRUGS:

Castor oil: a pale yellow oil obtained from the castor bean, used in medicine as a purgative, and in the nineteenth century in lamps.

Carbonate of soda: a white crystalline compound soluble in water; medicinally, it is used as an antacid.

Tartaric acid: derived from tartar, it is used to make cream of tartar.

Borax: a salt used medicinally to treat ulcerations and skin diseases; it also has antiseptic and disinfecting properties.

Phenacetin: an analgesic; introduced in 1887, it was one of the first synthetic fever reducers to go on the market.

Cream of tartar: purified and crystallized bitartrate of potassium, used in medicine and for culinary purposes.

Alum: a whitish transparent mineral salt used in medicine internally as an emetic and locally as an astringent.

Sulphur: in a refined state it is used medicinally as a laxative, and as an ingredient in various ointments.

Turpentine: an oleoresin from coniferous trees; oil of turpentine was used to kill tapeworm, and in the relief of conditions such as bronchitis, chronic rheumatism, and pleurisy.

Boracic acid: a weak antiseptic; also used as an eyewash.

24   *Saltpetre*: popular name for potassium nitrate; medicinally it was used for the treatment of various conditions including asthma.

     Sal ammoniac: ammonium chloride is a white crystalline powder used in medicine to treat bronchitis and pneumonia amongst other conditions.

     Linseed meal: the residue after the removal of the linseed oil by commercial processes; used medicinally as a laxative.

     Methylated spirit: a mixture of methyl alcohol and ethyl alcohol, used medicinally as a skin disinfectant.

     Vaseline: a brand of petroleum jelly, used as a topical ointment on cuts and burns.

26   *Oil cake*: the solid residue left after oil seeds have been pressed; commonly used in animal feed.

     Palate: here the palate of an animal as an article of food; beef palate is the most common.

27   *Snipe*: a medium-sized wading bird notoriously difficult to hunt; the word 'sniper' was originally applied to anyone skilled enough to shoot one.

28   *Lahori seer*: a seer of 20 *chittacks* rather than the imperial seer of 16.

30   *High Schools and University Extensions*: following the Elementary Education Act of 1870 which provided the foundation upon which the education system in England and Wales would be built, the later part of the nineteenth century saw the founding of a number of girls' high schools; the development of the university extension movement in the middle to late nineteenth century saw universities sending lecturers all over the country to give talks on topics of general interest.

33   *Black Monday*: i.e. the day credit with local merchants becomes due.

37   *Presidencies*: administrative units in British India. The three presidencies were the Bengal Presidency, the Bombay Presidency, and the Madras Presidency.

38   *Bon-accord enamel*: a brand of enamel paint.

     Japanese black: (Black Japan) a wood varnish that produces a very hard and glossy finish.

     Distemper: a form of whitewash, made from powdered chalk or lime and size (a glutinous substance such as hide glue).

     dados: lower part of interior walls when decorated by lining, painting, or papering.

     friezes: bands of decoration around interior rooms.

     A good jail [carpet]: the art of carpet weaving in India was revived in the mid-nineteenth century, and from the 1860s taught to prisoners in the country's jails, who produced some of the best quality carpets.

39   *Maypole soap*: popular brand of fabric dye for home dyeing, available in a variety of colours and sold throughout the Empire.

     gimps: ornamental braids, of silk or cotton around a cord or wire, used for trimming.

BOMBAY: one of the three Presidencies of British India, which by the late nineteenth century had grown to encompass much of western and central India and present-day Pakistan.

40 *in the Fort*: Fort St George, built by the East India Company and demolished in the 1860s by Sir Bartle Frere, the Governor of Bombay; the Fort area was the business district of the city.

MADRAS: (Presidency of Fort St George) one of the three Presidencies of British India, which encompassed much of southern India.

42 *Berlin black*: a wood varnish with a matte or eggshell finish.

cretonnes: a strong cotton or linen fabric used for chair covers and curtains.

the club: the Madras Club, founded in 1832; more generally, a venue where Anglo-Indians could socialize together; it was also a place where newcomers to India were initiated into the social codes of Anglo-Indian society.

vagrants: poor whites of the lowest order of the European community in India.

CEYLON: previously part of the Madras Presidency, Ceylon (now Sri Lanka) became a separate British Crown Colony administered by a governor in 1798.

43 *Cinghalese or Tamil*: the Sinhalese (Cinghalese) community formed the majority of the population of Ceylon; Tamils, including ethnic Tamils and those brought to Ceylon from India as indentured labour by the British to work in the plantation economy, formed the largest ethnic minority.

European servants: unlike British India, poor Europeans were commonly employed as domestic servants in Ceylon.

As the currency is different in Ceylon: the rupee in circulation in Ceylon in the late nineteenth century was the Indian rupee; however, from 1872 the rupee in Ceylon was divided into 100 cents rather than 16 annas as in India.

44 *calling*: visiting; the etiquette of calling was a firmly established ritual in Anglo-Indian society.

new-comers do not call first: in Victorian Britain it was usual for a lady to make calls soon after arriving in town in order to inform everyone that her family had arrived. In British India the etiquette differed and new-comers waited to be called on.

RANGOON: the commercial and political centre of British Burma.

BURMAH: part of British India from 1824 to 1937.

45 *Rangoon Central Jail*: built by the British in 1871 and modelled on the architecture of Pentonville prison in North London, with a central hub and radiating prison wings; prisoners were taught jail industries including the manufacture of furniture.

Sutherland tables: drop leaf tables with rectangular leaves, named after Harriet, the Duchess of Sutherland (1806–68).

46 *Burmah appears to be the last place on which the eye of annexation would be cast!*: a province of British India; the Arakan region on the west coast of Burma was annexed in 1826 following the First Anglo-Burmese War, Lower Burma, including Rangoon, was annexed after the Second Anglo-Burmese War in 1852, and Upper Burma was annexed in 1886 following the Third Anglo-Burmese War, bringing the whole of Burma under British control.

Lares and Penates: in Roman mythology, household gods; figuratively, household belongings.

Upper Burmah . . . Mandalay: Upper Burmah is the term used by the British to refer to the central and northern areas of Burma; Mandalay, the principal town of Upper Burmah.

47 THE *PUNJAB AND NORTH-WEST PROVINCES*: the Punjab, a province of British India, was one of the largest areas of the subcontinent to come under British rule, and included the important city of Lahore; it was annexed in 1849 following the Second Anglo-Sikh War (1848–9). The North-West Provinces refers to the upper basin of the Ganges and Jumna rivers, extending from Bengal to the Punjab; in 1902 the North-Western Provinces (distinct from the North-Western Frontier Provinces, created in 1901 from the north-western districts of the Punjab Province) became part of the United Provinces of Agra and Oudh.

50 *Supply*: the food and other stores needed for the household.

51 *CALCUTTA AND BENGAL*: Calcutta was established in 1690 by the East India Company; it was the capital of the Bengal Presidency and, until 1912, the capital of British India. Bengal (Presidency of Fort William), one of the three Presidencies of British India, eventually encompassed all the British territories north of the Central Provinces, and Burma.

52 *Hill Stations—Mahableshwar and Matheran*: *hill stations* were towns in the hills (usually between 3,281 feet (1,000 m) and 8,202 feet (2,500 m)) developed as refuges for the British from the summer heat of the Indian plains and as sanatoriums. They also provided the opportunity for military surveillance; several served as summer capitals of the various provinces, or, in the case of Simla, of British India. Mahableshwar (Mahabaleshwar) was the highest hill station in the Western Ghats, 4,718 feet (1,438 m) above sea level, and the largest in the Bombay Presidency; it was the summer capital of the Governor of the Bombay Presidency. Matheran, lies about 67 miles (108 km) from Bombay and 2,635 feet (803 m) above sea level in the Western Ghats. It was discovered in 1850 by Hugh Malet, the Collector of the Thane district of the Bombay Presidency, and developed under the patronage of Lord Elphinstone, who, as Governor of Bombay, visited Matheran in 1855; it is one of the smallest hill stations in India.

Bhandala: (Khandala) located in the Shayadri ranges of the Western Ghats, at an altitude of 2,051 feet (625 m), 62 miles (100 km) from Bombay; it was part of the territory of the great Maratha leader Chattrpati Shivaji, and afterwards in the hands of the Peshwas and the British.

Newera Elliya Hills: (Nuwara Eliya) the main hill station in Ceylon, located 112 miles (180 km) from Colombo at an altitude of 6,129 feet (1,868 m); it began as a retreat for European planters after being discovered by a hunting party led by John Davy in 1818, and was planned as an English village by Sir Samuel Baker in the mid-nineteenth century.

Ootacamund and Coonor: Ootacamund (Ooty), the largest hill station in the Nilgiri hills of Tamil Nadu in southern India, 9,078 feet (2,767 m) above sea level; Ooty was developed by the British in the early nineteenth century and served as the summer capital of the Madras Presidency. Coonor was the second largest hill station in the Nilgiri hills, about 11.8 miles (19 km) from Ootacamund.

Mesapolium: (Mettupalaiyam) a mountain railway from Mettupalaiyam to Coonor (first proposed in 1854) was opened in 1899 and extended to Ootacamund in 1908; prior to that Mettupalaiyam served as the railhead for the Nilgiri Hills.

53 *Kodai Kalnal*: (Kodaikanal) on the southern crest of the Palani hills about 75 miles (120 km) from Madurai, it was founded by American missionaries in 1845.

Darjeeling: located 367 miles (590 km) north of Calcutta in the Lower Himalayas, 6,982 feet (2,128 m) above sea level, it was developed as a sanatorium for the East India Company in the 1830s; tea was introduced to the area in the 1840s.

UPPER INDIA: the following hill stations are listed:

Naini Tal: developed in 1841 by P. Barron, a European merchant and enthusiastic hunter.

Ranikhet: in the Kumaon Hills, 37 miles (60 km) from Nainital, established as a cantonment town and hill station by the British in 1869.

Landour: a small cantonment town 1,476 feet (450 m) above Mussoorie, in the Dehra Dun district of the United Provinces, it is often considered part of Mussoorie. The first permanent house was built here in 1825 by Captain Young, and it became an important military convalescent station after a sanatorium was established here in 1827.

Mussoorie: one of the most popular British hill stations, situated in the Garhwal hills 21.1 miles (34 km) from Dehra Dun, it dates back to 1825 when Captain Young built a residence here. It became the summer capital of the United Provinces government.

Kasauli: a small cantonment town established in 1842, 48 miles (77 km) from Simla and 21.8 miles (35 km) from the railhead at Kalka.

Simla: the first European house was built in Simla in 1819, and the station was first visited by a Governor-General in 1827. It became the summer residence of the Viceroy and the summer capital of British India in 1864.

Dhurmsala: (Dharamsala) established as a cantonment town in 1849, largely for Gurkha regiments, it was made the headquarters of the Kangra district of the Punjab in 1855 and became a popular hill station and sanatorium.

53 *Dalhousie*: established in 1854 and named after the Governor-General, Lord Dalhousie, it was the summer capital of the Commissioner of Lahore.

Murree: a garrison town and sanatorium in the Rawalpindi district of the Punjab, founded in 1851 by Sir Henry Lawrence, Governor of Punjab, for British troops garrisoned on the Afghan frontier. Until 1876 it was the summer headquarters of the Punjab government. Only five hours from Rawalpindi by tonga, it was the most accessible hill station in the Punjab. The Murree Brewery Company was established here in 1860.

54 *'The Charleville'*: the Charleville Hotel, built around 1860. Rudyard Kipling stayed here during his visit to Mussoorie in 1888.

the Doon: (the Dun) a valley in the Dehra Dun district of British India in the Meerut division of the United Provinces.

Lahore: the capital of the Punjab, Lahore was under British rule from 1849 to 1947.

Kashmir: more correctly Jammu and Kashmir, a princely state to the north of the Punjab.

Ooty: see note to p. 52, *Ootacamund*.

bazaar followers: (or camp followers) people who follow military camps to provide the goods or services not supplied by the military.

Rawulpindi: (Rawalpindi) the largest military station in India and crucial to Britain's defence of the North-West Frontier.

the Gullies and Thandiani: the Gullies was a hill station between Abbottabad and Murree; Thandiani was a hill station in the foothills of the Himalayas established for officers stationed at the nearby cantonment town of Abbottabad.

55 *the English and the French fashions*: breakfast English fashion in the late nineteenth century—in country houses and adopted by the Anglo-Indian community in India—was a buffet-style meal with game, fish, breads, tea, and coffee; the French fashion for breakfast was simpler and often consisted of nothing more than a cup of coffee with breakfast being eaten later in the day (see note below, *the French dejeuner à la fourchette*).

the French dejeuner à la fourchette: a late breakfast or luncheon with meat, wine, etc.

vie intime: (French) intimate personal life, in this case, of the family.

56 *plastic art*: visual art that involves the use of material that can be moulded.

Hunter's sandwiches: sandwiches of cold meat.

kromeskys: croquettes made of minced meat or fish rolled in bacon or calf's udder and fried.

croutons: small pieces of toasted or fried bread added to soups and used to garnish stews.

57 *cold viands*: cold dishes of (leftover) food.

tiffins: light midday meals.

'*A sadder and a wiser man* | *He'll rise the morrow's morn*': the final lines of Coleridge's 'The Rime of the Ancient Mariner' (1798). The lines should read: 'A sadder and a wiser man, | He rose the morrow morn'. The wedding guest is one of three gallants on their way to a wedding feast, who is detained by an ancient mariner who tells him his tale.

58 *granitos and sorbets*: granitos are iced desserts, usually made with sugar syrup and fruit juice; sorbets are sherbet drinks.

59 *apostle spoons*: spoons with an image of one of the twelve Apostles at the top of the handle.

ennui: lethargy caused by lack of employment.

60 '*If they serve you up . . . the company round,*' *says the young husband in* '*Heartsease*' *to his tearful wife*: from chapter 2 of Charlotte M. Yonge's *Heartsease or Brother's Wife* (1854).

61 *récherché pudding*: a choice or popular pudding; the adjective was commonly applied to food, drink, and clothing in the nineteenth century.

bitters: a bitter digestif drink prepared with herbs and citrus.

Cuisinier des Cuisiniers . . . 'Cette pâte epaisse et gluante . . . dérange ses fonctions': Jourdan Lacointe's *Les Cuisinier des Cuisiniers* was published in Paris in 1825. 'This glutinous substance is always indigestible and upsets the stomach.'

à la Russe: *service à la russe*, or service in the Russian style; a manner of dining that involves the courses being brought to the table sequentially, as opposed to *service à la française*, or service in the French style, in which all the food is brought out at once to create an impressive display.

62 *blue*: laundry blue or washing blue, a household product used to improve the appearance of white fabrics, it adds a trace of blue dye to the fabric.

cloth-press: a wooden press; many designs incorporated drawers or cupboards to hold the finished linen.

troisième service: third course of a meal, which by the late nineteenth century was close to the modern concept of a dessert.

Punch: or *The London Charivari*, an illustrated weekly comic periodical founded in 1841.

63 *café noir*: a small cup of strong black coffee.

66 *Ear-wigging*: influencing a person through private communication.

67 *Punkahs and thermantidotes*: punkah, see Glossary; a thermantidote is a rotating fan fixed in a window opening and encased in wet tatties (grass screens) to drive a current of cool air into a room.

68 *godown*: a warehouse or, as here, a storeroom for goods.

cards: or visiting cards, presented when making a call, or left to indicate that a call has been made.

70 *Sapolio*: household soap; a cake of greasy, gritty soap, first manufactured in 1869 by Enoch Morgan's Sons Co., popular worldwide in the late nineteenth century.

72 *blotting-paper*: a type of paper used to absorb excess ink or other liquid substances.

Wooden spud: a tool for digging or lifting with the characteristics of a spade and a chisel.

entrée: (French) access.

74 *conservancy carts*: carts used for the collection of household refuse.

bathbrick: fine clay moulded in the form of a brick, made in Bridgwater, England, and patented in 1823 by William Champion and John Browne; used to clean metal.

75 *tripoli*: a fine earth used as a polishing powder.

76 *a kerosene oil stove with an oven*: the first pressurized portable stoves were invented by F. W. Lindqvist who was granted a patent in the 1880s and went on to develop the Primus brand of stove.

77 *Curry stone*: sil, see Glossary.

81 *a Dead Sea apple of dust and ashes*: or an apple of Sodom, a fruit which appears tempting, but dissolves into smoke and ashes when grasped; hence, a thing which does not live up to expectations.

blue pill: an antibilious pill.

Eno's Fruit Salt: fast-acting effervescent fruit salts used as an antacid, invented in the 1850s by James Crossley Eno (1827–1915) and one of the best-known proprietary medicines of the late nineteenth and early twentieth centuries.

82 *Pair butter spats*: wooden spatulas used for making up butter.

87 *Christy bread-knife*: a nickel-plated, serrated-edged bread knife, invented and patented by the Christy Knife Co., Fremont, Ohio, in 1889.

91 *Maw's feeding-bottle*: a glass feeding bottle with a glass 'straw' or pipe manufactured by S. Maw, Son and Sons, London.

92 *a sweeper or low-caste woman*: a sweeper is a person from the lowest caste traditionally employed to perform the most menial household tasks.

94 *a chapter on the management of children*: see Chapter XIV.

95 *pish-pash*: a soup or stew containing rice and small pieces of meat.

96 *'the cattle within her gate'*: a reference to Exodus 20: 10: 'But the seventh day is the sabbath of the Lord thy God: in it thou shalt not do any work, thou, nor thy son, nor thy daughter, thy manservant, nor thy maidservant, nor thy cattle, nor thy stranger that is within thy gates.'

97 *Remarks have been made*: by readers of earlier editions of the book.

curry-comb: a comb or metal instrument used for currying, or rubbing down, horses.

gram: any kind of pulse used as food for horses.

99 *Waler horses*: horses imported from Australia, especially from New South Wales. As the troop-horse reminds the old mule Billy in Rudyard Kipling's 'Her Majesty's Servants', a minor story included in the first of *The Jungle*

Books: 'Nearly all our horses for the English cavalry are brought to India from Australia, and are broken in by the troopers.'

101 *N. W. Soap Company at Cawnpore*: the North West Soap Company opened the first soap manufacturing plant in India in Meerut; it was awarded the only Gold Medal for soap manufactured out of Europe at the Calcutta International Exhibition of 1883.

103 *Butterick's, Schild's, or Weldon's paper patterns*: printed commercial dressmaking patterns; the first graded paper patterns were sold by the Butterick family from their home in Sterling, Massachusetts, in 1863.

dress form: a simple tailor's dummy with no head or limbs.

Redmayne's: not identified.

a scientifically-cut bodice pattern: a block, a basic bodice pattern made to the exact measurements of the wearer.

104 *éclaircissement*: a clearing up of something puzzling; an enlightening explanation.

'Sunlight,' 'Paraffin,' 'Scotsman,' and other soaps: soaps designed for washing clothes and general household use. Sunlight soap, originally produced by Lever Brothers in 1884 and sold in cut, wrapped bars, was one of the earliest internationally marketed branded products.

107 *treated by poultices, fomentations, expectorants, diaphoretics, and with stimulants*: poultices and fomentations, soft moist masses of bread or other cereals, often heated or medicated, are used to reduce swelling or relieve pain, and often applied to the lower legs of horses under a stable bandage; expectorants are used to promote the discharge of fluid from the respiratory system; diaphoretics are used to induce perspiration; stimulants are used to increase the function of various organs.

observing the state of the dejections: inspecting the faeces.

give a ball as a drench: administer a draught of medicine, or drench, to an animal in the form of a ball or large pill.

clyster . . . clyster pipe: a clyster is a medicine injected into the rectum to empty or cleanse the bowels; the clyster pipe is the tube or pipe used for injections.

108 *Elliman's embrocation*: a rub, first made in 1847 by James Elliman. *The Uses of Elliman's Embrocation for Horse, Dogs, Birds, Cattle* was published in 1899 by Elliman, Sons & Co., Slough, England, and ran to several editions.

Holloway's ointment: created in 1837 by Thomas Holloway (1800–83), a successful purveyor of patent medicines, as a 'cure anything' ointment. The sale of Holloway's Ointment and Pills around the world made Holloway a multimillionaire. As a philanthropist he is best remembered as the founder of Holloway Sanatorium in Virginia Water, Surrey, and Royal Holloway College for women (now part of the University of London), in Englefield Green, Surrey, which he built as 'Gifts to the Nation'.

109 *Regimental and jail dairies*: the first Regimental dairy was founded in the late eighteenth or early nineteenth century in the Deccan by a British regiment which had brought good quality cattle from England. By the late nineteenth century such dairies were deemed to hamper the movement of the regiment and they were converted into Government Military Farms, the first of which was established at Allahabad in 1889.

110 *the plan followed by the House of Commons in regard to factories consuming their own smoke*: the Public Health Act of 1875 required factories, as far as practicable, to 'consume the smoke arising from the combustible used therein'.

114 *cream separator*: a device invented by Martin Wiberg (1826–1905) in 1877 to separate cream from milk. When the separator spins, the milk is pushed out to the sides and the cream is collected in the middle.

atmospheric churn: similar to a plunge churn, the atmospheric churn operates on the principle of forcing air into the cream via a stopper and valve connected with a hollow cylindrical handle. At each plunge the valve closes and air is forced through the milk and the butter is separated and forms quickly.

ordinary plunge churn: a simple churn consisting of an upright vessel in which a plunger is worked up and down.

the Roorkee workshops: established as the Roorkee Workshop and Foundry in 1847 to support the Ganges Canal Works, the Roorkee Workshop severed its connection with the canal in 1852, and by 1871 it was employing over a thousand artisans and labourers manufacturing and repairing a wide variety of goods.

caseine: (casein) one of the chief constituents of milk; the product precipitated as curd which forms the basis of cheese.

116 *Stilton*: a type of English cheese named after the village of Stilton, on the main coaching route between London and Edinburgh, where, in the early 18th century, it was sold to travellers at the Bell Inn. Daniel Defoe mentions passing through Stilton, 'a town famous for cheese, which is called our English parmesan', in his *Tour through the Whole Island of Great Britain* (1724–6).

119 *Epsom salts*: popular name of magnesium sulphate; originally the salt, first obtained in 1675, from the water of a mineral spring at Epsom in Surrey, England.

Glauber's salts: hydrate of sodium sulphate, used as a cathartic; named after Johann Rudolf Glauber (1604–70), the German chemist and apothecary who discovered it in 1625.

121 *Light Brahmas or Houdans*: varieties of domestic fowl; Light Brahmas are named after the Brahmaputra river in India and are known for their meat; Houdans, originally called the Normandy fowl, are known for their fine meat and prolific laying.

Silver Dorkings: an ancient breed of poultry believed to have originated in Italy during the reign of Julius Caesar, prized for the quality of their meat.

123 *lazaretto*: a place for the reception of the diseased.

Hearsom's Champion: the British inventor Charles Edward Hearson developed a thermostat controlled hot-water incubator for poultry in the early 1880s which he transformed into an incubator for premature infants in 1884.

125 *Rouen, Pekin, and Aylesbury ducklings*: large, pure breeds of duck bred mainly for their meat. The Rouen duck, similar in appearance to a wild mallard, originated in France and was introduced to England in the 1800s; the Pekin duck, an all white bird, originated in China and spread elsewhere in the 1800s; the Aylesbury duck, developed in England in the early 18th century, also has white plumage.

126 *shoot the red*: at 10 weeks of age turkeys enter a period known as shooting the red in which the birds sprout their wattles.

128 *hydrophobia*: rabies; characterized by an aversion to water or other liquids and difficulty in swallowing.

130 *Hugh Dalziel's book on the 'Diseases of Dogs'*: Dalziel was one of the first British authorities on dogs. His *The Diseases of Dogs, their pathology, diagnosis, and treatment: to which is added a complete dictionary of canine 'materia medica'* was first published in 1874.

131 *Ethiops mineral*: black sulphide of mercury, prepared by triturating mercury and sulphur together; believed to have an alterative effect.

Goulard lotion: (Goulard's extract or Goulard water) named after Thomas Goulard (1697–1784), a French surgeon; a solution of subacetate of lead, used as a lotion in cases of inflammation.

133 *Carter, Sutton, Cannell, &c.*: Carter's Tested Seeds, London; Suttons Seeds, founded in Reading in 1806; and H. Cannell & Sons were all regular exporters of seeds from England in the late nineteenth century.

Haage & Schmidt . . . Erfurt, Germany: well-known firm of German horticulturists.

138 *kerosene oil*: a thin clear liquid formed from hydrocarbons; the name kerosene was coined by the Canadian geologist Abraham Gesner (1797–1864) in 1846.

144 *the summer of discontent*: a bad or difficult period in the garden, but with the expectation of better times to follow; probably an allusion to the opening line of Shakespeare's *Richard III*: 'Now is the winter of our discontent | Made glorious summer by this son of York; | And all the clouds that loured upon our house | In the deep bosom of the ocean buried' (I. i 1–4).

145 *large (what are called D. P. W.) bricks*: Indian-scaled bricks were larger than the standard British brick.

147 *'the cattle and the stranger that are within your gates'*: a reference to Exodus 20: 10. See p. 96.

'unflowerful ways': not identified.

148 *district bungalows*: (also dak bungalows) basic guest houses frequented by Government servants.

149 *deodar*: an important timber tree in India.

150 *Hitchcock's patent*: the most famous mechanically ventilated lamp, designed to be used without chimney, was patented by Robert Hitchcock who founded the Hitchcock Lamp Company in 1873.

D. P. W.: Public Works Department (PWD).

151 *Chollet's compressed vegetables*: Messres Chollet of Paris were producers of high-quality compressed, dried vegetables, which by the mid-nineteenth century—as Francis Galton informs us in the 1856 second edition of *The Art of Travel* (1st edn.1855)—could be bought at all provision merchants, including Fortnum and Mason's.

152 *Du reste*: (French) moreover.

154 *itinerating mission and the village mission*: an itinerating mission was a body of missionaries who travelled from place to place preaching, a village mission, a body of missionaries who preached in villages.

the bread of sorrows: a reference to Psalms 127: 2: 'It is vain for you to rise up early, to sit up late, to eat the bread of sorrows: for so he giveth his beloved sleep.' The word bread is used figuratively, suggesting that sorrow, like one's daily bread, plays a significant role in one's life.

Civil and Military Gazette: a local English language newspaper for the British in northern India, published in Lahore from 1876 to 1949. Rudyard Kipling worked as an assistant editor on the paper from 1882 to 1887; thirty-two of the forty stories published in *Plain Tales from the Hills* (1888) were first published in the paper.

158 *Civil Officer*: originally a servant of the East India Company who was not a member of the Army or Navy; here, a member of the Indian Civil Service.

159 *puttoo*: woollen fabric made from the coarse hair of a goat; here, garments made of this fabric.

160 *nursing*: breastfeeding.

161 *wet-nurse*: a woman hired to breastfeed a child; in Anglo-Indian household the wet-nurse would usually be a native woman.

Materia Medica: list of preparations used in the practice of medicine.

162 *Chavasse . . . 'Advice to a Mother'*: *Advice to a Mother on the Management of Her Children and on the Treatment of the Moment of Some of Their More Pressing Illnesses and Accidents* by Pye Henry Chavasse (1810–79) was first published in 1841. Chavasse was a Fellow of the Royal College of Surgeons of England, a Fellow of the Obstetrical Society of London, and formerly president of Queen's College Medico-Chirurgical Society, Birmingham.

The widely known book ran into numerous editions during the second half of the nineteenth century and into the twentieth; it was translated into various languages including Tamil.

Cashmiri women at Amritsar: Cashmiri, from Cashmere (Kashmir); Amritsar is a city and district in the Lahore division of the Punjab, notable as the centre of the Sikh religion and the site of the Golden Temple, the most holy shrine of the Sikhs.

Agra: for many years the seat of the great Mughal rulers, Agra is situated on the west bank of the Yamuna, about 124 miles (200 km) south of Delhi.

163 *violet powder*: a variety of toilet, or talcum, powder.

165 *bismuth*: a reddish white metal closely related to antimony, the salts are used in medicine.

ipecacuanha: a drug with emetic, diaphoretic, and purgative properties extracted from the root of *Cephaëlis Ipecacuanha*, a small shrubby plant native to South America.

Dover's Powder: an anodyne diaphoretic (see p. 166) made of ipecacuanha and opium originally compounded with nitrate and sulphate of potash and liquorice; it is named after Dr Thomas Dover (1662–1742), an English physician who first prepared the powder in 1732.

166 *Liebig's Extract*: a concentrated beef extract used as a tonic and named after Justus von Liebig, the nineteenth-century German organic chemist who developed it. A cheaper version of Liebig's Extract was introduced in 1899 under the name Oxo. The Oxo stock cube was introduced in 1910 as a cheaper alternative to the meat extract.

diaphoretic: a medicine that induces or promotes perspiration.

167 *Gregory's Mixture*: (or Gregory's Powder) a laxative powder containing calcined magnesia, powdered rhubarb, and powdered ginger. It was named after the British physician Professor James Gregory (1753–1821), Chair of Medicine at Edinburgh University, who published the remedy in 1780.

calomel: mercurous chloride, used in medicine in the form of a yellowish-white powder, taken internally as a purgative or cathartic until the twentieth century.

hydrobromic acid: the dilute form is made by adding one part absolute hydrobromic acid (one of the strongest mineral acids) with nine parts water. It relieves the symptoms of quinine, and also of migraines, headaches, and other neuralgias.

168 *Brand's Essence of Beef*: while working as chef to King George IV from 1824 to 1831, H. W. Brand created the sauce that would later be marketed as A1 Steak Sauce. After leaving Buckingham Palace in 1831 Brand started Brand & Co. and began manufacturing meat extracts and essences.

169 *syrup of squills*: made from the bulbs of *Urginea maritima* and used as an expectorant.

169 *acacia (liquid gum)*: the juice of the unripe fruit of acacia and mimosa used as a drug to treat inflammations of the throat or stomach.

grey powder: a purgative containing mercury.

compound kino powder: a preparation of kino (a gum used as an astringent), cinnamon, and opium.

170 *bacilli*: microscopic vegetable organisms found in tubercular diseases.

while the civilian European population . . . one of 69: David Bornstein suggests that by the early 1860s the death rate for British soldiers in India was six times higher than for civilian young men in England. Through sanitary reforms encouraged by Florence Nightingale, between 1863 and 1873 the annual mortality rate of soldiers in India was reduced by 75 per cent (*How to Change the World* (New York: Oxford University Press, 2004), 44).

neuræsthenia: a condition of lassitude with symptoms such as fatigue, headache, muscle pain, and sensory disorder; in the late 1800s it was primarily diagnosed among women.

171 *the Tropics*: literally the equatorial regions of the world bounded by the tropic of Cancer in the northern hemisphere and the tropic of Capricorn in the southern hemisphere, here the reference is to those parts of the British Empire that are found in the tropics.

nuns-veiling or thin serge: nun's veiling: a thin, light, plain-weave fabric originally used for veils and later used for blouses and dresses; serge: a durable twilled cloth or worsted.

Rampore chuddar: (Rampur chaddar) handwoven shawls from Rampur, renowned for their softness and durability. Rampur was a princely state of British India ruled by a Muslim nawab, under the political control of the commissioner for the Rohilkhand division of the United Provinces.

podophyllin pill: a patent medicine used to treat cases of constipation of hepetic origin.

172 *charcoal respirator*: an air-purifying device which uses charcoal as a filtering medium.

phthisis: tuberculosis.

173 *McKesson and Robbin's compound podophyllin*: a brand of podophyllin pill produced by McKesson and Robbins of New York, which in 1855 became one of the first pharmaceutical wholesalers to manufacture drugs; their products soon became known around the world.

antipyrin: a synthetic drug obtained from coal-tar, first prepared in 1884 by L. Knorr, and formerly used in medicine as an antipyretic and analgesic in place of quinine.

Salicylate of soda: a crystalline salt used as an analgesic and antipyretic.

Kaye's essence of linseed: (Kay's Essence of Linseed) an opium-based cough medicine manufactured by Kay Brothers of Stockport.

175 *Waring's book, 'Bazaar Medicines'*: Edward John Waring's *Remarks on the uses of some bazaar medicines, and on a few of the common indigenous plants of India, according to European practice*, first published in 1860 with parallel text in English and Tamil.

datura leaf: a powerful narcotic.

176 *cold effusions*: cold liquids.

177 *'saffron bag worn at the pit of the stomach,' as Mr. Caxton says*: a reference to *The Caxtons: A Family Picture* (1849), a novel of domestic life by Edward Bulwer-Lytton (1803–73).

Rubini's camphor: tincture of camphor, made by dissolving a piece of camphor in alcohol, became known as Rubini's Camphor after Dr Rocco Rubini, a pioneer of Italian homeopathy, successfully used it to treat cholera in Naples during the epidemics of 1854–5 and 1865.

salol: a white crystalline powder used as an antipyretic and antiseptic.

178 *The inoculation system is as yet on trial*: in the late nineteenth century Louis Pasteur, considered by many 'the Father of immunology', and others were experimenting with inoculation to treat various infectious or contagious diseases including cholera. The first human trial took place in 1885 when Pasteur successfully immunized Joseph Miester, a 9-year-old boy who had been bitten by a rabid dog.

stupes: moistened cloths used as fomentations.

179 *Fowler's solution*: a medication containing a 1 per cent solution of potassium arsenite developed by Dr Fowler of Stafford, England, in 1786; it was prescribed throughout the nineteenth century as a tonic and as a less reliable alternative to quinine to treat a range of ailments including malaria.

Mother Seigel's Syrup: a patent medicine containing tincture of capsicum, along with dilute hydrochloric acid, aloe, and water; it was advertised as 'a cure for impurities in the blood' as well as 'a cure for dyspepsia and liver complaints'.

180 *galls*: bitters.

181 *gum mastic*: an aromatic, ivory-coloured resin from the lentisk or mastic tree, it has chiefly been used medicinally as an astringent.

Eau-de-Suez: a popular brand of mouthwash, advertised widely in the late nineteenth century using the slogan 'Eau de Suez, Vaccine de la Bouche, le meilleur dentifrice connu'.

183 *Aconite*: a poisonous substance from the dried roots of the *Aconitum* species (also called wolfsbane) which was used internally as a sedative; it features in Oscar Wilde's story 'Lord Savile's Crime' (1891).

demulcent: a medicine or other mixture which soothes the irritation of inflamed mucous membranes.

Catechu: an astringent that has been used for centuries in Ayurvedic medicine.

184 *lute*: fix or fasten.

185 *tobasco sauce*: correctly Tabasco Sauce; a brand of hot sauce made
from Tabasco peppers, vinegar, and salt, invented in 1868 by Edmund
McIlhenny and patented in 1870. Lord Kitchener is said to have carried
Tabasco Sauce with him to Khartoum in 1898.

188 *Hill Capuas*: hill stations; the allusion is presumably to the 'New Capua'
that was built on a hilltop after the 'Old Capua', the greatest Roman city
of south Italy, was sacked by the Saracens, and thus refers to the British
propensity for developing hill stations.

189 *tapes*: wide tapes used to string a bedframe.

   '*Cholera is a dirt disease, carried by dirty people to dirty places from dirty
   places*': in an address delivered before the American Medical Association,
   Mr Ernest Hart described cholera as 'a filth disease, carried by dirty
   people to dirty places, and there spread by dirt and the use of dirty water'.
   See Ernest Hart, 'Cholera: Where it Comes from and how it is Propa-
   gated', *British Medical Journal* (1 July 1893), 1.

194 *the lucky-bag in the 'Swiss Family Robinson'*: Johann David Wyss (1743–
   1818), *The Swiss Family Robinson* (*Der schweizerische Robinson*, 1812),
   is a novel about a Swiss family shipwrecked in the East Indies. The wife
   carries a bag with her from the wrecked ship that proves to contain all
   sorts of useful things from seeds to needles and thread.

195 '*I will lift up mine eyes unto the hills, from whence cometh my help*': Psalm
   121: 1.

196 *which was Wellington and which was Blucher in the panorama*: on 18 June
   1815 the French army, under the command of Napoleon, was defeated
   at the battle of Waterloo by an Anglo-Allied army led by the Duke of
   Wellington and the Prussian army led by Field-Marshal Blücher; pan-
   oramic representations of the famous meeting between Wellington and
   Blücher at the close of battle include *The Meeting of Wellington and
   Blücher* (1859–61) by Daniel Maclise (1806–70), a huge painting over 12
   feet (3.7 m) high and 46 feet (14 m) long.

   In these times of depreciated currency: the fall of the rupee, a silver standard currency, in the late nineteenth century was brought about by the
   decline of the relative value of silver to gold. In Oscar Wilde's *The Impor-
   tance of Being Earnest* (1895) the prudish governess Miss Prism believes a
   discussion on the fall of the rupee may be too exciting for a young
   lady: 'Cecily, you will read your Political Economy in my absence. The
   chapter on the Fall of the Rupee you may omit. It is somewhat too
   sensational. Even these metallic problems have their melodramatic side'
   (Act 2).

197 *Northern India*: commonly used to refer to the region north of the Vindhya
   mountains, but excluding north-east India (Upper and Lower Bengal).

   Johnson's self-watering machine: a brand of thermantidote not identified.

will-he nill-he: whether he wishes it or not, without choice; now usually in the form willy-nilly.

198 *Bombay and Bengal punkahs*: those in the Bombay and Bengal presidencies as opposed to those in the Madras Presidency.

200 *So, as Pepys says, dinner at eight, and to bed about half-past ten*: Samuel Pepys's (1633–1703) detailed *Diary*, which he kept from 1660 to 1669, is an important primary source for the English Restoration period, combining personal detail, such as the time he ate dinner or went to bed, with accounts of events such as the Great Plague of London and the Great Fire of London.

   a Frankenstein monster: a reference to the monster created by Frankenstein in Mary Shelley's (1797–1851) gothic novel, *Frankenstein, or The Modern Prometheus* (1818).

201 *'Don't give in to your stomach, and your stomach will give in to you'*: from Wilkie Collins's (1824–89) play *The Frozen Deep: a Drama in Three Acts* (1857) which was written in collaboration with Charles Dickens and first performed at Dickens's home, Tavistock House, in January 1857. Based on the disastrous 1845 expedition by Sir John Franklin to discover the Northwest Passage, the play drew on Dickens's articles in *Household Words* rebutting the allegations of cannibalism made about the expedition members (later proved to be true). In this extract, John Want, the cook, is describing a cure for sea-sickness inflicted on him by a ship's captain early in his seafaring career. Collins later rewrote the play as a novella, first published in the magazine *Temple Bar* in 1874. The quotation should read: 'Never you give in to your stomach, and your stomach will end in giving in to you' (Second Scene: The Hut of the Sea-Mew, Chapter 7).

   Madras and parts of Lower Bengal: the Madras Presidency, and Lower Bengal, meaning Bengal (the division of Calcutta and four other districts), Behar, Orissa, and Chota Nagpore.

208 *Queen: The Queen: The Lady's Newspaper and Court Chronicle*, a women's periodical published in London by Samuel and Isabella Beeton and Frederick Greenwood, included material on a variety of topics including household management and women's fashions. It ran from 1861 to 1970.

209 *torchon lace*: a coarse bobbin lace of loose texture.

   Madeira edgings: a decorative lace edging pattern.

210 *beige . . . Harris tweed*: beige, a fine woollen fabric used as a dress-material; Harris tweed, a high-quality cloth handwoven by the inhabitants of the remote Outer Hebrides in Scotland using pure virgin wool produced on the islands.

   mousseline de laine tea-gowns: mousseline de laine (or delaine) is a wool muslin; afternoon- or tea-gowns were introduced in the 1840s by Anna, the Duchess of Bedford.

210 *pongee silks*: a kind of foulard; glossy, soft-textured fabric which consists of a silk warp and a woollen weft.

    cashmeres, vicunas: cashmeres, fabrics made from the wool of the Cashmere goat; vicunas, fabrics made from the fine silky wool of vicuñas (closely related to alpacas and llamas).

211 *demi-toilette*: half-dress, or informal evening wear.

    A habit: a riding-habit; a lady's riding-dress.

    hop-sacking: a woollen dress-fabric made with a roughened surface.

    Breeches and topboots: breeches (britches), trousers finishing just below the knee; topboots, riding boots, specifically high boots with a light-coloured leather band around the upper part of the leg.

    Wölmershausen: suppliers of quality riding attire.

212 *billycock hat . . . double terai*: a billycock is a round, low-crowned hat named after William Coke. A double terai is a double felt hat, believed to provide greater protection from the sun; a hat of this kind was worn by Stewart Granger in the 1950 film version of *King Solomon's Mines* (dir. Compton Bennett and Andrew Marton).

213 *combinations*: combination-garments; close-fitting under-garment consisting of combined chemise and drawers.

    ulster: a loose, long overcoat made of heavy fabric such as frieze.

214 *confection*: (French) an article of women's clothing such as a cloak or a wrap.

    the great Calcutta houses, such as Whiteaway, Laidlaw & Company: department stores; Calcutta was home to several large department stores including Whiteaway, Laidlaw & Co., a Scottish firm with stores throughout Britain's eastern empire, Hall and Anderson, and the Army and Navy Stores.

    Ultima Thule: the highest degree attainable.

215 *fine India long-cloth*: a soft cotton cloth or calico manufactured in long pieces, made in India.

    Summer cashmere . . . delaines: Summer cashmere, a lightweight, single-ply cashmere fabric; delaines, see note to p. 209, *mousseline de laine*.

    court plaster: sticking plaster made of silk or taffeta coated on one side with an adhesive substance such as isinglass.

    nankeen coats and skirts: garments made of nankeen cloth, a durable, firm-textured cotton cloth, named after the city of Nankeen (Nanjing) where it was first manufactured.

217 *bernous*: a cloak or loose outer garment.

218 *cloud*: a light, loose-knitted woollen scarf worn by women, often about the head.

    an Austrian blanket: a fine quality rug.

Karachi: seaport and district of British India and capital of the province of Sind.

219 *essence of coffee*: coffee essences are not true essences, but extracts mixed with other ingredients such as chicory and sugar. The most famous brand, Camp Coffee and Chicory, has been made in Scotland since 1885 when, allegedly, the Gordon Highlanders requested a coffee drink which could be brewed up easily when they were on field campaigns in India; until 2006 the label on the distinctive bottle depicted a Sikh soldier serving coffee to a kilted Scottish soldier.

Bovril: a salty beef extract (or beef tea) developed in the 1870s by John Lawson Johnston, originally known as Johnston's Fluid Beef; it is sold in a distinctive bulbous jar.

Paysandu ox tongue: tinned ox tongue from Uruguay. Following their shipwreck on the African coast, Holly and his companions gain comfort from 'a hearty breakfast of "Paysandu" potted tongue' in H. Rider Haggard's *She* (1887; Oxford World's Classics edn., 1998), 62.

a bicycle dress: a divided skirt; as cycling became popular with women in the 1890s the wearing of bifurcated garments or 'reform dress' in the form of Turkish trousers or split skirts, as well as bloomers, became widespread.

220 *Francatelli*: Charles Elme Francatelli (1805–76), regarded as the leading chef in Victorian London, worked for various aristocrats and noblemen, managed Crockfords Club, was chief cook to Queen Victoria, and chef at the Reform Club. He was the author of several books including *A Plain Cookery Book for the Working Classes* (1861).

222 *panade*: (panada or panard) a thick paste of flour or breadcrumbs.

223 *Roman Urdu*: Urdu written in the Roman script.

225 *if you have a place for everything, everything will be in its place*: the phrase 'A place for everything, everything in its place' is attributed to Benjamin Franklin (1706–90), one of the Founding Fathers of the United States of America and a major figure of the Enlightenment.

226 *mum-chance*: silent.

227 *cordon bleu*: first-class cook.

231 *brun-estew*: brown stew.

hashes, salmis, and rechauffés: hashes, dishes of previously cooked meat, cut up small and warmed up with gravy and sauce or other flavouring; salmis, ragout of roasted game with sauce, wine, bread, and condiments; rechauffés, reheated dishes.

234 *timbals*: (timbales) food cooked in a cone-shaped mould (also called a timbale) and turned out onto a plate or dish.

Wyvern Soup: 'Wyvern' (Colonel Arthur Robert Kenney-Herbert) includes a recipe *for consommé aux œufs pochés* in his *Culinary Jottings for Madras* (5th edn., 1885).

236 *sippets*: small pieces of toasted or fried bread used for dipping into soup or gravy.

 leason of eggs: a mixture of eggs and cream used to thicken soups or sauces.

237 *Mulligatawny Soup*: an Anglo-Indian version of the Tamil rasam (pepper water).

238 *Harvey sauce*: Harvey's Sauce (containing anchovies and soy) was one of the earliest and best known bottled sauces created in the nineteenth century. Mrs Beeton uses it as an ingredient in various recipes including 'A Good Beef Gravy for Poultry, Game, &c.' (*Mrs Beeton*, 131–2); in *Vanity Fair* (1847–8) William Thackeray writes: 'Those who know the English Colonies abroad know that we carry with us our pride, pills, prejudices, Harvey-sauces, cayenne-peppers, and other Lares, making a little Britain wherever we settle down.'

240 *Chilwas*: small bright silvery freshwater fish, similar to whitebait; the fish are described as 'very good eating' by the Adjutant in Kipling's story 'The Undertakers', collected in *The Second Jungle Book* (1895), the only story in which Kipling comments directly on the Indian Mutiny.

 mango fish: a small fish, the colour of ripe mango, found in coastal and estuarine waters.

241 *Aurora sauce*: a variety of béchamel sauce; see recipe in Chapter XXV.

 farce: forcemeat or stuffing. The 1898 edition included the following recipe: 'Farce.—Equal units of meat, panade, and butter. Add a unit or two of egg.'

242 *Findon haddocks*: haddock cured in peat smoke, originally in the Scottish village of Findon, north of Aberdeen, in the eighteenth century.

243 *Ravigotte sauce*: see recipe in Chapter XXV.

247 *tanny*: probably brown (Scottish).

 Espagnol sauce: see Third Group of sauces in this chapter.

250 *panard*: see note to p. 222, *panade*.

 Robert sauce: see recipe in Chapter XXV.

252 *dariol moulds*: (dariole moulds) small tin moulds shaped like flower-pots.

257 *Barataria prawns*: prawns from Barataria Bay, Louisiana, available in tins; in 1888 a tin cost 1s. 4d.

258 *epigrams*: (*épigrammes*) small cutlets of mutton, etc.

259 *Italian Sauce*: see recipe in Chapter XXV.

 salamander them: brown with a salamander, a circular iron plate which is heated and placed over a dish to brown it.

260 *allemande sauce*: see recipe in Chapter XXV.

 cockscombs: cockscomb oysters.

261 *Reform Garnish*: after the style of the famous London Reform Club in Pall Mall, founded in 1836; see note to p. 291, *The great Soyer*.

264 *Swinbourne's opaque gelatine*: a high-quality gelatine; George Swinborne (1822?–83) discovered and patented an improved method for refining isinglass and gelatine in 1847, and established a factory at Coggeshall in Essex.

Liebig's essence or Bovril: see notes to p. 166, *Liebig's Extract* and p. 219, *Bovril*.

pâté de foie: (pâté de foie gras) goose-liver paste.

Laodicean toast: a reference to Revelation 3: 15–16: 'I know thy works, that thou art neither cold nor hot: I would thou wert cold or hot. So then because thou art lukewarm, and neither cold nor hot, I will spue thee out of my mouth.' Figuratively, lukewarm toast.

266 *Cut the asparagus into peas*: as Nicola Humble explains, this is a process used for very young asparagus when the stems are too small to make a good appearance whole (*Mrs Beeton's Book of Household Management*, ed. Humble (Oxford: Oxford University Press, 2000), p. xv).

269 *gourmet*: a connoisseur in the art of food and food preparation.

The great Soyer: the French chef Alexis Benoît Soyer (1810–58), one of the most famous chefs in Victorian London, was *chef de cuisine* at the Reform Club from 1837 to 1850. He set up a soup kitchen in Dublin during the Great Irish Famine (1847) and during the Crimean War (1854–6) he persuaded the military to train soldiers as cooks, and to make use of his specially designed Soyer stove, that would remain in use until the late twentieth century. His books included *A Shilling Cookery for the People* (1854).

271 *shikar sticks*: shikar, see Glossary; sticks used for hanging game birds.

flock pillows: pillows stuffed with flock, a material consisting of waste wool or cotton.

272 *Florican*: a name used in India for two species of small bustard, the Bengal Florican and the Lesser Florican.

olla podrida: a Spanish stew made from a variety of meats and vegetables.

273 *trail*: the entrails of birds such as snipe and woodcock that are cooked and eaten with the rest of the flesh.

276 *Mrs. Beeton's recipe*: see *Mrs Beeton*, 274–5.

278 *Van Houten's Cocoatina*: a brand of instant cocoa beverage produced by Van Houten's of Amsterdam. In 1828 C. J. Van Houten patented a method of manufacturing cocoa powder which would become the basis of all chocolate products.

280 *annatto*: an orange-red dye used for colouring cheese and other foods.

281 *curaçoa, noyeau*: curaçoa, a liqueur flavoured with the peel of bitter oranges and sweetened; noyeau, a liqueur made of brandy flavoured with the kernels of stone fruits, almonds, citrus peel, and spices.

282 *plantain*: a variety of banana.

orgeat: a syrup or drink made from barley or almonds and orange-flower water.

284 *What Ruskin says of general ornamentation is true in cooking, 'Imitation is false art.'*: John Ruskin (1819–1900), a leading art and social critic whose essays on art and architecture were extremely influential during the Victorian period; the quotation, though not accurate, is a clear reference to *Modern Painters I* (1843).

285 *the new mills*: flour mills equipped with modern machinery, such as the Cawnpore Flour Mill, founded in 1886 by the Scotsman Edward Foy, were established in large centres and towns during the late nineteenth century, supplanting the grinding of wheat in hand-mills.

Feuilletage: (French) puff pastry.

brayed: beaten small or crushed.

290 *cornucopias*: horns of plenty; here, wafers rolled into horn-shapes.

'carways' or carraway comfits: a caraway seed enclosed in sugar.

arabesque: a decoration of Arabian design.

293 *Greengage*: a variety of plum. The use of green mangos in this recipe is a rare example of substitution.

Massepains: (French) marzipans.

298 *pomeloes*: (also called shaddocks) large citrus fruits, similar to grapefruits, with thick green rind and sweet yellow or pink flesh.

Tipparee: cape gooseberry, a fruit ideally suited to making jam.

299 *Byculla*: a residential suburb in South Bombay popular with the British in the nineteenth century. This recipe is probably named after the Byculla Club, the first of Bombay's residential clubs, opened in 1833, which was famous for the decadent, liqueur-filled Byculla Soufflé.

salamander: see note to p. 259.

301 *the native preparation of milk called koya*: boiled milk curd; see Glossary.

Swiss milk: canned condensed milk, first developed in the mid-nineteenth century by the American Gail Borden and produced in Switzerland in the late nineteenth century by companies such as the Anglo-Swiss Condensed Milk Company and Nestlé.

303 *bread-and-butter pastry*: thin rectangles of puff pastry, baked, then spread with various toppings.

305 *macedoines*: medleys of finely cut vegetables (or fruit).

308 *apostolic succession*: the Christian doctrine that contends ministerial authority has been transmitted through an unbroken line of bishops from the apostles onwards.

GLOSSARY

âbdâr an Indian servant whose duties include preparing water for drinking, and serving drinks, including wine, at the table

ajwain a plant that looks like wild parsley, the seeds are used as a spice and as a digestive after meals

almirah Anglo-Indian name for cupboard, wardrobe, or chest of drawers

alu bokhara type of plum

angethi/angithi a brazier-like stove

anna a denomination of money used in Anglo-India; one-sixteenth of a rupee

ardawa coarsely ground meal

atees aconite

atta/âtta wheatmeal flour

ayah an Indian female servant, housemaid, lady's maid, or nursemaid

bâbool the thorny mimosa

bael the aromatic fruit of an Indian tree; Bengal quince

bajra/bâjra millet

bârsi muttee a type of rice

bearer head servant, especially in Bengal; butler is used in Bombay, Madras, and Burmah; *appu* is used in Ceylon

bheesti/bheestie an Indian water-carrier

bhindi okra

bhoosa cattle food from husks and chopped straw

brinjal aubergine or eggplant

buksheesh a tip or present of money; can also be a bribe

bungalow originally a single-storeyed thatched house in Bengal and afterwards throughout India; now applied to a one-storeyed house anywhere

buniya (usually *bania*) a Hindu trader or merchant

butea gum the resin of the Indian palas or dhak tree, also known as the flame of the forest

charpoy a light Indian bedstead which has a wooden frame strung with light rope or webbing

chatty earthenware water pot (a *ghurra* in N. India)

cheechee disparaging Anglo-Indian term for a Eurasian or their accent

chick a screen made of split bamboo that can be rolled up and down as required

chini whiter variety of common sugar

chiretta plant found in northern India; the bitter tonic obtained from it is used medicinally like quinine

chit an employment certificate given to a servant, or a brief written message exchanged between officials

chitai a mat made of bamboo

chittâck 5 *tolas*; weight equivalent to 2 ounces

chokra generally, a boy or young man; here, one employed as a servant in an Anglo-Indian household

choolâ an Indian fireplace or cooking-place, often made of clay

chota hâzree/chôta hâzri/choti hâzree bed tea or early light breakfast (lit. little breakfast)

choukidar watchman or groundsman

chuddar a large sheet commonly worn as a shawl; a Rampore chuddar is a particularly fine quality shawl woven with pashmina wool and silk

chula/chûla *see* choolâ

chupâtti small, flat, thin cake of unleavened bread

chuprassi messenger or office orderly

coolie hired labourer or burden-carrier

cowrie small shell formerly used as currency in India and elsewhere

dai/dâi wet-nurse

dâk gâri mail cart

dâl lentils or split pulses

dali/dâli basket (to hold vegetables, fruit, or flowers)

dallia *see* Dulya

dandy a vehicle used in the hills, consisting of a strong cloth suspended like a hammock from a bamboo staff, carried by two (or more) men known as dandy-wallahs

dastur custom

dêgchi/degcha saucepan

dhaee *see* dai

dhal *see* dâl

dhobi/dhôbi an Indian washerman or washerwoman

dhooli covered litter suspended by bamboo poles and carried by four men

dhurrie an Indian cotton carpet

dhye (*dahi*) curds or yoghurt

dirzie an Indian tailor

doob *see* drubh

dooly *see* dhooli

drubh a kind of coarse rye grass

dulliya *see* Dulya

dulya/dulyâ semolina (made from hard wheat)

durri *see* dhurrie

dustoor *see* dastur

gêru red-coloured clay

gharra *see* ghurra

ghat steps leading down to a river; a quay

Ghauts Anglo-Indian name for the mountain ranges that run parallel to the east and west coasts of India, the Eastern and Western Ghauts

ghee clarified butter

ghurra earthenware water pot (a *chatty* in S. India)

goojurs members of large Hindu clan, formerly thieves; in Punjab they are Muslims. Gave name to Indian State of Gujerat and Pakistani district of Gujrat.

goor jaggery or coarse brown sugar; raw sugar

gow-wâlah/gow-wâla a cowherd or milkman

gowdown a store for goods

gûr *see* goor

gurrah *see* ghurra

guthri bundle, wrapped in cloth, used for personal things

hamal a domestic servant, especially in Bombay

hirmchi lime (quicklime)

hubble-bubble a rudimentary hookah

hukka Indian waterpipe for smoking tobacco

hulal (halal) killing an animal according to Muslim rites

Huzoor a respectful address used by Indians when talking to or about their master

isphagul seeds or husks of psyllium plants used in herbal remedies for constipation or digestion

jâfri lattice-work, usually of bamboo

jhampan a kind of sedan chair used in hill stations

jhampanni a man who carries a *jhampan*

jhool body clothing or quilt for a domesticated animal

jinricksha (jennyrickshaw) a light two-wheeled hooded carriage with two shafts, drawn by one or two men

jungli chambeli a twining shrub of the same family as jasmine

kabobs meat or fish roasted in small pieces on a skewer

kâla dâna dried black seeds of the twining plant *Impomoea hederacea*; made into a compound powder or tincture it is used as a purgative

kasoundé (*kasundi*) chutney or relish usually made with mustard

khânsâmâh/khansâmâh /khânsamah/khansâman in Anglo-Indian households, a native male servant, the butler, or head of the kitchen and pantry department

khit short form of *khitmutgâr*

khitmutgâr in Anglo-Indian households, a native male servant, the bearer and chief table-servant

khoya boiled milk curd

khus khus root of an Indian grass used to make screens, known as 'tatties', which are hung in windows and doorways and wetted to cool the air passing through them

kooltrie a type of grain

kootki a root

kotwâli chief officer of police for a town or city; also a native town magistrate

koya *see* khoya

kujâwah/kujâwar camel pannier; also a camel litter used for conveying women and fitted to the camel in pairs on each side

kunnât tent flysheet or similar

lobeas black-eyed peas

lota round (brass or copper) pot used for drinking water

malathi liquorice

mâli an Indian gardener

masaul in the Bombay Presidency, a male servant who waits on tables (cf. *khitmutgâr*)

matey in the Madras Presidency, an assistant under the head servant (cf. *khitmutgâr*)

maund Anglo-Indian weight; approx. 88 lb (40 kg)

Mem Sahib a European married woman, often used as a respectful form of address by Indians

mofussil rural as opposed to urban

mom roghan a preparation used to preserve leather

mudhâni wooden churner

mushk *see* mussack

mussack a leather water-bag carried by a *bheesti*

musolchi/musolchee a general servant, someone who grinds the spices, a cook's assistant, a dishwasher, or scullion, especially in Madras

nim (neem) the margosa tree sacred to Hindus; the leaves and bark are used medicinally

numdah saddle-cloth or rug made of coarse Indian felt

omum *see* ajwain

pagri *see* pugri

paisa one-hundredth of a rupee

pice a small copper coin used in Anglo-India; one-quarter of an anna

pilau rice cooked in stock with spices, and meat or other ingredients

Poorbeâh in upper India, a native of Oudh, the Benares district and Bihar

pugri/pugree a turban or headscarf

punkah a fan; often a large swinging fan made of cloth stretched over a wooden frame suspended from the roof and worked by a rope pulled by a *punkah-wallah*

purdah lit. a curtain, used to signify the seclusion of women from the sight of men and strangers

rupee standard monetary unit of Anglo-India: in India 1 rupee is divided into 16 annas; in Ceylon it is divided into 100 cents

sahib lôg/sahib logue Europeans in India (lit. 'master-race')

sais *see* syce

salaam a Muslim salutation meaning peace

seer 16 *chittâcks*; weight equivalent to 2 lb (0.9 kg)

shikar/shikâr the hunting of game for sport

sikka rupee a rupee coined by the Government of Bengal of a greater weight than a Company rupee (192 grains)

sil stone slab on which spices are ground

soojee/sujee semolina (made from soft wheat)

surâhi a long-necked metal or earthenware water pot

sweeper a low-caste Indian servant employed to perform the most menial tasks including the emptying and cleaning of latrines

syce an Indian servant who attends to horses; a groom

tâhseel a revenue subdivision within a district in India

tâhseel chuprassi an orderly attached to a revenue subdivision

tamis a drum sieve; a wide, round, low-walled sieve

tawa circular iron griddle used for cooking *chuppatis*

tezâl a large earthen utensil-cum-oven

til sesame

tizâl *see* tezâl

tola Indian weight; about 0.03 oz (12 g), the weight of a *sikka* rupee

tonga small two-wheeled horse-drawn carriage

toorees red lentils

ujwain *see* ajwain

wallah suffix—person

INDEX

American Literature

Authors in Context

British and Irish Literature

Children's Literature

Classics and Ancient Literature

Colonial Literature

Eastern Literature

European Literature

History

Medieval Literature

Oxford English Drama

Poetry

Philosophy

Politics

Religion

The Oxford Shakespeare

A complete list of Oxford World's Classics, including Authors in Context, Oxford English Drama, and the Oxford Shakespeare, is available in the UK from the Marketing Services Department, Oxford University Press, Great Clarendon Street, Oxford OX2 6DP, or visit the website at www.oup.com/uk/worldsclassics.

In the USA, visit www.oup.com/us/owc for a complete title list.

Oxford World's Classics are available from all good bookshops. In case of difficulty, customers in the UK should contact Oxford University Press Bookshop, 116 High Street, Oxford OX1 4BR.

	Late Victorian Gothic Tales
JANE AUSTEN	Emma
	Mansfield Park
	Persuasion
	Pride and Prejudice
	Selected Letters
	Sense and Sensibility
MRS BEETON	Book of Household Management
MARY ELIZABETH BRADDON	Lady Audley's Secret
ANNE BRONTË	The Tenant of Wildfell Hall
CHARLOTTE BRONTË	Jane Eyre
	Shirley
	Villette
EMILY BRONTË	Wuthering Heights
ROBERT BROWNING	The Major Works
JOHN CLARE	The Major Works
SAMUEL TAYLOR COLERIDGE	The Major Works
WILKIE COLLINS	The Moonstone
	No Name
	The Woman in White
CHARLES DARWIN	The Origin of Species
THOMAS DE QUINCEY	The Confessions of an English Opium-Eater
	On Murder
CHARLES DICKENS	The Adventures of Oliver Twist
	Barnaby Rudge
	Bleak House
	David Copperfield
	Great Expectations
	Nicholas Nickleby
	The Old Curiosity Shop
	Our Mutual Friend
	The Pickwick Papers

A SELECTION OF   **OXFORD WORLD'S CLASSICS**

CHARLES DICKENS	**A Tale of Two Cities**
GEORGE DU MAURIER	**Trilby**
MARIA EDGEWORTH	**Castle Rackrent**
GEORGE ELIOT	**Daniel Deronda**
	The Lifted Veil and Brother Jacob
	Middlemarch
	The Mill on the Floss
	Silas Marner
SUSAN FERRIER	**Marriage**
ELIZABETH GASKELL	**Cranford**
	The Life of Charlotte Brontë
	Mary Barton
	North and South
	Wives and Daughters
GEORGE GISSING	**New Grub Street**
	The Odd Women
EDMUND GOSSE	**Father and Son**
THOMAS HARDY	**Far from the Madding Crowd**
	Jude the Obscure
	The Mayor of Casterbridge
	The Return of the Native
	Tess of the d'Urbervilles
	The Woodlanders
WILLIAM HAZLITT	**Selected Writings**
JAMES HOGG	**The Private Memoirs and Confessions of a Justified Sinner**
JOHN KEATS	**The Major Works**
	Selected Letters
CHARLES MATURIN	**Melmoth the Wanderer**
JOHN RUSKIN	**Selected Writings**
WALTER SCOTT	**The Antiquary**
	Ivanhoe

ANTHONY TROLLOPE

The American Senator

An Autobiography

Barchester Towers

Can You Forgive Her?

The Claverings

Cousin Henry

The Duke's Children

The Eustace Diamonds

Framley Parsonage

He Knew He Was Right

Lady Anna

Orley Farm

Phineas Finn

Phineas Redux

The Prime Minister

Rachel Ray

The Small House at Allington

The Warden

The Way We Live Now